RACIAL INTEGRATION IN CORPORATE AMERICA, 1940–1990

In the space of about thirty years – from 1964 to 1994 – American corporations abandoned racially exclusionary employment policies and embraced some form of affirmative action to diversify their workforces. It was an extraordinary transformation, which most historians attribute to civil rights activists, federal legislation, and labor unions. This book examines the role of corporations in that transformation. Whereas others emphasize corporate obstruction, this book argues that there were corporate executives and managers who promoted fair employment and equal employment opportunity long before the federal government required it and who thereby helped prepare the corporate world for racial integration. The book examines the pioneering corporations that experimented with integration in the 1940s and 1950s, as well as corporate responses to the civil rights movement and urban crisis in the 1960s and 1970s and the widespread adoption of affirmative action in the 1980s and 1990s.

Jennifer Delton received her Ph.D. in history from Princeton University and is currently associate professor of history at Skidmore College. She is the author of *Making Minnesota Liberal: Civil Rights and the Transformation of the Democratic Party* and several articles on race, politics, and labor.

Racial Integration in Corporate America, 1940–1990

JENNIFER DELTON

Skidmore College

CAMBRIDGE
UNIVERSITY PRESS

CAMBRIDGE
UNIVERSITY PRESS

University Printing House, Cambridge CB2 8BS, United Kingdom

One Liberty Plaza, 20th Floor, New York, NY 10006, USA

477 Williamstown Road, Port Melbourne, VIC 3207, Australia

314-321, 3rd Floor, Plot 3, Splendor Forum, Jasola District Centre, New Delhi - 110025, India

79 Anson Road, #06-04/06, Singapore 079906

Cambridge University Press is part of the University of Cambridge.

It furthers the University's mission by disseminating knowledge in the pursuit of
education, learning and research at the highest international levels of excellence.

www.cambridge.org
Information on this title: www.cambridge.org/9780521730808

First published 2009

A catalogue record for this publication is available from the British Library

Library of Congress Cataloging in Publication data
Delton, Jennifer A. (Jennifer Alice), 1964–
Racial integration in corporate America, 1940–1990 / Jennifer Delton.
    p.   cm.
Includes bibliographical references and index.
ISBN 978-0-521-51509-2 (hardback) – ISBN 978-0-521-73080-8 (pbk.)
1. Discrimination in employment–United States.   2. African Americans–Economic conditions.
3. Affirmative action programs–United States.   I. Title.
HD4903.5.U58D55   2009
331.13´3097309045–dc22   2009010921

ISBN 978-0-521-51509-2 Hardback
ISBN 978-0-521-73080-8 Paperback

Contents

List of Tables

Statistical Tables

Introduction

Like other steel companies in the early twentieth century, the Lukens Steel Company in Coatesville, Pennsylvania, hired large numbers of immigrants and African Americans. Lukens executives regarded both groups as racially separate from themselves but dealt with each differently. Charles Lukens Huston, Sr., who was in charge of operations and production, preferred immigrant labor to black labor. Concerned about high turnover among his immigrant workers, he engaged a consultant to instruct Lukens foremen and supervisors on how to be more culturally sensitive when dealing with foreign-born workers. In an effort to stem his increasing dependence on black labor, he lobbied against anti-immigration laws.[1]

In Huston's eyes, black workers were dangerous, disruptive, and inefficient. He was fearful of them and felt inconvenienced by the special attention he felt they required – that is, segregation and policing. The main problem with black workers was where to put them. Housing was not a problem for immigrants because they could live anywhere, but blacks required a segregated space, even in Pennsylvania, and space was scarce. During World War I, Lukens had hired several hundred black southerners. Like other steel companies in the area, Lukens housed them in an encampment on plant grounds, watched over by Lukens's own police force. Huston referred to it as their "colored colony."[2] Huston worried constantly that noise and activities in the black encampments would disturb the neighbors. In an attempt to gain control

---

[1] See Charles L. Huston to John T. Clark, July 23, 1923, in Lukens Steel Company, Executive Officer Files, 1903–1979, Series II, Box 1999, File: Urban League of Pittsburgh and Charles L. Huston, Sr., to George K. Irwin, Jan. 12, 1920, in Lukens Steel Company, Executive Officer Files, 1903–1979, Series II, Box 1993, at Hagley Museum and Library, Wilmington, Delaware (hereafter HML).

[2] See, for instance, Charles L. Huston to John T. Clark, July 23, 1923, in Lukens Steel Company, Executive Officer Files, 1903–1979, Series II, Box 1999, File: Urban League of Pittsburgh, HML.

over the situation, he engaged a Negro welfare worker from the Armstrong Association of Philadelphia, an organization that worked to prepare African Americans for steady employment.

George W. Royall arrived at Lukens in December 1918. The understanding was that Royall would help improve the condition of the Negro workers and, Huston hoped, thereby relieve the policing burden.[3] From the start, however, Royall's methods excited suspicion. In a January 1919 letter to the Armstrong Association, Huston was concerned that Royall was "taking up the question of wages, employment, etc., with the men." While allowing that it was natural that the men would come to Royall with complaints, he thought it unwise for him to try to address those complaints. Rather, he should, as Huston put it, "devote himself to the matters of improving the men's habits in the way of spending their leisure time, and in adopting saving habits."[4]

George Royall accordingly refocused his energies on leisure issues. But this too proved problematic. Huston wrote in horror, "He wanted to introduce boxing amongst our colored men; also proposed to have occasions when he would invite visitors to our colored camp and have dances. . . . " A devout Quaker, Huston had an aversion to boxing, which he felt was warlike, and modern dancing, which bordered on evil. But he had a particular aversion to black men boxing, because as he put it, boxing "is only fit for the training of soldiers and policemen," and hence unsuitable for blacks.[5] Royall was discharged. Huston attempted to remedy the problem by reducing the black workforce.[6]

Charles L. Huston, Sr., exhibited the classic elements of white American racism. He feared blacks' physicality, their sexuality, their closeness to life. His horror that the welfare worker would have introduced to *these* people boxing or dancing was prompted by his belief that they already embodied, inherently, the worst elements of these activities – violence, merriment, sex. The reason they had to be kept separate from whites was not to prevent racial violence but to quarantine their social behavior and prevent miscegenation. His view of black people as licentious, lazy, and fun loving was a common one among whites at this time and clearly informed company employment policies.

---

[3] Charles L. Huston to John T. Emlen, Nov. 23, 1918, in Lukens Steel Company, Executive Officer Files, 1903–1979, Series II, Box 1988, File: Armstrong Association, HML.

[4] Both quotes from Charles L. Huston to John T. Emlen, January 2, 1919, in Lukens Steel Company, Executive Officer Files, 1903–1979, Series II, Box 1988, File: Armstrong Association, HML.

[5] Both quotes in Charles L. Huston to John T. Emlen, Feb. 6, 1919, in Lukens Steel Company, Executive Officer Files, 1903–1979, Series II, Box 1988, File: Armstrong Association, HML. There were Quakers with abolitionist roots who continued to be sympathetic to the plight of African Americans. Huston was not part of this faction.

[6] Charles L. Huston to A. L. Manley, Feb. 27, 1919, in Lukens Steel Company, Executive Officer Files, 1903–1979, Series II, Box 1988, File: Armstrong Association, HML.

Color mattered, though executives were unaware of the extent to which it did. Executive communications about specific workers, which actually show a great deal of warmth, always identified nonwhite employees by their race or nationality, as in, "Rev. Wm A. Creditt, colored, of Downingtown, asked me to look up H.L. Webster, colored, who is working for us . . . "[7] Huston's sons, who helped run the company from the 1940s through the 1960s, were more circumspect but likewise carried within them unconscious assumptions about color and work. When Arthur A. Smith was denied employment at the Lukens Steel Company in 1941, he wrote to the company's president for an explanation. It turned out that at five feet two inches and 130 pounds he was too small. Charles Lukens Huston, Jr., the director of Personnel Relations, explained, "Since Smith is a colored man, and since most colored men are required to do heavy work, I am inclined to agree . . . that the man in question is too light to work safely, without danger to others and to himself."[8] Sensing the delicacy of the situation, he added that someone should meet with Smith personally to explain why it was not in his interest to be hired at this time. It was not his color that was a problem, you see, but his size.

American employers regularly denied that they participated in racial discrimination. As the previous examples indicate, however, they did not understand what racial discrimination was. This book is about how they learned.

It is the premise of this book that American corporations played a significant role in opening the American workplace to racial minorities. Historians have attributed the racial integration of American workplaces in the late twentieth century to activists, the state, and labor unions. They have not only ignored corporations' contributions to integration but have also portrayed them as impediments to it.[9] Yet not all corporations were obstructionist. Just as certain

---

[7] Charles L. Huston, Sr., to George K. Irwin, Sept. 30, 1920, in Lukens Steel Company, Executive Officer Files, 1903–1979, Series II, Box 1993, File: George K. Irwin, HML.

[8] Charles L. Huston, Jr., to George K. Irwin, August 4, 1941, in Lukens Steel Company, Executive Officer Files, 1903–1979, Series II, Box 1993, File: Charles L. Huston, Jr., HML

[9] On the role of activists in integration, see Nancy MacLean, *Freedom Is Not Enough: The Opening of the American Workplace* (New York: Russell Sage Foundation; Cambridge: Harvard University Press, 2006); Terry H. Anderson, *The Pursuit of Fairness: A History of Affirmative Action* (New York: Oxford University Press, 2004); Timothy Minchin, *Hiring the Black Worker: The Racial Integration of the Southern Textile Industry, 1960–1980* (Chapel Hill: University of North Carolina Press, 1999), and Minchin, *The Color of Work: The Struggle for Civil Rights in the Southern Paper Industry* (Chapel Hill: University of North Carolina Press, 2001). On the role of the state, see Judith Stein, *Running Steel, Running America: Race, Economic Policy and the Decline of Liberalism* (Chapel Hill: University of North Carolina Press, 1998); Hugh Davis Graham, *The Civil Rights Era: Origins and Development of National Policy, 1960–1972* (New York: Oxford University Press, 1990); Bruce J. Schulman, *From Cotton Belt to Sunbelt: Federal Policy, Economic Development, and the Transformation of the South, 1938–1980*, rev. ed.

unions championed racial integration, so too did certain corporations. My aim in recognizing corporate efforts is not to celebrate their enlightened antiracism but rather to provide a more complete understanding of how a key sector of American society was integrated in the latter half of the twentieth century. There were executives and managers at large corporations who promoted fair employment, equal employment opportunity, and, later, affirmative action. There is abundant evidence that large employers embraced some form of affirmative action long before the federal government required it. We can choose to ignore this or we can attempt to explain it.

Activism on the part of African Americans and their allies was the original impetus for the changes I examine in this book, which is why the first chapter examines the African American struggle for fair employment. But once the demands were made, once the laws were legislated, how did employers respond? Most historians have argued that they responded negatively. Many did. Others were more positive. I focus on those executives and managers at large corporations who experimented with hiring and advancing racial minorities into traditionally white positions in the 1940s, who tried to convince their peers to do the same in the 1950s, who adopted affirmative action plans in the 1960s, who hired and trained unemployed black youth in the 1970s, and who defended affirmative action in the 1980s.

Large corporations set the pace of racial integration in the workplace. Small businesses, which made up the majority of businesses in the United States, were slow to hire minorities and are not the subject of this study. The executives and managers I examine had leadership positions in major corporations that employed at least forty thousand workers, such as General Electric, Ford Motor Company, General Motors, Du Pont, International Harvester, IBM, Lockheed, RCA, and Control Data Corporation. Although large corporations represented less than 5 percent of all business enterprises in the United States, they had

(Durham, NC: Duke University Press, 1994); Paul Moreno, *From Direct Action to Affirmative Action: Fair Employment Law and Policy in America, 1933–1972* (Baton Rouge: Louisiana State University Press, 1997); Timothy Thurber, "Racial Liberalism, Affirmative Action, and the Troubled History of the President's Committee on Government Contracts," *Journal of Policy History* 18, no. 4 (2006): 446-75; Gavin Wright, "The Civil Rights Revolution as Economic History," *Journal of Economic History* 59, no. 2 (June 1999): 267–89; William J. Collins, "The Labor Market Impact of Anti-Discrimination Laws, 1940–1960," *Industrial and Labor Relations Review* 56, no. 2 (January 2003): 244–72. On the conflicted role of labor, see Robert Zieger, *For Jobs and Freedom: Race and Labor in American since 1865* (Lexington: University of Kentucky Press, 2007); Paul Moreno, *Black Americans and Organized labor: A New History* (Baton Rouge: Louisiana State University Press, 2006); Bruce Nelson, *Divided We Stand: American Workers and the Struggle for Black Equality* (Princeton, NJ: Princeton University Press, 2001); and Terry Boswell et al., *Racial Competition and Class Solidarity* (Albany: State University of New York Press, 2007).

tremendous influence in society and over the business community. They positioned themselves as leaders in post–World War II economic life. They established prices, wages, and the pattern of union-management relations. They had the ear of the government, with whom they also held large military contracts. Because the heads of large corporations saw their organizations as engines of change, they were attentive to their public image and social obligations, which helps explain their tacit support for fair employment and, later, their quick compliance with the government's affirmative action requirements.[10]

Support for fair employment and equal opportunity was not located in one economic sector or industry but was expressed at different times for different reasons by a variety of actors across industries. Corporate liberals, business conservatives, manufacturers, industrialists, bankers, retailers, personnel managers, management experts, and even the leaders of the National Association of Manufacturers were among those who supported fair employment and equal employment opportunity for minorities beginning during World War II. The number of executives and managers willing to practice fair employment was very small at first, consisting of a few "pioneers." But it grew over time, so that by the 1960s, the climate of opinion among corporate executives, as among white people in general, was favorable to equal employment opportunity.[11] It would of course take much more than a favorable climate of opinion to change discriminatory employment practices, but a supportive atmosphere was a necessary precondition.

Chronologically, this book traces corporations' movement away from traditional policies of exclusion and segregation to the ostensibly color-blind policies of nondiscrimination (called "fair employment" or "equal employment opportunity") and then to proactive, color-conscious policies specifically designed to increase the number of racial minorities in traditionally white positions (known as "affirmative action"). Although initially skeptical of quotas, large employers of the late-1960s had little difficulty making the transition from color-blind proscriptions against discrimination to color-conscious strategies to hire minorities. This was in part because the ostensibly

---

[10] On the defense of corporations as influential in even if not "representative" of American business, see Peter Drucker, *The New Society: The Anatomy of Industrial Order* (New York: Harper, 1949, 1950, paperback ed., 1962). See also Kim McQuaid, *Uneasy Partners: Big Business in American Politics, 1945–1990* (Baltimore: Johns Hopkins Press, 1994).

[11] See Stephen M. Gelber, *Black Men and Businessmen: The Growing Awareness of a Social Responsibility* (Port Washington, NY: Kennicat Press, 1974), 7–22. In June 1964, 67 percent of nonsouthern whites preferred a candidate who supported civil rights as opposed to one who did not, whereas 47 percent of all people interviewed thought the "racial problem" was the most important problem facing the country in 1964. See July 26 and July 29 in *The Gallup Poll: Public Opinion, 1935–1970*, 3 vols. (New York: Random House, 1972), 2:1894.

color-blind policies of fair employment and equal employment opportunity already involved implicitly color-conscious strategies. But it was also the case that large employers felt a sense of relief to be done with the uncertainties of antidiscrimination policies, which were impossible to enforce because no one could define "discrimination," and the policies themselves prohibited keeping racial statistics that could monitor progress. When the Equal Employment Opportunity Commission (EEOC) and the Office of Federal Contract Compliance (OFCC) suggested that large employers worry less about discrimination and just start hiring minorities, integration became much easier.[12] The new focus on "results" was unambiguous; everyone knew what was expected. A corporation's progress toward compliance could be quantified and measured in objective terms on which all sides could agree.

The firms I examine in the first part of the book were not typical. Their experiments in minority employment in the 1940s and 1950s were regarded as daring innovations. While the business community at large – its official spokesmen, its business and management schools, its publications – was open to the idea of fair employment and equal opportunity in the 1950s, few corporations actually took steps to integrate minorities into their firms unless they needed the labor. In business, as in other areas, no one wanted to disrupt the status quo. As one management consultant explained, "Most businessmen are not bigots, but they are cowards."[13] This is why the pioneering firms were so crucial to workplace integration – they provided a model, they took the first risky steps, they worked closely with the federal government to prove to others that it could be done. Within these pioneering corporations, there were particular individuals who made minority employment a priority. These executives and personnel directors were not heroes, not in the way that Fannie Lou Hamer, Robert Moses, or other activists who risked their lives daily were. But they were historical agents. They tried to make things happen, and to a large degree, they succeeded.

Executives who supported and practiced fair employment or equal employment opportunity in the 1940s and 1950s did not usually support federal legislation (although some did). They preferred voluntary methods for achieving integration, such as adopting and promoting antidiscrimination policies; establishing relationships with black colleges and institutions; desegregating

---

[12] In a meeting with National Association of Manufacturers officials, an OFCC official said that employers should focus on producing "results." See "OFCC Equal Employment Opportunity Commission Compliance Efforts" (n.d. presumed 1968), p. 3, in National Association of Manufacturers, Records, 1895–1990 (hereafter NAM Records), Series 5, Box 64, Philadelphia Plan folder, HML. This will be discussed in Chapters 7 and 8.

[13] Quoted in Gelber, *Black Men and Businessmen*, 81.

facilities; educating white workers, managers, and executives about the principles of fair employment; hiring blacks into white positions; formulating strategies for integration; participating in studies of biracial employment; testifying on behalf of integration; and changing established employment patterns that inhibited integration. Civil rights historians have made support for antidiscrimination legislation a litmus test for a group's commitment to integration, often treating employers' preference for voluntary methods and education as a sign of *opposition* to fair employment and civil rights.[14] While voluntary efforts may not have yielded immediate results, they were not merely obstructionist feints. They acclimated employers to the problems of discrimination and racism. They provided models for others to follow. They helped reshape attitudes. They laid the groundwork for integration so that when federal law finally required companies to integrate their workforces in 1964, many companies were not only prepared but willing to comply.

Indeed, the most surprising aspect of this story is how quickly large employers in the 1960s moved to comply with government orders to hire and advance minorities. By the mid-1960s, the heads of most major corporations professed a desire to end racial discrimination, were willing to cooperate with government enforcement officials, and had taken steps to target and train minorities for employment. Although there were corporations and executives who continued to resist hiring minorities, the dominant attitude had changed and the vocally recalcitrant became the outliers.

Executives' profession of support for equal employment opportunity and their adoption of affirmative action policies, however, did not mean that discrimination did not continue to occur at their firms. Like labor leaders, corporate heads who supported equal employment opportunity presided over organizations that had institutionalized discriminatory practices and that resisted change. What has been said of United Auto Workers (UAW) president Walter Reuther (that he was always glad to integrate anything except his own union) could easily have been said about any number of employers as well. We forget how mammoth an undertaking it was to undo institutionalized assumptions and practices that appeared to be "natural." It took a long time for employers and managers to actually see how traditional employment practices *were* discriminatory, and then they had to convince others to not only see discrimination but to end it, despite the adverse effects antidiscrimination measures

---

[14] Examples can be found in MacLean, *Freedom Is Not Enough*, and Anthony Chen, "The Hitlerian Rule of Quotas: Racial Conservatism and the Politics of Fair Employment in New York State, 1941–45," *Journal of American History* 92, no. 4 (March 2006): 1238–64.

could have on those being asked to change. Then, too, the pressure for employers to integrate occurred at the precise moment that the jobs most African Americans were best prepared to step into – semiskilled and production jobs – were disappearing because of automation or the movement of facilities out of cities. Integration was a Herculean task; that employers were not immediately successful is hardly surprising. Employers could adopt all of the experts' recommendations, including affirmative action, and still be unable to attain the desired goals. Thus, I am less interested in results than I am in the efforts.

This is not a story about liberal triumph, nor is it one of conservative backlash. The story of workplace integration confounds our assumptions about liberalism and conservatism. Both corporate liberals, who tended to accept unions and government activism, and business conservatives, who actively opposed unions and government activism, were favorably disposed to fair employment and even affirmative action. Indeed, the National Association of Manufacturers, a paragon of antiunion conservatism, urged its members to practice fair employment beginning during World War II and opposed the Reagan administration's attempts to prohibit affirmative action in the 1980s. Among businessmen, then, neither ideological demeanor nor political party indicated support for or against racial integration.

One reason corporations were not more averse to civil rights legislation and affirmative action was because it had the potential to disable unions. Policies and trends that were good for racial minorities tended to be bad for unions. The human relations in management movement is a case in point. Developed in the 1930s and 1940s, the human relations approach promised to curb industrial strife through such innovations as management training, formal employment procedures, and personnel offices. Human relations experts urged executives to let go of traditional laissez-faire principles and to be more socially responsible and sensitive to community needs. Although human relations advocates were sympathetic to workers, the employers who adopted their methods were not. Indeed, many historians regard human relations managerial techniques as fundamentally antiunion.[15] Nonetheless, human relations techniques were necessary to – and strengthened by – racial integration in the workplace.

Labor unions themselves had a mixed history with regard to racial integration. After a century of exclusionary policies and a sprinkling of failed biracial organizing attempts, American unions actively began to include blacks in the

---

[15] I will fully discuss the issue in Chapter 4. In the meantime, see Sanford Jacoby, *Modern Manors: Welfare Capitalism since the New Deal* (Princeton, NJ: Princeton University Press, 1997), and Elizabeth Fones-Wolf, *Selling Free Enterprise: The Business Assault on Labor and Liberalism, 1945–1960* (Urbana: University of Illinois Press, 1994).

1930s, under the leadership of the Congress of Industrial Unions (CIO). But while CIO leaders endorsed nondiscriminatory policies, the union membership was sometimes slow to follow. The craft unions in the American Federation of Labor (AFL) were even less inclined to accept blacks. While the CIO's industrial unions had a practical reason to include blacks (excluded blacks could provide employers with a nonunion source of labor), the AFL's elite craft unions, whose power rested on their restriction of the skilled labor market, stood to lose this advantage if they allowed blacks in. Quite apart from issues of membership, union practices that were intended to strengthen unions' position vis-à-vis management (such as apprenticeships, seniority lines, and the closed shop) hurt blacks and institutionalized their exclusion from skilled positions.[16]

Even when union leadership fully endorsed the idea of equal employment opportunity, the interests of racial minorities and the interests of labor unions were often at odds. The Wagner Act (1935) protected workers' right to choose their own representation, but when white workers chose to be represented by exclusionary unions, blacks were eased out of jobs they had long held in an open shop or were excluded from any future employment.[17] Seniority was good for unions but usually worked against minorities seeking advancement. During the years that unions' power declined, the fortunes of minorities rose. Large corporations laid off thousands of union workers during the economic downturn of the 1970s but retained or increased the percentage of minority workers in jobs not covered by union seniority clauses. In the early 1970s, a time of recession, Lockheed Aircraft Corporation increased the number of minority workers in every nonunion category.[18] I am not suggesting a causal relationship between the decline of unions and the rise of affirmative action, but I am noting a historical pattern that provides context for employers' acceptance of affirmative action.

[16] The literature on blacks and unions is voluminous. Start with the following: Zieger, *For Jobs and Freedom;* Moreno, *Black Americans and Organized Labor;* Nelson, *Divided We Stand;* and Herbert Hill, *Black Labor and the American Legal System: Race, Work and Law* (Madison: University of Wisconsin Press, 1985), originally published by the Bureau of National Affairs, Inc., 1977.

[17] See Moreno, *Black Americans and Organized Labor,* 167; Robin D. G. Kelley and Earl Lewis, *To Make Our World Anew: A History of African Americans* (New York: Oxford University Press, 2000), 415; and Hill, *Black Labor and the American Legal System,* originally published by the Bureau of National Affairs, 1977, p. 102. Eric Arneson notes that the Wagner Act's failure to include an antiexclusion clause did not totally eliminate blacks from the railroad industry. See Arneson, *Brotherhoods of Color: Black Railroad Workers and the Struggle for Equality* (Cambridge, MA: Harvard University Press, 2001).

[18] "Acting Affirmatively to End Job Bias," *BusinessWeek,* January 27, 1975, 94.

The rise of affirmative action in the 1970s and 1980s corresponded not only to the decline of unionism but also to the decline of liberalism. Historians often view the Reagan-era backlash against affirmative action as the end of affirmative action, as if the backlash were successful. But the backlash against affirmative action occurred in the political arena, not the corporate boardroom. While large employers cheered the Reagan administration's antiunionism and antiliberalism, they opposed the attempt to curtail and prohibit affirmative action. Though politically disabled, affirmative action survived and thrived in the corporate world under a new name – "diversity." Major corporations held on to their affirmative action programs, now justified as a means to maintain the diversity deemed crucial to success in a global marketplace. In 2003, the heads of major corporations submitted briefs on behalf of the University of Michigan's affirmative action polices. Affirmative action in college admissions was different from affirmative action in employment, yet corporate heads understood the crucial link between the two, arguing that diversity in education was necessary both to fulfill their manpower needs and to prepare students for a diverse workplace. *BusinessWeek* called the Supreme Court's decision in *Grutter v. Bollinger* (2003) to uphold Michigan's race-conscious admissions policy a victory for corporate America. Given the disappearance of unions and the dismantling of the welfare state, however, the triumph of affirmative action and diversity in the corporate world can hardly be considered a victory for liberalism. Nor can it be seen as a victory for conservatives, who, after all, opposed affirmative action. The survival of affirmative action is best seen as a victory for employers, who, after years of negotiation and compliance, finally regained control over the social and racial changes that had first disrupted traditional employment policies back in the 1940s.[19]

The focus of this study is racial integration. When a southern congressman inserted "sex" into the list of categories in which discrimination was prohibited in Title VII of the 1964 Civil Rights Act, the struggle for racial integration became merged with the struggle for gender equality and historians have since combined race and gender in their studies of workplace integration. It is true that the segregated, subordinate position of women of all races in the workplace resembled that of African American men. Just as there was "white work" and "black work," there was "men's work" and "women's work." But before 1964, the two struggles, while related, had separate histories. Black women, of course, fought both struggles simultaneously, but to the extent that

[19] On corporations' embrace of affirmative action, see John D. Skrentny, *The Minority Rights Revolution* (Cambridge, MA: Harvard University Press, 2002); Anderson, *The Pursuit of Fairness*; "Don't Scuttle Affirmative Action," *BusinessWeek*, April 15, 1985, 174; and "Businessmen Prefer Affirmative Action Goals," *Fortune*, September 16, 1985, 26.

this book discusses black women, it will be in regard to their efforts to break into positions traditionally held by white women, rather than their efforts to attain male positions.

Defining Terms

Let me define the terms most often used to refer to the idea of integrating black workers into the workplace: *fair employment, equal employment opportunity,* and *affirmative action.* Each term connoted an eventual expectation of racial integration, and yet none was equivalent to integration. "Fair employment," a term used in the 1940s and 1950s to connote the hiring and advancement of workers without regard to race, was synonymous with nondiscrimination and could include anything from the adoption of a color-blind nondiscrimination policy to the desegregation of facilities to the hiring of blacks into white positions. None of these things necessarily achieved integration, but each was part of a gradual process toward that end. Color-blind nondiscrimination policies by themselves were generally ineffective because white people were unable to recognize how their personal biases and assumptions determined their hiring practices. However, fair employment advocates regarded the sort of color-conscious policies that could have led to integration, such as hiring blacks into previously white positions, as tokenism. The mere presence of black employees in white positions did not, according to antidiscrimination agencies, mean that a company practiced fair employment. If the company had hired the black worker because he or she was black in order to comply with state antidiscrimination laws, then that would not have been fair employment. Yet, the agencies themselves counted the number of black employees in a company as evidence of nondiscrimination and fair employment.[20]

"Equal employment opportunity" was used regularly beginning in the 1950s. Like fair employment, it referred to a color-blind policy of nondiscrimination – equal opportunity without regard to race, nationality, or faith – but in practice, it included much more than mere nondiscrimination. Equal employment opportunity could also include the active recruitment of minority applicants, the use of black employment agencies, special training for whites, or even the rearrangement of seniority lines to accommodate black advancement. Both fair employment and equal employment opportunity were ostensibly color-blind and appealed to the ideal of individual opportunity, but both also included practices that specifically targeted minorities.

---

[20] On the origins and evolution of fair employment, see Moreno, *From Direct Action to Affirmative Action.*

Historians attribute the origin of the term "affirmative action" to the Kennedy administration's Executive Order 10925 (1961), which required firms to not just passively practice nondiscrimination but to "take affirmative action to ensure that applicants are employed ... without regard to their race, creed, color, or national origin."[21] But the types of affirmative actions recommended (targeted recruitment, use of black employment agencies, etc.) were already in use by those companies that had fair employment or equal employment opportunity policies. Affirmative action was in many ways a new name for well-established practices. Unlike fair employment or equal employment opportunity, however, affirmative action was not regarded as color-blind. It was a color-conscious policy, justified as a way to make up for past injustices. Affirmative action did not include quotas until 1968, when the OFCC developed the Philadelphia Plan to force the integration of the construction unions, and then applied the same techniques to all government contractors.[22] By 1970, quotas had become "goals and timetables" – a more palatable concept for executives who were used to setting goals and timetables.

Let me also explain my use of certain terms that have since become obsolete due in large part to the changes described in this book. First, throughout most of the book, I regularly use the gender-specific term "businessmen." There were, of course, businesswomen, but they were exceptional, not the rule. Aside from Sarah Southall, who held a leadership position in International Harvester's Employee Relations Department, the main actors in this story are male. The gender-specific term captures the white-maleness of the historical moment in a way that a gender-neutral term cannot. Second, there are instances when I use the term "Negro," rather than the more current "African American" or "black," which can be anachronistic in some contexts. I know this is jarring to some readers, but Negro was once the preferred, respectful term for people of African American heritage, and in reference to certain sources and situations, the term better captures the historical moment described.

Sources

This book combines a general overview of positive business responses to fair employment and racial integration with a number of detailed case studies

---

[21] Quoted in Anderson, *The Pursuit of Fairness*, 60.

[22] On the origins and evolution of affirmative action, see Anderson, *The Pursuit of Fairness*; John David Skrentny, *The Ironies of Affirmative Action* (Chicago: University of Chicago Press, 1996); and Graham, *The Civil Rights Era*.

focused on specific corporations. The material for the general overview comes from the business press, sociological studies, management textbooks, executive memoirs, state fair employment agencies, and the archives of business organizations such as the National Association of Manufacturers. The case studies are, for the most part, based on corporate archives.

Because of the sensitive legal nature of the topic, corporate archives are somewhat unreliable. One suspects that incriminating material has been removed, while what is left shows only the company's positive actions with regard to minority hiring. Nonetheless, when available, archival materials from corporations provide a perspective that is missing from the EEOC archives, which have been the most common historical source for the study of workplace integration. Where it exists, materials on race and minority employment are embedded in the context of a company's other concerns and priorities. It comes from certain offices and not others. For this reason, it can tell us where racial policies fit into the company's concerns, what they complemented and supplemented, and which parts of the company favored them. Archival material from corporations can also confirm or disprove common conjectures about fair employment, such as the role of top leadership in instigating change or the profitability of nondiscriminatory policies.

The companies examined in detail are International Harvester (Chicago, Illinois), Pitney-Bowes, Inc. (Stamford, Connecticut), Control Data, Inc. (Minneapolis, Minnesota), E. I. Du Pont de Nemours and Company (Wilmington, Delaware), and Lukens Steel Company (Coatesville, Pennsylvania). They are large manufacturing corporations from the Northeast and Midwest, although International Harvester and Du Pont had plants in the South. International Harvester, Lukens, and Du Pont had unions; the others did not. I chose International Harvester, Pitney-Bowes, and Control Data, not on the basis of their representativeness in the business world but rather on the basis of their reputations for "progressive" racial policies (which made them, if anything, unrepresentative). I chose to look at E. I. Du Pont de Nemours and Company and Lukens Steel Company, neither of which was regarded as "progressive," solely on the basis of the availability of archival material pertaining to their racial policies.

Nothing in this book is intended to suggest that racial integration in the workplace has been achieved or that economic and racial injustices have been eliminated from American life. Its aim is to understand the changes that have occurred in employment policies since 1940, not to suggest that further change is unnecessary.

PART I COLOR-BLIND GROUNDWORK, 1940–1961

1   The African American Struggle for Jobs

The struggle to be gainfully employed is one of the central stories of African American history. Segregation, racism, violence, and a large supply of immigrant labor limited black workers' participation in the American workforce to a few circumscribed areas at the lower end of the pay scale.[1] The details of exclusion varied geographically and changed over time, but until the latter half of the twentieth century, labor unions, employers, and the state upheld or promoted exclusionary employment policies that barred blacks from what came to be called "traditionally white jobs." In the late nineteenth and early twentieth centuries, strikebreaking and labor shortages had been the surest paths into traditionally white jobs for African Americans. By World War I, however, black leaders began to pursue economic opportunities in a more organized fashion. The National Association for the Advancement of Colored People (NAACP), founded in 1909, the National Urban League, founded in

---

[1] The literature on race, labor, and employment is voluminous. My understanding has been shaped by Thomas Sugrue, *The Origins of the Urban Crisis: Race and Inequality in Postwar Detroit* (Princeton, NJ: Princeton University Press, 1997); Robert Zieger, *For Jobs and Freedom: Race and Labor in America since 1865* (Lexington: University of Kentucky Press, 2007); Judith Stein, *Running Steel, Running America: Race, Economic Policy, and the Decline of Liberalism* (Chapel Hill: University of North Carolina Press, 1998); Paul Moreno, *Black Americans and Organized Labor: A New History* (Baton Rouge: Louisiana State University Press, 2006); Bruce Nelson, *Divided We Stand: American Workers and the Struggle for Black Equality* (Princeton, NJ: Princeton University Press, 2001); Gavin Wright, *Old South, New South* (New York: Basic, 1986); William H. Harris, *The Harder We Run* (New York: Oxford University Press, 1982); David Roediger, *The Wages of Whiteness: Race and the Making of the American Working Class*, rev. ed. (New York: Verso, 1999); Herbert Hill, *Black Labor and the American Legal System: Race, Work and Law* (Madison: University of Wisconsin Press, 1985), originally published by the Bureau of National Affairs, 1977; Gunnar Myrdal, *An American Dilemma* (New York: Harper and Bros., 1944); Nancy MacLean, *Freedom Is Not Enough: The Opening of the American Workplace* (New York: Russell Sage Foundation; Cambridge, MA: Harvard University Press, 2006); and Robert Weaver, *Negro Labor: A National Problem* (New York: Harcourt Brace, 1946).

1920, and black leaders such as A. Philip Randolph, W. E. B. Du Bois, Walter White, and Clarence Mitchell worked tirelessly for what eventually became known as "fair employment" and later "equal opportunity." After years of cajoling, lawsuits, protests, boycotts, data collecting, and industry-by-industry "experiments," their arguments and efforts would eventually convince organized labor, employers, and the state that racial discrimination was bad for unions, bad for business, and bad for the nation. Although this book focuses on employers' role in integrating the workplace, it has to begin with the black struggle for jobs, because without this impetus, it is unlikely that employers would have taken it upon themselves to change the long-standing habits and customs that had congealed into discriminatory economic structures.

Patterns of Exclusion and Discrimination

The metaphors of "carving out" or "breaking through" to describe black gains comport with a labor market segmented, guarded, and stratified by ethnic and racial blocs. As late as the 1940s, U.S. Steel's Ohio Works plant consisted of, in the words of one worker, "little islands of ethnic concentrations," with the Irish and Scotch working the open hearths, blacks in the blast furnaces, English and Germans in the machine shop, and the Italians laying bricks.[2] Whites monopolized southern textile jobs until the 1960s. Blacks held a virtual monopoly on the portering jobs on the railroads. Technological innovation and economic cycles created new opportunities and closed others, and groups competed, moved around, and resettled into different segments, as if employment opportunity were a game of musical chairs.[3]

Until World War I, the overwhelming majority of African Americans resided in the southern states, working as sharecroppers and tenant farmers in the South's largely agricultural economy. Beginning in the late nineteenth century, an increasing number moved to cities and towns to take advantage of the industrialization of the southern economy. By the early twentieth century, black southerners had carved out spaces in coal mining, tobacco, lumber, dock work, and the steel industry.[4] Southern industrial labor was defined by strict segregation, which meant that black and white workers competed not as

[2] Quoted in Nelson, *Divided We Stand*, 155.

[3] On ethnic segmentation, see Nelson, *Divided We Stand*; Lizabeth Cohen, *Making a New Deal* (New York: Cambridge University Press, 1990); Richard Edwards, *Contested Terrain: The Transformation of the Workplace in the 20th Century* (New York: Basic, 1979), 163–70; Orvis Collins, "Ethnic Behavior in Industry: Sponsorship and Rejection in a New England Factory," *American Journal of Sociology* 51 (January 1946): 293–98; W. Lloyd Warner and J. O. Low, *The Social System of the Modern Factory* (New Haven, CT: Yale University Press, 1947).

[4] Moreno, *Blacks Americans and Organized Labor*, 153; Wright, *Old South, New South*, 156–97.

individuals on their respective merits, but en bloc as work groups. Employers of menial labor hired either Negro or white. A "mixed" labor force was not an option, although blacks could be found in physically separate menial jobs in otherwise white industries.[5]

Southern blacks often broke into the industrial sector in those areas where white workers were attempting to organize: steel, coal mining, and dock work. Employers brought blacks into the workforce either as strikebreakers or as nonunion alternatives. Black coal miners in the nonunion Appalachia coal fields accounted for a rise in black mining employment of 5 percent in the 1920s, while total employment in mining declined by 14 percent. In 1923, New Orleans shippers avoided longshoremen's unions by delegating control of hiring to a black labor contractor who kept out unions and hired only blacks.[6] Southern unions excluded blacks, but some, like the United Mine Workers, were forced to welcome blacks as a way to circumvent employers' divide-and-conquer tactics. However, as long as segregation and economic exclusion defined southern society, black workers would be an available alternative for employers seeking to subvert unions.

Racial segregation also existed in the North and Midwest, but it did not dictate labor relations the same way it did in the South. Far more significant was a seemingly endless supply of European immigrants, each arriving group willing to work for less than the previous group, and like their native-born counterparts, hoarding jobs for their own kind. Native-born white workers organized unions to protect themselves from the wage-reducing immigrant onslaught. Since the purpose of organizing was to control and limit the available labor supply, unions were by nature exclusionary. This was especially true of craft, or skilled, unions. Mass industrial unions were different – and, before the government's help in the 1930s, less successful. Because they organized unskilled workers with little bargaining power, mass unions, such as the Knights of Labor, the Industrial Workers of the World, and later the CIO, had more incentive to organize the entire labor force, regardless of race or ethnicity. Despite the strategic incentive for multiracial solidarity, however, it was difficult for unions to overcome ethnic bonds, racism, and white entitlement at the local level. Often blacks were admitted into unions only to find themselves in

[5] Donald Dewey, "Negro Employment in Southern Industry," *Journal of Political Economy* 60 (1952): 279; Edward Ayers, *The Promise of the New South: Life after Reconstruction* (New York: Oxford University Press, 1992); Wright, *Old South, New South*; and Allison Davis, Burleigh Gardner, and Mary R. Gardner, *Deep South: A Social Anthropological Study of Caste and Class* (Chicago: University of Chicago Press, 1941), 423–80.

[6] Moreno, *Black Americans and Organized Labor*, 153; Nelson, *Divided We Stand*, 102–3. For a different interpretation, see Eric Arnesen, *Waterfront Workers of New Orleans: Race, Class, and Politics, 1863–1923* (New York: Oxford University Press, 1999).

segregated locals. Even when union leaders wanted blacks in their unions, they found it difficult to keep them because white unionists created an unwelcome atmosphere.[7] The North's workforce was much more cosmopolitan and diverse than the South's, but immigrants and native whites exhibited strong, strategic loyalties to their own communities that excluded blacks.

With World War I, European immigration declined, while the demand for steel, war material, and other manufactured items increased. Employers turned south for workers, and northern cities' black populations quadrupled. Detroit's black population went from 5,741 in 1910 to 40,838 by 1920, a sevenfold increase. Fifty-thousand southern blacks arrived in Chicago between 1910 and 1920. Black migrants found work in steel factories and packing plants. In 1920, at least one Chicago packing plant employed more than five thousand black workers, more than a quarter of its workforce. Executives at International Harvester, also in Chicago, worried that the company was hiring too many Negroes by 1920 and urged that the number be kept at 20 percent of the workforce. Illinois Steel's Gary Works, which employed 66 blacks in 1909, had 1,295 by 1918. Carnegie Steel had four thousand black employees in 1917.[8] Some employers regarded blacks as ideal workers: compliant, grateful, and antiunion. Most famously, Henry Ford hired black workers in his River Rouge plant and paid them a very generous $5 a day, at a time when other automobile companies would not employ them. By 1940, the Ford Motor Company employed half of the black men in Detroit, compared with only 14 percent of the white men.[9]

In 1924, Congress restricted immigration. This was potentially good for black workers since it reduced competition for jobs. However, because employers were forced to pay higher wages, they began to develop laborsaving technologies and to look for ways to develop a stable, reliable, homogeneous workforce. Because workers were scarce and no longer expendable, compan-ies invested more in keeping them, developing, for instance, formalized

---

[7] Moreno, *Black Americans and Organized Labor*, 44–47; Horace Cayton and George Mitchell, *Black Workers and the New Unions* (Chapel Hill: University of North Carolina Press, 1939), 266–67.

[8] St. Clair Drake and Horace Cayton, *Black Metropolis: A Study of Negro Life in a Northern City* (New York: Harcourt Brace, 1945), 303; Robert Ozanne, *A Century of Labor-Management Relations at McCormick and International Harvester* (Madison: University of Wisconsin Press, 1967), 184; and Nelson, *Divided We Stand*, 164. See also Rick Halpern, *Down on the Killing Floor: Black and White Workers in Chicago's Packinghouses* (Urbana: University of Illinois Press, 1997).

[9] Sugrue, *The Origins of the Urban Crisis*, 25; See also Thomas N. Maloney and Warren Whatley, "Making the Effort: The Contours of Racial Discrimination in Detroit's Labor Markets, 1920–40," *Journal of Economic History* 55 (September 1995): 465–93; and Thomas Maloney, "Higher Places in the Industrial Machinery? Tight Labor Markets and Occupational Advancement by Black Males in the 1910s." *Social Science History* 26 (2002): 475–502.

promotion ladders and in-house training. It was hoped that promising workers advancement opportunities, benefits, and a stable career would induce them to stay with the company rather than seeking higher wages at a competing firm. This hurt black employment because now employers were looking for something called "promotability," which entailed qualities such as education and supervisory skills, qualities that few black workers had and which white employers would have refused to see even in those who had them.[10]

If black workers succeeded in securing employment, they faced hostility from white managers and workers. A 1944 poll conducted for the National Association of Manufacturers indicated that 65 percent of 2,145 polled white business owners, managers, white-collar, and manual workers favored segregated workplaces. Of these, owners, managers, and white-collar workers were more inclined than manual workers to favor segregated workplaces, a result that seems to challenge the notion that the lower classes were more racist than others. Of 1,208 white respondents, 68 percent said white jobs should not be opened to Negroes. Again, owners, managers, and white-collar workers were least inclined to open jobs for blacks: 74 percent said no, while only 26 percent said yes. According to this poll, manual laborers and those residing in the Northeast were the most amenable to integration and opening job opportunities, but even so, the majority was inclined to discriminate and segregate.[11]

By World War II, patterns of economic exclusion were firmly in place. Employers, white workers, and unions worked together to reinforce exclusionary "customs" in the workplace. That these policies were called customs and traditions tended to naturalize their occurrence as the normal state of things. And in many ways they were natural. Exclusion was not always the result of concerted antiblack efforts but rather the unintended consequences of policies designed to further the interests of unions or employers. Employers hired the friends and relatives of people who already worked for them because it was cost-effective. Employers looked for promotability to curb turnover. Exclusionary policies gave unions control over the labor supply. Seniority – which disadvantaged blacks – was a way for unions to mitigate arbitrary productivity demands. Whites defended exclusionary policies, and most regarded racial minorities as inferior. But exclusionary policies were not solely the result of

---

[10] See Sanford Jacoby, *Employing Bureaucracy: Managers, Unions, and the Transformation of Work in American Industry, 1900–1945* (New York: Columbia University Press, 1985); and Thomas N. Maloney, "Personnel Policy and Racial Inequality in the Pre–WWII North," *Journal of Interdisciplinary History* 30 (1999): 235–58.

[11] "The Color-Line in Industry: A Report of the Public Opinion Index for Industry," Princeton, NJ, April 1944, in National Association of Manufacturers, Records, 1895–1990 (hereafter NAM Records), Series 7, Box 136, Hagley Museum and Library, Wilmington Delaware (hereafter HML).

white racism but rather of different groups of whites trying to protect their interests from other groups of whites. The result was what sociologists have since called "institutional racism": discrimination against minorities that could not necessarily be traced to intentional racism but was embedded in the way things were done.[12]

World War II gave rise to a confluence of factors favorable to black employment and activism. It created economic opportunities. It increased the power of the federal government. It highlighted the dangers of racial strife and the importance of democracy. It required centralized economic and social planning. It spurred black migration out of the South. It forced corporations to work with the state. Researcher and fair employment advocate Robert Weaver, who was not given to hyperbole, called the war a "revolution" for America's racial minorities. There would be no going back to traditional race relations.[13]

Overcoming Color: Fair Employment and Equal Opportunity Activism, 1940–1964

Because color mattered, because there were "black jobs" and "white jobs," because the job market was segregated and segmented by color, black employment activists after World War II focused their efforts on convincing employers that color should not matter, that employers should be color-blind in their hiring and promotion policies. Black employment activists demanded not jobs per se but rather antidiscrimination policies that prohibited the consideration of race, nationality, and religion in employment and emphasized the meaninglessness of color and the importance of individual opportunity.

It hadn't always been this way. Before the 1940s, there had been black leaders who sought to secure jobs for blacks specifically, rather than pursuing universal antidiscrimination policies. Urban League officials, for instance, visited industrialists with the aim of getting them to hire a certain number of blacks, often in proportion to the local population.[14] The "Don't Shop Where You Can't Work" boycott campaigns of the 1930s took a more coercive approach, demanding

---

[12] See, for example, Sugrue, *Origins of the Urban Crisis*; John Perry, "Business – Next Target for Integration," *Harvard Business Review* 41, no. 2 (March–April 1963): 104-15; and William Sundstrom, "The Color-Line: Racial Norms and Discrimination in Urban Labor Markets, 1910–1950," *Journal of Economic History* 54, no. 2 (June 1994): 382–96.

[13] Weaver, *Negro Labor*, preface.

[14] Whitney Young, "History of the St. Paul Urban League" (master's thesis, University of Minnesota, 1947), 34–39, at the Minnesota Historical Society, Minneapolis, Minnesota, and the Minnesota Governor's Interracial Commission, *The Negro Worker in Minnesota* (St. Paul: the Commission, 1945), 21–22.

that white store owners hire blacks in proportion to their population in the area or in proportion to their patronage.[15] But the idea was the same – to secure jobs for blacks, not antidiscrimination policies for all. Similarly, both the Tennessee Valley Authority and the Public Works Administration (PWA) practiced a quota system that reserved jobs for blacks.[16] Originally, the PWA had tried to ban discrimination in the program, but discrimination turned out to be extremely difficult to identify since there were so many structural factors hindering black employability. So the agency instituted quotas to ensure that blacks would be employed in skilled and semiskilled public works positions at the same levels that they had been in 1930.[17] At one level, these race-conscious strategies were not unlike what other ethnic groups had always done in establishing a labor monopoly for their group in a particular market.

White employers disliked the idea of racial quotas and boycotts, but so too did many black leaders. The "Don't Shop" boycott campaigns triggered for some blacks recollections of Booker T. Washington's segregationist strategies. Writer George Schuyler felt that the boycotts and demands for proportional hiring were too narrowly racial and fostered "an unhealthy race consciousness."[18] Everywhere, he wrote, progressive workers were turning away from racial and nationalist slogans and seeking solutions in rational, mutual, interracial, international cooperation. The segregationist overtones of the boycott strategy were a step in the wrong direction. Similarly, Ralph Bunche, who was at this time chair of the Political Science department at Howard University, felt that the boycotters misunderstood the nature of the problem, which was not necessarily discrimination or racism but rather the inadequacy of the economic system to create an adequate number of jobs for all. The problem was American capitalism and the solution for Bunche was not to displace white workers from their jobs (which was what the boycotters sought) but to work with white workers to change an economic system that beggared both white workers and black.

[15] On the boycott campaign, see Robin D. G. Kelley and Earl Lewis, *To Make Our World Anew: A History of African Americans* (New York: Oxford University Press, 2000), 429; Gilbert Ware and William Hastie, *Grace under Pressure* (New York: Oxford University Press, 1984), 67; Paul Moreno, *From Direct Action to Affirmative Action* (Baton Rouge: Louisiana State University Press, 1997), 32–33.

[16] Moreno, *From Direct Action to Affirmative Action*, 55–57, and John Kirby, *Black Americans in the Roosevelt Era: Liberalism and Race* (Knoxville: University of Tennessee Press, 1980), 22–23, 127.

[17] See T. Arnold Hill, "The Plight of the Negro Industrial Worker," *The Journal of Negro Education* 5, no. 1 (January 1936): 40–47, and Moreno, *From Direct Action to Affirmative Action*, 55–64.

[18] George Schuyler, *Black and Conservative: The Autobiography of George S. Schuyler* (New Rochelle, NY: Arlington House, 1966), 217.

Putting the competition for jobs on a strictly racial basis, Bunche felt, widened the already wide gap between the white and black working classes.[19]

NAACP and Urban League officials such as Walter White and Lester Granger were likewise skeptical of a divisive "black only" approach to employment. They felt blacks' interests were best pursued by building political alliances with other whites in what would later be called the New Deal coalition. Although the New Deal was not always helpful to blacks (indeed, in some cases, it harmed black interests), it did offer some benefits.[20] The New Deal accepted once-shunned groups, such as organized workers, as modern realities that had to be included in the body politic to achieve social peace. It emphasized the interdependence of social groups and the role of the state in balancing, integrating, and harmonizing the many groups in society. It emphasized how American traditions such as individualism, laissez-faire economics, and states' rights were inadequate for dealing with the realities of a complex, multigroup, economically interdependent modern society.[21] It recognized that economic hardship created racial conflict and encouraged dangerous ideologies such as fascism and communism. But mostly, the New Deal gave the federal government the power to achieve the sort of massive economic and social intervention that racial progress required. Not for nothing did conservatives call the New Deal "social engineering."[22]

The NAACP was especially critical of any kind of quotas. The demands for hiring blacks in proportion to their numbers, that is, quotas, would backfire. Blacks were after all a small minority in most areas of the nation. If such quotas were adopted everywhere, it followed that blacks would be relieved of, or denied, positions in white majority areas, which were in fact most areas. Quotas created employment ceilings. Employers would hire the minimum number of blacks and then just stop.[23] In Minnesota, for instance, where the Urban League had convinced industrialists to hire blacks in proportion

---

[19] Ralph Bunche, "A Critical Analysis of the Tactics and Programs of Minority Groups," *Journal of Negro Education* 4, no. 3 (July 1935): 308–20. On Bunche's views, see John Kirby, "Ralph J. Bunche and Black Radical Thought in the 1930s," *Phylon* 35, no. 2 (1974): 129–41.

[20] For African American critiques of the New Deal, see, for instance, Ralph Bunche, "A Critique of New Deal Social Planning as It Affects Negroes," *Journal of Negro Education* 5, no. 1 (January 1936): 59–65; Harvard Sitkoff, *New Deal for Blacks* (New York: Oxford University Press, 1978).

[21] The best contemporary expositions of New Deal philosophy is Henry Wallace, *New Frontiers* (New York, 1934). See also David Plotke, *Building a Democratic Political Order* (New York: Cambridge University Press, 1996); David Truman, *The Governmental Process* (New York: Knopf, 1951); and Alan Brinkley, *The End of Reform: New Deal Liberalism in Recession and War* (New York: Vintage, 1996). On black intellectuals' support of these ideas, see Kirby, *Black Americans in the Roosevelt Era*.

[22] Kirby, *Black Americans in the Roosevelt Era*, 32–33, 130–32.

[23] Schuyler, 216–17; Moreno, *From Direct Action to Affirmative Action*, 35–37.

to their population, Twin City companies would typically hire ten blacks.[24] Such policies did nothing to end employment discrimination. Indeed, they allowed employers to hire a token number of black workers to escape charges of discrimination. While securing jobs for a few, then, proportional hiring, or quotas, did little to create employment opportunities for the many, it did little to ameliorate the problem of black employment in the long run.

What the NAACP wanted instead were color-blind policies of nondiscrimination, which were not divisive or parochial but rather universal and just. They called it fair employment, and by the end of World War II, the idea that race should not be a consideration in hiring and advancement decisions was the goal of black employment activism. All talk of quotas and proportional hiring stopped. Several factors contributed to the ascent of this color-blind approach to the problem of minority employment. Perhaps the most influential was the experience of the wartime Fair Employment Practice Committee (FEPC) and its aftermath.

The Wartime FEPC and the Movement for Fair Employment

In late 1940, America's industrial plants were beginning to deliver on President Roosevelt's promise to an embattled England that the United States would be an "arsenal for democracy." Countless white workers had been hired, but, as usual, few blacks. Black leaders, including Walter White of the NAACP, T. Arnold Hill of the National Urban League, and A. Philip Randolph of the Brotherhood for Sleeping Car Porters, met with President Roosevelt in September 1940 to discuss black participation in the armed forces and the defense industries. Promises were made. The president professed belief in equal opportunity. But Randolph was skeptical. He proposed instead that ten thousand Negroes march down Pennsylvania Avenue to protest black exclusion from the armed forces and the defense industries. The movement caught on, and though the traditional black organizations were lukewarm about a mass movement, they offered tentative support. Randolph headed the new March on Washington Committee. The march was scheduled for July. The more it looked like the march might actually happen, that there might actually be ten thousand Negroes on their way to Washington, DC, the more alarmed liberal

---

[24] Minneapolis Moline Company, Northland Greyhound Lines, St. Paul's Ford plant, and a St. Paul mail-order house all employed ten Negroes. Young, "History of the St. Paul Urban League," 34–39, at MHS, and Governor's Interracial Commission, *The Negro Worker in Minnesota*, 21–22.

allies became. Even Eleanor Roosevelt wanted Randolph to call it off. It would create, she argued, a tremendous backlash that would set back Negro progress. But Randolph stood his ground. He wanted an executive order against employment discrimination. Fearing the ramifications of a Negro march, President Roosevelt eventually acquiesced to Randolph's demand. On June 25, 1941, he signed Executive Order 8802, prohibiting discrimination in employment in the defense industries or the government because of race, creed, or national origin. He also created a temporary Fair Employment Practices Committee (FEPC) to enforce the order. Randolph called off the march, declaring that its goal had been achieved.[25]

The wartime FEPC consisted of representatives from industry, labor, and black leadership. The presidents of RCA, United Fruit Company, and the Federal Cartridge Company represented industry, as did Sara Southall, the employee relations supervisor from International Harvester. Black members included Earl Dickerson, a Chicago alderman; Milton Webster of the Brotherhood of Sleeping Car Porters; and attorney Charles Houston. William Green (AFL) and Philip Murray (CIO) represented labor. Black activists and ordinary black workers filed 11,200 complaints of racial discrimination with the FEPC over the course of its six-year existence (1941–46), 80 percent of the total complaints received.[26] The FEPC's powers were limited by lack of funding, bureaucratic infighting, and a cumbersome legal process that required the plaintiff to prove intentional discrimination. Despite these shortcomings, however, its hearings and investigations began the important work of publicly identifying and discrediting discrimination. Its investigations yielded solid statistical evidence of widespread systematic exclusion of black workers in traditionally white positions. They found companies that explicitly refused to hire Negroes. They found unions that excluded black workers. They found that black workers were limited to laboring positions and that employers were hiring white women but not black women. They also declared that segregated workplaces were instances of discrimination and hence prohibited. FEPC investigators acted with the authority of the federal government behind them. They talked to company presidents about promoting black workers, hiring black women,

---

[25] On the creation of the wartime FEPC, see Malcolm Ross, *All Manner of Men* (New York: Reynal and Hitchcock, 1948); Denton Watson, ed., *The Papers of Clarence Mitchell, Vol. 1, 1942–1943* (Athens: Ohio University Press, 2005), esp. xliii–lxxxiii; Andrew Kersten, *Race, Jobs, and the War: The FEPC in the Midwest, 1941–1946* (Urbana: University of Illinois Press, 2000); and Merl Reed, *Seedtime for the Modern Civil Rights Movement* (Baton Rouge: Louisiana State University, 1991).

[26] Six percent of complaints claimed religious discrimination, mainly against Jews, and 14 percent were complaints from Mexican Americans on account of national origin. See Ross, *All Manner of Men*, 23–25.

and ending segregation in cafeterias and workplaces. They elicited promises from company presidents and checked back to measure progress and hold them to their word. Although the FEPC was hamstrung in any number of ways, its work provided useful data and experience, which activists would continue to draw on in the postwar years.[27]

The formation of the wartime FEPC was significant on several levels. First, it proved the power of organized mass political pressure. Second, it indicated that the government, or at least the president, was prepared to intervene in the business of private industry in the interests of social peace. Third, it denaturalized discrimination, transforming it from something that just happened to something that was unfair, un-American, and preventable. Fourth, it collected data. Finally, and most significantly, the FEPC, with its charge to enforce fair employment, became the focal point of all subsequent employment activism, as Negro groups focused their energy on monitoring its effectiveness, its failures, and its future.

After the war, Randolph continued to organize and lobby for a permanent federal FEPC or, failing that, FEPCs at the state level. The FEPC strategy was to seek an end to racial discrimination in employment. The hope was that, in prohibiting discrimination, individual black workers would secure employment commensurate with their qualifications. FEPC activists did not focus on securing jobs for blacks but rather on ending barriers to black employment. With its adoption, all other strategies for securing black employment (such as proportional hiring) were abandoned, as employment activists focused on winning state-level FEPCs. "Opportunity" and "fair employment" became the bywords of black employment activism until the late 1960s.

Activists found that the FEPC's rhetoric of individualism and opportunity, together with its legal authority, made it persuasive to many whites. There was nothing radical about opportunity. Indeed, it affirmed white Americans' fundamental beliefs about their nation and themselves. The strategy integrated Negro Americans into the fabric of economic life, not as burdens or wards but as contributors. They asked for no special treatment, only the right to contribute to the war effort and to compete fairly in the labor market. It was unfortunate that legislation was required to make Americans live up to their principles, but the coercive power of law, backed by the federal authority, made the FEPC particularly effective in changing attitudes.[28]

---

[27] On the wartime FEPC see Ross, *All Manner of Men*; Watson, *The Papers of Clarence Mitchell*, esp. 1: xliii–lxxxiii; Reed, *Seedtime for the Modern Civil Rights Movement*. Ross was committee chair from 1943 to 1945; Mitchell was a field investigator for the FEPC.

[28] FEPC chairman Malcolm Ross reported that "federal authority is an enormously effective instrument.... When it was put into play a new attitude toward intolerance ran like a wave

Black activists also emphasized the material benefits fair employment would deliver to whites. Fair employment would create loyal customers, affirm individualism and free-market values, transform a beggar class into a market, and ensure social equilibrium and harmony. Don't do us any favors, activists pronounced; our value to society will be evidenced as you pursue your own economic interests. As one civil rights activist put it during the House Committee on Labor's 1944 hearings for a permanent FEPC, if Negroes were assured full employment, "their buying power and practices would create a revenue greater than all the revenue from our exports."[29] This same claim, bolstered by income and population estimates, recurred endlessly in postwar articles touting fair employment.

Proponents of fair employment deftly tied their agenda to the less radical but still liberal postwar agenda of "full employment." Full employment required government action, but, as fair employment advocate Robert Weaver pointed out, it did not require government control. Full employment required government expenditure to maintain consumer demand. If there was sufficient consumer demand, the Negro employment problem would be resolved with little coercion.[30] By equating fair employment with full employment, Weaver was tying black aims to a larger, color-blind, postwar liberal economic agenda and assuring those who worried about heightened race consciousness or government control that their concerns were unmerited. Thus, despite fair employment's rhetoric of individualism, its underlying philosophy of purchasing power and government guidance indicated its comportment with the new state-centered, postwar liberalism.[31]

Another reason that fair employment became the focus of black employment activism in the 1940s and 1950s was because it affirmed the color-blind message of the emergent antiracist movement in a way that other strategies (such as proportional hiring or quotas) did not. Race, and, more to the point, racial tension, was a palpable subtext to World War II, whether it was Hitler's

---

through government offices, director's meetings, and union halls. Prejudice could no longer be totally ignored." Ross, *All Manner of Men*, 168.

[29] Testimony of Beulah Whitby, the national president of Alpha Kappa Alpha Sorority in Detroit, Michigan, June 6, 1944, in U.S. Congress, House Committee on Labor, *To Prohibit Discrimination in Employment* (Washington, DC: U.S. GPO, 1944), 49.

[30] Weaver, *Negro Labor*, 261–63; see also essays in Raymond Logan, ed., *What the Negro Wants* (Chapel Hill: University of North Carolina Press, 1944).

[31] On the development of postwar liberalism, see Brinkley, *The End of Reform*, and Kevin Mattson, *When America Was Great: The Fighting Faith of Postwar Liberalism* (New York: Routledge, 2004). On the development of consumer-oriented economic policy, see also Meg Jacobs, *Pocketbook Politics: Economic Citizenship in Twentieth Century America* (Princeton, NJ: Princeton University Press, 2005).

persecution of the Jews; race riots in Beaumont, Texas; Japanese internments on the West Coast; or the fate of European and American colonies. A four-day race riot in Detroit in June 1943 not only held up war production, it also required federal troops to restore peace.[32] The army was required in Philadelphia as well, after white transit workers went on strike to protest the FEPC-enforced hiring of African Americans. African American activists took advantage of the threat of fascism and riots to make their case for racial reform, which further focused the nation's attention on racial injustice. In his landmark *An American Dilemma*, Gunnar Myrdal famously pointed out the hypocrisy that hung over America's purported championing of democracy and justice. Large numbers of white Americans suddenly became alarmed, not only by the race riots but also by racism itself, as if they were seeing it for the first time. Thousands of interracial, intergroup committees and citizens groups sprung up in cities across the United States, some even in the South. Their aim was to quell racial tension and promote interracial cooperation through education and example. They produced books, articles, pamphlets, filmstrips, role-playing scripts, and museum exhibits designed to educate the public about racial tension and racism.[33]

Armed with the anthropological theories of Franz Boas and Margaret Mead, antiracist educators sought to combat the pervasive influence of nineteenth-century scientific racism, which held that racial categories were discrete and rankable and that race determined a person's moral character, intelligence, and potential. Since the belief that race was real and character-forming was so embedded in American culture, antiracist educators focused their energies on dismantling that belief and offering in its stead the idea that race "doesn't matter," that we are all human beings, that we all experience the same trials and tribulations of humanity, and hence are entitled to the same rights, regardless of color, nationality, or religious faith. One of the most effective ways of illustrating to whites the falseness of race-based thinking was to show the plight of some smart, worthy, ambitious Negro individual, who was treated according to unflattering racial stereotypes, rather than on the basis of his or her

---

[32] See Daniel Kryder, *Divided Arsenal: Race and the American State during World War II* (New York: Cambridge University Press, 2000); and Ross, *All Manner of Men*.

[33] On interracial committees, see Jennifer Delton, *Making Minnesota Liberal* (Minneapolis: University of Minnesota Press, 2002), 40–60. Much has been written about the grassroots nature of activism during the war. See especially Robert Korstad and Nelson Lichtenstein, "Opportunities Found and Lost: Labor, Radicals, and the Early Civil Rights Movement," *Journal of American History* 75, no. 3 (December 1988): 786–811; and appropriate chapters in John Dittmer, *Local People: The Struggle for Civil Rights in Mississippi* (Urbana: University of Illinois Press, 1994); Arnesen, *Brotherhoods of Color*; Kelley and Lewis, *To Make Our World Anew*; and Sugrue, *The Origins of the Urban Crisis*.

individual merits. Getting white people to see black Americans as individuals, rather than a group defined and embodied by race, was a major goal of the antiracist movement and it bolstered the fair employment movement. Denying a qualified person employment on the basis of his race alone epitomized the perils of race-based thinking. Alternative employment strategies, such as proportional hiring or quotas, contradicted the new color-blind ideals that would deliver white Americans from scientific racism and the potential threat of a homegrown fascism.[34]

Opposition to the FEPC was nonetheless virulent. White southerners felt that the FEPC was a communistic, federal dictatorship designed to ensure "social equality" between whites and Negroes. FEPC proponents ritually denied that their aim was social equality, which everyone understood to mean miscegenation. During the hearings for a permanent FEPC, supportive House members always asked those testifying on its behalf whether they wanted social equality, and the answer was always no. No one wanted social equality, only economic equality (only the specter of interracial sex could make "economic equality" the acceptable choice in capitalist America).[35] But white southerners understood better than most the ways in which economic marginalization upheld white supremacy.

A large number of business owners and employers also opposed the FEPC. For many it represented unprecedented and unwanted state intrusion into the affairs of private industry. The New Deal had already expanded the power of the state over industry in unproductive ways with the National Labor Relations Board and the Wagner Act, and the FEPC was another indication of the federal government's unconstitutional will to power. Surely the employer was in a better position than a bureaucratic committee to decide who would and would not be a useful, productive employee at his firm. How could one disprove accusations of discrimination? To keep statistics that would exonerate an employer would itself constitute discrimination, according to the proposed legislation. Employers feared a rush of lawsuits filed by professional agitators. They feared that they would have to meet quotas. Businessmen did not even agree that

---

[34] Typical examples of the antiracist literature for the time include Ruth Benedict, *Race: Science and Politics* (New York: Modern Age Books, 1940); Ashley Montagu, *Man's Most Dangerous Myth: The Fallacy of Race* (New York: Columbia University Press, 1942); Bucklin Moon, ed., *Primer for White Folks* (Garden City, NY: Doubleday, Doran, 1945); Cary McWilliams, *Brothers under the Skin* (Boston: Little, Brown and Co., 1951). For a discussion of changing conceptions of race during the time, see Matthew Jacobson, *Whiteness of a Different Color* (Cambridge, MA: Harvard University Press, 1998); and Walter Jackson, *Gunnar Myrdal and America's Conscience: Social Engineering and Racial Liberalism, 1938–1987* (Chapel Hill: University of North Carolina Press, 1990).

[35] U.S. Congress, *To Prohibit Discrimination in Employment*.

discrimination was such a bad thing. As the Minnesota Employers Association declared, "Discrimination is simply American freedom to do business free of governmental control."[36]

Public opinion was more measured, although hardly enthusiastic. A *Fortune* poll conducted in September 1948 asked whether people agreed or disagreed with candidates who supported a law making it illegal for employers to discriminate on the basis of race or religion. Forty-nine percent agreed, while 44 percent disagreed and 7 percent had no opinion.[37] This meant more people supported such a law than did not. Truman and Wallace supporters were even more likely to support the law. But the question did not specify whether the law would be at the federal or state level. A 1949 Gallup poll conducted just six months later asked how far the federal government should go in requiring employers to hire people without regard to race or religion. Phrased this way, only 34 percent thought "all the way," while 45 percent thought "none of the way." While a similar percentage opposed the law, the positive response was smaller when the role of federal government was made explicit.[38] In a 1952 Gallup poll that asked whether there should be a national law requiring employers to hire without regard to race or religion or whether the matter should be left to the states, 32 percent supported a national law, while 44 percent said it should be left to the states. The rest said neither or no opinion. It is unclear from this poll whether the people who wanted to leave it to the states actually supported a state-level law. In the South, for instance, 70 percent wanted the matter left to the states, which were unlikely to pass such legislation. Only 17 percent of white southerners said "neither/no." But in the Midwest, where 44 percent wanted to leave it with the states, 28 percent said "neither/no opinion," which could mean that 44 percent accepted a state law, since people who opposed the law chose the "neither/no opinion" category.[39] In sum, these polls indicate that support for a federal FEPC was lukewarm and ambivalent, especially when compared with the passionate and committed opposition.

Civil rights organizations succeeded in making fair employment a national political issue. In 1946, President Truman set up a Committee on Civil Rights,

---

[36] Otto Christenson, "Fair Employment Practices Act, A Communication from Otto Christenson to the Minnesota League of Women Voters" (St. Paul: Minnesota Employers' Association, 1949), 10, at MHS. See also L. M. Evans, "Freedom or Regimentation," in *Vital Speeches of the Day* 13, no. 17 (June 15, 1947): 541–44.

[37] *Public Opinion Quarterly*, Winter 1948–49, 764.

[38] Interview dates: March 19–24, 1949, in *The Gallup Poll: Public Opinion, 1935–1971*, 3 vols. (New York: Random House, 1972), 2:810.

[39] Interview dates: July 13–18, 1952, in *The Gallup Poll: Public Opinion, 1935–1971*, 3 vols. (New York: Random House, 1972), 2:1083.

which explicitly called for a permanent federal FEPC. Truman repeatedly introduced legislation for a permanent FEPC. In 1948, the Republican, Democratic, and Progressive party presidential candidates all endorsed a permanent FEPC.[40] At the state level, activists had managed to win actual FEPCs. New York state adopted an FEPC in 1945. By 1950, New Jersey, Massachusetts, Connecticut, New Mexico, Oregon, Rhode Island, and Washington, DC, had followed New York's lead. By 1960, twenty-eight states and fifty municipalities were operating under some sort of fair employment law.

Civil rights pressure also induced post–World War II presidents to issue executive orders barring racial discrimination in the defense industries to be enforced by presidential compliance committees. President Truman created the Committee on Government Contract Compliance (1952–1953); President Eisenhower, the Committee on Government Contracts (1953–1961); and President Kennedy, the Committee on Equal Employment Opportunity (1961–1963), which instituted the voluntary Plans for Progress program. In a familiar story, the compliance committees were underfunded, weak, slow, and regarded as "window dressing." But recently, some historians have argued that these agencies had a more sophisticated understanding of discrimination than has been recognized and that their experiences and research paved the way for the affirmative action programs of the 1970s.[41]

Activists were unsuccessful in securing federal fair employment legislation. The push for a federal FEPC was hobbled by southern Democrats' control of the Senate and congressional rules, which required a two-thirds majority to end a filibuster. Nonetheless, activists tried. In 1949, the NAACP helped form the Leadership Conference on Civil Rights, consisting of twenty national civil rights and labor groups, to aid congressional liberals in their attempts to pass national fair employment legislation. With the help of the Leadership Conference, liberals introduced legislation for a permanent FEPC almost every year from 1946 to 1964. At the same time, they introduced legislation to allow cloture on "debate" (i.e., filibuster) with just a simple majority. Both of these efforts failed repeatedly. The best that was achieved were occasional committee hearings, which allowed civil rights groups to present evidence about widespread discrimination against racial minorities in the workplace.

[40] See William Berman, *The Politics of the Civil Rights in the Truman Administration* (Columbus, OH: Ohio State University Press 1970), Hugh Davis Graham, *The Civil Rights Era: Origins and Development of National Policy, 1960–1972* (New York: Oxford University Press, 1990), 9–17.

[41] On the federal agencies, see Paul Norgren and Samuel Hill, *Toward Fair Employment* (New York: Columbia University Press, 1964), 149–79, and Timothy Thurber, "Racial Liberalism, Affirmative Action, and the Troubled History of the President's Committee on Government Contracts," *Journal of Policy History* 18, no. 4 (2006): 446–476.

Between 1940 and 1956, black economic life improved considerably, mainly as a result of blacks finally leaving the agricultural sector. Per capita black income tripled during this time from $364 (1956 dollars) in 1940 to $1,070 in 1956, climbing from 30 percent of per capita white income to 53 percent. Moreover, black men and women were getting slightly better jobs. In 1940, only 19.1 percent of black males worked in semiskilled, skilled, or clerical positions. By 1956, that percentage had risen to 39.8 percent, although within that category they occupied the lowest jobs. The percentage of black women working in semiskilled, skilled, or clerical positions increased almost threefold during those years.[42] In 1940 nonwhites made up 10.6 percent of the semiskilled, skilled, and white-collar workforce, while by 1960, they comprised 19.2 percent of that sector.[43]

Still, despite apparent progress and despite state FEPCs and government compliance committees, employment discrimination persisted. Indeed, what each new FEPC, congressional hearing, or contract compliance committee confirmed was that discriminatory hiring patterns continued nationwide and that blacks were egregiously underrepresented in higher-status, better-paying positions. To give just one example: in 1960, Detroit blacks made up only 0.3 percent of skilled Chrysler workers and 0.6 percent of skilled General Motors workers.[44] And those were ostensibly enlightened companies where blacks were part of the racially enlightened UAW-CIO. In Detroit and other cities, the antidiscrimination legislation and activism appeared to have little to no effect on black employment opportunities. As historian Thomas Sugrue points out, those Detroit auto plants that were largely white in 1940 remained so in 1960; those with large black workforces in 1940s retained them in 1960.[45] Urban League studies confirmed that companies' hiring policies were haphazard, undocumented, and typically relied on employee family networks. Black economic progress slowed during the latter half of the prosperous 1950s, as technological innovations in industry began replacing the lower-level jobs that blacks typically occupied. While there was improvement from where blacks had been before the war, then, by the end of the 1950s blacks still lagged far behind whites in family income, savings, education, and occupational status and far ahead of whites in terms of unemployment and infant mortality. (See appendix.)

[42] Statistics from Emmet John Hughes, "The Negro's New Economic Life," *Fortune*, September 1956, 127–31.
[43] Norgren and Hill, *Toward Fair Employment*, 64.
[44] Sugrue, *The Origins of the Urban Crisis*, 105, citing the Detroit Urban League.
[45] Sugrue, *The Origins of the Urban Crisis*, 98.

The Southern Civil Rights Movement, Title VII, and the EEOC

In the South, a very different civil rights movement had developed in the 1950s, based largely in black churches and communities, and with the specific goal of ending Jim Crow segregation in the South. Its leaders were everyday people – students, teachers, preachers, sharecroppers – but whites would come to associate it with Dr. Martin Luther King, Jr. Dr. King spoke the language of human brotherhood, harmony, and justice and promised to redeem America, to cleanse it of its sins. His tactics were civil disobedience, boycotts, and nonviolent resistance, and they forced white Americans to see the ugliness of white racial hatred. He was no lobbyist.

The headlines of the civil rights movement have become iconic, heroic, and righteous: *Brown v. Board of Education*, the Little Rock Nine, Rosa Parks, the Montgomery Bus Boycott, the Freedom Riders, Birmingham, Medgar Evers, Freedom Summer, Fannie Lou Hamer, Selma. These events, these people, inspired white Americans outside the South to want to be better, to do better, to repent, to change. So too did the violence of white southern resistance: Bull Connor's fire hoses and dogs; the Birmingham church bombings; the murder of the three civil rights workers in Philadelphia, Mississippi; the assassination of Medgar Evers and countless others. For these crimes, too, white Americans sought redemption. Other names inspired something different, not so much hope and brotherhood as fear. Malcolm X, Elijah Muhammad – names that portended the urban riots of the late 1960s and embodied white fears of black uprising and retributive violence.

Between the hope and the trembling, between the desire for brotherhood and the fear of retribution, white Americans slowly made their way toward change. It is true that not all white Americans accepted Dr. King's message. Segregationist presidential candidate George Wallace found many supporters in Michigan, Ohio, and Pennsylvania in 1964, the alleged high point of white racial liberalism.[46] But Wallace was a marginal candidate, and the Republican candidate who opposed civil rights, Barry Goldwater, was soundly defeated by a pro–civil rights president in one of the largest landslides in election history. Public opinion polls indicated that white nonsoutherners were more supportive of integration, civil rights, and racial equality than ever before. When asked if they would vote for a candidate who strongly favored civil rights, as opposed to one who was strongly opposed to civil rights, only 17 percent supported the candidate opposed to civil rights. Even among white southerners,

[46] Ibid., 209–30.

28 percent would support a pro–civil rights candidate.[47] After a decade of listing civil rights near the end of the list of "most important problems facing the nation today," it was at the top of the list in 1964 and 1965, alternating between first and second position with "international problems." In Washington, DC, southern Democrat and master politician Lyndon Baines Johnson had vowed to make real a slain president's civil rights program. The nation was ready for the Civil Rights Act of 1964, in which Title VII would finally prohibit racial and religious discrimination in employment. But that did not mean that there would not be a fight.

Liberals and civil rights activists had been working for this opportunity since 1945. In the intervening twenty years, they had strategically rechristened "fair employment" as "equal opportunity" to appeal to business leaders who saw opportunity as a fundamental principle of capitalism. This affirmation of color-blind principles, however, was distinctly at odds with what liberals and activists had learned from state FEPCs and government compliance committees. They had learned, for instance, that it was almost impossible to prove *intentional* discrimination; that removing racial categories from application forms and employee records left no way of measuring compliance; that statistical underrepresentation or imbalances were the best way to determine and correct discriminatory patterns; that merely practicing nondiscrimination did not lead to integration; that some kind of race-conscious affirmative action – that is, special recruitment efforts, training, or revised job qualifications – was necessary to bring black Americans into the workforce; that, in short, the color-blind assumption on which equal opportunity rested did not – and could not – correct discriminatory employment practices.[48]

Nonetheless, the liberals who hammered out Title VII on the House and Senate floors in 1963 and 1964 affirmed, and indeed, strengthened, the color-blind principles of the proposed equal opportunity legislation. To do otherwise would have impeded the passage of the entire civil rights bill, something the president and the nation could ill afford. Liberals, of course, genuinely believed that employment decisions should be made without regard to color or creed and that proportional hiring, or quotas, constituted a form of discrimination. But conservatives' obstructionist claims that Title VII would force employers to fulfill quotas, practice reverse discrimination, and adopt race-conscious hiring policies forced liberals to ban these practices in the bill. Thus, the final version

---

[47] Interview dates: June 25–30, 1964, in *The Gallup Poll: Public Opinion, 1935–1971*, 3 vols. (New York: Random House, 1972), 2:1894.

[48] Graham, *The Civil Rights Era*, 100–21; Moreno, *From Direct Action to Affirmative Action*; Thurber, "Racial Liberalism," and Norgren and Hill, *Toward Fair Employment*.

of the bill specifically prohibited the use of racial quotas to make up for racial imbalances. It also specified that inadvertent, or accidental, discrimination did not violate Title VII.[49] Signed into law in July 1964, the bill set up the Equal Employment Opportunity Commission (EEOC) to receive and to investigate complaints.

The new EEOC was notoriously feeble. It lacked the cease-and-desist authority of other regulatory agencies. It took more than a year to appoint its commissioners and find a leader. Its relationship to the President's Committee on Equal Employment Opportunity (PCEEO), the Office of Federal Contract Compliance (OFCC), and the Civil Rights Commission was confused and resented. Its commissioners had to figure out how to enforce Title VII while complying with the proscriptions against race-conscious assessment methods or record keeping. Despite these handicaps, however, the EEOC eventually found its voice, held hearings, and, with the help of other federal civil rights agencies and the U.S. Supreme Court, was able to force employers to promote African Americans into supervisory positions.[50] As the decade wore on, companies began to respond to the presence of the EEOC, keeping statistics, filling out forms, and incorporating its suggestions into company policy.[51] The key to its success, however, lay in the abandonment of its color-blind charge.

Bringing Color Back In: Boycotts, Riots, and Affirmative Action

The decade following the Civil Rights Act of 1964 would see a concerted effort on the part of the nation's employers to integrate their workplaces. As this book will document, there were employers and other members of the business community who had been supportive of, even advocates for, fair employment and integration long before the tumultuous events of the mid-1960s. But most employers had taken few if any steps to promote black workers into traditionally white jobs. It took the social crisis of the late 1960s – the urban riots, the militant racialism – together with the widespread use of boycotts, an activist EEOC, and court-sanctioned affirmative action to prompt employers into action. These factors would replace the passive call for equal opportunity with an urgent, race-conscious imperative to hire, to promote, and to integrate African Americans into the corporate structure to achieve what has sometimes been called "equality of result."

[49] Graham, *The Civil Rights Era*, 132–52.
[50] Ibid., 177–254.
[51] See, for instance, Employee Relations Department Annual Report 1965, in Du Pont Human Resources, Accession 1615, Series I: Employee Relations Department, HML.

Grassroots pressure on the part of black workers and their allies was key. In Philadelphia, the Reverend Leon Sullivan of the Zion Baptist Church helped organize boycotts against Sunoco Gas, Breyer's Ice Cream, and Tastykakes in the early 1960s. Inspired by the sit-ins in the South, Sullivan and others in the movement demanded that companies hire specific numbers of Negroes in specific positions. [52] Sullivan and a group of ministers, for instance, demanded that Sun Oil Company hire or upgrade thirty Negroes within thirty days or they would organize a boycott. As management consultant Jack Gourlay told the story, Sunoco hired seven, but that wasn't enough. The boycott lasted ten weeks ("No more Sunoco till your preacher says so!"). One station's sales dropped from thirty thousand gallons per month to fourteen thousand and went out of business.[53] The company ultimately complied with demands, agreeing to hire "25 Negro girls in clerical, three drivers and one salesman."[54] Ministers and the Congress for Racial Equality activists in other cities adopted the technique and, one company at a time, succeeded in opening up new jobs for blacks.[55]

This story and others like it were related endlessly in the "how-to" guides of the mid-1960s, which were designed specifically to help companies deal with "Negro demonstrations and boycotts."[56] The author of one of these guides, Jack Gourlay, stressed that the threat of boycotts was the number one reason companies were hiring African Americans into traditionally white jobs. There was no reason, he concluded, to think your company could avoid a boycott.

In addition to boycotts, black workers actively made real the changes promised by the new antidiscrimination legislation in their workplaces. They documented patterns of discrimination in advancement. They testified about discrimination to the EEOC. They educated other workers of their rights. They sued companies for discrimination under Title VII. They made the heavy,

---

[52] See Stacy Kinlock Sewell, "The 'Not-Buying Power' of the Black Community: Urban Boycotts and Equal Employment Opportunity, 1960–1964," *Journal of African-American History* 89, no. 2 (Spring 2004): 135–51; Kathy Newman, "The Forgotten Fifteen Million: Black Radio, 'the Negro Market,' and the Civil Rights Movement," *Radical History Review* 76 (2000): 115–35; August Meier and Elliot Rudwick, *CORE: A Study in the Civil Rights Movement, 1942–1968* (New York: Oxford University Press, 1973); and Jeanne Theoharis and Komozi Woodard, eds., *Freedom North: Black Struggles Outside the South, 1940–1980* (New York: Palgrave MacMillan, 2003).

[53] Jack Gourlay, *The Negro Salaried Worker* (New York: American Management Association, 1965), AMA Research Study 70, 27–28.

[54] Quoted in Sewell, "The 'Not-Buying Power' of the Black Community," 135–51, quote on p. 140.

[55] On the Congress of Racial Equality (CORE) boycotts, see Meier and Rudwick, *CORE.*

[56] Gourlay, *The Negro Salaried Worker.* See also Stephen Habbe, *Company Experience with Negro Employment*, 2 vols., Studies in Personnel Policy No. 201 (New York: National Industrial Conference Board, 1966).

bureaucratic machinery work for them. As a lead plaintiff in the 1973 case of *Ellison v. Rock Hill Printing and Finishing Company* testified, "I brought the lawsuit because I believe in justice and equality to all people."[57]

During the late 1960s, the focus of employment activism shifted from convincing employers to practice nondiscrimination to urging them to hire and advance blacks. The term "affirmative action" signified the break from color-blind principles of equal opportunity. Although it has come to be associated with preferential hiring and quotas (or, if you prefer, "goals and timetables"), it initially referred to any kind of outreach to and cultivation of potential black employees. The term was used in John F. Kennedy's Plans for Progress program, begun in 1961, for which companies promised to take "affirmative action" in recruiting minorities, training minorities, and keeping records of their progress in minority hiring. This type of affirmative action did not involve racial preferences, but it did signify a consciousness of color. The "actions" were race specific. They had to be to be effective. The growing body of civil rights bureaucrats in state FEPCs and government compliance agencies had discovered that simply removing discriminatory intentions, or being color-blind, did not lead to racial integration. In many cases, such blindness perpetrated existing structural inequities.[58] Actual integration would require seeing and seeking out color, not ignoring it. Executives accepted this. Du Pont and Lukens Steel Company were just two Plans for Progress companies that enthusiastically reached out to local Urban Leagues, black colleges, and black community organizations.[59] Indeed, even the conservative National Association of Manufacturers suggested that its members seek out black applicants and make connections to local black organizations. What executives rejected and opposed, at least at first, was the idea of quotas and proportional hiring.

Those employers and politicians who supported fair employment and equal opportunity legislation did so in part because the legislation seemed to uphold fundamental American ideals: individual opportunity, merit, fair play. They

---

[57] Quoted in Minchin, *Hiring the Black Worker: The Racial Integration of the Southern Textile Industry, 1960–1980* (Chapel Hill: University of North Carolina Press, 1999), 225. For more examples of grassroots activism enforcing the new legislation, see also Timothy Minchin, *The Color of Work: The Struggle for Civil Rights in the Southern Paper Industry, 1945–1980* (Chapel Hill: University of North Carolina Press, 2000), Robin D. G. Kelley, *Race Rebels: Culture, Politics, and the Black Working Class* (New York: Free Press, 1996); Venus Green, *Race on the Line: Gender, Labor, and Technology in the Bell System, 1880–1980* (Durham, NC: Duke University Press, 2001); and Arnesen, *Brotherhoods of Color.*

[58] Graham, *The Civil Rights Era*, 51–59; Thurber, "Racial Liberalism."

[59] As I will discuss later. See Charles Brelsford McCoy Papers, 1967–74, Boxes 11–13, 31; and Lukens Steel Company, Executive Officer Files, 1903–1979, Boxes 2164 and 2018, both at HML.

had long regarded the use of quotas or racial preferences to resolve racial inequities as contrary to those ideals. In congressional debates at the state and federal level, they expressed concern that the legislation might lead to a situation in which employers would have to hire a certain number of black workers, to fill a quota, and waited for liberals and activists to assure them that would not happen.[60] Activists who had advocated proportional hiring in the 1930s and who saw the inadequacies of the color-blind fair employment strategy nonetheless understood the political difficulty of convincing white Americans to abandon cherished beliefs in merit, individualism, and opportunity. To point out that white Americans had not cherished these beliefs in regard to black people only begot affirmations that they would in the future; hence there was no need to abandon them now. White Americans who supported Title VII's prohibition on discrimination were uncomfortable with hiring black workers to correct racial imbalances or to reflect their proportion in the community.

The Republican Nixon administration flouted public opinion and instituted an extreme version of affirmative action that required government contractors to set goals and timetables for hiring minorities in proportion to their numbers in the local population. Developed and administered by the OFCC, the plan revived what many civil rights activists had long held to be the only solution to structural economic inequity: hiring and training black people. The Nixon administration had initiated the plan against the notoriously exclusionary construction trade unions of Philadelphia in 1969, but by 1970, the OFCC adopted the plan for all government contractors.[61] There are several explanations for Nixon's unlikely sponsorship of such an unpopular and radical policy. Because it was initially directed against unions, some have argued that it was an attempt to drive a wedge between two key constituents of the Democratic Party (blacks and unions). Memos indicate that the Nixon people were aware of (and amused by) this. But the plan was broadened to include all government contractors, and thus baiting the Democratic Party cannot be the whole explanation. Others suggest that Nixon was uninterested in domestic policy and delegated it to advisors and agency bureaucrats, who, charged with resolving an explosive racial situation, applied solutions that had been talked

---

[60] See Anthony Chen, "The Hitlerian Rule of Quotas: Racial Conservatism and the Politics of Fair Employment in New York State, 1941–45," *Journal of American History* (March 2006): 1238–64; and Graham, *The Civil Rights Era*.

[61] On affirmative action, see Graham, *The Civil Rights Era*, 322–45; Dean Kotlowski, *Nixon's Civil Rights* (Cambridge, MA: Harvard University Press, 2001); Terry H. Anderson, *The Pursuit of Fairness: A History of Affirmative Action* (New York: Oxford University Press, 2004); and John David Skrentny, *The Ironies of Affirmative Action: Politics, Culture and Justice in America* (Chicago: University of Chicago Press, 1996).

Table 1.1 *Distribution of African Americans in Particular Occupational Groups, 1950–1980 (percent)*

Occupation	1950	1960	1970	1980
Total	100.0	100.0	100.0	100.0
White-collar	**9.9**	**16.1**	**27.9**	**39.2**
Professional, technical	3.4	4.8	9.1	12.7
Managers	1.8	2.6	3.5	5.2
Sales	–	1.5	2.1	2.9
Clerical	4.7*	7.3	13.2	18.4
Blue-collar	**40.3**	**40.1**	**42.2**	**35.8**
Craft	5.3	6.0	8.2	9.6
Operatives	19.0	20.4	23.7	19.4
Nonfarm labor	15.9	13.7	10.3	6.9
Service	**31.0**	**31.7**	**26.0**	**23.1**
Farmwork	**18.8**	**12.1**	**3.9**	**1.8**

* This number includes salesworkers.

Compiled from *U.S. Bureau of the Census, Statistical Abstract of the United States, 1955, 1981.*

about for years but never implemented. Still others, including Nixon, have suggested that he was concerned about the legitimacy of the capitalist system in the eyes of black Americans and knew from his experience on Eisenhower's President's Committee on Government Contracts (PCGC) that more drastic measures had long been necessary.

Despite their initial unpopularity among whites and despite their questionable legality, affirmative action policies that used goals and timetables to correct racial imbalances at all levels of an organization finally became the way that large numbers of African Americans began to be integrated into "traditionally white positions." One can see the initial results in Table 1.1.

The Supreme Court upheld and bolstered the use of color-conscious methods in hiring for correcting specific historical injustices. By the 1980s, American companies had crafted and implemented affirmative action programs that employed a combination of techniques to encourage hiring and promoting racial minorities at all levels, including executive leadership.[62] A 1984 Harris poll indicated that 61 percent of the American public said they supported affirmative action in employment. Although many white Americans and conservatives remained resentful of affirmative action policies, employers and managers had come to appreciate them because they made it easier for

---

[62] These programs are described in Frank Dobbin and John Sutton, "The Strength of the Weak State: The Rights Revolution and the Rise of Human Resources Management Divisions," *American Journal of Sociology*, 104, no. 2 (September 1998): 441–76, and Skrentny, *The Ironies of Affirmative Action.*

companies to avoid lawsuits and to plan their compliance with Title VII and other civil rights legislation. Thus, when Ronald Reagan attempted to reverse several Supreme Court decisions and prohibit affirmative action in the early 1980s, the business community opposed his efforts.[63]

Conclusion

In the relatively short space of forty years, then, American employers and unions changed their hiring and promotion practices. Although racial minorities remain underrepresented in many areas and although whites retain a vast economic advantage in most areas, there has been change, even progress, in the integration of American workplaces. No one today would advertise for "whites only." Few corporations today would consider limiting the applicant pool to friends and family of current employees. Whereas once employers refused to declare themselves "equal opportunity employers" lest they raised false hopes, this is standard practice for today's employers.[64] Indeed, companies that have all-white departments or all-white managerial staffs are regarded with suspicion.

Credit for these changes lies primarily with African Americans, whose investment in education, unrelenting pressure, and refusal to stand down in the face of injustice opened worlds once closed to them. But other factors contributed as well, including federal and state agencies, union activism, liberal politicians, and historical circumstances and events. Although less recognized, corporations, employers, and managers also played a role in this transformation. Management and corporations not only shouldered a great deal of the cost and effort of integration, they also helped determine its shape and scope. It is to that story we now turn.

[63] Poll cited in "The Issues behind Opposition to Reagan," *Business Week*, January 23, 1984, 24. See also Dobbin and Sutton, "The Strength of the Weak State," 441–76.
[64] See Greenewalt to E. F. Du Pont, June 17, 1957, in Papers of Crawford E. Greenewalt, President and Chairman of the Board of E. I. Du Pont de Nemours and Co., 1947–67 (1928–68), Box 11; Series II Employee Relations Department, File: Personnel – employment, 1954–57; HML. Discussed further in Chapter 6.

2 Fair Employment Is Good Business

Businessmen generally want to do the right thing for their workers just because it is right, but if they say it as simply as that, they think it makes them sound naïve. So they feel they have to rationalize any decent move they make as a plan for increasing productivity and profits.

Walter Wheeler, President of Pitney-Bowes, Inc.[1]

If inequities and frictions arising from discrimination in the employment relationship are permitted to continue, they will not only interfere with the development of harmonious industrial relations, but will invite government legislation.

National Association of Manufacturers, memo, 1948[2]

There were many reasons employers might hire black workers into white positions before the Civil Rights Act of 1964. The most common were labor shortages, state or municipal fair employment laws, defense contract requirements, pressure from civil rights organizations, and moral (or religious) considerations.[3] But those business leaders who were most enthusiastic about promoting fair employment in the post–World War II decades rarely mentioned these. Instead, echoing fair employment activists, they emphasized how

---

[1] In Hadley Donovan, "Watch the Yankees," *Fortune,* March 1950.

[2] Proposed Program of Education re: Non-Discrimination . . . , April 5, 1948, in National Association of Manufacturers, Records, 1895–1990 (hereafter NAM Records), Series 7, Box 135, at Hagley Museum and Library, Wilmington, Delaware (hereafter HML)

[3] See Paul Norgren, et al., *Employing the Negro in American Industry: A Study of Management Practices* (New York: Industrial Relations Counselors, 1959), 37; Stephen M. Gelber, *Black Men and Businessmen: The Growing Awareness of a Social Responsibility* (Port Washington, NY: Kennicat Press, 1974), 23–122; and Stacy Kinlock Sewell, "The Best Man for the Job: Corporate Responsibility and Racial Integration in the Workplace, 1945–1960," *The Historian* 65 (Fall 2003): 1125–46.

fair employment was "good business." Variations on the phrase "fair employment is good business" appeared in just about every account of fair employment from World War II through the 1970s. Originally a slogan, it turned up repeatedly in articles, books, and pamphlets. Some time in the mid-1950s, it became "merit employment is good business" and then "equal opportunity is good business." The phrase persisted because businessmen really wanted to believe that the free market fostered equal opportunity for all. What it expressed was theoretically true. Fair employment, in theory, could be profitable. If a company could overcome employee resistance and white consumer boycotts and summarily change deeply embedded, long-standing job structures and promotion practices, then hiring and promoting African Americans into traditionally white positions could, potentially, expand a company's consumer and labor markets.

One can't help observing, however, that if fair employment was really good business, that is, profitable, more employers would have practiced it. The truth was that effective fair employment policies required elaborate planning and costly implementation that challenged both traditional racial norms and ascendant color-blind ideals. Fair employment was disruptive and difficult to oversee, and it rarely improved the bottom line. This is why only a handful of large corporations in the 1940s and 1950s pursued it. When large numbers of employers finally committed resources to integration in the late 1960s, it would be because of urban riots, boycotts, and federal legislation, not the alleged economic benefits of an enlarged labor pool or the so-called Negro Market. Still, there were a few pioneering employers who supported or practiced fair employment during the 1940s and 1950s, and their arguments, possible motivations, and experiences are the topic of this chapter.

The varied meanings of "fair employment" make it difficult to determine the number of corporations that actually practiced it during the 1940s and 1950s. Many firms adopted nondiscrimination policies, but few enforced them. Not all firms advertised their policies. Very few kept records of employees by race. Yet there are studies that indicate that integrated companies did in fact exist. Paul Norgren et al. found forty-four integrated companies for their study, *Employing the Negro in American Industry* (1959); Steven Habbe's *Company Experience with Negro Employment* (1966) examined forty-seven. One could (arguably) interpret the 5,251 companies that the New York State Commission Against Discrimination found in compliance with the state's antidiscrimination law between 1945 and 1961 as evidence of more widespread practice of fair employment. I am less interested in determining the number of corporations that practiced fair employment than in understanding what motivated their leaders to support it.

American Business at Midcentury

The racial integration of America's workforce occurred within the context of economic, political, and technological changes that transformed the way American businesses operated after World War II. Post–World War II business trends, such as defense spending, automation, and the crisis in manpower utilization, led to a closer relationship between the federal government and major corporations that ultimately allowed the government to have a greater influence on corporate employment policies.

In 1946, 95 percent of all American companies had fewer than 100 employees.[4] Most Americans worked at small companies. But the large manufacturing corporations – General Electric, U.S. Steel, Du Pont, RCA, General Motors, Ford Motor Company, International Harvester, IBM, Lockheed Aircraft, and the Standard Oil companies – dominated the business community. Unlike smaller companies, they had the resources to take on the risks of innovative, forward-looking policies. Their executives headed the major business policy and interest groups, including the Business Advisory Council (BAC), the National Industrial Conference Board (NICB), and the Committee for Economic Development (CED), and represented industry on numerous government committees at the municipal, national, and international levels.

World War II rehabilitated the tattered Depression-era image of large corporations and softened Americans' traditional fears of "bigness." The wartime cooperation between business leaders and government agencies, exemplified by the War Production Board and the "dollar-a-year" men in Washington, DC (executives loaned to the government for service in wartime agencies), not only redeemed the reputation of big business but also demonstrated what could be achieved when old animosities were set aside. A 1945 Roper poll indicated that the public credited shipbuilder Henry Kaiser above all other civilians with securing the war victory.[5] The organizational demands of the U.S. war effort brought a new appreciation and demand for the administrative and managerial techniques honed by American corporations.[6]

---

[4] Cited in Kim McQuaid, *Uneasy Partners: Big Business in American Politics, 1945–1990* (Baltimore: Johns Hopkins University Press, 1994), 23.

[5] Stephen B. Adams, *Mr. Kaiser Goes to War: The Rise of a Government Entrepreneur* (Chapel Hill: University of North Carolina Press, 1997), 9.

[6] The Harvard Business School, for instance, trained military officers. Rakesh Khurana, *From Higher Aims to Hired Hands: The Social Transformation of American Business Schools and the Unfulfilled Promise of Management as a Profession* (Princeton, NJ: Princeton University Press, 2007), 198–99; on the organizational capacity of the U.S. war effort, see David Kennedy, *Freedom from Fear: The United States in Depression and War* (New York: Oxford University Press); on the wartime industrial-state cooperation, see Adams, *Mr. Kaiser Goes to War*.

The heads of the major corporations, in turn, emerged from World War II with a new appreciation for government's role in the economy. Cold war defense spending fueled the postwar economy and turned otherwise conservative businessmen into unwitting Keynesians. Seventy percent of President Dwight D. Eisenhower's budget was military spending, with twenty companies receiving half of the total dollar value of all military contracts. By the mid-1950s, 80 percent of the aerospace industry's business was with Washington, DC.[7] Businessmen tolerated enormous tax burdens in the 1950s to sustain this relationship. From 1951 to 1963, the personal income tax rate for those earning more than $400,000 was 91 percent; the federal tax on corporate profits over $50,000 during the same years ranged from 50 to 52 percent.[8] Industry had always been intertwined with government through contracts, subsidies, and fiscal policies, but there were indications that the heads of major corporations in the post–World War II years were becoming more comfortable admitting this – even as they continued to defend "free enterprise." No longer alarmed by government power, they sought to use it to their advantage – not in a nefarious, robber baron way but rather in their capacity as self-proclaimed guardians of society. They allied themselves with the government to establish economic policies, to shape American society, and to contribute to social progress.[9]

At the same time, however – perhaps because of their newfound coziness with (and dependence on) government – business leaders remained antipathetic to "New Dealism," "government interference," and, especially, unions. They understood that unions were a new political reality and toned down their traditional antiunion rhetoric, but, with a few exceptions, they continued their efforts to subvert union power through increased use of human relations techniques and political lobbying.[10] Although business leaders were willing

---

[7] Figures cited in McQuaid, *Uneasy Partners*, 74–75.

[8] See "Personal Exemptions and Tax Rates, 1913–2002," and "Corporate Income Tax Brackets, 1909–2002," in *IRS Statistics of Income (SOI) Bulletin* (Spring 2002).

[9] On the conditions for postwar industry's cooperation with the state, see Peter Drucker, *The New Society: The Anatomy of Industrial Order* (New York: Harper, 1949, 1950, paperback ed., 1962); McQuaid, *Uneasy Partners*; Bruce J. Schulman, *From Cotton Belt to Sunbelt: Federal Policy, Economic Development, and the Transformation of the South, 1938–1980*, rev. ed. (Durham, NC: Duke University Press, 1994); Jonathan Soffer, "The National Association of Manufacturers and the Militarization of American Conservatism," *Business History Review* 75 (Winter 2001): 775–805; and William Novak, "The Myth of the Weak American State," *American Historical Review* (June 2008): 752–72.

[10] See Elizabeth Fones-Wolf, *Selling Free Enterprise: The Business Assault on Labor and Liberalism, 1945–1960* (Urbana, IL: University of Illinois Press, 1994); Howell John Harris, *The Right to Manage: Industrial Relations Policies of American Business in the 1940* (Madison: University of Wisconsin Press, 1982); and Sanford Jacoby, *Modern Manors: Welfare Capitalism since the New Deal* (Princeton, NJ: Princeton University Press, 1997).

to cooperate with the government on economic regulation, trade policy, and lucrative defense contracts, they remained wary about specific government interventions that impinged on their authority in the workplace, such as labor laws and fair employment legislation.

One postwar business trend that invited government intervention into employment policies was automation. With technological innovation, fewer workers were necessary to produce an increased amount of goods. Manufacturers' total output between 1947 and 1963 increased by 58 percent, for instance, but the number of employees required to produce that output increased by only 9 percent.[11] Lost in this transformation were thousands of unskilled and semiskilled union jobs, first in mining and the extractive industries and then in the mass production industries, which had hired the largest numbers of African Americans. Historian Thomas Sugrue has demonstrated automation's devastating effect on African Americans and Detroit's autoworkers in the late 1950s, an era of aggregate growth.[12]

Industrialists claimed that automation contributed to economic growth and the creation of new and better jobs. This was true. But the new jobs required higher levels of education. Laid-off production line workers did not necessarily have the education, skills, or training to take advantage of the new jobs in emerging hi-tech, white-collar administrative fields. This led to both unemployment and labor shortages, or what was termed a crisis in "manpower utilization." In anticipation of such a crisis, Eisenhower, then president of Columbia University, had established the Conservation of Human Resources Project in 1950. Sponsored by fifteen large corporations, including Du Pont, General Dynamics, General Electric, Standard Oil (New Jersey), and RCA, and directed by Eli Ginzberg, professor of economics at Columbia Graduate School of Business, the project studied the nation's manpower inefficiencies and proposed policy recommendations to alleviate anticipated labor shortages. Of particular concern was the large number of illiterate and uneducated Americans, who had once worked in the unskilled and semiskilled jobs.

Although automation initially hurt African American employment prospects by contracting the need for labor, the crisis it created focused government attention on the need for more comprehensive employment policies. As president, Eisenhower signed the National Defense Education Act of 1958, largely regarded as a response to *Sputnik* but also a policy response to the manpower

[11] Eli Ginzberg, *Manpower Agenda for America* (New York: McGraw-Hill, 1968), 42.
[12] Thomas Sugrue, *The Origins of the Urban Crisis: Race and Inequality in Postwar Detroit* (Princeton, NJ: Princeton University Press, 1997), 125–52. See also Judith Stein, *Running Steel, Running America: Race, Economic Policy, and the Decline of Liberalism* (Chapel Hill: University of North Carolina, 1998).

crisis. In 1962, Congress passed the Manpower Development and Training Act, which allocated federal funds to prepare unqualified, undereducated workers for new jobs in emerging industries.[13]

"Fair Employment Is Good Business"

Businessmen who hired blacks into traditionally white positions almost always denied any moral motivation and said that it was just "good business." An advertising executive from BBD&O was typical in explaining his decision to hire African American ad man Clarence Holte in 1952: "I'm not a crusader. This is a cold calculated move on my part for the dollar sign only. I was not pushed. I was not shoved. I was only moved by the dollar sign."[14] Echoing the sentiment, researcher Paul Norgren noted that executives experimenting with integration sought to avoid a "crusade attitude" and emphasized the primacy of profit in their decisions.[15] It is not difficult to see why businessmen emphasized profit in their explanations for why they had broken with tradition and hired blacks. In a capitalist society, among capitalists, "profit" was a compelling and persuasive justification for almost any controversial change. Two types of economic opportunities awaited the enlightened entrepreneur's exploitation: the so-called Negro Market and a black labor pool eager for work.

"The Negro Market"

At the end of World War II, black leaders and the Negro press touted the emergence of "the Negro consumer." Having gained access to wartime jobs, black consumers made up a lucrative $8 billion to $10 billion market, a market, fair employment activists claimed, that was larger than Canada's and, potentially, equal to the entire U.S. non-European export market.[16] Fourteen million

---

[13] Ginzberg, *Manpower Agenda for America*, 11–21.

[14] Quoted in "The Negro Market: As Customers and Citizens," *Tide* (July 25, 1952), 44. On Holte's pioneering career, see Jason Chambers, *Madison Avenue and the Color Line: African Americans in the Advertising Industry* (Philadelphia: University of Pennsylvania Press, 2007), 88–95.

[15] Norgren, et al., *Employing the Negro in American Industry*, 55.

[16] See, for instance, Testimony of Beulah Whitby, the national president of Alpha Kappa Alpha sorority in Detroit, Michigan, June 6, 1944, in United States Congress, House Committee on Labor, *To Prohibit Discrimination in Employment* (Washington, DC: U.S. GPO, 1944), 49; John A. Davis, "Negro Employment: A Progress Report," *Fortune*, (July 1952), 102–3, 158–62. On the development of the Negro market, see Chambers, *Madison Avenue and the Color Line*, and

customers, boosters claimed, were waiting to spend their money on the other side of the color line. But, activists and boosters warned, the potential of this market depended on the continued employment of black workers in good jobs. If white companies wanted to reap the benefits of the Negro Market, they would have to employ more Negroes.

There were employers who shared this reasoning. In his 1954 Senate testimony in support of fair employment, RCA president Frank Folsom affirmed that increasing Negro purchasing power was a primary motivation for RCA's policy of fair employment: "Equal job opportunities for Negroes and other minority groups will increase the income of this part of the population and hence widen the market for many products, including our own."[17] Joseph J. Morrow, personnel director at Pitney-Bowes, Inc., estimated that increasing the earning power of the 6.5 million Negroes employed in 1949 would increase their consuming power from $10 billion to $16 billion a year. Morrow urged employers to develop this internal market before trying to expand foreign markets. The U.S. Negro Market, Morrow noted, needed "no expensive, high pressure selling, but just an opportunity to increase its power to purchase the goods and services it is already willing and anxious to have."[18] U.S. Chamber of Commerce President Eric Johnston concurred: "The withholding of jobs and business opportunities from some people does not make more jobs and business opportunities for others.... Perpetuating poverty for some merely guarantees stagnation for all."[19]

During the 1930s, Esso Oil, American Tobacco Company, and Pabst Brewing Company, among others, hired black sales representatives as "goodwill ambassadors" to drum up business in the black communities. But while these companies were hiring blacks into the traditionally white job of sales representative, they were not necessarily practicing "fair employment," since those few who were hired were hired because of, not despite, their race. Indeed, regular

---

Robert Weems, Jr., *Desegregating the Dollar: African American Consumerism in the Twentieth Century* (New York: New York University Press, 1998).

[17] U.S. Congress. Senate Committee on Labor and Public Welfare. Antidiscrimination in employment. Hearings before the Subcommittee on Civil Rights of the Committee on Labor and Public Welfare, U.S. Senate, 83rd Congress, 2d Session, on S. 692 (1954), p. 12; On RCA's fair employment policy, see Theodore Kheel, *Guide to Fair Employment Practices* (Englewood Cliffs, NJ: Prentice-Hall, 1964), 43.

[18] Quoted in John Popham, "Race Bias Cost Put at 6 Billion a Year," *New York Times*, July 9, 1949, 7. See also Joseph Morrow, "Employment on Merit: The Continuing Challenge to Business," *Management Review* (February 1957): 10.

[19] Quoted in "Job Color Line Hit as 'Bad Business' by Chamber of Commerce President," *Chicago Defender* (National Edition), January 20, 1945, 5.

sales positions would be among the hardest positions for African Americans to break into.[20]

The experience of Pepsi-Cola illustrates the promises and pitfalls of the Negro Market and is worth exploring in some depth. In 1940, Pepsi-Cola President Walter S. Mack, Jr. hired black newspaperman Herman T. Smith to head Pepsi's foray into the untapped Negro soda market.[21] Mack's decision received little notice in the mainstream press, but the *Chicago Defender* announced, "Pepsi-Cola Co. Names Smith to Sales Post," with subhead, "Has Charge of Planning Promotions for Race Market in South."[22] The headline served a dual purpose. It announced Smith's appointment, which was, after all, real news in black communities, but it also rewarded Pepsi's decision by giving Pepsi what amounted to free advertising. In a historically segregated society, any move toward integration was news for the black press. Companies that hired African Americans into traditionally white positions, such as sales, received publicity in the black community long before the new employee even began the job. "Pepsi-Cola Gives Jobs to Negroes," declared the *Defender* in January 1943, in an even more explicit illustration of how the black press rewarded white employers who hired blacks.[23]

Although Pepsi desired this kind of publicity in the black communities whose customers it sought, it was not always useful in the white world. Indeed, it was potentially detrimental for a company to become too associated with the Negro Market – as Walter Mack, Jr., acknowledged in 1949 when he told a roomful of Pepsi bottlers that he intended to give Pepsi a little more class; it wasn't just going to be a "nigger drink."[24] This remark disappointed and

---

[20] On lack of progress in sales, see Occupational Tables in appendix. On "goodwill ambassadors," see "The Negro Market," *Opportunity* (February 1935), 38; David Sullivan, "The Negro Market Today and Postwar," *Journal of Marketing* 10 (July 1945): 68–69; Chambers, *Madison Avenue and the Color Line*, and Weems, *Desegregating the Dollar*.

[21] This story has been told most recently by Stephanie Capparell, *The Real Pepsi Challenge: The Inspirational Story of Breaking the Color Barrier in American Business* (New York: Wall St. Journal Books/Free Press, 2007). See also Chambers, *Madison Avenue and the Color Line*, 83–84, 94–95; Weems, *Desegregating the Dollar*, 50; Joseph T. Johnson, *The Potential Negro Market* (New York: Pageant Press, 1952); and "Pepsi-Cola's Campaign to the Negro Market," *Printer's Ink* (Sept. 9, 1949): 38–40.

[22] *Chicago Defender*, March 23, 1940, 8. Compare to the *New York Times*, "Business Notes," March 18, 1940, 24, which mentions it in two sentences.

[23] "Pepsi-Cola Gives Jobs to Negroes," *Chicago Defender*, January 30, 1943, 22.

[24] This story is from Capparell's interviews with the black sales team, recounted in Capparell, *The Real Pepsi Challenge*, 3. Chambers, *Madison Avenue and the Color Line*, 94–95, also recounts, citing the Pepsi-Cola Papers, National Museum of American History, Washington DC, Series 3, Box 18.

angered Pepsi's new black employees, but for the most part, Mack was skillful at straddling the separate markets.

Herman Smith and the black sales team he hired for Pepsi exploited the historical significance of Pepsi's decision to court the Negro Market, which is to say, they advertised Pepsi's role in racial progress. In their campaigns, the Pepsi-Cola Company became a friend to the race. Assistant sales manager Edward Boyd reminded Pepsi's Negro customers how the company "has consistently endeavored to make sure that the benefits of [Pepsi's social contributions] were extended to each and every segment of our society regardless of race, creed, or color."[25] In 1950, the black sales team even produced flyers calling on consumers to boycott Coke because of its discriminatory policies.[26] The role of boycotts in the civil rights movement is well known, of course, but we don't usually think of them as originating in advertising campaigns. But then, the members of Pepsi's black sales team were not merely, or solely, sales reps, but active leaders in the black community, members of the NAACP, pioneers in the corporate world.[27]

The members of the black sales team cultivated ties to the NAACP and the Urban League that at once advertised black gains and Pepsi-Cola. They were featured speakers at Urban League conferences, discussing the possibilities and pitfalls of corporate life. They used Urban League resources to learn about blacks in different communities. They contacted the NAACP about the discrimination in lodging and travel they experienced while conducting business for Pepsi. To the extent that the black news media covered the conferences and the resulting lawsuits, Pepsi also received good publicity.[28] Even as Arthur Miller mourned the spiritual death of a white salesman, Pepsi's black sales team embodied the spiritual vitality of all those who had ever fought for justice and liberty.

By 1950, Smith had left Pepsi, and Edward Boyd presided over the twelve-member Negro Marketing Division. But this would soon change. Walter Mack stepped down as president in March 1950 and was replaced by Alfred H. Steele, a former vice president of Coca-Cola. Initially, Steele kept the Negro marketing team organized at the national level, but in 1951, he reorganized the company, breaking up the all-Negro national division and assigning its

---

[25] Quoted in Capparell, *The Real Pepsi Challenge*, 158–59.

[26] Ibid., 202–3.

[27] For a description of that first generation of black businessmen and women, see George Davis and Glegg Watson, *Black Life in Corporate America: Swimming in the Mainstream* (New York: Anchor Books, 1985), 11–25.

[28] See "How Big Is Your Negro Market?" *Modern Industry* 15, no. 4 (April 15, 1948); and Capparell, *The Real Pepsi Challenge*, 210–11.

members to regional offices. Now, instead of being part of a team of twelve, they were each a token, lone African American working under a white regional office manager. The team members that Stephanie Capparell interviewed had mixed reactions to the reorganization. While recognizing the ways in which it made sense to focus on regional markets, the move required them to rethink what had been a successful national marketing strategy and weakened their ties to the National Urban League and the NAACP. They had to focus on fulfilling individual sales quotas, not national advertising campaigns. Moreover, they missed the camaraderie of the old group. Many of them quit. Despite these problems, however, it was a more integrated arrangement. In their regional offices, they were able to recruit and train more blacks to work in sales.[29]

The initial centralization of Pepsi's Negro sales representatives reveals the limitations of the Negro Market strategy of employment integration. Negro marketing divisions replicated within a company the segregation that existed in society. These separate marketing divisions did not represent integration, as fair employment activists saw it. As the movement for color-blind fair employment policies proved successful and northern states began passing fair employment legislation, separate Negro marketing divisions became problematic and, theoretically, illegal. In 1951, for instance, an African American man applied for a sales position at American Tobacco Company's Syracuse, New York, office. According to the applicant, he was told that the company limited the employment of Negroes to its large Negro markets, such as Harlem, New York City, and the South. He filed a discrimination suit with the New York State Commission Against Discrimination (NYSCAD).[30] During the interview with the NYSCAD commissioner assigned to the case, the personnel director denied having told the plaintiff that the company limited employment of Negroes to those areas, but he insisted that it made sense to assign employees to areas "in which they could make full use of their qualifications." NYSCAD investigator Caroline Simon disagreed: "If salesmen have all their qualifications evaluated and it is determined that a man has special skills which would assist him in specialized neighborhoods, that would be in conformance with the law . . . [but] it would be illegal to send a Negro into a Negro neighborhood just because he was a Negro."[31] This, of course, is what Pepsi and dozens of other firms with "Negro

---

[29] Capparell, *The Real Pepsi Challenge*, 229, 241, 252.
[30] C-2681–51, *John A. Williams v. American Tobacco Co.*, filed January 25, 1951. In New York (State). State Division of Human Rights, Discrimination case files, Master case files for 1951–1968, New York State Archives, Albany.
[31] C-2681–51, *John A. Williams v. American Tobacco Co.*, filed January 25, 1951, Conference Report, April 16, 1951. In New York (State). State Division of Human Rights, Discrimination case files, Master case files for 1951–1968, New York State Archives, Albany.

marketing divisions" had been doing.[32] By the 1960s, some businessmen were wary of hiring blacks to help them develop the Negro Market, believing that they would regard it as a "segregated opportunity."[33]

But Harvey C. Russell, who had come to Pepsi in 1950, believed the logic of the Negro Market defied color-blind fantasies: "A special markets approach is necessary because Negroes have been excluded for so long and have developed different consumption patterns."[34] In 1957, Russell proposed that the company reinstitute the national division, which it did in 1958. Chosen to head it, Russell renamed the new department Special Markets. He rebuilt the department, cultivating a new generation of African American talent and heading the company's foray into the African market. In 1962, Pepsi made him the first African American vice president of a major corporation.[35]

Despite the ballyhoo over the Negro Market in the trade press, few employers were ultimately persuaded to pursue it. Retailing is an area, for instance, in which one might expect to find employers hoping to attract black customers by hiring black employees. But that was not the case. For most retailers, the fear of losing white customers outweighed the potential gain of new black customers. In those stores that did hire black sales clerks, it was not always clear that economics had been the main prod, even though the accompanying stories always proclaimed it was. Beatrice Fox Auerbach, president of the G. Fox & Co. department store in Hartford, Connecticut, and a well-known philanthropist, began a policy of upgrading Negro workers into all positions in 1942.[36] In an interview with the National Urban League's journal *Opportunity*, Auerbach stressed that it made good "business sense," but if that was the case, why was Fox's policy so noteworthy, and why were so many other department stores reluctant to follow? During the late 1940s, activists targeted department stores in major cities, and eventually, after much cajoling and negotiation with

---

[32] Other firms with Negro marketing divisions included Pabst Beer, American Tobacco Company, Seagram's, Vaseline, Lever Brother's, Inc., and Esso Standard Oil Co. See Chambers, *Madison Avenue and the Color Line*, 84–112; "How Big Is Your Negro Market?" *Modern Industry*; and "The Brown Hucksters," *Ebony* (May 1948).

[33] Quoted term from *The Selection and Training of Negroes for Managerial Positions: Proceedings of the Executive Study Conference*, held November 10–11, 1964 (Princeton, NJ: Educational Testing Service, 1965), 55; see also Davis and Watson, *Black Life in Corporate America*.

[34] Philip Shabecoff, "Negro Executive Finds There Is Room at the Top," *New York Times*, July 1, 1962, 79.

[35] Jackie Robinson held a similar position at Chock Full O' Nuts, a much smaller company. Capparell, *The Real Pepsi Challenge*, 252–53, 264, and Shabecoff, "Negro Executive Finds There Is Room at the Top," 79.

[36] Marjorie Greene, "Fair Employment Is Good Business at G. Fox of Hartford," *Opportunity* (April/June 1948): 58–59, 73.

other retailers in the same community, reached agreements to integrate.[37] This decision was not the result of abstract economic considerations, but rather pressure from activist groups and agreements with peers. Similarly, major corporations and advertising agencies would not use African Americans in mainstream advertisements until after the Congress of Racial Equality's Image campaign in the early 1960s.[38]

The Labor Market

Labor shortages were the main reason employers hired blacks into traditionally white jobs.[39] This did not necessarily lead to integration, however. Labor shortages and economic growth meant that whites moved on to better jobs, and blacks took the vacated jobs. Blacks gained access to better-paying, traditionally white jobs and thus bettered their economic condition, but they were still not advancing with whites. Following traditional patterns, manpower shortages merely turned previously white departments into predominantly minority ones. Noted one researcher about New York in 1959, "In production work, Negroes, Puerto Ricans, and women have largely replaced the immigrants of an earlier generation."[40]

Proponents of fair employment argued that adding blacks to the labor pool increased the chances of hiring the best people for the job, implying that considering blacks for all positions would increase the labor supply and hence lower overall wages.[41] Studies indicated that employers found black workers to be as productive and reliable as whites, sometimes more so (this was because the blacks hired into breakthrough positions were often overqualified). Moreover, because they were "pioneers" for the race, black individuals who had

---

[37] See Robert O. Blood, Jr., *Northern Breakthrough* (Belmont, CA: Wadsworth, 1968), and Gelber, *Black Men and Businessmen*, 81–83.

[38] Chambers, *Madison Avenue and the Color Line*, 133–55.

[39] Gelber, *Black Men and Businessmen*, 103–10; Norgren, et al., *Employing the Negro in American Industry*, 36. See also H. Ellsworth Steele, "Jobs for Negroes," *Social Forces* 32, no. 2 (1953): 152–62, Bucklin Moon, *The High Cost of Prejudice* (New York: Julian Messner, 1947).

[40] Bernard Rosenberg and Penney Chapin, "Management and Minority Groups: A Study of Attitudes and Practices in Hiring and Upgrading," in *Discrimination and Low Incomes*, eds. Aaron Antonovsky and Lewis Lorwin (Albany: New York Interdepartmental Committee on Low Incomes, 1959): 147–194, 188; see also Gelber, *Black Men and Businessmen*, 106.

[41] See, for instance, Sara Southall, *Industry's Unfinished Business: Achieving Sound Industrial Relations and Fair Employment* (New York: Harper & Brothers, 1950), 135–36; John Perry, "Business – Next Target for Integration," *Harvard Business Review* 41, no. 2 (March–April 1963): 104–15; and Caroline Bird, "More Room at the Top," *Management Review* 52 (March 1963): 4–16.

been given a chance in a white position were keen to prove their capability and productivity.[42] These arguments were persuasive inasmuch as they led to the hiring of highly qualified "token" blacks in white-collar and skilled positions during the 1950s. But as the pressure to hire African Americans increased in the 1960s, the pool of highly qualified black labor shrunk, and the argument lost much of its power.

Like the arguments for the Negro Market, the arguments about the economic benefits of an increased labor supply failed to motivate employers to hire significant numbers of African Americans. The economic benefits to be gained from a larger, interracial labor pool have to be weighed against the high costs associated with introducing black workers into traditionally white positions in a manufacturing setting. The hiring of black workers into white jobs was usually met with suspicion and resistance from white workers, especially during the 1940s when white workers regularly refused to work with blacks. The problem got better in the 1950s, but only because companies committed resources to helping white workers adapt to the new situation. Even in the 1950s, there were instances of walkouts after blacks were promoted into white positions.[43] There was the additional problem of restrooms and cafeterias. Even if white workers acquiesced in working with blacks, they demanded – or, in southern states, the law demanded – separate facilities. This could be prohibitively expensive and kept many smaller companies from integrating, even in northern states.[44] In addition, black workers typically cost more to train because of the limited educational and training opportunities available to them at this time.

Activists and historians have long regarded employers' claims about white workers' resistance and blacks' lack of qualifications as excuses. They argue that fears of resistance were exaggerated and that judgments about black applicants' qualifications were clouded by prejudice. There is a great deal of truth in these assertions. There were many cases in which integration occurred without

---

[42] On black employees' eagerness to please, see Everett Cherrington Hughes, "The Knitting of Racial Groups in Industry," *American Sociological Review*, 11, no. 5 (October 1946): 512–19, and Steele, "Jobs for Negroes," 152–62.

[43] See Andrew Kersten, *Race, Jobs, and the War: The FEPC in the Midwest, 1941–46* (Urbana: University of Illinois Press, 2000); Denton Watson, ed., *The Papers of Clarence Mitchell, Vol. 1, 1942–43* (Athens: Ohio University Press, 2005); and Burleigh Gardner and David Moore, *Human Relations in Industry*, rev. ed. (Chicago: Richard D. Irwin, 1945; repr. 1950), 308–11. In the 1950s, see "To All Employees," memo from International Harvester Company, General Office, Chicago, April 23, 1953, in International Harvester Company, Corporate Archives Central File (documented series), 1819–1998, 6Z M2001–125 IH Relationship with African Americans (Materials), 1939–1972, at Wisconsin Historical Society, Madison (hereafter WHS), and Michael Honey, *Going Down Jericho Road: The Memphis Strike, Martin Luther King's Last Campaign* (New York: Norton, 2007), 38.

[44] *Gelber, Black Men and Businessmen*, 63–65.

incident, and it is well documented that employers understood "qualified" to mean "white."[45] But just because employers used white resistance and blacks' low skill levels as excuses to avoid integration, doesn't mean that these problems did not exist. White employees did resist black promotions and many African Americans' skills and experience were insufficient for more advanced jobs. Even the most sympathetic researchers acknowledged this, which is why they recommended special training programs for both whites and blacks.[46]

To illustrate the high costs of fair employment practices, let us briefly examine the experiences of International Harvester, a Chicago-based manufacturer of farm equipment. In 1941, Harvester president Fowler McCormick instituted an official policy of nondiscrimination in its twenty-three plants, making it company policy to hire, train, and upgrade Negroes according to the same rules that applied to other workers. To implement the policy in its southern plants, the company devised a plan to avoid "misunderstandings" and violence. This plan involved the following: researching the plants and communities affected; meeting with white employees and community members to explain the reason for the policy; winning the cooperation of white employees, union leaders, and community members; working with the local Urban League to find qualified black workers; intergroup training programs for white employees and supervisors; training programs for black workers; maintaining statistics about employees' racial and ethnic background; and changing seniority policies. Nor was this extensive (and expensive) preparation any guarantee that there would not be strikes or work disruptions.[47] Not all companies deployed these measures. Indeed, many scoffed at them and said that all that was necessary was to simply hire and promote blacks. But Harvester was more ambitious and, initially, more effective than other companies when it came to fair employment.

The enormity of Harvester's efforts helps explain why employers were reluctant to pursue a real program of fair employment. The question is, why did Harvester invest so much? Sara Southall, who worked in Harvester's industrial relations department and was an advocate for fair employment, recalled that

[45] Jack Gourlay, *The Negro Salaried Worker*, AMA Research Study 70 (New York: American Management Association, 1965), 12; see also Rosenberg and Chapin, "Management and Minority Groups," 147–94, 154; Gelber, *Black Men and Businessmen*.

[46] See Allison Davis, "The Motivation of the Underprivileged Worker," in *Industry and Society*, ed. William Foote Whyte (New York: McGraw-Hill, 1946); Eli Ginzberg, *The Negro Potential* (New York: Columbia University Press, 1956), 92–115; and Thomas N. Maloney, "Personnel Policy and Racial Inequality in the Pre-WWII North," *Journal of Interdisciplinary History* 30 (1999): 235–58.

[47] Robert Ozanne, *A Century of Labor-Management Relations at McCormick and International Harvester* (Madison: University of Wisconsin Press, 1967), 190; this will be discussed in greater detail in the following chapters.

such a policy made good business sense in the South. Harvester needed to hire the best people and could not afford "to get into it" every time it sought to hire a well-qualified Negro worker. Having a formal company-wide policy and procedures alleviated the risk of boycotts every time the company hired or promoted a Negro into a white position.[48] As we will see in later chapters, however, there was more to Harvester's policy than maintaining an efficient and talented labor force.

Manpower Utilization

Because integration could be costly to individual employers in the short run, those interested in promoting it emphasized the macroeconomic advantages of full "manpower utilization." Bradshaw Mintener, the vice president and general counsel of Pillsbury Company, lobbied his businessmen friends in 1949 to support a Minnesota Fair Employment law by arguing that "our production today, and therefore, our wealth, is less than it might be, because we refuse to let certain people perform tasks for which they are particularly fitted, solely because of a prejudice against their race."[49] In a 1951 speech, Inland Steel Container Company President William G. Caples urged employers to tap underutilized groups, such as women and racial minorities, to meet their manpower needs. That minorities had been unequally treated he found hard to understand. After all, he chided, "we insist in bargaining with unions that 'ability' be our yardstick . . . and yet we don't allow the use of the ability yardstick in our own employment offices."[50] He suggested that manpower shortages would "force real education and a real solution" to the problem of racial discrimination, thus alleviating the need for federal meddling in the form of a permanent Fair Employment Practices Committee (FEPC) law.

Manpower utilization became an alternative way to discuss fair employment and integration. The American Management Association declared that the need for manpower "effectively removed Negro employment from the realm of social reform."[51] Perhaps no person better illustrates this than

---

[48] Sara Southall, *Industry's Unfinished Business*, 135–36.

[49] Bradshaw Mintener to "friend," January 3, 1949, in Testimony in Support of a Minnesota Fair Employment Practice Bill [February 1949] in Genevieve Steefel Papers, Box 13, Minnesota Historical Society, St. Paul, MN.

[50] William G. Caples, "How to Survey and Plan for Your Future Manpower Needs," November 14, 1951, in Collection 5250, Box 1, Folder 1950–51, at Kheel Center.

[51] Quoted in Robert Weaver, *Negro Labor: A National Problem* (New York: Harcourt Brace, 1946), preface.

economist Eli Ginzberg, whose thirty-plus-year career in manpower utilization focused heavily on training minority and disadvantaged workers. An advisor to eight U.S. presidents, Ginzberg headed the Conservation of Human Resources Project at Columbia University beginning in 1950 and served on the National Manpower Council from 1952 to 1961. While aware of the unique history of blacks and race in America, Ginzberg saw black employment not as a racial problem but rather as an economic problem. Most of Ginzberg's books were not about African Americans per se but rather were about the problem of manpower utilization. In books such as *Manpower Agenda for America,* he traces the history of education and training legislation as if it were as important to black employment as civil rights legislation.[52]

In *The Negro Potential* (1956), Ginzberg argued that the 15 million Negroes living in the United States were "the single most underdeveloped human resource in the country."[53] The book analyzed the factors that inhibited African Americans' potential contributions to the economy and described the changes necessary in education, housing, government, and the economy for American society to reap all of the benefits of Negro talent.[54] It included a chapter on the integration of the U.S. armed forces, which had been one of the first major institutions to integrate and hence provided a model for others. The armed forces also offered blacks the training and work experience denied to them in the private sector. Ginzberg argued that white fears about integration were unwarranted. It turned out that whites were more accepting of racial change than even they had suspected. The benefits of integration far outweighed the initial costs of adjustment. Directed mainly at the nation's employers, the book gave sociological and empirical ammunition to the arguments of fair employment activists.

Joseph J. Morrow, the head of Industrial Relations at Pitney-Bowes, endorsed Ginzberg's argument in a 1957 article for *Harvard Business Review,* which referred to African Americans as a "wasted resource." While U.S. industry had advanced technologically, the labor force had not kept pace. As a result, American industry would soon face a severe shortage of skilled labor.[55] That African American talent was allowed – even encouraged – to remain underdeveloped was a waste that American industry could ill afford, especially in light of its competition with the Soviet Union (to be discussed in the section

[52] Ginzberg, *Manpower Agenda for America.*
[53] Ginzberg, *The Negro Potential,* 124.
[54] Ibid.; see also "U.S. Negro Held Neglected Asset," *New York Times,* May 14, 1956, 1.
[55] Joseph J. Morrow, "American Negroes – A Wasted Resource," *Harvard Business Review* (January–February, 1957): 65–74.

"The Cold War"). Morrow's article drew heavily from Ginzberg's book, framing black employment as a costly economic problem for the nation – in other words, a policy issue.

Closely related to manpower utilization were the social costs of racial discrimination. As long as blacks were denied access to jobs, they would be a burden on their communities and the state. In explaining its nondiscrimination policy to its employees, a Harvester publication considered the harm done when "manpower resources remain unused – when large numbers of people do not contribute to the wealth of the community to the extent of their abilities and when many of them regularly burden the community through dependence and government relief."[56] In the wake of urban riots and racial unrest in the 1960s, businessmen would apply the idea of "social costs" to black unemployment and invest in training unqualified, or "disadvantaged," blacks. But such investments did not usually improve the bottom line.

Though everywhere, then, the argument that fair employment was good business was not necessarily true or even very persuasive in terms of cost effectiveness. It usually had to be tweaked to remind businessmen that the *social* costs of discrimination could in the long run eat into a company's profits. Years later, while commenting on whether business should invest in training the disadvantaged, John Harper, the president of Alcoa, pointed out that the individual company that invested in training the downtrodden did not see a short-term profit from such an action, even if in the long run it benefited from a healthy economy.[57] But just because fair employment wasn't necessarily profitable does not mean that it wasn't good for business. It turns out that fair employment was very good for the ideologies and self-image of mid-twentieth-century businessmen.

The Cold War

After economic incentive, the most common argument employers and industry officials made on behalf of fair employment was that it was necessary in the cold war fight against the Soviet Union and communism. In a 1957 *Harvard*

---

[56] "The Negro Employe at Harvester" (n.d.), 11, found in International Harvester Company, Corporate Archives Central File (documented series), 1819–1998, McCormick Mss 6Z, Box 881, Folder 13908, WHS.

[57] Robert C. Albrook, "Business Wrestles with Its Social Conscience," originally published in *Fortune*, August 1968, included in Neil W. Chamberlain, ed., *Business and the Cities* (New York: Basic Books, 1970): 25–29.

Business Review article intended to stir his colleagues into action, Pitney-Bowes executive Joseph J. Morrow opened with a typical appeal to cold war concerns:

> Our race relations have far reaching implications for democracy – for the struggle against communism, as well as the endeavor to overcome discord within our own borders. The progress of the non-White citizen in the United States is of deep concern to the non-White people of Asia and Africa, where Russia's challenge is the strongest.[58]

Soviet propaganda made the race problem urgent. It meant that the nation could not afford a gradual approach to the problem, nor could it take comfort in the progress that had been made. As FEPC advocate John A. Davis told the readers of *Fortune* in 1952: "In a world that is about 65 percent nonwhite the Communist charge of racial exploitation in American reverberates with a crashing emphasis. Thus it is not the fact of progress, but the pace that becomes the crucial problem."[59] Businessman-turned-Senator William Benton argued that the United States' civil rights problems undermined international good will and thus threatened national security. For this reason, he advocated a permanent, federal FEPC.[60]

The righteousness of its aims meant that the cold war was able to justify a wide assortment of federal policies and programs during the 1950s, including income tax rates over 90 percent, interstate highways, farm subsidies, space programs, education, foreign aid, and even desegregation. For fair employment activists, the cold war was a continuation of World War II, a fight for democracy that drew attention to America's distinctly undemocratic racial traditions. Like the war against fascism, the cold war against communism drew attention to America's racial inequities and hypocrisy. If national security concerns could force southern conservatives to accept the desegregation of the military, then surely employers could be persuaded to integrate their workplaces. All of this comports with what historians of this era have found: that the cold war persuaded white people in power that racial inequality was damaging to American foreign policy and democratic credibility.[61]

Businessmen regarded the Soviet Union and communism with the utmost horror, but most believed that the main threat was not the Soviet army but

[58] Morrow, "American Negroes – A Wasted Resource," 65–74.
[59] John A. Davis, "Negro Employment: A Progress Report," *Fortune*, July 1952, 102–3, 158, 161–62.
[60] "Bias Seen Harming U.S. in Cold War," *New York Times*, May 10, 1950.
[61] See, for instance, Mary Dudziak, *Cold War Civil Rights: Race and the Image of American Democracy* (Princeton, NJ: Princeton University Press, 2000), and Thomas Borstelmann, *Cold War and the Color Line: American Race Relations in the Global Arena* (Cambridge, MA: Harvard University Press, 2001).

the ideologies of communism and socialism, which had already diluted the traditional, individualistic creed of American capitalism and democracy. The cause of fair employment, based as it was on individual rights and opportunity, thus became a bulwark against communism. Keenly aware of the communist threat, Harvester's Ivan L. Willis called on his peers to enact the democratic principles of individual rights and equal opportunity at their own companies. Almost as if he was a reformer (despite his adamant denials), he exhorted, "Do you have the courage to take positive measures in the direction of making democracy really work?"[62] He told a Senate subcommittee that International Harvester was committed to "economic equality": "We believe very deeply that a man has a right to earn a living. We believe that the kind of living he earns should be what his own talents and abilities, his education, his application entitle him to earn in a competitive market."[63] Thus, there were principles at work – it was not all hard-hearted profit – but the principles supported business leaders' conception of democracy as fundamentally about individual freedom and economic opportunity.

Cold war military spending strengthened the interdependent relationship between the state and industry that had existed during World War II, which allowed the government to require government contractors to practice nondiscrimination. Since Franklin D. Roosevelt, all U.S. presidents have required government contractors to practice fair employment. Roosevelt's wartime FEPC (1941–1946), which monitored fair employment practices of defense contractors, was followed by Harry S. Truman's Committee on Government Contract Compliance (1952–1953), Eisenhower's Committee on Government Contracts (1953–1961), and John F. Kennedy's President's Committee on Equal Employment Opportunity (1961–1963). These committees had a dismal record in terms of holding companies accountable for racial discrimination (see Chapter 6). But they educated contractors about the problems of underutilization of minority workers, normalized the idea that racial discrimination was wrong, and provided those businessmen who participated on them an opportunity to administer the compliance requirements to which their industries would be bound.

---

[62] Ivan Willis's address before the Conference on Human Relations in Industry, July 15, 1948, quoted by R. L. Seigel in minutes of the Industrial Relations Managers Conference, French Lick, Indiana, November 8–12, 1948, p. 18, in International Harvester Company, Corporate Archives Central File (documented series), 1819–1998, McCormick Mss 6Z, M2001-125, Box 7, Folder 25, WHS.

[63] Statement of Ivan L. Willis...before the Senate Subcommittee on Labor and Labor-Management Relations, April 16, 1952, p. 3, in International Harvester Company, Corporate Archives Central File (documented series), 1819–1998, McCormick Mss 6Z, Box 758, folder 09131, WHS.

Averting Legislation

Those executives who promoted fair employment and equal opportunity often did so to avert government legislation. This is how International Harvester's Ivan L. Willis put it at a 1948 Harvester Managers' Conference:

> You men know what unfavorable experiences we have had with government intervention in the field of human relations. We don't want it in this phase of human relations [minority groups]. We think it can be avoided if all of industry will undertake to resolve this problem voluntarily. But in the event legislation does some day enter the picture, we want our progress to have been so great on a voluntary basis that we will have progressed well beyond the requirements of any such legislation.[64]

William G. Caples, another Chicago employer, also endorsed fair employment and equal opportunity to stave off the heavy hand of government. Caples was president of Chicago-based Inland Steel Container Company from 1950 to 1953 and, in 1953, became vice president of human relations for the parent company, Inland Steel, a multiplant company of about twenty-five thousand employees. Like Willis, he urged employers to integrate their plants voluntarily to avoid government interference. He saw fair employment as good management and, like Willis, traveled the country preaching this message. Given Chicago's racial demographics, and given that Harvester and Inland Steel were the type of manufacturing firms that typically hired large numbers of black workers, it may be unremarkable that the industrial relations directors of both companies had an interest in fair employment and equal opportunity. It is their public support of fair employment as a way to avert legislation that holds interest.[65]

The National Association of Manufacturers (NAM) likewise sought to avoid a legislative solution to discrimination. NAM officials believed that legislation was coercive. Tolerance could not be legislated, they argued. Antidiscrimination laws would create a backlash that would deepen racial divisions and hinder progress. New laws would require more freedom-limiting bureaucracy.[66] These became the standard arguments against civil rights

[64] Minutes of the Industrial Relations Managers Conference, French Lick, Indiana, November 8–12, 1948, p. 17, in International Harvester Company, Corporate Archives Central File (documented series), 1819–1998, McCormick Mss 6Z, M2001-125, Box 7, Folder 25, WHS.

[65] On Caples, see Williams F. Whyte, *Pattern for Industrial Peace* (New York: Harper & Brothers), 69–70, 97–113, 221. See also William G. Caples Speeches, Collection No. 5250 at Kheel Center, Cornell University, Ithaca, NY.

[66] "Substance of Remarks Made by Phyllis H. Moehrle," pp. 2–4, November 8, 1949, in NAM Records, Series 7, Box 135, HML.

legislation, but they should not be taken to mean that the NAM opposed integration or fair employment. On the contrary, the desire to avoid fair employment legislation spurred the NAM to begin its own program of antidiscrimination. Pointing to its success in thwarting guaranteed wage legislation by persuading employers to stabilize employment, a 1950 memo about expanding NAM's antidiscrimination program stated, "By the same token, if we are able to point to a positive NAM program which has for its purpose the elimination of discriminatory practices in industry, we will be on solid ground in questioning the necessity of fair employment legislation."[67] Historians of the civil rights movement have been quick to dismiss "educational" or "voluntary" efforts as watered down and ineffective, if not obstructive.[68] As a result, we have not considered how such efforts contributed to preparing employers for integration.

The NAM's educational campaign for the "enhancement of individual opportunity" was self-serving, but it was also substantive and backed by the same research state-level Fair Employment Practices (FEP) committees were using. NAM officials skipped platitudes about "getting along" and went straight to identifying the structural problems that replicated patterns of racial exclusion: seniority, housing restrictions, nepotism, and restricted educational and training opportunities. During the early 1950s, NAM officials cultivated relationships with the leading Negro organizations, particularly the Urban League. They reached out to Negro colleges. They sponsored workshops about equal opportunity. Cribbing from fair employment activists' how-to-integrate pamphlets, they stressed the importance of leadership at the top, training, and sound employment policies based on objective criteria. They even recommended working with unions to ensure smooth integration, which is quite remarkable, given that the NAM had only recently recognized the right of unions to exist.[69] As early as 1945, with the passage of New York State's antidiscrimination law, NAM officials were dispensing advice on how companies could

[67] "Some Questions in Connection with Expansion of NAM Program re Discrimination," September 27, 1950, in NAM Records, Series 7, Box 135, HML.

[68] See, for instance, Gelber, Black Men and Businessmen; Nancy MacLean, Freedom Is Not Enough: The Opening of the American Workplace (New York: Russell Sage Foundation; Cambridge, MA: Harvard University Press, 2006).

[69] Ivan Willis, "Personnel Practices for Enhancement of Individual Opportunity and Advancement," address given at the N.A.M. Institute on Industrial Relations, June 21–25, 1948, in NAM Records, Series 7, Box 135, HML. See also "Some Questions in Connection with Expansion of NAM Program re Discrimination," September 27, 1950, "Antidiscrimination in Industry," The Conference Board, October 1945, 286–90, and "Suggested Outline for Booklet Implementing NAM's Position Against Discrimination," September 27, 1950, all in NAM Records, Series 7, Box 135.

comply with state laws.[70] NAM officials recommended the relevant literature
on the topic, including such familiar names in race relations as Robert Weaver,
Herbert Northrup, Ruth Benedict, Charles Johnson, and Horace Cayton. They
recommended the publications of liberal organizations such as the National
Conference of Christians and Jews and state FEPCs. Indeed, the NAM urged all
businesses, whether they resided in a state with FEP legislation or not, to follow the recommendations of the state FEP committees charged with enforcing
state antidiscrimination laws in the 1950s.[71] There was no watering down, no
ignoring the issue. The extent to which individual companies followed through
on these recommendations is difficult to know, but the amount of research
and materials on fair employment and discrimination in the NAM Archives
indicates that the NAM very actively promoted nondiscrimination policies.

NAM members such as Ivan Willis and Pitney-Bowes chairman Walter
Wheeler urged their peers to act, not just talk. Willis was critical of those
businessmen who favored "education" instead of legislation but offered few
suggestions "as to the educational or the non-legislative steps that can be taken
to integrate minority groups."[72] In 1963, after years of failing to convince his
peers to practice fair employment (and after it became apparent that legislation
would be passed), Walter Wheeler finally endorsed federal legislation. These
men were activists, although their activism was guided initially by the desire
to thwart the heavy hand of government. In practice, there was not much
difference between them and those who sought legislation. Joseph Morrow of
Pitney-Bowes supported legislation and urged his peers to do so as well, but
other than that, there was little difference between his efforts and those of Ivan
Willis. Both used the same data and made the same arguments. Both sought
to eliminate practices that perpetrated blacks' exclusion from the workplace.
The endgame was the same: to get employers to hire and advance blacks into
traditionally white positions.

---

[70] "Report on the Operation of the New York Antidiscrimination Law," January 23, 1945, in
NAM Records, Series 7, Box 135, HML.
[71] Phyllis Moehrle to John J. Fallon, November 14, 1949; Phyllis Moehrle to Robert Hill, April 19,
1955; Willis, "Personnel Practices for Enhancement of Individual Opportunity and Advancement" address given at the N.A.M. Institute on Industrial Relations, June 21–25, 1948; "Some
Questions in Connection with Expansion of NAM Program re Discrimination," 9/27/50 and
"Report on Operation of New York Anti-Discrimination Law," 1–23-45, all in NAM Records,
Series 7, Box 135, HML.
[72] Ivan Willis address before the Conference on Human Relations in Industry, July 15, 1948,
quoted by R. L. Seigel in Minutes of the Industrial Relations Managers Conference, French
Lick, Indiana, November 8–12, 1948, p. 18, in International Harvester Company, Corporate
Archives Central File (documented series), 1819–1998, McCormick Mss 6Z, M2001-125, Box
7, Folder 25, WHS.

Public Relations and Corporate Social Responsibility

There is a tendency to see employers' support for fair employment as "public relations" or "window-dressing." In part it was, but we need to be careful about discussing the public relations value of nondiscrimination policies before 1964. Integration was threatening to the traditional social order, after all, and just as likely to receive bad publicity as good (which is why the articles on fair employment always stressed the good publicity companies received). For this reason, companies in the 1950s – in contrast to today for instance – did not usually publicize their intentions to hire and to promote blacks into white positions. Walter Mack sought no publicity (among whites) for his decision to hire black advertising executives. General Electric very quietly and with no fanfare hired a small number of black engineers and administrative professionals after the war.[73] RCA's policies were unannounced.

Companies had to explain their decision to hire and promote blacks and assure the community that they were not interested in social change. Harvester's handbook, "The Negro Employe at Harvester," is a good example. The booklet reminds the reader (Harvester employees and their families) that Harvester had no official position on "general social problems" of black Americans, it neither supported nor opposed a program of black civil rights. It did, however, have a policy of nondiscrimination in employment, which it justified in practical terms pertaining to the company only.[74] As Ivan Willis affirmed in a speech to Indiana Methodists, the company "had no intention of approaching [employment policy] from the standpoint of a reform movement."[75] And as the works manager of Harvester's integrated Memphis plant put it to the

---

[73] See *Inside Brown America*, a periodical published by Joseph Baker Associates, Inc., and the Institute of Industrial Race Relations, and "At Work in Industry Today: 50 Case Reports on Negroes at Work in the General Electric Company," published by General Electric in 1964, both at HML. In a New York radio interview with Channing Tobias, January 10, 1950, Tobias confirmed that GE tapped Howard University for six engineers the previous year. See transcript in Radio Reports, Inc., to International Harvester, in International Harvester Company, Corporate Archives Central File (documented series), 1819–1998, 6Z M2001-125 IH Relationship with African Americans (Materials), 1939–1972, (WHS). Clarence Dart, a Tuskegee Airman originally from Saratoga Springs, New York, was hired by GE as an engineer after the war.

[74] Stated explicitly in "The Negro Employe at Harvester," 10, found in International Harvester Company, Corporate Archives Central File (documented series), 1819–1998, McCormick Mss 6Z, Box 881, Folder 13908, WHS.

[75] See, for instance, Ivan L. Willis speech, "American Industry and Its Human Relations," Indianapolis, May 22, 1949, p. 13, in International Harvester Company, Corporate Archives Central File (documented series), 1819–1998, McCormick Mss 6Z, M2001-125,, Box 7, Folder 24, WHS.

people of Memphis, "We have no intention of attempting to change custom or tradition. We have not urged other employers to follow our example" (which was untrue – they had urged others to follow their example).[76] In addition, executives were reluctant to be seen as boasting of their fair employment policies. They worried that seeking publicity for antidiscrimination policies might be seen as self-serving or, worse, "political." They also worried that self-publicity would give the impression that they thought the problem was solved, and they were always careful to point out that there was "still work to be done" and that their company was not alone in its efforts.[77]

The public relations value of fair employment during the 1940s and 1950s, then, was limited specifically to three related areas: (1) corporate leadership, (2) labor conflict, and (3) the rehabilitation of the terms "individualism" and "opportunity."

Corporate Leadership

The most outspoken executives on behalf of fair employment – people such as International Harvester's Ivan Willis, Pitney-Bowes president Walter Wheeler, and Inland Steel's William Caples – believed that corporations needed to play a leadership role in society. They wanted business to be out in front on the fair employment issue, not forced into complying with laws or capitulating to black activism. They saw themselves in particular and corporations in general as social arbiters and trendsetters, harbingers of progress. While they told the white public and their employees that they were not interested in "social progress" or reform, the truth is they were interested in making sure that social progress happened in an orderly, socially responsible fashion, and the best way to ensure this was to play a role in it. This is why so many of them became involved in the National Urban League and the various government committees charged with investigating the state of race relations in America.

The National Urban League was an interracial organization dedicated to integrating black Americans into the economic life of the United States. Funded largely by the Rockefeller Foundation, its leaders included such dedicated

---

[76] R. G. Mahal to Fellow Memphian, May 4, 1953. In International Harvester Company, Corporate Archives Central File (documented series), 1819–1998, 6Z M2001-125 IH Relationship with African Americans (Materials), 1939–1972, WHS.

[77] See, for instance, Ivan L. Willis speech, "American Industry and Its Human Relations," Indianapolis, May 22, 1949, cited above; and Joseph Morrow's testimony in U.S. Congress, Senate, Committee on Labor and Public Welfare, Subcommittee on Employment and Manpower, Hearings Equal Employment, 88 Congress, 1st sess., July 24–August 20, 1963, p. 215.

African American activists as T. Arnold Hill, Lester Granger, Clarence Mitchell, Jr., and Whitney Young, Jr., who appealed to businessmen's interest in economic gain and social stability. So-called responsible businessmen became advisors and benefactors of the organization. Chaired by Winthrop Rockefeller in the early 1950s, the Urban League's Commerce and Industry Council included Henry Luce, William S. Paley, and executives from Standard Oil, Western Electric, Union Carbide, RCA, Gimbel Brothers, Pitney-Bowes, and Bristol-Meyers.

The same sort of businessmen participated on the various government committees dedicated to the race problem. Charles E. Wilson, the president of General Electric (not to be confused with Charles E. Wilson, the president of General Motors during the same years), chaired President Truman's Committee on Civil Rights in 1947, which produced a report entitled *To Secure These Rights*, the first official federal condemnation of employment and housing discrimination, segregation, and racial injustice.[78] Industry representatives on Eisenhower's Committee on Government Contracts included Harvester's Ivan L. Willis, Fred Lazarus of Federated Department Stores, Inc., and John Roosevelt of Allied Industrial Research Consultants. In these positions, executives had some influence over the committees' proposed "solutions," which during the 1950s usually emphasized voluntary measures over legal coercion. The desire to play a leadership role in integration was motivated in part by the desire to avoid government legislation, but it was also larger than that. It affirmed the idea that business and enterprise, not the state and certainly not unions, were the source of social progress.

Labor Conflict

Racially progressive policies could detract attention from what might otherwise appear to be contentious, even backward, labor-management policies. Despite constant battles with their unions, employers who made fair employment a priority retained credibility as enlightened employers. Many of the companies that embraced fair employment policies, such as International Harvester, RCA, and General Electric, for instance, were notoriously wracked by labor strife after the war. International Harvester experienced a strike with almost every contract it negotiated with its unions between 1945 and 1958, but this did not stop vice president of Industrial Relations Ivan L. Willis from testifying before Congress on behalf of good human relations and fair employment – or

---

[78] NAACP Chairman Walter White recommended Wilson for the position on the basis of Wilson's alleged concern for the race problem. See Walter White, *A Man Called White* (New York: Viking Press, 1948), 332.

from receiving favorable publicity from both management groups and black newsletters and journals.[79] This headline in a National Urban League publication says it clearly, "The Negro Employee at International Harvester: Proof of Enlightened Industrial Policy."[80] RCA likewise experienced constant labor trouble, but its president, Frank Folsom, appeared before Congress to testify on RCA's success in moving blacks into skilled positions.[81] General Electric, torn by labor strife after the war, was also known in some circles for its progressive racial policies during this era.

Employers' commitment to equal opportunity proved useful in what was one of the main labor contests of the postwar era: the struggle against the communist-dominated, left-wing unions. Left-led unions were a factor at International Harvester, General Electric, and RCA. It would be a mistake to apply a simple management-versus-labor template on postwar labor struggles that involved left-led unions. Both management and the so-called right-wing unions – led in the Congress of Industrial Organizations (CIO) by Walter Reuther – sought to defeat, or purge, the left-wing, communist-dominated unions. Harvester's management was in almost constant battle with the left-led United Farm Equipment Workers (FE) union from 1945 to 1955. And so was Reuther. Like so many liberals of this era, Walter Reuther had worked with communists and their allies during the 1930s and had come to see them as detrimental to the cause of workers' rights. If the labor movement was to succeed in the postwar era, the left would have to be purged. In 1949, the CIO expelled eleven unions, among which were the United Electrical, Radio, and Machine Workers of America (UE) and the FE, and engaged in a series of raids against them.[82] Subsequently, the FE sought affiliation with the larger UE and became the FE-UE. The story of General Electric and the UE has

---

[79] Ozanne, *A Century of Labor-Management*, 208; statement of Ivan L. Willis ... before the Senate Subcommittee on Labor and Labor-Management Relations, April 16, 1952, p. 2, in found in International Harvester Company, Corporate Archives Central File (documented series), 1819–1998, McCormick Mss 6Z, Box 758, folder 09131, WHS.

[80] "The Negro Employee at International Harvester ... " *PAR – People Above Race* (February 1953) Supplement, found in International Harvester Company, Corporate Archives Central File (documented series), 1819–1998, McCormick Mss 6Z, Box 898, folder 14870, WHS.

[81] U.S. Senate, Antidiscrimination in Employment, Hearings before the Subcommittee on Civil Rights of the Committee on Labor and Public Welfare, 83d Cong., 2d Sess., Feb. 23, 1954, p. 11. Folsom had appeared at the Senate hearings two years earlier. On RCA's labor trouble, see Jefferson Cowie, *Capital Moves: RCA's Seventy Year Quest for Cheap Labor* (New York: New Press, 2001). Originally published in 1999.

[82] On which, see Bert Cochran, *Labor and Communism: The Conflict That Shaped American Unions* (Princeton, NJ: Princeton University Press, 1977), 305–15; and Robert Zieger, *The CIO, 1935–1955* (Chapel Hill: University of North Carolina, 1995).

been told elsewhere.[83] But it is worth summarizing the situation at International Harvester, since Harvester is so central to our story. Harvester dealt with twenty different international unions, but the two largest (after 1949) were the FE-UE and the UAW-CIO. Of Harvester's twenty-three plants, eight were organized by the FE (East Moline, Illinois; Farmall, Illinois; Louisville, Kentucky; McCormick, Chicago; Richmond, Indiana; Rock Falls, Illinois; Tractor Works, Chicago; and West Pullman Works, Chicago), representing 22,837 employees.

Like other communist-led, left-wing unions, the FE practiced a more radical unionism than its rivals. It saw capitalism as the cause of economic inequality. It was suspicious of compromise and negotiation and sought more than simple bread-and-butter gains for its members. It claimed to be a union of principle, critical of U.S. foreign policy, free-market capitalism, racial discrimination, and cold war red-baiting. And it was, until 1955 or so, a fairly powerful union, the source of a good deal of Harvester's labor problems.[84] Although ultimately defeated by Harvester and the CIO, it accomplished what has been the left's role in America: pulling its antagonists/rivals to the left. The FE forced Harvester to cooperate more readily with the UAW, which Harvester officials regarded as the lesser of two evils. It pushed the CIO to enforce its antidiscrimination clause.[85]

Left-led unions paid special attention to racism and racial discrimination. They made explicit appeals to black workers and were generally regarded as more racially inclusive and antiracist than nonleft CIO locals. The competition between the FE and the UAW for Harvester workers forced the CIO to be attentive to its locals' discrimination.[86] This helps explains Ivan Willis's public celebration of Reuther and the CIO for their cooperation in enforcing Harvester's antidiscrimination policy – praising the CIO's racial liberalism reminded employees and particularly black employees that the CIO was every bit as vigilant against discrimination as the left-led union.[87]

Similarly, Harvester emphasized its own commitment to fair employment and equal opportunity in an effort to combat the left's charges about capitalism

---

[83] See Zieger, *The CIO*.

[84] The management of the West Pullman plant spent a good deal of its time and resources countering information issued by the FE-UE. See International Harvester Company, Corporate Archives Central File (documented series), 1819–1998, 6Z M2001-125, Box 3, Folder 49, WHS.

[85] Kevin Boyle, *The UAW and the Heyday of American Liberalism, 1935–1968* (Ithaca, NY: Cornell University Press, 1995), 118.

[86] Ibid., 118; see also Steve Rosswurm, ed., *The CIO's Left Led Unions* (New Brunswick: Rutgers University Press, 1992).

[87] For example, see statement of Ivan L. Willis... before the Senate Subcommittee on Labor and Labor-Management Relations, April 16, 1952, p. 2, in found in International Harvester Company, Corporate Archives Central File (documented series), 1819–1998, McCormick Mss 6Z, Box 758, folder 09131, WHS.

and racial discrimination. Harvester's Public Relations Department carefully monitored information about its strikes, especially if it involved the FE and race. In a 1949 article for the *Milwaukee Journal*, "Whites in South Helping End Negro's Dark Night," African American author and observer Roi Ottley wrote, "In a magnificent demonstration of unity, 3,000 workers at Harvester's Louisville plant walked off their jobs in February in protest against the firing of two Negroes."[88] Harvester's assistant director of Public Relations, John Vance, wrote to Ottley and the *Milwaukee Journal* to correct what the company regarded as an "unfavorable" and incorrect story. The two Negroes had been discharged not because they were Negroes, as Ottley had implied, but because they – along with ten white men who had also been discharged – were leaders of a wildcat strike that violated the FE union's contract with the company. Vance stated that Harvester had a policy of fair employment and that the Louisville plant had received several commendations by Negro publications for its efforts at job equality.[89] This story indicates that Harvester officials were very much aware of the ways race operated in labor politics and sought to control information. In this regard, the company's proven record of fair employment and activism helped establish its credibility.

Fair Employment and Rugged Individualism

Support for equal opportunity also aided the corporate community in its rhetorical struggle against the left and liberals to define American democracy. The language of fair employment revived the almost obsolete concepts of "individualism" and "opportunity." After years of languishing in conservative backwaters, individualism and opportunity were suddenly deemed "progressive" and "socially responsible" when attached to race and black employment. Employers saw equal opportunity as a defense of the free enterprise system. It affirmed their belief that America was a land of opportunity and healthy competition. They relentlessly emphasized individualism, merit, and opportunity in speeches, in testimony, and in company newsletters, connecting fair employment to the working-class experiences of Irish, Italian, and Jewish immigrant

---

[88] Roi Ottley, "Whites in South Helping End Negro's Dark Night," *Milwaukee Journal*, June 27, 1949; clipping in International Harvester Company, Corporate Archives Central File (documented series), 1819–1998, 6Z M2001-125 IH Relationship with African Americans (Materials), 1939–1972, WHS.

[89] John W. Vance to *Milwaukee Journal*, July 7, 1949, in International Harvester Company, Corporate Archives Central File (documented series), 1819–1998, 6Z M2001-125 IH Relationship with African Americans (Materials), 1939–1972, WHS.

workers. International Harvester president John McCaffrey's speeches drew on his own experiences as an Irish American, emphasizing that judging men on their individual merits rather than skin color, religion, or the country they came from, was "a grass roots matter" and concluding colloquially, "so that's the first thing I'm for – I'm for looking at men and women as individuals and judging them on their individual merits."[90]

The NAM – an organization not known for its progressive views – officially endorsed equal employment opportunity for racial minorities and women beginning in 1941. The issue of hiring minorities provided the NAM with a way to promote its philosophy of individualism over unions' philosophy of collective action and modern liberalism's tendency to divide people into groups. In 1947, a NAM-affiliated organization called the Congress of American Industry adopted a statement of "Freedom and Opportunity for the Individual," which reminded American employers that "the principles of the sanctity and dignity of the individual and freedom of opportunity in the work relationship are cornerstones of the American way of life.... Any conditions of employment which are not related to qualifications for satisfactory job performance, safety and security violate these principles and constitute a threat to sound employer-employee relations and good management."[91] In a 1949 speech at the Women's International Exposition, NAM representative Phyllis Moehrle restated NAM's stand "against discrimination in employment because of age, race, sex," in hiring, promoting, retaining an employee in layoff, dismissal, or any other aspect of the employer-employee relationship. Manufacturers "know that there is no color-line in skills, in loyalty, in efficiency."[92] Commenting on the NAM's merit employment policy in 1954, another officer said, "Free competition demands recognition of merit."[93] These statements are virtually indistinguishable from statements made by Urban League officials and fair employment activists, and yet they endorse a conservative view of the world.

When fair employment activists chose to emphasize individual opportunity and merit in their arguments, it was to persuade conservative employers to adopt nondiscriminatory policies and the American public to accept them. The strategy sought to hold Americans to their alleged principles. It

---

[90] Excerpts from John McCaffrey's speech [to mayors], March 22, 1949, found in International Harvester Company, Corporate Archives Central File (documented series), 1819–1998, McCormick Mss 6Z, Box 715, Folder 07688, WHS.

[91] "Freedom and Opportunity for the Individual, Resolution, Congress of American Industry, December 1947," in NAM Records, Series 7, Box 135, HML.

[92] "Substance of Remarks made by Phyllis H. Moehrle," November 8, 1949, in NAM Records, Series 7, Box 135, HML.

[93] Kenneth Miller, "The American Negro in Industry," address at the Annual Press Awards Dinner, for release on June 5, 1954, in NAM Records, Series 7, Box 135, HML.

had the unintended effect of strengthening those principles. It tied a progressive, forward-looking policy (integration) to what many liberals regarded as a backward-looking economic philosophy (free-market liberalism). In doing so, it undermined liberals' attempts to wean Americans from their traditional "bootstraps" mentality.

Conclusion

In practice, fair employment was not always "good business," in that it could be costly to implement and risked alienating customers, employees, and colleagues. In principle, however, fair employment was consistent with executives' belief in free enterprise, merit, and individualism, their antipathy toward unions, and their aims of profitability, efficiency, and corporate leadership. A handful of executives at large corporations found these arguments compelling enough to "experiment" with nondiscrimination policies in the 1940s and 1950s. Their experiments provided data and became models for convincing other companies to consider integration. Another factor that contributed to employers' willingness to experiment with fair employment was the rise of racial liberalism among educated white elites, the topic of the next chapter.

3 Racial Liberalism and the Mid-Twentieth-Century Businessman

> Rare is the citizen who can bring himself to say, "Sure I'm a conservative." ... Any American would sooner drop dead than proclaim himself a reactionary.
>
> Robert Bendiner about the 1950s[1]

Many corporate executives were receptive to the arguments of black employment activists after World War II because, like other white elites, they were becoming increasingly concerned about the prevalence of racism, discrimination, and bigotry in American society. They may have been unaware of their own prejudices, but they valued racial fairness and tolerance. Their racial liberalism fit neatly within the "liberal consensus," a term used to describe the broad bipartisan acceptance of New Deal and cold war policies that dominated American politics from the late 1940s until the election of Ronald Reagan in 1980. Not yet tainted by the excesses of the Great Society, the Vietnam War, and racial extremism, liberalism in the 1950s still connoted open-mindedness, enlightened thinking, and a modern desire to be progressive. Nor was it the provenance of any one political party. There were liberal Democrats and liberal Republicans. Among a certain type of people – educated, informed, public-spirited, influential whites – liberalism was superior to the narrow-minded parochialism associated with conservatives and the lower classes.

In an era of liberal dominance, one's tolerant attitudes about race came to signify, affirm, announce, one's enlightened, liberal character. Among white elites of the 1950s, liberalism was a positive quality. Illiberal, however, meaning bigoted or narrow-minded, was a negative term. Republicans in the

[1] Quoted in Peter Vierick, "The Philosophical 'New Conservatism,'" in *The Radical Right*, ed. Daniel Bell (Garden City, NY: Anchor Books, 1964): 185–208, p. 187.

72

1950s used to point to southern racism as a sign of Democrats' illiberality. Not for the last time in his life, a young Richard Nixon exploited southern racism for his own political benefit by accusing Democrats of being beholden to the racist South.[2] Racial liberalism united moderate Republicans, liberal Democrats, and a new breed of "industrial statesmen" who made up the liberal establishment.

It is important not to overstate the prevalence of racial liberalism in the post–World War II decades.[3] Racism continued to influence grassroots politics and national elections. Employers in all regions continued to subscribe to the idea of white jobs and blacks jobs. Racism continued to be a fact of life for African Americans. But among a certain type of northern white elites, racial tolerance became a normative ideal.

Changing Racial Attitudes

During the war, government agencies and local community organizations had educated Americans about the dangers of bigotry and discrimination, producing documentaries, newsreels, and exhibits about the contributions of America's racial minorities to the war effort and to the nation. After the war, Hollywood films like *Gentleman's Agreement* (1947), *Pinky* (1949), *Home of the Brave* (1949), and *Crossfire* (1947) depicted the tragic effects of anti-Semitism, discrimination, and racism. A substantial array of antiracist fiction was published in the late 1940s, including a novel by the young Arthur Miller, called *Focus* (1945). There were numerous journalistic investigations and sociological studies about the problem of race relations. Ashley Montagu's *Man's Most Dangerous Myth: The Fallacy of Race*, Ruth Benedict's *Race: Science and Politics*, and Lillian Smith's *Killers of the Dream*, all by white authors, explained to popular audiences how demagogues manipulated race to exploit economic divisions. Montagu's book was a best seller. Museums and libraries,

---

[2] "Nixon Says Rivals Dodge Rights Issue," *New York Times*, September 5, 1952, 13.

[3] Historians have recently challenged the prevalence and influence of racial liberalism in the post–World War II decades, arguing that racism continued to shape grassroots politics. See Thomas Sugrue, *The Origins of the Urban Crisis: Race and Inequality in Postwar Detroit* (Princeton, NJ: Princeton University Press, 1997), Gary Gerstle, "Race and the Myth of the Liberal Consensus," *Journal of American History*, 82 (September 1995): 579–86, Robert O. Self, *American Babylon: Race and the Struggle for Postwar Oakland* (Princeton, NJ: Princeton University Press, 2003). See also Michelle Brattain, "Race, Racism, and Antiracism: UNESCO and the Politics of Presenting Science to the Postwar Public," *American Historical Review* 112, no. 5 (December 2007): 1386–1413, which argues that postwar scientists backed away from the constructivist view of race presented by Ruth Benedict and Ashley Montagu.

churches and community centers sponsored programs designed to foster inter-cultural understanding and help white Americans overcome their parochial tendencies.[4]

The new racial liberalism created a tolerant, multiracial, multifaith, color-blind Americanism that ran counter to, and indeed rejected, older, more exclusive versions of Americanism, which were tied to whiteness, racial con-sciousness, and Protestantism.[5] Born in part out of a need for wartime unity, the new racial liberalism was patriotic. It promised to make real the stories white Americans told about their nation: that it was a land of freedom for all, that it was a land of opportunity, that it was a land where individual where-withal mattered more than one's racial or ethnic background. Because the United States was a nation of minorities, the story went, because its unity was not based on common blood or one faith, the only thing that united its people was a set of principles or ideals. Thus, it was essential that these principles applied to all Americans, regardless of race, religion, nationality, or color.

Bolstered by the ecumenicalism of the newly discovered Judeo-Christian tradition, the new racial liberalism could be religious. Indeed, the language of "interracial brotherhood" was one of the most popular ways the new racial liberalism was disseminated.[6] The National Conference of Christians and Jews, the YMCA, the YWCA, and churches of all denominations sponsored "broth-erhood weeks" and intercultural education programs.

The new racial liberalism sought to counteract the assumptions that made color matter. Because skin color had mattered, because it had determined who would work in certain areas, because it had led to discrimination and racial resentment, the logical way to correct these ills was to make color meaningless, to erase its unmerited power. The new attitudes toward race affirmed the moral correctness of a color-blind world and upheld the idea that race was

---

[4] On the emerging antiracist consensus, see Walter Jackson, *Gunnar Myrdal and America's Con-science: Social Engineering and Racial Liberalism, 1938–1987* (Chapel Hill: University of North Carolina Press, 1990); Stuart Svonkin, *Jews against Prejudice: American Jews and the Fight for Civil Liberties* (New York: Columbia University Press, 1999). See also Henry Yu, "Ethnicity and Race," in *The Encyclopedia of American Cultural and Intellectual History Social Sciences*, ed. Mary Kupiec Cayton and Peter W. Williams (New York: Scribner's Sons, 2001), Vol. 3, 109-20; and Jennifer Delton, *Making Minnesota Liberal: Civil Rights and the Transformation of the Democratic Party* (Minneapolis: University of Minnesota Press, 2002), 40–60.

[5] On the contest between competing versions of Americanism, see Gary Gerstle, *American Cru-cible: Race and Nation in the Twentieth Century* (Princeton, NJ: Princeton University Press, 2002). For a statement of multiracial Americanism, see Eric Johnston, "Hate Challenges America," *Negro Digest* (March 1946): 3–5.

[6] On the postwar creation of the "Judeo-Christian tradition," see Will Herberg, *Protestant, Catholic, Jew: An Essay on American Religious Sociology* (Chicago, University of Chicago Press, 1983).

meaningless, a chimera used to foster hatred and political advantage. The new racial liberalism opposed all forms of racial privilege, particularly anti-Semitism and white supremacy.

Despite the controversy it engendered, the new racial liberalism was compatible with mainstream, capitalist, cold war values. Hence, the left and black intellectuals such as James Baldwin, W. E. B. Du Bois, and Ralph Ellison were skeptical of its ability to address the structural inequities that perpetrated racial injustice.[7] They regarded the talk of human brotherhood and intercultural cooperation as sentimental, a way for white people to assuage their guilt, but not a solution for racial injustice, which was, the left believed, deeply rooted in the economic structures of American capitalism.

The new celebration of racial tolerance did not mean that racism vanished. Far from it. A 1944 poll conducted by the Opinion Research Center found that 74 percent of nonsouthern white workers, managers, and owners favored segregated lunchrooms and washrooms, while 73 percent would object to a Negro family moving next door.[8] Even though only 4 percent of whites advocated explicit employment restrictions, a majority objected to working with or next to Negroes. In 1944, the War Department and the USO refused to distribute Ruth Benedict and Gene Weltfish's antiracist pamphlet, *The Races of Mankind*, because it claimed that northern Negroes achieved higher scores on intelligence tests than white southerners.[9] Nonsouthern whites disapproved of southern bigotry and segregation (in 1955, 70 percent of nonsouthern whites approved of *Brown v. Board of Education*[10]); yet a national 1958 poll indicated that 92 percent of polled whites objected to interracial marriage. Despite their

[7] See, for instance, Ralph Ellison, "An American Dilemma: A Review," written in 1944, republished in John F. Callahan, ed., *The Collected Essays of Ralph Ellison* (New York: Modern Library, 1995), 328–40; and James Baldwin, "The Image of the Negro," *Commentary* 5 (April 1948): 378–80. Historians as well have seen postwar racial liberalism as a weaker, conciliatory alternative to the left's economic/international critique. See Patricia Sullivan, *Days of Hope: Race and Democracy in the New Deal Era* (Chapel Hill: University of North Carolina Press, 1996), and Robert Korstad and Nelson Lichtenstein, "Opportunities Found and Lost: Labor, Radicals, and the Early Civil Rights Movement," *Journal of American History* 75 (1988): 786–811.

[8] "The Color-Line in Industry: A Report of the Public Opinion Index for Industry," April 1944, in National Association of Manufacturers, Records, 1895–1990 (hereafter NAM Records), Series 7, Box 136, Hagley Museum and Library, Wilmington, Delaware (hereafter HML).

[9] "Army Drops Race Equality Book; Denies May's Stand Was Reason," *New York Times*, March 6, 1944, 1. This decision was widely criticized, see "Plans New Edition of Race Pamphlet," March 8, 1944, 11, "Tead Defends Race Book," April 29, 1944, 13; and "A Plea for Racial Truth," letters, March 14, 1944, 18, all in the *New York Times*.

[10] Interview, date: April 14–19, 1955, in *The Gallup Poll: Public Opinion, 1935–1970*, 3 vols. (New York: Random House, 1972), 2:1332.

disapproval of southern Jim Crow, whites in northern, midwestern, and western cities fought against fair housing laws and residential integration into the 1960s. There were employers in northern and midwestern firms who refused to hire blacks into any position that involved "personal intimate relationships" with whites on the basis of their fears of intermarriage.[11]

White racism still existed, then, but it was in many areas increasingly frowned on, regarded as coarse, problematic, and alien to one's own tolerant middle-class sensibility. Whatever one's antipathy toward other races, one did not want to be perceived as a racist or a bigot. In his 1947 best-selling novel *Kingsblood Royal*, Sinclair Lewis captured how the white middle class struggled to reconcile new ideas about tolerance with its ingrained racism. The novel is about a Minnesota banker who, upon discovering a black ancestor, decides to "resign" from the white race and thereby learns what it really means to be black in America. Before his awakening, he and his wife are typical northern, middle-class whites who know that racism is wrong but harbor their own racist views. They believe the North is better than the South ("I'm glad that in the north there is no discrimination against 'em going to the same public schools as our own white kids," says the protagonist[12]), but at the same time, they are suspicious of their black maid. They know that "a Negro is just as good as we are," but secretly have their doubts.

This schizophrenic view of race seems to describe someone like Pepsi-Cola president Walter Mack, who, on the one hand, offered blacks opportunities and sat on antibias commissions but, on the other hand, was known to use racial epithets. It can be seen in Lyndon B. Johnson, who humiliated his black aides and colleagues with racist comments but also ensured the passage of sweeping civil rights legislation.[13] It can be seen in the many employers who claimed that they opposed racism and bigotry but continued to believe that black workers were not suited for particular kinds of work.[14] The old racist attitudes and practices mixed easily with new aspirations of tolerance.

Many members of the business community were nonetheless increasingly quick to condemn racism and discrimination. IBM president Thomas Watson,

---

[11] Poll: Interview dates: September 24–29, 1958; September 24–25, 1958, in *The Gallup Poll: Public Opinion, 1935–1970*, 3 vols. (New York: Random House, 1972), 2:1573. Employers: recounted in Stephen M. Gelber, *Black Men and Businessmen: The Growing Awareness of a Social Responsibility* (Port Washington, NY: Kennicat Press, 1974), 56.

[12] Sinclair Lewis, *Kingsblood Royal* (New York: Bantam Books, 1949), 11.

[13] See especially Robert Caro, *Master of the Senate: The Years of Lyndon Johnson* (New York: Knopf, 2002).

[14] Recounted in Gelber, *Black Men and Businessmen*.

Jr., took a stand against discrimination at a 1956 conference of IBM executives. Watson was delivering a long speech detailing IBM's new corporate structure, and in the middle of the speech, he stopped to read the letter of an unhappy applicant who was interviewed several times, told he was overqualified, and then denied employment at IBM. The letter was signed Irving J. Schlumowitz. The implication was that he wasn't hired because he was Jewish. In his 1990 memoir, Watson recalls that he lost his temper and really let the men have it.[15] The transcript of the proceedings confirms this:

> I'm getting so dam [sic] sick of talking up in my office about hiring minorities and not getting any answers – and any results, that by golly if I don't get results after this reorganization .... God almighty fellas, we live in America – this country was created by people who were persecuted overseas, and because a guy's name is Schlumowitz or Watson – or because he happens to be colored or white or yellow or anything else how can I stand up and tell people – tell chairmen of organizations how wonderful we are with our lack of discrimination and look at the action you fellas and your associates are taking .... What do you think I do talk out of both sides of my mouth[?] Do you think I say hire colored people – don't hire them?[16]

He promised to discover the people who had engaged in this instance of discrimination and ask them to resign. Then he concluded, "I'm sorry to get worked up, but I've tried all my life to not have racial prejudice in myself and to not have religious prejudice in myself, and I think that any of you who know my intimate friends will find in them representatives of every religion and most races."[17]

One sees in this statement the white liberal anxiety about one's own racial virtue, the attempt to show one's own sincerity through outrage, anger, and action in the form of threats. This is not to say that Watson was insincere – not at all. It is rather to point out that white antiracism took predictable, patterned forms during these years. The assurance that one's friends were people of all races and religions, the outrage that discrimination could occur at all, the tough stand that disrupts polite gatherings – these were (and are still) recurring themes in white people's stories about themselves and racism. A story like this is akin to self-reported tales of white people escorting an

---

[15] Thomas Watson, Jr., with Peter Petre, *Father Son & Co.: My Life at IBM and Beyond* (New York: Bantam Books, 1990), 306.

[16] Reel no. 3, pp. 6–7, Thomas J. Watson, Jr., Transcript of a speech at Williamsburg Conference, November 1956, Box TM 119, IBM Technical History Project, IBM Archives, Somers, NY. I would like to thank Ross Bassett for sending me the transcript.

[17] Ibid., p. 7.

African American into a restricted dining hall, theater, train car, and, with all eyes upon them, demanding service. My aim is not to belittle these acts, which were heroic stories to be imitated and praised, but to situate them in history, to see them as part of white peoples' collective awakening to their own culpability in America's racial tragedy.

Watson's tirade echoed that of other businessmen who also tried to instigate change in employment customs. Federal Cartridge Company president Charles Lilley Horn recalled that when skilled white workers refused to work with blacks (in 1942), he went to the plant, stuck his head in the door, and said, "Anyone who wants to walk, can get the hell out of here."[18] International Harvester's R. L. Siegel likewise berated Harvester's managers for not enforcing the company's nondiscrimination policy.[19] Human relations experts would later caution against scolding white workers, but such scolding is testimony to executives' expression of new racial attitudes in the workplace. However self-serving the tirades were, they also conveyed and normalized the new antiracist viewpoint.

Some businessmen who hired blacks into white positions expressed discomfort at making "a big deal" about it. They did not want to be seen as exploiting the race problem for their own advantage. In a 1952 speech to the National Conference of Christians and Jews, William Caples, president of the Inland Steel Container Corporation, criticized those who indulged in "race relations dramatics," which he regarded as political exploitation.[20] Nor did businessmen want to be seen as reformers. Silence about race, then, in speeches, memoirs, and reports did not necessarily mean that someone was uninterested in racial progress, or worse, opposed to it. Silence could be an attempt to make race meaningless by ignoring it, removing it, changing the subject. It could be a sign of color-blind principles. The more educated whites became about race, the more silent they often became, both because they risked "saying the wrong thing" and because they wanted to give the appearance that race just "didn't matter" to them. Black, white, red, purple – a person's skin color was irrelevant.

[18] Quoted in Delton, *Making Minnesota Liberal*, 58.

[19] "Minutes of the Industrial Relations Managers Conference, French Lick, Indiana, Nov. 8–12, 1948," in International Harvester Company, Corporate Archives Central File (documented series), 1819–1998, McCormick Mss 6Z, M2001-125, Box 7, Folder 25, WHS, pp. 17–18, at Wisconsin Historical Society, Madison (hereafter WHS).

[20] See, for instance, William G. Caples, "Teamwork in Industry," Speech before the Institute of Teamwork in Industry and the National Conference of Christians and Jews, Rutgers University, July 31–August 1, 1952, in William Goff Caples Transcripts of Speeches, Collection 5250, Box 1, Folder 1952, at Kheel Center for Labor-Management Documentation and Archives, Cornell University, Ithaca, New York (hereafter Kheel Center).

In his 1982 memoir, Pepsi-Cola president Walter Mack was largely silent about the significance of race in his life. As we saw in the previous chapter, Walter Mack hired a black advertising team for Pepsi in 1938. Yet, his memoir contains no mention of the team, Herman T. Smith, or Pepsi's pioneering experience in the Negro market. Nor does he tell us anything about his service on the New York State Commission Against Discrimination (NYSCAD) or the recognition he received from the NYSCAD and the Negro press for his work.[21] He does not even include the obligatory "it was good business." The only times he mentions race is to chastise himself for paying attention to it. The first reference is to a Pepsi scholarship contest he first sponsored in July 1940, just a few months after hiring Herman Smith. The Walter Mack Job Award for American Youth offered the winners of an essay contest a one-year, salaried position with Pepsi. The "interns" would receive on-the-job training and at the end of the year be offered a position at Pepsi or assisted in finding employment in another company. Originally, each state was to choose two students who would compete in the national essay contest. But, as Mr. Mack recalled, it became clear that no black students would ever win because of the segregated educational system. So, writes Mack, "I established separate scholarships for blacks in each state . . . every state had the right to choose four students, two whites and two blacks, since that was the only way I could get blacks on scholarship." Operating from the ascendant color-blind norm, he adds, "I knew it wasn't fair or proper, but I also knew it was the only way it could be done."[22] The scholarship contest was a hit in the black press, which followed it closely, but Walter Mack seems almost ashamed of it.[23] This story leads him to the second reference to race, which was how the unions at his Long Island Pepsi plant would not allow blacks on the production line. Writes Mack, "So I built two more lines and made them all black and forced the unions to take them."[24] Again, he expresses regret at the lack of fairness, by which he

[21] "Bias Unit Warned to Bar Sentiment," *New York Times*, February 1947. Mack actually does mention a "Herman Smith," which indicates the name stayed with him, but it is used in reference to a soft-drink dealer bought off by the Coca-Cola Company. Walter Mack, *No Time Lost* (New York: Antheum, 1982), 127–28.

[22] , Mack, *No Time Lost*, 158. Interested in bolstering the market's color-blind credentials, Stephanie Capparell, *The Real Pepsi Challenge: The Inspirational Story of Breaking the Color Barrier in American Business* (New York: Wall St. Journal Books/Free Press, 2007) doesn't mention this or another instance of Mack ignoring color-blind expectations.

[23] "Beverage Co. Launches Job Awards Plan," *Chicago Defender*, July 13, 1940, 6; "Pepsi-Cola Scholarships," *Opportunity* (January 1947): 43, 47; "Congratulate Winners," *Chicago Defender*, August 2, 1941, 6.

[24] Mack, *No Time Lost*, 159.

seems to mean his acceptance of segregation but again insists it was the only way to deal with the situation.

Walter Mack was a forward-looking, progressive businessman who cared about politics and who fraternized in a sophisticated, liberal social milieu. He was active in the New York Republican Party at a time when New York City Republicans were the liberal alternative to Tammany Hall. He ran for office in 1932. He supported Fiorello LaGuardia, even praising the prolabor Norris-LaGuardia Act of 1932. He admired Franklin Roosevelt, whom he believed saved the nation from economic disaster. (He did not share his colleagues' antipathy for Roosevelt because he did pretty well during the Depression, financially speaking.) He supported liberal Republicans: Wendell Willkie in 1940 and Thomas E. Dewey in 1948. But he was also friendly with President Truman, with whom he played poker. Some of his best friends were liberal Democrats. He detested Barry Goldwater and organized the Independent Republicans and Citizens for Johnson in 1964. Ordinarily a person with these liberal credentials uses race to bolster his or her moral character. In contrast, Walter Mack decided to downplay race – his own Jewishness (which he would not have considered "racial," although others did), his hiring of African Americans, his service with the New York Commission Against Discrimination. Given his liberal inclinations, his silence about his role in creating a Negro marketing team for Pepsi suggests an adherence to deeply held color-blind principles.

White peoples' racial virtue could connote a variety of virtues in some parts of the corporate world. A man who was able to reject the encrusted tradition of racism was truly independent minded, daring, creative, and forward looking, all desired qualities in the 1950s, especially after William H. Whyte's *The Organization Man* condemned the mindless conformity in American corporations. In an effort to cultivate the dynamic creativity that capitalism promised and indeed required, business journals often warned against thinking that stifled creativity and potentially profitable ideas. A commonly reprinted list, titled variously "Killer Phrases" or "How to Kill Ideas," included such phrases as, "it costs too much," "customers won't stand for it," "doesn't conform to our policy," "Don't move too fast," "the union will scream," and "hasn't been done before – why stick our necks out" – all of which were, verbatim, oft-stated reasons a company could not hire and promote blacks. White people at the time probably did not notice this connection, but these phrases indicate that tradition and conformity were associated with a meek narrow-mindedness, while the questioning of accepted norms was seen as daring and good. By 1960, segregation was definitely on the side of traditionalism, conformity, and fear. To the extent that certain segments of the business community wanted to see themselves as progressive – not in a narrow political sense but rather in a cultural, always-moving-forward-to-the-next-new-thing sense – it was clear that segregation and racism belonged to the age of the horseless carriage (the vehicular analogy favored by American businessmen to connote backwardness). One could oppose segregation, not because it was unjust or immoral but because it was so old-fashioned. Certainly many young people entering business in the 1960s shared with their cogenerational peers a general suspicion of tradition, conformity, and segregation.[25]

Not surprisingly, racial cosmopolitanism was initially exhibited by outsiders, by people not representative of either the old-line northeastern Protestant elite or the middle-class Rotarians of Main Street but who were influential in the business world nonetheless. Edward Bernays, known as the father of public relations, and Peter Drucker, the legendary management consultant, were both successful, innovative promoters of their respective businesses, public relations and management. Both were also of Austrian-Jewish heritage and critics of American racism. Their commitment to antiracism could have been due to their own experiences as minorities, but it was framed in terms of a forward-looking, cosmopolitan commitment to open-mindedness and change.

A nephew of Sigmund Freud, Edward Bernays was the consummate modern. He was an advocate for women's rights. He took on projects that flouted sexual taboos and norms. He had once lived in Greenwich Village, and his friends were the denizens of bohemian America. He believed in change and often used progressive social developments as a tool in public relations. For instance, in 1929, to tap the female market for his client, the American Tobacco Company, Bernays equated smoking with women's liberation. Smoking in public was an activity restricted to men. In what was essentially an exploitation of the women's movement, Bernays organized a campaign called "Torches of Freedom," wherein women marched down Fifth Avenue smoking in defiance of patriarchic norms.[26] But exploitation was a two-way street for Bernays, who also believed that public relations could help further the progressive development of society.

One of Bernays' first major clients was the National Association for the Advancement of Colored People (NAACP), which contacted Bernays to help with publicity for its 1920 convention in Atlanta. It would be the first time

[25] Thomas Frank, *The Conquest of Cool: Business Culture, Counterculture, and the Rise of Hip Consumerism* (Chicago: University of Chicago, 1997), 28–33.

[26] Larry Tye, *The Father of Spin: Edward L. Bernays and the Birth of Public Relations* (New York: Crown, 1998), 23–35, and Edward L. Bernays, *Biography of an Idea: Memoirs of Public Relations Counsel Edward L. Bernays* (New York: Simon and Schuster, 1965).

the NAACP had convened in the South. Despite fears of violence, the NAACP hoped to get positive press coverage in both the South and the North for the event. Bernays and his team arranged to have local dignitaries attend the event. They convinced the governor to provide security. They got southern newspapers to report the convention as news, rather than travesty. Bernays felt that his work for the NAACP proved that the fight for civil rights could reach the South through its media. He left Atlanta, "gratified at what had been accomplished, disgusted with southern bigots, and happy no violence had broken up the meeting."[27] In a 1928 article, Bernays used his work with the NAACP to illustrate how propaganda, or what he called "manipulating public opinion," was not necessarily a bad thing, and that in fact it could contribute to positive social and economic development, such as changing white attitudes about Negroes (or influencing the style of hat fashionable women will wear).[28]

Bernays worked for large corporations, unions, civil rights groups, and artistic organizations alike. He helped the United Fruit Company depose the Arbenz regime in Guatemala in 1954. Yet he also testified on behalf of workers at General Electric against what he saw as GE's use of antiunion "impropaganda."[29] He portrayed himself as a foe of racism, describing how he urged clients to hire Negroes, and how he fought to deny southern racists like Theodore Bilbo and Eugene Talmadge the opportunity to use television news to spout their "hate propaganda against the Negro."[30] He worked with antiracist associations to develop awards that would highlight the importance and progress of interracial relations. The Society for the Psychological Study of Social Issues (SPSSI) actually has an award called the Edward L. Bernays Intergroup Relations Award. And yet one gets the sense from reading his memoirs that his interest in racial justice was tied to his hatred of southern bigots and hidebound traditionalism. He was a cosmopolite, not an activist.

Peter Drucker shared Bernay's forward-looking cosmopolitanism, although when it came to American race relations, he also exhibited a curious sort of nineteenth-century sentimentalism. An Austrian émigré, Drucker was not an American businessman per se, but he was one of the few management experts that businessmen respected, and more than anyone else's, his ideas about management shaped late-twentieth-century American corporate culture. In his 1975 memoirs, Drucker used race to convey the maverick character of a

[27] Bernays, *Biography of an Idea*, 215.

[28] Edward Bernays, "Manipulating Public Opinion: The Why and the How," *American Journal of Sociology* 33, no. 6 (May 1928): 958–71.

[29] On Guatemala, see Tye, *The Father of Spin*, 155–184. Anticommunism in the 1950s was perfectly compatible with antiracism. On GE, see Bernays, *Biography of an Idea*, 581.

[30] Bernays, *Biography of an Idea*, 349, 687.

promising General Motors executive named Nick Dreystadt. Dreystadt's refusal to be bound by social conventions such as racism signified for Drucker his leadership qualities. Drucker claimed that Dreystadt, who headed the Cadillac and Chevrolet divisions, saved Cadillac during the Depression by marketing to wealthy blacks, overturning an alleged General Motors policy prohibiting the sale of Cadillacs to black consumers.[31] Drucker also claimed that Dreystadt, to the horror of GM's upper management, hired two thousand Negro prostitutes during the war to make bombsights.

According to Drucker, Dreystadt defied GM upper management to bid on a federal contract to produce high-precision, electronic bombsights. GM had not bid on the project because there was a severe shortage of the highly skilled mechanics necessary for such work. But Dreystadt believed that he could instruct illiterate prostitutes on how to do the work, which he did by devising some sort of electronic flow chart. While others jeered at Cadillac's "red-light district," writes Drucker, Dreystadt defended the women: "These women are my fellow workers and yours. They do a good job and respect their work. Whatever their past they are entitled to the same respect as any of our associates."[32] The union objected and demanded that the women be fired after the war. This allows Drucker to remind readers of how unprogressive unions were on matters of race. Though taunted as a "nigger-lover," Dreystadt heroically tried to save the jobs for the women. Again Drucker quotes Dreystadt, "For the first time in their lives, these poor wretches are paid decently, work in decent conditions, and have some rights. And for the first time they have some dignity and self-respect. It is our duty to save them from being again rejected and despised."[33] In a melodramatic flourish, Drucker reports that some of the women committed suicide after being let go. He ends the story with Dreystadt in tears, asking God to forgive him for having "failed those poor souls."

This would be a remarkable story if it were true. But it is not. Journalist Andrea Gabor found no evidence to support the story.[34] A 1943 UAW survey indicated that, of approximately 2,200 black workers at three Cadillac plants in the Detroit area, fewer than a hundred were women, and two-thirds were janitors or matrons. GM managers and employees recalled no bombsight project and no prostitutes, black or otherwise.[35] It is unclear where Drucker got this story, but its contours are familiar. It indulges in common stereotypes of black women as prostitutes to emphasize the degradation from which they

[31] Peter Drucker, *Adventures of a Bystander* (New York: Harper & Row, 1979), 269.
[32] Ibid., 271.
[33] Ibid., 271.
[34] Andrea Gabor, *The Capitalist Philosophers* (New York: Time Business, 2000), 310–11.
[35] Ibid., 311.

were lifted. At the same time, its sentimental melodrama reflects how decent white Americans had long thought about the long-suffering, downtrodden black race, a view that derives from the abolitionists' crusades against slavery. With its "poor wretches," dramatic suicides, and failed salvation, Drucker's story could have been written by Harriet Beecher Stowe.

Drucker devotes an entire chapter of his memoir to the American race problem. Like the old nineteenth-century abolitionists, he believed America's racial woes were fundamentally a spiritual problem. In this regard, his views contrasted with those of Edward Bernays, for whom racism was a problem of stunted social evolution. For Drucker, racism and discrimination would not be solved by social reform but rather by atonement. Race, Drucker wrote, was a white problem, and until whites freed themselves through contrition and repentance, blacks would continue to suffer.[36] This was a prevalent attitude among mid-twentieth-century white liberals. It was the message of Sinclair Lewis's *Kingsblood Royal* and the reason Martin Luther King, Jr.'s message of redemption and hope appealed to so many white Americans. It was this attitude of contrition and redemption that led hundreds of middle-class American youth to go south in 1964 to put their lives "on the line" for a cause larger than themselves.

Businessmen were not immune to the moral appeals of the civil rights movement. There were those who wanted to do the right thing. Admittedly, it is difficult to "prove" moral sincerity. But there is no reason to think that business-men, alone among white people, were somehow resistant to the moral appeal of civil rights. The American Friends Service Committee (AFSC) enlisted Christian businessmen who tried to persuade other religious employers of the moral imperative of integration. Indeed, the interviews that the AFSC con-ducted as part of its Merit Employment program indicate that many employers struggled to reconcile their Christian values with exclusionary customs.[37] In the pages of *Management Review*, Pitney-Bowes's personnel director Joseph J. Morrow urged his peers to recognize the moral correctness of equal economic opportunity, writing, "there is really only one impelling and unanswerable argument in its behalf for any human – any businessman – who honestly believes in the teachings of the Christian or Jewish religions."[38] Morrow's lead-ership roles in the Urban League, the National Conference of Christians and Jews, and various local and national equal opportunity groups, and his many

---

[36] Quoted in Drucker, *Adventures of a Bystander*, 312, see also 307–12 for Drucker's explanation of the U.S. race problem.

[37] Gelber makes heavy use of these interviews. See Gelber, *Black Men and Businessmen*, 92–95.

[38] J. J. Morrow, "Employment on Merit: The Continuing Challenge to Business," *Management Review* (February 1957): 10.

awards for interracial cooperation, suggest that he, like so many other whites at this time, wanted to do his part to eradicate racism from American life.[39]

As the civil rights movement grew in the 1960s, many businessmen increasingly emphasized the moral imperatives of antiracism and became ever more poetic in their entreaties. When Pitney-Bowes president John O. Nicklis announced shortly after President Kennedy's assassination that his company would hire Negro applicants over whites, he gave a moral reason that echoed Malcolm X's "chickens coming home to roost" remark about the assassination. In an address to the National Social Welfare Assembly, Nicklis linked "two hundred years of outright slavery and another hundred years of discrimination" with the "dark horror" of the assassination, and called for a purge of the nation's soul: "Now is the time to do the purging, and the Negro and his struggle for justice and opportunity should be the place to begin."[40] In a private letter to his brother about an equal opportunity conference he attended, Lukens Steel Company's Stewart Huston, a devout Quaker, singled out for quotation an admonishment from one of the speakers that the necessary reforms must come from the heart.[41] *Fortune* editor Charles Silberman's 1963 article, "The Businessman and the Negro," rejected expediency and reminded readers of the moral issues at stake, ending with Jefferson's famous quotation: "I tremble for my country, when I reflect that God is just."[42] Urging American employers to rebuild the Negro's faith in American society, a senior vice president at Crown Zellerbach Corporation declared, "The light of America, darkened by the racial cloud, would brighten and shine more brilliantly than ever before."[43]

Thus, in addition to the economic and practical motivations we examined in the previous chapter, new attitudes about race and racism influenced many American executives to support and promote equal employment opportunities. Such attitudes would serve them well in the liberal political atmosphere

[39] See "Review Family Progress at Urban League Meet," *Chicago Defender*, September 10, 1956, 8; "Parley Stresses Civil Rights Issue," *New York Times*, August 1, 1952, 33; "Cite 2 For Interracial Cooperation," *Chicago Defender*, November 7, 1953, 23; and "Joseph J. Morrow, Former Official at Pitney-Bowes and Civic Leader," *New York Times*, June 23, 1981. It is worth noting that four out of the seven leaders of the National Conference of Christians and Jews have been businessmen.

[40] Emma Harrison, "Company is Giving Negroes Priority," *New York Times*, December 4, 1963; "Pitney-Bowes Announces New Negro Preferential Hiring Plan," *Chicago Defender*, December 5, 1963, 3; John Nicklis, "A Statement," *PB News*, December 13, 1963 in Collection 5583/2, Box 51, Folder: communication, at Kheel Center.

[41] Stewart Huston to Charles L. Huston, Jr., June 12, 1964, in Lukens Steel Company, Executive Officer Files, 1903–1979, Series III, Box 2018, File: Equal Employment Opportunity, HML.

[42] Charles Silberman, "The Businessman and the Negro," *Fortune*, September 1963.

[43] James P. Mitchell, "Business and Civil Rights," a speech delivered to the Commonwealth Club of California, June 5, 1964, in *Vital Speeches of the Day* 30, no. 18 (July 1, 1964): 549–51.

of the 1950s and 1960s. The new racial liberalism went hand in hand with a new openness to the expansion of the federal government.

Racial Liberalism and the Liberal Consensus

With the help of Keynesian economic policies, a progressive tax structure, and a politically powerful labor movement, liberal Democrats had contained and stabilized capitalism. As a result, they no longer sought to curb it but rather based their entire political program on its controlled expansion and growth. Long-standing class conflicts, which liberals believed were rooted in a scarcity of resources, would be resolved through an ever-expanding economic pie. Having solved the economic problem, liberals turned the power of the state onto social problems, such as racial discrimination. Historian Alan Brinkley called liberals' embrace of economic growth "the end of reform." But it began forty years of liberal rule, progressive taxes, and activist government.[44]

Businessmen played a critical role in creating the "liberal consensus." The traditional antipathy between business and government had begun to erode during the New Deal, when certain businessmen, whom historian Stephen B. Adams called "government entrepreneurs," began to perceive the "entrepreneurial opportunities presented by the growth of the administrative state."[45] Shipbuilder Henry J. Kaiser, the subject of Adams's book, was known as the "New Deal's businessman" because, whether he was building dams or ships, the federal government was his biggest client. IBM's Thomas J. Watson, Sr., was another businessman whose company benefited from New Deal programs: IBM's punch card computers made possible the implementation of Social Security and agricultural subsidies.[46] Bankers and aspiring multinational firms benefited from the Roosevelt administration's internationalist, open-door foreign policy and were willing to accept the New Deal's prolabor policies in exchange for policies that encouraged international trade and economic stability. As historian Thomas Ferguson explains, the older, labor-intensive industries (steel, mining, textiles), which had demanded high tariffs and antilabor laws, were no longer the sole representatives of American

---

[44] On the liberal consensus, see Godfrey Hodgson, *America in Our Time* (Garden City, NY: Doubleday, 1976); Alan Brinkley, *The End of Reform: New Deal Liberalism in Recession and War* (New York: Vintage, 1996); and Kevin Mattson, *When America Was Great: The Fighting Faith of Postwar Liberalism* (New York: Routledge, 2004).

[45] Stephen B. Adams, *Mr. Kaiser Goes to Washington: The Rise of a Government Entrepreneur* (Chapel Hill: University of North Carolina Press, 1997), 3.

[46] David Stebenne, "IBM's New Deal: Employee Policies of the IBM Corporation, 1933–1956," *Journal of the Historical Society* 5, no. 1 (Winter 2005): 47–77.

capitalism. Industries and bankers with interests in low tariffs and conciliatory labor policies were finding influence in the Roosevelt administration.[47] Industrial leaders, such as John D. Rockefeller, Jr., Walter Teagle of Standard Oil New Jersey, Gerard Swope of GE, and Thomas Watson of IBM, not only supported Roosevelt and the Democratic Party but also helped craft New Deal legislation.[48] Some of the most powerful (and liberal) Democrats in the postwar years began their careers as investment bankers, including Averill Harriman, Herbert Lehman, James Forrestal, and Sidney Weinberg.

World War II further fostered the relationship between industrial leaders and the federal government. There were lucrative government contracts, of course, but executives also went to Washington to head wartime agencies, such as the Office of Price Administration, the War Production Board, and even the FEPC. Their service softened their attitudes toward the government, and they would later look back fondly on it. Neil McElroy, chairman of the board of Proctor and Gamble, Inc., for instance, wrote to Philip D. Reed, GE's chairman, about his service with the Department of Defense: "I found, as you did when you were serving the Government, that the life was strenuous but that in leaving such an assignment a man feels an intangible inner satisfaction which probably would come to him in no other way."[49] Although few executives were so sentimental, the war had awakened in many a sense of service to the nation. There was among the leaders of the largest corporations a growing sense that corporations had a positive role to play in the governance of the country, one that recognized the interdependence of economic prosperity, national security, and government action.[50]

The new relationship between industry and government allowed executives to play a larger role in government. Recast as "industrial statesmen," executives from large corporations and internationally focused business sectors founded the Business Advisory Council (later the Business Council, or BC), within the Department of Commerce to provide counsel and guidance

---

[47] Thomas Ferguson, "Industrial Conflict and the Coming of the New Deal: The Triumph of Multinational Liberalism in America," in *The Rise and Fall of the New Deal Order*, ed. Steve Fraser and Gary Gerstle (Princeton, NJ: Princeton University Press, 1989), 3–31.

[48] Ferguson, "Industrial Conflict and the Coming of the New Deal," 19; see also Kim McQuaid, *Uneasy Partners: Big Business in American Politics, 1945–1990* (Baltimore: Johns Hopkins University Press, 1994).

[49] Neil McElroy to Philip Reed, December 15, 1959, in Philip D. Reed Papers, 1937–1989, Series II, Box 7, HML.

[50] This viewpoint can be found in William Benton, "The Economics of a Free Society: A Declaration of American Business Policy," *Fortune*, October 1944; see also Sidney Weinberg to GE board, May 31, 1957, in Series II, Box 7 of Philip D. Reed Papers, 1937–1989. Attached is a copy of Fred Hovde's remarks to GE management trainees about how GE has to be good for the nation.

to New Deal programs. In 1942, members of the Department of Commerce founded the Committee for Economic Development (CED) as a temporary, independent committee, whose purpose was to help plan for postwar reconversion. Eventually, it became a permanent research and planning organization, formulating quasi-Keynesian monetary and tax policies and promoting free enterprise and industry-government cooperation.[51] Like so many wartime planning organizations, it consisted of a familiar group of federal power brokers and public-minded executives, such as R. R. Deupree of Proctor and Gamble, Marion Folsom of Eastman Kodak, Secretary of Commerce and former head of the Reconstruction Finance Corporation, Jesse Jones, Paul Hoffman of the Studebaker Corporation, U.S. Chamber of Commerce president Eric Johnston, advertising executive William Benton, and the ubiquitous Beardsley Ruml, all of whom straddled the worlds of government, philanthropy, banking, and business.

If liberals were in charge of Washington, DC, businessmen were willing to adapt to their game. As William Benton, a former advertising executive and cofounder of the CED, wrote to another CED member: "I believe that we need the intellectual and liberal forces of the country behind us. I think we can get them." Benton continued, "We must be prepared to take some raps from 'the right' if we are to maintain and hold our position with the great middle group [liberals] who will prove our long term strength."[52] Benton and his allies in the CED hoped to persuade the liberals and intellectuals in Washington that the business community was redeemable. They saw the CED as an "enlightened" alternative to the conservative National Association of Manufacturers (NAM). Some historians ignore Benton's distinctions and lump the CED together with the hard-line NAM conservatives, arguing that both were part of the antiliberal, antilabor postwar campaign for free enterprise, individualism, and productivity.[53] It is true that moderates and conservatives shared a missionary zeal for the free enterprise system and that there was overlap between the leadership of the CED and the NAM, but it is important to recognize that businessmen such as Benton made the decision to accept postwar liberalism and reject conservatism. In their eyes, this was the only way to save free enterprise.

William Benton had begun his career in advertising in the 1930s, as cofounder (with Chester Bowles) of the highly successful firm Benton & Bowles.

---

[51] On the CED, see McQuaid, *Uneasy Partners*, 19–20, Sidney Hyman, *The Lives of William Benton* (Chicago: University of Chicago Press, 1969), 263–96; and Elizabeth Fones-Wolf, *Selling Free Enterprise: The Business Assault on Labor and Liberalism, 1945–1960* (University of Illinois Press, 1994), who portrays the CED as more conservative than liberal.
[52] Quoted in Sidney Hyman, *The Lives of William Benton*, 277–78.
[53] See Fones-Wolf, *Selling Free Enterprise*.

Both Benton and Bowles later became liberal Democratic politicians and power brokers – Fair Dealers – and both supported the numerous attempts to pass a permanent federal FEPC bill. Benton was the Democratic senator from Connecticut from 1949 through 1953 (he was appointed by Bowles to fill out a term but won election in his own right in 1950 – against Republican challenger Prescott Bush). Of the two, Benton remained more closely connected to the business community during his years in politics. He was a member of the CED and continued to run his own business, Encyclopedia Britannica, Inc. Politically, Benton was a very liberal Democrat. He was endorsed by the Congress of Industrial Organizations (CIO) and consistently supported and voted with the Senate's most principled liberals, Paul Douglas Hubert Humphrey, and fellow businessman Herbert Lehman. Long before Edward R. Murrow ever criticized Joseph McCarthy, Benton was fighting to have the Senate censure him, beginning in 1951.

Benton's liberalism did not prevent corporate executives from supporting him. Although he was a Republican, General Electric chairman and CED member Philip D. Reed supported Benton's reelection in 1950. In fact, Reed sent campaign solicitations to CED members and telegrammed two hundred of his Connecticut industrialist friends to support the liberal Benton.[54] This electioneering on the part of General Electric's CEO was widely criticized, mainly by Connecticut Republicans, who resented the outside meddling. Marion Folsom, president of Eastman Kodak Company, Republican, and CED member, also complained that Reed's action suggested a CED endorsement of Benton, which did not exist and certainly was not the purpose of the CED.[55] Reed's support for Benton's campaign indicates that party lines were weaker than the "old boys" network, but it also suggests that the old boys were more open to liberal ideas than historians have appreciated. Reed's inclinations were not purely cronyism. Like Benton, Reed despised Wisconsin Senator Joseph McCarthy and sent money to defray Benton's legal expenses after McCarthy sued him for libel.[56]

The new racial tolerance fit comfortably within this political agenda. Racially intolerant people tended to be intolerant also of the federal government, free trade, and international cooperation, whereas the racially tolerant

---

[54] Edward Michelson, "GE Chief's Support of Benton Irks GOP," *Bridgeport Sunday Herald*, October 29, 1950; and Reed to Hayes Murphy, Wiremold Co., Hartford, Conn., October 30, 1950, and other letters in Philip D. Reed Papers, 1937–1989, Series IV, Box 33, HML.

[55] See Benton to Marion Folsom, Kodak Eastman Co. November 7, 1950, and Philip Reed to Hayes Murphy, Wiremold Co., Hartford, Conn., October 30, 1950, in Philip D. Reed Papers, 1937–1989, Series IV, Box 33, HML.

[56] William Benton to Philip Reed, July 11, 1952, in Philip D. Reed Papers, 1937–1989, Series IV, Box 33, HML.

were tolerant, even encouraging, of such liberal ideas. Given their comfort with government activism, CED members had no problem supporting fair employment legislation. In 1948, a group of businessmen and professionals urged the Senate to pass the Ives-Fulton bill against employment discrimination. The group included such self-styled industrial statesmen and Republicans as Nelson Rockefeller, Henry Luce, and Eric Johnston. Northeast Yankee types such as Rockefeller and William Benton despised bigotry, which they associated with the benighted South, the right, and the demagogic politics of McCarthyism. Their racial tolerance connoted a particular political and cultural worldview that was everything the South was not: liberal, cosmopolitan, tolerant. For moderates and liberals, the South's commitment to states' rights was reason enough to support a stronger federal government. In this regard, Benton's support for a federal FEPC sometimes seems to be more antisouthern than problack. It was Benton who suggested cutting off federal funds to the South to stop southern filibustering against FEPC legislation.[57] In a 1952 campaign speech, Benton reminded his audience that the moral and electoral strength of the Democratic Party lay "in the enlightened Northern states."[58] The South for Benton represented the same sort of narrow-mindedness and irrational fear mongering that characterized McCarthyism. Racial tolerance was inseparable from a belief in political tolerance.

Racial tolerance also signified a willingness to learn about and from other cultures. The extraordinarily active Benton was also a cofounder of the United Nations Educational, Science, and Cultural Organization (UNESCO), an international agency devoted to intercultural education, racial tolerance, and cultural democracy. Author of a statement against scientific racism, UNESCO was the cultural part of a new internationalist vision of global cooperation, peace, and free markets. Articulated originally by Woodrow Wilson and later honed by Henry Luce and Wendell Willkie, postwar internationalism justified American intervention in the world but, at the same time, enjoined Americans to recognize their common ties to those they might regard as "foreign." Internationalism required an appreciation for other cultures and peoples, a willingness to reach across boundaries, to create a new world in which, as Wendell Willkie proclaimed, "there shall be an equality of opportunity for every race and every nation." The rise of internationalism in American foreign

---

[57] "Cut-Off Suggested on Funds to South," *New York Times*, October 3, 1951, 27 – although he claimed he wasn't really serious about it.

[58] "Benton Scores G.O.P.," *New York Times*, Sept. 8, 1952, 13. Benton was responding to vice-presidential candidate Richard Nixon's (correct) accusation that the Democrats were beholden to southerners. See "Nixon Says Rivals Dodge Rights Issue," *New York Times*, September 5, 1952, 13.

policy recast isolationists as xenophobic, racist, and close-minded.[59] More-over, as more American corporations opened foreign operations, parochial attitudes could prove detrimental to success. Standard Oil of New Jersey's M. J. Rathbone explained his company's policy of interviewing the wives of execu-tives who were assigned to overseas offices: "We have to appraise if they are the kind that can readapt themselves to foreign living.... We try to interest them in learning the foreign language, but the main thing we look for is emotional stability. If she's a whiner, thinks foreigners are inferior, she can do a lot of harm."[60]

Since the idea that racism correlates to conservative, isolationist politics is still a common assumption, it may seem like I am stating the obvious, but my point is that racial tolerance became tied to particular political agendas (government-industry cooperation, the cold war, free trade) favored by the most influential businessmen and their allies. This does not mean that they were free of racism but that racism was incompatible with their vision of the world in a way that it hadn't been fifty years before. Thus, when civil rights activists and demonstrators pushed for the issue of employment discrimi-nation, liberal businessmen did not push back and indeed, in 1964, largely supported legislative efforts to end discrimination.

By 1964, things were beginning to change even at Lukens Steel Company. Charles Huston, Jr. and Stewart Huston were enthusiastic about equal oppor-tunity, and Lukens was signed up for Plans for Progress, a voluntary affirma-tive action program for defense contractors. In June 1964, Stewart attended the Philadelphia Regional Conference on Equal Opportunity and Economic Growth and returned with much to report to his brother. The letter is a some-what gushy account of the conference: who said what, who the good speakers were, who seemed "not entirely enthusiastic about the program" (a labor rep-resentative – of course). The vice-president of the President's Committee on Equal Employment Opportunities gave an excellent luncheon talk in which, Stewart noted favorably, he said that the "problem of individual freedom and equal opportunity should be not only in our factories, etc., but in our hearts." A Negro businessman talked about expanding black purchasing power. Stewart concluded, "The general spirit of the meeting was excellent and should produce

[59] Wendell Willkie, "Isolation Policies and the League of Nations," delivered May 11, 1942, at Union College, printed in Vital Speeches of the Day 8 (June 1, 1942): 485–86. On the political implications of cold war internationalism, see Robert Griffith, "Old Progressives and the Cold War," Journal of American History 66 (September 179): 334–47; and Lary May, ed. Recasting America: Culture and Politics in the Age of the Cold War (Chicago: University of Chicago, 1989). On UNESCO's antiracism, see Brattain, "Race, Racism, and Antiracism," 1386–1413.
[60] Quoted in Osborn Elliott, Men at the Top (New York: Harper and Brothers, 1959), 109.

some sound thinking in what can easily be an explosive situation."[61] This was a private letter to a brother, not a public statement, and it indicates a genuine interest in and openness to the ideas presented at the conference. Within a generation, attitudes had changed. Actually, what this letter illustrates is that the problems associated with black workers had changed. In their father's day, the problem had been how to segregate and control black workers. For his sons in 1964, it was how to incorporate and promote them. But this change was necessarily accompanied by a change in attitudes within some segments of the business community, one that was not just about racial attitudes but also about attitudes toward the government.

Foundations, Professional Associations, and Research Organizations

No matter how liberal they were, employers had tremendous difficulty reconciling their professions of tolerance with the discriminatory practices that occurred in their firms. There were other sectors of the business community, however, that managed to match racial liberalism to their mission and provided a place where liberal, public-minded executives could put their energies and do something for racial progress in a way they could not in their own companies. Their efforts in foundations, professional associations, and research organizations signified and furthered the normalization of racial liberalism both within the business community and society.

Foundations

The three great philanthropic institutions founded by American titans – the Rockefeller Foundation, the Carnegie Corporation, and the Ford Foundation – each made major contributions to racial progress and the study of race relations. Through the General Education Board (GEB), the Laura Spelman Rockefeller Memorial, and the Phelps-Stoke Fund, the Rockefeller Foundation funded black schools and colleges, studies of American race relations, and the National Urban League.[62] Whatever its motivations and however conservative its vision, the Rockefeller Foundation nonetheless helped create a generation

---

[61] Stewart Huston to Charles L. Huston, Jr., June 12, 1964, in Lukens Steel Company, Executive Officer Files, 1903–1979, Series III, Box 2018, File: Equal Employment Opportunity, HML.

[62] See Nancy Weiss, *The National Urban League* (New York: Oxford University Press, 1974), and Jackson, *Gunnar Myrdal and America's Conscience*.

of black activists, including T. Arnold Hill, Lester Granger, Clarence Mitchell, Jr., and Whitney Young, Jr., who cajoled, pressed, and demanded that employers practice equal employment opportunity. Under the direction of Beardsley Ruml, the Laura Spelman Rockefeller Memorial focused on the social sciences, funding new social science research centers at the University of Chicago (which was created by the Rockefeller Foundation), Columbia University, Harvard, Stanford, and the University of North Carolina.

Social scientists played a crucial role in integrating the American workplace. They collected the empirical data that helped government officials, employers, and the public actually see discrimination and promulgated the theories that connected racial discrimination to unemployment, poverty, and social alienation. They gave people the tools not only to identify injustice but also to correct it. Beginning in the 1920s, their work was funded in large part by the Rockefeller funded organizations mentioned earlier, the Carnegie Corporation, the Russell Sage Foundation, the Julius Rosenwald Fund, and other philanthropic organizations. Foundation monies supported the work of the great black social scientists, including E. Franklin Frazier, W. E. B. Du Bois, St. Clair Drake, Allison Davis, Charles Johnson, Ira De Reid, Bertram Doyle, Horace Cayton, and Oliver Cox, as well as the race relations research of white social scientists, such as John Dollard, Louis Wirth, Hortense Powdermaker, Margaret Mead, Ruth Benedict, Howard Odum, W. Lloyd Warner, Guy Johnson, Melville Herskovits, Gordon Allport, Will Alexander, Edwin Embree, M. F. Ashley Montagu, Samuel Stouffer, Arnold Rose, and Everett C. Hughes. Foundation monies paid for the empirical evidence that made discrimination a demonstrable scientific reality and not merely an emotional accusation. Social science research lifted racial discrimination out of the realm of custom and inevitability and made it a problem to be solved.

One of the most influential studies of race relations was Gunnar Myrdal's *An American Dilemma* (1944), commissioned by the Carnegie Corporation, which revealed to white Americans – as if for the first time – the extent to which racial discrimination violated the nation's founding tenets. With the Carnegie Corporation's funds, Myrdal, a Swedish economist, put together an ideologically diverse research team that included Dorothy Thomas, Ralph Bunche, Doxie Wilkerson, Paul Norgren (a Harvard-trained economist who would go on to become an expert on fair employment), Charles Johnson, Ashley Montagu, Louis Wirth, Edward Shils, Guy Johnson, Allison Davis, E. Franklin Frazier, Sterling Brown, T. Arnold Hill (from the Urban League), St. Clair Drake, and Ira De Reid. Arnold Rose and Samuel Stouffer helped write the book.[63] Myrdal

[63] Jackson, *Gunnar Myrdal and America's Conscience*, 89–127.

believed that social science should be used on behalf of public policy, and he intended the book to provide a basis for legislation and change. Its recommendations became the goal of civil rights activists, and it was cited in the 1954 *Brown v. Board of Education* decision, which ended segregation in the schools. Although one finds it difficult to believe that many Americans actually read the 1,482 pages of sociological data, the book sold well and went through twenty-five printings before it was revised in 1963. The *New York Times* called it a "book that changed American life."[64]

Critics, however, found it timid. They felt Myrdal underestimated white resistance to change, that he put too much faith in education, and that he saw black culture as pathology. Ralph Ellison faulted the book's implicit anti-Marxism and questioned how the book served the interests of those who commissioned it: "Here the profit motive of the Right – clothed, it is true, in the guilt-dress of philanthropy – has proven more resourceful, imaginative, and aware of its own interests than the overcautious socialism of the Left."[65] The left's criticisms were not misplaced. Despite the intentional foreignness of its author, *An American Dilemma* was a quintessential expression of the postwar liberal establishment. It assumed the fundamental correctness of the American system and that whatever problems existed within it could be resolved through social science and public policy.

Established in 1936, the Ford Foundation entered the philanthropic community in full force in 1948 when Henry Ford II reorganized it to focus on five areas: peace, democracy, the economy, education, and human relations. In 1950, Ford chose CED cofounder Paul Hoffman (who was at that point administering the Marshall Plan in Washington) to head the foundation. Hoffman brought with him University of Chicago president Robert M. Hutchins. The pair delighted in shocking businessmen with their liberal views.[66] The foundation funded international exchange programs, foreign language education, and intercultural training, anything that would help educate Americans about the world they lived in. Its Fund for the Republic was dedicated to strengthening civil liberties and the study of right-wing extremism. These programs caught the eye of congressional conservatives, who, under the leadership of Georgia Democrat Eugene Cox, began an

---

[64] Oscar Handlin, "A Book That Changed American Life," *New York Times Book Review*, April 21, 1963, 1.

[65] Quote from Ellison, "An American Dilemma: A Review," written in 1944, republished in Callahan, *The Collected Essays of Ralph Ellison*, 328–40, p. 336. On critics, see Jackson, *Gunnar Myrdal and America's Conscience*, 257–66.

[66] See Dwight McDonald, *The Ford Foundation: The Men and the Millions* (New York: Reynal, 1956), 50–94. Originally published in the *New Yorker*.

investigation of the possibly seditious, apparently "communistic" activities of wealthy tax-exempt organizations. Conservatives' suspicions that the wealthy Ford Foundation harbored communists mirrored their suspicions that Dean Acheson's "stripy-pants" manners connoted treachery, and were part of what postwar liberals had identified and marginalized as "status-anxiety" and right-wing extremism. But while conservatives exaggerated the radicalism of the Ford Foundation's initiatives, it is not as though they had no cause to be alarmed. The Ford Foundation's agenda was liberal.

To deflect right-wing criticism, Henry Ford II replaced Hoffman and Hutchins with quieter, less provocative bureaucrats but did not change any of the programs they had set up.[67] The Ford Foundation continued to support the causes of postwar liberalism, from the CIA's "cultural front" in the war against communism, to minority scholarships, to dozens of civil rights organizations, including the Congress of Racial Equality , which was responsible for the string of boycotts in the late 1950s and early 1960s that prompted many companies to integrate. It is not surprising that McGeorge Bundy, a paradigmatic liberal from the Kennedy and Johnson administrations, would be chosen to head the foundation after his failure in Vietnam.

The Alfred P. Sloan Foundation was founded by General Motors president and chairman of the board Alfred P. Sloan, Jr., in 1934. Sloan put together a board of trustees that consisted mainly of General Motors executives. The foundation's program focused on technology, science, and business, but it was also the sponsor of the Public Affairs Committee, Inc., a nonprofit educational organization, whose purpose was to "make available in summary and inexpensive form the results of research on economic and social problems to aid in the understanding and development of American policy."[68] The Public Affairs Committee regularly published pamphlets on the race problem, including Ruth Benedict and Gene Weltfish's *The Races of Mankind*, which argued that "race" was a myth and that apparent differences between so-called races were the result of culture and education, not biology. When a House Committee supported the army's refusal to circulate the pamphlet, the director of the Alfred P. Sloan Foundation, Harold S. Sloan, stood behind the pamphlet, stating, "It is a pity that the Military Affairs Committee of the House sees fit to withhold from our armed forces the simple facts of science that completely refute the enemy's conception of a superrace."[69] The authors of Public Affairs Committee

---

[67] Ibid.

[68] From the back of Public Affairs Pamphlet No. 128, *Our Negro Veterans* (1947).

[69] "Plans New Edition of Race Pamphlet," *New York Times*, March 8, 1944, 11. Other Public Affairs Committee pamphlets included *The Negro in America* (1944), *Race Riots Aren't Necessary* (1945), and *Our Negro Veterans* (March 1947).

Pamphlet No. 128, *Our Negro Veterans*, identified jobs, housing, and education as key to the full citizenship demanded by – and owed to – Negro veterans.

The world of foundations is usually regarded as "philanthropy" and thus somehow separate from the business world. Many of the individuals who headed the great foundations, however, were part of a coterie of public-minded executives who sought to stabilize the American economy and liberalize American society. People such as Beardsley Ruml, Paul Hoffman, William Benton, Henry Ford II, Alfred P. Sloan, and the Ford Motor Company's Arjay Miller flitted among corporations, government committees, and foundation work, no longer representatives of one narrow sector but rather the ecumenical, broad-minded, coalition-building liberal leaders of society. Having identified racial injustice as a threat to social stability and continued economic growth, corporate foundation heads cooperated with social scientists and professional administrators to address the underlying causes of racial inequality, as well as the resulting social discontent. Sometimes this meant supporting activist organizations that would boycott and sue corporations for discrimination.

The elements of racial liberalism can also be seen in the business community's schools and professional and research associations, such as the American Management Association (AMA), the National Industrial Conference Board (NICB), Industrial Relations Counselors, Inc., the National Planning Association, and the Personnel Research Foundation. Business schools and professional organizations sought to professionalize management and corporate administration.[70] Their many publications – research studies, conference papers, journals, books·– kept corporate executives and managers apprised of the latest developments in their fields and provided a forum for social science researchers to reach the practitioners of everyday business and management. Their insistence on the value of social science research as a tool for managers reveals the growing influence of liberalism on corporate culture in the 1950s.

Beginning in the 1940s, these organizations regularly published studies and articles about minority workers, fair employment, and integration, offering managers practical tips for integration and alerting them to potential problems. They tended to avoid editorializing either for or against integration but rather presented data, objective information, about how other companies had integrated, what their experiences had been, and how to go about it if one chose.[71] Long before the U.S. government, the AMA and the NICB

---

[70] On the liberalization of midcentury business schools, see Rakesh Khurana, *From Higher Aims to Hired Hands: The Social Transformation of American Business Schools and the Unfulfilled Promise of Management as a Profession* (Princeton, NJ: Princeton University Press, 2007).

[71] See, for example, "The Elimination of Discrimination," *Personnel Journal* 24 (January 1946): 255–59; "A Successful Voluntary FEPC," *Personnel Journal* 28 (July–August 1949): 111;

were conducting surveys of minorities in the workplace. Indeed, the AMA's first research study was *The Negro Worker*, issued in 1942 to supply American industries with much-needed information on African American workers.[72] As its foreword explained: "The growing interest in the employment of Negroes in industry and the numerous requests from employers and personnel executives for information on how to initiate and carry through a program of integration of colored employees have prompted this study."[73] *The Negro Worker* framed the issue in terms of manpower utilization, noting in its summary that many Negroes were working below their level aptitudes, abilities, and skills and providing data about the numbers of trained and skilled Negro workers in the United States. The publication encouraged employers to use Negro workers and provided them with "tried and true guideposts" to help them overcome resistance on the part of supervisors, managers, and employees. Company heads were more likely to follow advice from one of these organizations, which were headed by their peers and served the interests of the business community, than advice from the government or civil rights organizations.

Like philanthropies, business schools and professional organizations are rarely acknowledged as being representative of the business community, but the executives and managers who made up "the business community" had very often graduated from a prestigious business school, were members of professional associations, served on their boards, subscribed to their services, wrote for their journals, and attended their conferences. Given the weakness of traditional business interest groups such as the National Association of Manufacturers among businessmen (see Chapter 7), the schools and the professional and research associations played a significant role in creating a cohesive corporate culture. That they regularly addressed the problem of minority workers and encouraged employers and managers to do so as well speaks to the prevalence of racial liberalism within the business community.

During World War II, white Americans' racial attitudes and behavior began to undergo what would be a stunning transformation from frankly racist

American Management Association, *The Personnel Job in a Changing World* (New York: American Management Association, 1964); Stephen Habbe, *Company Experience with Negro Employment*, 2 vols., Studies in Personnel Policy No. 201 (New York: National Industrial Conference Board, 1966); Jack Gourlay, *The Negro Salaried Worker*, AMA Research Study 70 (New York: American Management Association, 1965); Paul Norgren et al., *Employing the Negro in American Industry: A Study of Management Practices* (New York: Industrial Relations Counselors, Inc., 1959).

[72] American Management Association, *The Negro Worker: An Analysis of Management Experience and Opinion on the Employment and Integration of the Negro in Industry*, Special Research Report No. 1 (New York: American Management Association, 1942).

[73] Ibid., foreword.

assumptions and exclusionary practices to the color-blind, tolerant tenets of mainstream racial liberalism. It was a bumpy and, in many ways, incomplete transformation; while whites wanted to be tolerant, they did not always recognize their own racist assumptions. Businessmen were not exempt from this transformation, and this chapter has tried to demonstrate the prevalence of racial liberalism within certain parts of the business community. The prevalence of racial liberalism did not mean the absence of racism or discrimination. It did, however, indicate a social atmosphere that discouraged open opposition to workplace integration.

4   Human Relations in Management

The idea of employing competent industrial relations personnel is no longer on trial.... Today it is considered good business to employ individuals whose handling of employer-employee relations is expected to result in more favorable management-employee understanding ... and therefore more production at less cost.

Sara Southall, 1950[1]

The development of equal employment opportunities cannot be divorced from the structure of an organization, especially its overall management of administrative matters.

Lewis Ferman, 1968[2]

Making the decision to hire or promote black workers into traditionally white jobs was one thing. Implementing it was quite another. The transition to an interracial workforce during and after World War II was often accompanied by violence and resistance, but it was made easier by the prevalence of managerial practices that stressed "human relations." Designed to alleviate labor tension and increase productivity, the human relations approach to management was especially attuned to issues of assimilation, adjustment, and social change and thus proved sensitive to the problems raised by fair employment and workplace integration. It is difficult to see how integration could have proceeded without human relations innovations such as formalized employment procedures, a recognition of group dynamics, in-house training and education, community relations programs, and sensitivity training. Essential to the eventual success of integration was the human relations belief that the workplace was a social

---

[1] Sara Southall, *Industry's Unfinished Business: Achieving Sound Industrial Relations and Fair Employment* (New York: Harpers & Brothers, 1950), 40.
[2] Louis Ferman, *The Negro and Equal Employment Opportunities: A Review of Management Experiences in Twenty Companies* (New York: Praeger, 1968), 81.

system, not a collection of individuals. To the extent that workplace discrimination was systemic, and not the sum of individual discriminators, human relations experts understood the ways in which the process of integration had to be proactive, affirmative, and holistic, rather than individualistic and color-blind.

The field of industrial human relations was closely related to the study of race relations. The two areas shared the same assumptions about the group-based nature of society and the same body of social research. Many of the case studies that made up the curriculum of business and management schools were based on race relations research. Those trained to be managers and personnel officers were familiar with the social science ideas that informed the movement for fair employment. They understood better than company and division heads that discrimination was rooted in a system of social relations and structural inequities.

While human relations policies eased integration, integration, in turn, could reinforce and strengthen human relations policies and, more significantly, the industrial relations departments that championed them. There was a mutually beneficial, interdependent relationship between the movements for fair employment and industrial relations. It is no accident that the executives who most actively promoted fair employment were heads of industrial relations departments: Ivan L. Willis of International Harvester, Joseph Morrow of Pitney-Bowes, William Caples of Inland Steel Container Corporation – who were introduced in Chapter 2 – were all vice-presidents of industrial relations departments. James D. Hodgson, who helped develop the Philadelphia Plan and mandatory affirmative action policies, had spent twenty-eight years in industrial relations at Lockheed Aircraft Corporation. They were "staff men" as opposed to "line men." They were not, typically, entrepreneurs or engineers. They had gone to college and been trained to manage organizations. Not all industrial relations officers championed fair employment – indeed, few in practice did – but in those companies that first experimented with fair employment, a strong industrial relations department was essential. Indeed, the expansion and acceptance of human relations techniques helped prepare the business community for the requirements of integration.

The Rise of Human Relations in Management

The human relations in management movement sought to end the "drive system," the traditional style of managing workers that consisted of foremen controlling workers through an arbitrary system of threats, rewards, and punishment. The drive system created an antagonistic relationship between workers and their employers that led to decreased productivity, high rates of turnover, and labor violence. The idea that harmonious employer-employee relations might yield more productive workplaces first gained popularity in the Progressive era.[3] Ordway Tead, Mary Parker Follett, Elton Mayo, and other management experts further developed the idea in the 1920s and 1930s, reminding workers and employers of their interdependence and urging employers to create more open, cooperative workplaces. Evidence for this proposition was discovered in the Hawthorne experiments. While directing experiments at Western Electric's Hawthorne Plant in Chicago between 1927 and 1932, Elton Mayo found that workers' productivity was not necessarily linked to such material incentives as pay or working conditions (lighting, seating, or lunch breaks) but rather to more intangible factors like work-group dynamics, belongingness, and sense of purpose. Thus, Mayo advised employers to facilitate a spirit of connectedness among his workers, while at the same time "adjusting" them to the realities of industrial society through personnel counseling. Human relations experts later dismissed Mayo's conclusions as nostalgic and simplistic, but they remained committed to Mayo's basic insight – that workers were influenced by the groups and culture around them.[4]

Holding out the promise of industrial peace and increased productivity, human relations experts urged industrial leaders to see their factory as a microcosm, a web of social relationships, statuses, and cliques, interconnected, dynamic, constantly seeking equilibrium.[5] Just as managers had figured out how to integrate a variety of machines and tasks into assembly lines, they could also learn to integrate the different human components of an organization to create an efficient, well-integrated, productive system. In this conception, troublemakers did not cause problems; disequilibrium did. Disequilibrium could not be fixed by punishment or coercion. Rather, employers had to reestablish equilibrium through adjusting and manipulating the groups within the system.

---

[3] The following account draws from Sanford Jacoby, *Modern Manors: Welfare Capitalism since the New Deal* (Princeton, NJ: Princeton University Press, 1997); Richard Gillespie, *Manufacturing Knowledge: A History of the Hawthorne Experiments* (New York: Cambridge University Press, 1991); Henry A. Landsberger, *Hawthorne Revisited: Management and the Worker, Its Critics, and Developments in Human Relations in Industry,* Cornell Studies in Industrial and Labor Relations. Vol. 9. (Ithaca: New York State School of Industrial and Labor Relations, Cornell University Press, 1958); and Loren Baritz, *The Servants of Power: A History of the Use of Social Science in American Industry* (Middletown, CT: Wesleyan University Press, 1960).

[4] William Foote Whyte, *Participant Observer: An Autobiography* (Ithaca, NY: ILR Press, 1994), 143. See also W. F. Whyte, "Human Relations Theory – a Progress Report," *Harvard Business Review* 34, no. 5 (September–October 1956): 125–32.

[5] See Burleigh Gardner, "The Factory as Social System," in *Industry and Society,* ed. William Foote Whyte (New York: McGraw-Hill, 1946): 4–20.

Experts instructed employers to understand what motivated different groups of workers, their fears, their anxieties, their hopes, their need to belong. With this knowledge, they promised, employers would be in a position to reestablish equilibrium and cooperation among the competing parts. Employers would be referees not commanders.

What distinguished the human relations approach from simple "welfare capitalism" was its stress on communication, opportunity, and fairness. Whereas welfare capitalism tended to workers' physical needs in the form of daycare, recreational facilities, and pension plans, the human relations approach sought to elevate workers to participating members of a community. Workers would work harder and stay longer if they felt they were valued members of a community, if they understood their role in that community, and if they had a future in it. This required more than creating an atmosphere of camaraderie and "connectedness," although that too was necessary. It required the creation of open channels of communication, where workers' concerns would be aired and addressed. It required the development of clear, formal job ladders and transparent procedures, fairly applied, for hiring, promotion, demotion, and dismissal. It required the company's commitment to cultivating and training individuals for future opportunities. It required that foremen and supervisors be retrained to communicate with their workers.

By the end of World War II, Harvard, University of Chicago, Yale, and MIT had all established major human relations research centers.[6] Much of the funding for these programs came from forward-thinking industrial leaders, who were convinced that a stabilized and motivated workforce was the key to increased productivity. They offered researchers access to their workplaces in order that researchers might conduct field research among real workers in real industrial situations. If, at the same time, the researchers happened upon a solution to an employer's specific labor problem, well, then, so much the better. A famous example of this academic-industrial cooperation was the University of Chicago's Committee on Human Relations in Industry (CHRI), founded in 1943 by a group of social scientists, including Burleigh Gardner, a former director of the Employee Relations Research Section at the much-studied Hawthorne plant, Allison Davis (the first African American tenured at a major research institution), economist Frederick Harbison, and sociologists W. Lloyd Warner, Everett C. Hughes, and William Foote Whyte. Sears Roebuck and Company, Container Corporation of America, Link-Belt Ordnance Company, and Visking Corporation were among the committee's corporate sponsors.[7] In its

---

[6] Daniel Bell, "Adjusting Men to Machines," *Commentary* 3 (January 1947): 79–88.
[7] On this story, see Jacoby, *Modern Manors*, and W. F. Whyte, *Participant Observer*, 141–49.

seven years of existence, the committee held seminars and lectures on "human relations," which were attended by personnel officers, managers, CEOs, and students. It met regularly with officers from supporting companies and conducted research in employee-management behavior, producing a number of case studies of midcentury American workplace relations.[8] The University of Chicago also helped International Harvester Company set up a central training program for its supervisors and managers. According to Sara Southall, supervisor of employment, the university and International Harvester signed a five-year contract, "providing that for the sum of $25,000 a year the University of Chicago would allow any of its personnel who could contribute to a specific program to serve in an advisory or research capacity."[9] In addition to research enterprises, human relations advocates also started journals and consulting firms and had succeeded in influencing the curriculum of major business schools.[10]

Employers adopted human relations techniques in response to specific historical and economic circumstances. In the 1920s, immigration restriction led to tight labor markets and high rates of employee turnover, which compelled employers to invest in workers' training and promotion as a way to tie workers to the company.[11] Union demands and New Deal labor laws in the 1930s, as well as the regulatory demands of World War II, necessitated the expansion of personnel offices, industrial relations departments, and education programs.[12] But it was perhaps the growth and diversification of American corporations during the postwar era that were most responsible for the dissemination of human relations techniques in the American corporation.

The development of human relations as a management technique went hand in hand with the expansion of administrative management positions in the modern corporation. As American corporations grew into complicated multidivisional, multiproduct, multiregional conglomerations, they created

[8] W. F. Whyte, *Participant Observer*, 145, and "Committee on Human Relations in Industry...Research Program," dated July 11, 1946, in the President's Papers 1950–55, Special Collections Research Center, University of Chicago Library.

[9] Southall, *Industry's Unfinished Business*, 46.

[10] Rakesh Khurana, *From Higher Aims to Hired Hands: The Social Transformation of American Business Schools and the Unfulfilled Promise of Management as a Profession* (Princeton, NJ: Princeton University Press, 2007), 43–49.

[11] Sanford Jacoby, *Employing Bureaucracy: Managers, Unions, and the Transformation of Work in American Industry, 1900–45* (New York: Columbia University Press, 1985).

[12] Frank Dobbin et al., "Equal Opportunity Law and the Construction of Internal Labor Markets," *American Journal of Sociology* 99, no. 2 (September 1993): 396–427, pp. 401–2; Frank Dobbin and John Sutton, "The Strength of the Weak State: The Rights Revolution and the Rise of Human Resources Management Divisions," *American Journal of Sociology* 104, no. 2 (September 1998): 441–76, p. 444; Jacoby, *Modern Manors*, 44–46.

Table 4.1. *The Impact of Diversification on U.S. Corporations (in percent)*

	1920	1950	1960	1970
Ratio of administrative to production employees	15.6	23.6	28.9	30.3
Industrial employment	32.3	32.9	30.8	28.2
Staff employment	39.5	54.4	59.5	66.8
Diversified firms	11.0	38.0	60.0	76.0
Multidivisional firms	0.0	20.0	57.0	73.0

Source: Rakesh Khurana, *From Higher Aims to Hired Hands: The Social Transformation of American Business Schools and the Unfulfilled Promise of Management as a Profession* (Princeton, NJ: Princeton University Press, 2007), 208.

new tiers of management to coordinate and manage their unwieldy parts and labor forces. Professionally trained managers seeking to justify and expand their services developed new administrative offices, programs, and positions. Between 1920 and 1970, the ratio of administrative to industrial employees in America's top 100 corporations increased from 15.6 percent to 30.3 percent[13] (See Table 4.1).

American corporations made the transition into their new multidivisional largeness through a restructuring process called decentralization that began in the mid-1930s and continued into the 1950s. Under a traditional central-ized organization model, all authority resided in the president or executive leadership at the top. Division heads had little power or autonomy to make decisions. And yet division heads were often most familiar with the particular situation in a given plant or product line and therefore in a better position to make decisions than the president or top executives. In addition, although the traditional system allowed men to work their way up from line positions into the executive suite, it provided no opportunity for men who would one day run the corporation to attain an understanding of how it operated as a whole. Their experience was specialized and particular, rather than general and integrative. They had little experience in actual leadership, since all power was concentrated at the top. Indeed, the top-down leadership model discouraged initiative. Divisional heads became "yes-men" in their bid to get ahead, rather than challenging the status quo to come up with better methods or products. When a man arrived at the top, his ability as a leader had not been tested. All of this led to a crisis in executive leadership.[14]

The solution, described by Peter Drucker in his study of General Motors' reorganization (in which he participated), was decentralization, the redistribution of power and autonomy from the top down to divisional

[13] Khurana, *From Higher Aims to Hired Hands.*
[14] Described in Peter Drucker, *Concept of the Corporation* (New York: John Day, 1946), 26–40.

heads.[15] The idea was to develop independent thinking and autonomy in division heads, not only to give them the leadership experience necessary to run the company but also to encourage creative initiative that would make the company more efficient and productive. By giving divisional heads the power to innovate, the company also created a standard by which to measure their leadership abilities, thereby identifying those best suited to be in executive positions. Of course, leadership at the top was still necessary to provide coherence and unity to the corporation, to appraise divisional progress, to deal with legal and financial issues, and to make sure that the organization's resources were made available to all of the parts.

While the restructuring decentralized productive departments, it tended to centralize industrial relations functions at the corporate staff level and strengthen administrative positions in general. The new industrial relations departments mediated between divisions and central management, informing division heads of new methods and innovations, while at the same time informing central management of important developments within the divisions.[16] Drucker was careful to stress that staff agencies acted in an advisory capacity only. They had no authority over divisional managers.[17] Despite their lack of formal power, however, the new centralized staff agencies wielded a higher degree of influence than similar offices had before decentralization. Industrial relations staff made policy recommendations and advised division heads on training and employment practices. They had the opportunity to "sell themselves" – and their techniques – to division heads and central management. In this way, they were able to disseminate human relations ideas throughout the corporate structure.

By the end of the 1950s, the human relations approach, with its holistic, anthropological, group-oriented view of industrial life, had been adopted by most major corporations. Large corporations were increasingly dedicating resources to studying their organizations, fostering cooperation, and training managers and foremen. In 1955, Du Pont's Employee Relations Department

[15] Ibid., ch. 2; see also Kim McQuaid, *Uneasy Partners: Big Business in American Politics, 1945–1990* (Baltimore: Johns Hopkins University Press, 1994), 92, and Ralph Cordiner, *New Frontiers for Professional Managers* (New York: McGraw-Hill, 1956), 49–78.

[16] Drucker, *Concept of the Corporation*, 54–56; on the relationship between personnel staff and the line organization, see Burleigh Gardner and David Moore, *Human Relations in Industry* (Chicago: Richard D. Irwin, 1945; rev. ed., 1950), 82–96.

[17] This admonition was regularly echoed by staff agencies in major corporations, as if to tell divisional heads they knew their place. See Minutes of the Industrial Relations Managers Conference, French Lick, Indiana, November 8–12, 1948, pp. 34, 35, in International Harvester Company, Corporate Archives Central File (documented series), 1819–1998, McCormick Mss 6Z, M2001-125, Box 7, Folder 25, at Wisconsin Historical Society, Madison (hereafter WHS).

reported, "Research continues in the effort to improve employee relations functions in the company by applying the principles and methods derived from the best thinking in the social sciences with due consideration of factors which are unique to each practical situation."[18] Corporate interest in human relations is further evidenced in employees' handbooks, the speeches of innumerable industrial relations managers, the management training seminars, the numerous articles in trade and management journals, and the widespread expansion of personnel officers and industrial relations offices.

Intellectuals at the time and historians since have been critical of human relations techniques. Their main concern has been that in "persuading" and manipulating resistant workers to accept technological changes, new policies, or reorganization schemes, management was merely pursuing its own ends, making invisible its power, and ignoring the legitimate issues behind workers' resistance, such as deskilling and control. Human relations' emphasis on equilibrium, stasis, and adjustment ignored the dynamism of history; it ignored the possibility of any substantive, real change in the structural relationship between management and labor. Human relations experts, critics charged, regarded change as disruption, as something to be avoided, managed, deftly adjusted to the status quo.[19]

There is some truth to those charges. The human relations approach reframed the management-labor relationship from one of coercion and confrontation to one of persuasion and cooperation, the latter being more effective in maintaining harmony and binding workers to the company. Rather than pitched battles in the street or authoritarian dictates, managers used programs such as HOBSO ("How Our Business System Operates") to get their point of view across to employees, peacefully, in auditoriums and lunchrooms. It was also true that employers used human relations to fight unionization. Under the guise of "taking the pulse" of the organization, managers solicited information about union activity.[20] Similarly, when faced with unionization drives,

---

[18] Employee Relations Department Annual Report 1954, February 11, 1955, in Du Pont Human Resources, Accession 1615, Series I, Box 1, Hagley Museum and Library, Wilmington, Delaware (hereafter HML).

[19] See Bell, "Adjusting Men to Machines," 79–88; C. Wright Mills, *White Collar* (New York: Oxford University Press, 1951); Mills, "Review of *Social Life of a Modern Community*," *American Sociological Review* 7 (April 1942): 263–71; Elizabeth Fones-Wolf, *Selling Free Enterprise: The Business Assault on Labor and Liberalism, 1945–1960* (Urbana: University of Illinois Press, 1994); Baritz, *The Servants of Power*; and Wilbert E. Moore, "Industrial Sociology: Status and Prospects," American Sociological Review 13 (August 1948): 382–91.

[20] See, for instance, Robert Michael Smith, "From Blackjacks to Briefcases: Commercial Anti-Union Agencies, 1865–1985," Ph.D. diss., University of Toledo, 1989, and Jacoby, *Modern Manors*, 130–44.

companies often turned to more training and education programs, which industrial leaders saw as ways to influence and change attitudes about work, about the company, and about the free enterprise system. Du Pont's Labor Relations Institute was designed specifically to instruct plant managers on "the relationship of good employee relations to the maintenance of a no-union status."[21]

While some saw the human relations movement as a threat to unions, others criticized it for its "collectivism." William H. Whyte's 1956 classic *The Organization Man* is remembered as a critique of 1950s conformity, but it was more specifically a critique of the group-oriented approach of human relations ideology. An editor at *Fortune*, Whyte argued that the individualistic Protestant ethic was being superseded in American corporate life by what he called the "social ethic," which emphasized cooperation, teamwork, and fitting in over and above competition and individual initiative. The dogma of human relations, Whyte wrote, was promulgated by evangelistic social engineers masquerading as "scientists" who believed they offered industry a progressive, modern alternative to the inefficiencies of competition and rugged individualism. But, in fact, Whyte argued, singling out Elton Mayo and Lloyd Warner, what they offered was a return to the Middle Ages, where "everyone is tightly knit into a belongingness with one another," and where "there is no restless wandering, but rather the deep emotional security that comes from total integration with the group."[22] Whyte acknowledged the shortcomings of competitive individualism. But he was deeply troubled by this new ideology, which he believed required the sublimation of the individual to the organization. And he found it both amusing and disturbing that managers and executives saw themselves as defenders of American enterprise and individualism even as they adopted and disseminated the contrary values of the social ethic.

Although the human relations approach permeated corporate culture in the 1950s, it is also true that its prescriptions were unevenly applied and, indeed, even resisted. Many industrial leaders and divisional heads ("line men") resisted or mocked what they regarded as fads, such as written procedures and respect for workers' rights and feelings. While a company's industrial relations staff might advocate a human relations approach, its top executives or divisional heads could remain skeptical of the approach's contributions to the bottom line. Divisional heads often adopted only selected techniques, rejecting much

[21] Employee Relations Department, Annual Report, 1955, p. 6 in Du Pont Human Resources, Series I, Box 1, HML.
[22] Joseph Norcera, foreword to *The Organization Man*, by William H. Whyte (Philadelphia: University of Pennsylvania Press, 2002), 32–33.

of the underlying philosophy.[23] Despite the talk about formal procedures and standards, executives continued to base promotions on personal biases, such as a preference for height and physical stature.[24] Human relations experts seemed to recognize the foot-dragging because a plaintive tone of persuasion suffused almost all of their writings. Despite the pervasiveness of human relations ideology in corporate culture, industrial relations staff members seemed to be constantly struggling to prove their worth to corporate leadership. Fair employment would present them with an enormous opportunity.

Background in Race Relations

Looking back, it is striking how many of the leading human relations advocates had cut their methodological teeth in the other area of "human relations," that is, race relations. Almost all of the founders of the University of Chicago's CHRI had some training or background in race relations. Burleigh Gardner and Allison Davis had spent two years in Natchez, Mississippi, conducting research for their book, *Deep South: A Social Anthropological Study of Caste and Class* (1941), written under the guidance of W. Lloyd Warner. Warner wrote *Color and Human Nature: Negro Personality Development in a Northern City* (1941) and *Social Systems of American Ethnic Groups* (1945) and directed the research for St. Clair Drake and Horace Cayton's classic *Black Metropolis* (1945). Everett Hughes, a Robert Park student, wrote about ethnic identity and conducted several important studies on race in the workplace. In addition to co-authoring *Deep South*, Allison Davis was the first African American tenured at the University of Chicago and devoted his life to the study of race relations in the United States. Everett Hughes, Frederick Harbison, and Allison Davis were active in the University of Chicago's Committee on Education, Training, and Research in Race Relations. John Dollard, the director of Yale University's Human Relations Institute during the 1940s, was closely associated with this group. Dollard used Warner and Gardner's idea about caste in his own *Caste*

---

[23] See William Breen, "Social Science and State Policy in WWII: Human Relations, Pedagogy, and Industrial Training, 1940–1945," *Business History Review* 76 (Summer 2002): 233–66; F. Stuart Chapin, "Social Obstacles to the Acceptance of Existing Social Science Knowledge," *Social Forces* 26 (October 1947): 7–12; Melville Dalton, "Conflicts between Staff and Line Managerial Officers," *American Sociological Review* 15, no. 3 (June 1950): 342–51; Robert Ozanne, *A Century of Labor-Management Relations at McCormick and International Harvester* (Madison: University of Wisconsin Press, 1967); and Rosabeth Moss Kanter, *Men and Women of the Corporation* (New York: Basic Books, 1977, 1984).

[24] See anecdotes in Osborn Elliot, *Men at the Top* (New York: Harper and Brothers, 1959), 106.

and Color in a Southern Town (1937) and co-authored, with Allison Davis, *Children of Bondage.*

The CHRI identified race and ethnicity as key factors prohibiting cooperative working relationships, and race relations was one of its perennial topics of study.[25] CHRI members directed and encouraged their students, especially their African American students, to secure a job in industry in order to conduct fieldwork. Mozell Hill, an Everett Hughes student who went on to become a prominent sociologist, secured a job at Ajax Aluminum Company and kept a detailed "work diary" of labor and race relations at the plant in 1943.[26] From the moment Hill arrived at the plant with a fellow student and was told by the Irish foreman that "nice colored fellows" like them should beware of the "goddam colored bums we have working here," Hill's narrative confirmed that race and ethnicity were central determinatives of workplace culture. William Foote Whyte, a white graduate student who studied with Warner and Hughes, landed a job at the Inland Steel Company, where blacks made up 65 percent of the employees and occupied positions of power in the union. He published his analysis of the experience in *Pattern for Industrial Peace* (1951), which likewise touched on the racial aspects of industry.[27]

Warner, Davis, Gardner, and Dollard developed an entire school of race relations inquiry based on their caste theory. It is worth reviewing their ideas about caste because the same ideas informed their work in human relations. Like most social anthropologists at this time, Warner, Davis, and Gardner understood that "race" was a social construct, not a biological reality. But they did not belabor this point. They were more interested in what the construct looked like. How does "race" work? What does it look like? How does the construct stay in place, and why do Negroes go along with it?[28] They rejected the idea that race antagonism, prejudice, or difference explained the system of racial subordination and dominance. They also rejected the idea that the Negro represented a minority group because their conception of minority groups was

---

[25] See General Research Program of the Committee on Human Relations in Industry, July 11, 1946, "The Committee on Human Relations in Industry presents eight lecture-Conferences on . . ." 1945, found in President's Papers, 1950–1955, Human Relations in Industry Committee, Special Collections Research Center, University of Chicago (hereafter SCRC). See also the book that grew out of the conference series, W. F. Whyte, *Industry and Society.*

[26] "Memorandum and Work Diary: Ajax Aluminum and Foundry Company," in Everett Hughes Papers, Box 31, Folder 22, SCRC.

[27] William Foote Whyte, *Pattern for Industrial Peace* (New York: Harper & Brothers, 1951).

[28] Allison Davis, Burleigh Gardner, and Mary R. Gardner, *Deep South: A Social Anthropological Study of Caste and Class*, directed by W. Lloyd Warner (Chicago: University of Chicago Press, 1941), 6.

that they were flexible and escapable.[29] One could leave minority groups by assimilating into the dominant culture or by marrying someone outside the group. One could not leave the Negro group through assimilation or marriage because legal and social strictures prohibited such actions. Indeed, the whole social system in the South, and even in the North, they felt, was set up to prevent exactly that type of movement.[30] To understand race in America, they felt, it wasn't enough to understand prejudice or race antagonism. Rather one had to see "race" as a constitutive element of the social, or caste, system of the United States.

That America had a caste system was hardly a new idea. Sociologist Robert Park had always argued precisely that. Like Park, Warner and the others saw the caste system as an accommodation or agreement between the races. In Park's famous "race relations cycle," accommodation was the third stage, following the conflict stage (second) that arose with contact (first).[31] Accommodation was a process of adjustment and social control whereby the politically dominant race worked out a social arrangement that allowed the two races to live together. It was in this stage that "race" congealed into an entrenched social arrangement of status and subordination. Eventually, it would be followed by assimilation, the final step in the cycle, which was a "process of interpenetration and fusion," in which persons or groups acquired the memories, traditions, and attitudes of other persons and groups.[32] The process showed the importance of status, negotiation, and equilibrium in social arrangements. Indeed, their methodological technique focused on the social and status relationships between various groups within the black and white communities. Although their elaborate taxonomies, which distinguished the lower-lower classes from the lower-middle and the upper-lower classes, for instance, or the upper-upper classes from the upper-middle classes, were widely mocked, they were an honest attempt to map the social classes and expectations that informed the lives of both blacks and whites.

While Park had once seen the caste system as permanent, by 1937 he believed it was on the verge of fading away because the Negro group had made so much social and economic progress that it had "gradually ceased to

---

[29] W. Lloyd Warner and Buford H. Junker, *Color and Human Nature: Negro Personality Development in a Northern City* (Washington, DC: American Council on Education, 1941), 10.

[30] Ibid.; see also W. Lloyd Warner, "American Caste and Class," *American Journal of Sociology*, 42 (September 1936): 234–37.

[31] Robert Park, "Our Racial Frontier," in *Race and Culture*, ed. Robert Park (Glencoe, IL: Free Press, 1950), 149–50.

[32] Robert Park and Ernest Burgess, *Introduction to the Science of Sociology* (Chicago: University of Chicago Press, 1921), 735.

exhibit the characteristics of a caste and had assumed rather the character of a racial or national minority."[33] Similarly, although Warner, Gardner, and Davis believed that the caste system was normative, entrenched, and still relevant, they acknowledged that industrialization and the New Deal were eroding its economic underpinnings.[34]

Critics faulted Warner, Davis, Gardner, and Dollard for not having a theory so much as a description of the way things were. But their real outrage was directed at their seeming refusal to acknowledge the system's injustices and the need to change it. In a blistering review of their work, Marxist sociologist Oliver Cox castigated Warner and the rest for failing to recognize segregation as a problem, an injustice, an affront to Negroes.[35] Cox objected to their suggestion that southern segregation was somehow normal or natural and that those who deviated from or resisted it were "maladjusted." Cox rejected the caste theorists' view that southern Negroes were part of something called a society.[36] Cox maintained that Negroes were not part of society and that the basis of race relations was not any kind of accommodation but rather constant conflict. Later critics would raise the same points, adding that a static conception of southern race relations discouraged change.[37]

By 1945, industrialization and war had disrupted American race relations and segregation, and, as Gardner and Davis had predicted, the caste theory no longer described things "as they were." While sociologists debated caste theory at least until 1947, Warner, Davis, Dollard, and Gardner never published a formal defense of their theory and all moved on to different projects in the area of industrial relations. (Dollard and Gardner became management consultants; in 1954, Dollard was analyzing plot summaries for Du Pont's *Cavalcade* television series.[38]) But the basic contours of the caste school – its ideas about adjustment and equilibrium, its explanation of why Negroes constituted neither an ethnic group nor a class, and its view that economic growth would

[33] Park, *Race and Culture*, 243; and Robert E. Park, introduction to *The Etiquette of Race Relations in the South: A Study in Social Control*, by Bertram W. Doyle (Chicago: University of Chicago Press, 1937), xvii, quoted in Warner and Junker, *Color and Human Nature*, 9.

[34] Davis, et al, *Deep South*, 479–81; See also Edgar T. Thompson and Everett C. Hughes, eds., *Race Individual and Collective Behavior* (Glencoe, IL: Free Press, 1958). Thompson and Hughes were students of Robert Park and Hughes was active in the CHRI.

[35] Oliver Cox, "The Modern Caste School of Race Relations," *Social Forces*, 21 (December 1942): 218–26. See also Maxwell Brooks, "American Class and Caste: An Appraisal." Social Forces, 25 (December 1946): 207–11.

[36] Ibid., 223.

[37] Herbert Blumer, "Social Science and Desegregation," *The Annals of the Academy of Political and Social Science* (March 1956): 137–43.

[38] John Dollard, "Attitudes of Cavalcade Viewers toward Du Pont," May 5, 1956, in E.I. Du Pont de Nemours & Company, Advertising Department. Subseries I, Box 6, HML.

end Jim Crow – remained relevant to the field of race relations for some time. Such prominent sociologists of race relations as E. Franklin Frazier, Charles S. Johnson, Horace Cayton, and Gunnar Myrdal endorsed the caste theory.[39]

The remnants of caste theory also informed the growing field of human relations. In the late 1940s, Warner, Davis, Dollard, and Gardner shifted their focus to workplace relations and brought to it their ideas about status, equilibrium, accommodation, adjustment, in-groups, and out-groups.[40] Essentially these were the ideas of early twentieth-century sociology, but they had been best illustrated and given theoretical validity through the study of American race relations. Human relations advocates simply took ideas that had described race tensions and caste and applied them to the workplace.

HR Techniques and Racial Integration

Companies that decided to hire and promote black workers into traditionally white positions implemented the decision through the managerial infrastructure created by human relations advocates: personnel offices, formal hiring and advancement procedures, training and education programs, and community relations programs. Perhaps the best way to illustrate the role of human relations in integration is to consider Drucker's aforementioned book, *The Concept of a Corporation* (1946). Ostensibly a study of General Motors, it was really Drucker's attempt to define the Good Corporation, to present the corporation as a solution to modernity, not as a problem in it. Although he doesn't mention race or racial discrimination, one of his main themes is "equal opportunity," which he argues is a positive attribute of the modern corporation. Yet, he laments, people fail to see how corporations represent equal opportunity. This is because corporations have not lived up to their promise. They have not organized opportunities rationally. They have emphasized formal training rather than promotion from within. They have failed to provide outlets for people to demonstrate their talents and skills. Because of employers' failure to adopt and adhere to clear, transparent, and rational personnel policies based on objective

---

[39] On Park's relationship to black sociologists, see Jerry G. Watts, "On Reconsidering Park, Du Bois, Frazier and Ried: Reply to Benjamin Bowser's 'The Contributions of Blacks to Sociological Knowledge,'" *Phylon* 44 (1983): 273–91.

[40] See especially Gardner and Moore, *Human Relations in Industry*; W. F. Whyte, introduction to *Industry and Society*; Everett Cherrington Hughes, "The Knitting of Racial Groups in Industry," *American Sociological Review* 11 (October 1946): 512–19; and CHRI, "General Research Program," July 11, 1946, in the President's Papers, 1950–1955, University of Chicago Library, Special Collections Research Center.

criteria, workers were attracted to unions' attempts to bring fairness to promotion procedures (in the form of seniority).[41] With such procedures in place and followed by all, workers would be aware of opportunities for advancement, which would solidify their ties to the company, and management could prove its fair treatment of workers.

Nowhere does Drucker mention race, discrimination, or fair employment. But the impediments to "equal opportunity" he identifies (personal bias, favoritism, capricious foremen, unclear and selectively enforced policies), and to which he offers solutions, also impeded black employment. While testing later came to be considered an impediment to racial integration, initially it was regarded by activists as a fair, objective measure for selection, preferable to the supervisor's potentially arbitrary and biased preference. In the 1950s and into the 1960s, companies depended on tests to protect themselves from accusations of racial bias.[42] Human relations reforms designed to provide equal opportunity to whites would later provide equal opportunities for racial minorities as well. In 1963, *Management Review* noted, "Many companies . . . have made the change [to merit employment] because they have found that work performance improves up and down the line when merit promotion is practiced without exception."[43] But more important than merit employment, which after all would soon be regarded as an impediment to real integration, was the power of an industrial relations office to enforce a centralized employment policy. A researcher for the New York State Commission Against Discrimination similarly noted that "one particular trend in modern corporations" – scientific management – encouraged minority hiring by eliminating the personal element.[44] Another researcher attributed the success of one company's equal employment opportunity program to its organizational structure: "The company has pioneered in scientific personnel administration with a heavy emphasis on merit employment and an active recruitment unit based in the personnel department."[45]

[41] Drucker, *Concept of the Corporation*, 145–46; see also Cordiner, *New Frontiers for Professional Managers*, who says virtually the same things about decentralization.

[42] See Stephen M. Gelber, *Black Men and Businessmen: The Growing Awareness of a Social Responsibility* (Port Washington, NY: Kennicat Press, 1974), 173, who cites C. E. Yount, "Antidiscrimination in Industry," *Conference Board Management Record* (October 1945): 288; and Ray Marshall, "Some Factors Influencing the Upgrading of Negroes in the Southern Petroleum Refining Industry," *Social Forces* 42 (December 1963): 186–95.

[43] Caroline Bird, "More Room at the Top," *Management Review*, 52 (March 1963): 5, preamble.

[44] Sally Backer and Harry Harris, "Progress toward Integration: Four Case Studies" in *Discrimination and Low Incomes*, ed. Aaron Antonovsky and Lewis Lorwin (New York: New York Interdepartmental Committee on Low Incomes, 1959), 281–304.

[45] Ferman, *The Negro and Equal Employment Opportunities* , 78.

Objective procedures, job specifications, and formal criteria, however, were no guarantee of fair treatment for minorities. In fact, most of these reforms initially worked against black advancement. Job specifications and formal criteria, for instance, meant that employers had to consider a new applicant's "promotability" into positions all along the ladder. Promotability was typically measured by high school diplomas or tests. Due to their limited access to education and high dropout rates blacks were less likely to have high school diplomas and they performed badly on tests. Tests were also used for promotion and entry into training programs. But even if a black person passed all of the tests, he or she still would not be considered for advancement because management advanced only those who would continue to ascend the entire ladder. To the extent that the highest positions were regarded as "white," management was unlikely to waste time and energy advancing someone who could only go halfway up the ladder.[46] The increased use of psychological testing to evaluate potential managerial hires would also have been detrimental to blacks (had they applied) since the tests were designed to measure how well an individual would fit in with the group of white, middle-class men who would become managers.

Moreover, the human relations emphasis on "workplace cultures" and ethnic homogeneity as factors in harmony and productivity led many industrial relations officers to reject fair employment. Citing the Hawthorne experiments, William R. Thomas, an industrial relations officer at Ford Motor Company, worried that a Fair Employment Practices Commission (FEPC) would disrupt the congeniality of informal, ethnically homogeneous work groups necessary for industrial efficiency. The new FEPC laws prohibited common practices that led to friendly work relations, which were in large part based on majority and minority groups' identification with particular jobs. "Negroes associate themselves with porter jobs; Irish with police positions; Poles with heavy construction work; and Greeks with foodservices," Thomas wrote, continuing, "Any disruption of these job associations would be met with obstinancy [sic]."[47] Such obstinacy created problems for the personnel director. While Inland Steel president William G. Caples advocated racial integration, his commitment to

---

[46] Thomas N. Maloney, "Personnel Policy and Racial Inequality in the Pre–WWII North," *Journal of Interdisciplinary History* 30 (1999): 235–58, 238–39; Bernard Rosenberg and Penney Chapin, "Management and Minority Groups: A Study of Attitudes and Practices in Hiring and Upgrading," in *Discrimination and Low Incomes*, ed. Aaron Antonovsky and Lewis Lorwin (New York: New York Interdepartmental Committee on Low Incomes, 1959), 147–94, 179–80. See also Logan Wilson and Harlan Gilmore, "White Employers and Negro Workers," *American Sociological Review* 8, no. 6 (December 1943): 698–705.

[47] William R. Thomas, "Problems under the FEPC," *Personnel Journal* (May 1951): 14–19, quote on pp. 17–18.

human relations principles led him to caution employers who were interested in integrating their firms to respect workplace tradition and custom and to proceed slowly.[48]

Still, once companies decided to integrate, it would be human relations techniques that allowed them to overcome these impediments. If blacks were not being hired because they were unable to meet certain criteria, personnel departments could change the criteria. Companies could reassess their specifications to determine whether high school diplomas or tests were in fact necessary. If tests were found to be biased, companies could change them or drop them, as the Illinois FEPC famously ordered Motorola to do in 1963. While employers associations were outraged by this presumption of state power, those companies that wanted to integrate followed suit. Pitney-Bowes changed its testing requirements in 1963, Ford in 1964, Du Pont in 1965. Executives could be educated to understand the biases inherent in tests.[49] If qualified blacks could not be found, companies could hire unqualified ones and train them or pay their tuition for technical classes.[50] Companies had experience in addressing personnel shortcomings with training programs. While the existing specifications of training programs might have initially hindered black advancement, the actual structure of training programs and formal procedures carried within it the means to overcome such hindrances.

Similarly, concern about workplace culture and traditions led companies that sought to integrate to change, sidestep, or reconfigure workplace culture

---

[48] William G. Caples, "Teamwork in Industry," July 31–August 1, 1952, in Collection 5250, Box 1, Folder 1952, at Kheel Center for Labor-Management Documentation and Archives, Cornell University, Ithaca, New York (hereafter Kheel Center).

[49] Hugh Davis Graham, *The Civil Rights Era: Origins and Development of National Policy, 1960–1972* (New York: Oxford University Press, 1990), 149–50; see also Marshall, "Some Factors Influencing the Upgrading of Negroes in the Southern Petroleum Refining Industry," 186–95, which indicates that Cities Service Company changed test standards in 1958.

[50] Stephen Habbe, *Company Experience with Negro Employment*, 2 vols., Studies in Personnel Policy No. 201 (New York: National Industrial Conference Board, 1966), 39–44; Jack Gourlay, writing on behalf of the American Management Association, suggested the word "qualified" was subjective and hence open to redefinition. Gourlay, *The Negro Salaried Worker*, AMA Research Study 70 (New York: American Management Association, 1965), 12. On Pitney-Bowes, see "Pitney-Bowes Announces New Negro Preferential Hire Plan," *Chicago Defender*, December 5, 1963, 3. On Du Pont's reassessment of testing, see Habbe, *Company Experience with Negro Employment*, 28, and Employee Relations Department, Reports to the Executive Committee, 1965, p. 7, in Du Pont Human Resources, Accession 1615, Series I, Box 1. See also *The Selection and Training of Negroes for Managerial Positions*, proceedings of the Executive Study Conference held November 10–11, 1964 (Princeton, NJ: Educational Testing Service, 1965), and "Report on the Workshop Panels, Regional Conference on Equal Opportunity and Economic Growth, June 10, 1964," p. 4. These are Vice-President J. Stewart Huston's notes on the conference, as found in Lukens Steel Company, Executive Officer Files, 1903–1979, Series III, Box 2018, File: Equal Employment Opportunity, at HML).

to achieve a harmonious transition. Researchers conducted a variety of studies designed to determine the best type of work group into which to integrate "breakthrough" black workers. Sociologist William Foote Whyte went further and suggested using the groups themselves to engineer a change in racial attitudes: "The successful adjustment of the various races in industry can be achieved only by working through the informal organization. It is only in this area that it is possible to manipulate the mental and emotional processes of people so as to build a harmonious organization."[51] Whyte understood more than most that the formal procedures that ensured fair treatment were only as effective as the informal networks that implemented them. Human relations research like Whyte's not only recognized the systemic nature of discrimination but also devised ways to "educate" and influence the informal networks and practices that perpetuated discrimination. This research first proved useful during World War II, when one of the major management problems was the integration of a traditionally segregated workforce.

World War II provided an opportunity for human relations experts and industrial relations officers to prove their value to industry. A tight labor market, increased production demands, and an executive order against segregation and discrimination presented American industry with a nightmarish situation. To it fell the task of integrating a traditionally segregated workforce, which would have been a monumental feat in the best of times, but it had to be done at a time of urgent demand and with an inexperienced, untrained workforce. Large numbers of the white men who typically manned American factories were overseas. Their replacements were unfamiliar with industrial work. The foremen and supervisors who were supposed to train the new workers were not only inexperienced but also hostile to blacks and women working in industrial positions. Then, too, white southerners, with their expectations of segregation and antipathies toward the interaction between black men and white women, were also a part of the new mix. This green, hostile, culturally disparate, and newly gendered workforce created a new set of workplace problems, including racial tension, sexual tension, unfamiliarity with workplace rules, and inappropriate behavior. It would perhaps have been most efficient to separate the blacks from the whites, as many companies did, but Executive Order 8802 discouraged that solution.

Into this explosive situation stepped the human relations experts. Working closely with the agencies in charge of enforcing the new antidiscrimination

---

[51] W. F. Whyte, *Industry and Society*, 192. See also Paul Norgren et al., *Employing the Negro in American Industry: A Study of Management Practices* (New York: Industrial Relations Counselors, 1959), 94; John A. Davis, "How Management Can Integrate Negroes in War Industries" (New York State War Council, Committee on Discrimination in Employment, 1942), 17–18; Hughes, "The Knitting of Racial Groups in Industry," 512–19.

measures, human relations experts developed guidelines and advice for companies transitioning to a biracial workforce. Longtime human relations advocate
and International Harvester representative Sara Southall was appointed to the
President's Fair Employment Practices Committee, the agency charged with
facilitating and enforcing Executive Order 8802, and talked to employers across
the nation about how to integrate their plants.[52] John A. Davis, the director
of Research and Planning for the FEPC and later a political science professor
in the field of civil rights, authored a 1942 booklet entitled *How Management
Can Integrate Negroes in the War Industries*. Published by the New York State
War Council's Committee on Discrimination in Employment, the booklet was
based on the experiences of a handful of successfully integrated companies
and human relations research. The information in this booklet would inform
subsequent attempts at integration and is thus worth examining in some
detail.[53]

Davis's pamphlet begins by emphasizing the economic and patriotic importance of fair employment. He assures employers that Negroes are productive
and compliant workers. However, employers could expect trouble from their
white employees, and the main concern of the pamphlet was how to avert
such trouble. Note the powerful work that Davis has already accomplished,
positioning himself, the consultant, with management against a problematic
workforce. By focusing on the specific problem of the workers, Davis was able
to adopt the familiar, counseling, sympathetic tone of one who understands
management's difficulty with "labor." Labor was always an impediment for
managers, so it would have been unsurprising to hear that it was an impediment to integration. Moreover, by focusing on how to allay white racism, on
how to introduce Negroes without friction, on gaining employee acceptance,
on selecting, placing, and handling Negro workers, Davis assumes the reader
to be in favor of this policy, and not an impediment to it – even though a NAM
poll from 1944 indicated that employers and managers tended to be more resistant to black workers in traditionally white jobs (especially their own) than
manual workers.[54] But assuming managers to be racist would not have helped
win them over. Davis's tone presumes support and attempts to normalize the
idea of fair employment as a leadership issue, not a social reform. As Davis told
the employer how to "educate" his workers about the need for integration and

---

[52] Southall, *Industry's Unfinished Business*, 61–2.

[53] Davis, "How Management Can Integrate Negroes in War Industries." For information on
Davis, see also the author blurb for John A. Davis, "Negro Employment: A Progress Report,"
Fortune, July 1952.

[54] "The Color-Line in Industry: A Report of the Public Opinion Index for Industry," Princeton, New Jersey, April 1944, in National Association of Manufacturers, Records, 1895–1990
(hereafter NAM Records), Series 7, Box 136, HML.

the danger of racism, he was at the same time subtly, and without accusation or condescension, "educating" the employer.

Following human relations philosophy, Davis warned against strong-arming employees into acceptance, which would undermine workplace harmony.[55] Employers needed to understand the deep, underlying causes of resistance in order to adjust their workers to working with African Americans. Davis identified two main causes for white workers' resistance to working with blacks. First, white workers feared a loss of status. Negroes traditionally held low-status jobs, so a Negro in the same job as a white worker would automatically lower the status of that job. Second, white supremacy was a deeply held, unquestioned organizing principle of white workers' lives. Its disruption would necessarily be accompanied by emotional shock, anger, and resistance.

To overcome white racism, Davis counseled employers to be firm and forthright in their decision to integrate and to convey this firmness to employees. They needed to explain the necessity for the company's new policy. Most important, they needed to pay careful attention to the placement, introduction, and appearance of Negro hires. To address white workers' status anxiety, experts recommended that new black workers be hired into white-collar positions first.[56] This recommendation came directly out of human relations research in factory hierarchies, which indicated that most employees, whether factory workers or white-collar office workers, regarded the white-collar office workers as socially superior. Placing new black workers in white-collar positions decreased the chance of resistance since white-collar workers were relatively more secure in their social status. This action assured anxious factory workers "that they are not being asked to do what white collar workers will not do," thus presumably quieting fears of status loss.[57] Second, as staff workers, the personnel charged with introducing black workers were more effective in staff departments than with the line workers, who typically resented and ignored the personnel department's directives.[58] Such a move also ensured the hiring of "the higher type" of Negro worker, one who was educated, well dressed, and personable. This was intended to dispel stereotypes among white workers and increase the chances of acceptance. Another placement suggestion was to put new Negro workers in areas where there was high labor turnover, "for here white workers will hardly have a

---

[55] Gardner and Moore, *Human Relations in Industry*, 310–11.
[56] Davis, "How Management Can Integrate Negroes in War Industries," 8.
[57] Ibid., 17–18.
[58] Dalton, "Conflicts between Staff and Line Managerial Officers." See also Kanter, *Men and Women of the Corporation*, 167.

vested interest in social organization or arrangements."[59] This, too, drew from human relations research on work-group dynamics and factory hierarchies. A sympathetic foreman was also crucial to the successful integration of black workers. Once Negroes were hired, employers were urged to create opportunities for establishing and maintaining good race relations, such as athletic programs, social activities, and musical groups.

In addition to preparing white workers, employers also had to prepare the black workers, by helping them to assimilate and "fit in." While the idea that blacks, or anyone for that matter, should curb their identity to fit in is somewhat abhorrent today, we must remember that fitting in was the goal of all human relations advice – it was the basis of the equilibrium so necessary for smooth industrial relations. One is struck when reading early accounts of integrated workplaces how focused they are on the work group rather than on race or racism. In a 1946 study, for instance, Everett C. Hughes concluded that black workers had a particularly hard time adjusting to integrated workplaces because they were loners, what Elton Mayo called "solitaires." Hughes stressed that workplace morale depended on informal teams or cliques. Denied access to informal cliques, black workers posed a threat to them. Moreover, the employers' stress on hiring blacks as individuals, "on their own merit," seemed to reinscribe their threatening individualism as opposed to their ability to be part of the group (which often meant curbing individual merit).[60] While most scholars today might venture that white workers were more likely threatened by black workers' blackness than their individualism, Hughes's study is nonetheless instructive in helping us see the prevalence of human relations theory in these first early experiments. Moreover, Hughes's observations do not seem that off the mark. FEPC experts presented much evidence that black workers who did manage to fit in were accepted and valued, "despite the color of their skin" and hence helped change white attitudes. And changing white attitudes about working with blacks was one necessary step on the road to integrating American workplaces.

The wartime experiment with racial integration was enormously beneficial for human relations enthusiasts and industrial relations executives, who finally proved their worth to central management. Human relations advocates saw the so-called Negro worker as just another source of disequilibrium, easily incorporated into the workforce if one used the proper methods. Writing about her experiences on the FEPC, Sara Southall noted that the problem of fair employment was fundamentally a problem of industrial relations. If a company had

---

[59] Davis, "How Management Can Integrate Negroes in War Industries," 17.
[60] Hughes, "The Knitting of Racial Groups in Industry," 512–19.

sound and fair industrial relations policies (by which she meant human relations policies), integration would occur smoothly.[61] One of the most successful human relations programs of the war seemed to confirm this. The War Manpower Commission's Training Within Industry program (TWI) was designed to train supervisors and foremen to deal with the disruptive issues that came with the new mixed-race, mixed-gender workforce.[62] The new workforce generated potentially explosive issues that could not go unaddressed, and yet a typical foreman or supervisor was unlikely to even notice them, let alone deal with them in a noncoercive, sensitive fashion. Indeed, most of the foremen were themselves inexperienced and unqualified to hold such leadership positions. Thus, experts advised that they be trained in managerial techniques that could deflate workplace tension. The TWI program introduced supervisors and foremen to the human relations approach, inculcating them with the idea that they could get the best output and cooperation from their workers, not by driving them but by understanding them.[63] Commentator Stuart Chase believed that this "new art of management," with its dictum that workers work best when treated as human beings, was one of the most important things to come out of the war.[64] He may have exaggerated its importance, but he was right that the success of TWI encouraged many companies to adopt such training programs for foremen, supervisors, and managers after the war.

The wartime experiment with racial integration had somewhat more mixed results for blacks. On the one hand, there were successful cases about which FEPC officials and activists wrote and on which they based subsequent suggestions.[65] On the other hand, there was also violence, noncompliance, continued segregation, and the reversion to discriminatory policies after the war. But the wartime experiences with integration – both the good and the bad – provided data for postwar researchers studying how companies should approach racial integration.

---

[61] Southall, *Industry's Unfinished Business.*

[62] Breen, "Social Science and State Policy in WWII," 233–66. For a contemporary puff piece on the program, see Stuart Chase, "Educating the Boss: The Job Relations Program of the TWI" in *Men at Work: Some Democratic Methods for the Power Age* (New York: Harcourt Brace, 1941, 1945), ch. 4.

[63] Chase, *Men at Work,* 40.

[64] Ibid., 47.

[65] See especially Malcolm Ross, *All Manner of Men* (New York: Reynald and Hitchcock, 1948); Cecil Newman, "An Experiment in Industrial Democracy," *Opportunity* (Spring 1944): 52–56; Southall, *Industry's Unfinished Business*; and John A. Davis, "Negro Employment," 102–3, 158, 161–62. On the effectiveness of the wartime FEPC, see William J. Collins, "Race, Roosevelt, and Wartime Production: Fair Employment in WWII Labor Markets," *American Economic Review* 91, no. 1 (March 2001): 272–86.

Kurt Lewin, Group Dynamics, and the T-Group

The management research field exploded in the postwar years, and researchers took the basic premises of "human relations" in different directions, determined often by academic discipline and social networks. At MIT's Sloan School of Management, a group of social psychologists centered around German Jewish émigré Kurt Lewin conducted and promoted research on group dynamics, participative management, and what became known as sensitivity training (or "T-groups"). Lewin had immigrated to the United States in 1935. He occupied a succession of positions before being recruited by MIT in 1946 to set up the Research Center for Group Dynamics (which was moved to the University of Michigan after his death in 1947). Along the way, he attracted a large coterie of colleagues and students, which included Margaret Mead, Gregory Bateson, Horace Kallen, Gordon Allport (author of *The Nature of Prejudice*), Rensis Likert, Alex Bavelas, Alfred Marrow, Chris Argyris, and his collaborator Ronald Lippitt. Like other refugee scholars from Nazi Germany, Lewin was interested in the problems of democracy: how to end racial prejudice, how to identify authoritarian leadership, how to translate good will into social change, how to wed theory to practice. For some reason, perhaps because of its applicability within industry, his work proved most attractive to the fields of management theory and human relations, which was becoming known as behavioral science. Certainly, his followers believed his influence on industry was great. "The views that enlightened executives express are clearly recognizable to those who know their origins as emanating largely from Lewin," wrote Alfred Marrow, who was Lewin's acolyte and biographer, as well as an enlightened executive at the Harwood-Weldon Company.[66]

According to psychologist Gordon Allport, the unifying theme in Lewin's work was that "the group to which an individual belongs is the ground for his perceptions, his feelings, and his action."[67] Lewin was interested in the dynamic relationship between the individual and the group, how the influence of one determined the other. Lewin was one of the few (white) researchers at this time who felt that minority group identification was more important in ending prejudice than individual achievement. While others believed that blacks had to overcome their race to succeed, Lewin thought they had to embrace it. Discrimination and hatred, after all, were not brought on by individuals but

---

[66] Alfred Marrow, *The Practical Theorist: The Life and Work of Kurt Lewin* (New York: Basic Books, 1969), 152.

[67] Kurt Lewin, *Resolving Social Conflicts: Selected Papers on Group Dynamics*, edited by Gertrude Weiss Lewin, foreword by Gordon Allport (New York: Harper, 1948), a publication for the Research Center for Group Dynamics, Ann Arbor, MI.

by their group membership.[68] A group for Lewin could never be simply a collection of individuals. Rather, it was an organic, autonomous entity. To change human behavior – and that was the goal of much of Lewin's research – one had to change group behavior, not individual behavior. Although his acolytes seem to think this insight was original to Lewin, it was already a staple assumption of human relations. Perhaps what was original was that Lewin founded a research center to theorize and apply what he called "group dynamics" to create social change.[69]

Founded in 1946, the Research Center for Group Dynamics was committed to interdisciplinary research on all types of groups (racial, religious, professional, work, civic, labor, students, etc.), which could be useful in a variety of organizations, including the military, government, education, medical, and business. The members of the original group assembled by Lewin at MIT saw themselves as pioneers, opening up a new subfield in the behavioral sciences. Dorwin Cartwright recalls the avant-garde sense that they were starting something wholly new and revolutionary: "We were members of an organization with no history or established tradition and with few precedents anywhere in the social sciences; we were committed to new techniques of research and the utilization of established procedures in investigating new kinds of problems."[70] Yet this wasn't entirely true. In the second edition of the textbook, *Group Dynamics: Research and Theory* (1960), Cartwright himself recognized that group dynamics had grown out of the field of human relations, even citing the work of Mary Parker Follett, Elton Mayo, Lloyd Warner, and Conrad Arensberg as important predecessors. What was different was that while Mayo and Warner had always tried to maintain the neutral, objective stance of scientists, the pioneers of group dynamics saw themselves as agents of change. Lewin's followers had a mission, a large part of which was to combat the lingering assumptions of "rugged individualism" in American society, which they believed to be a great impediment to democracy. Although they never mentioned the New Deal, or anything involving politics, they did promote "interdependence," an idea that was used to justify the New Deal and government activism. Interdependence referred to the state of mutual dependence between and among individuals or groups or both. It usually connoted a repudiation of American bootstraps ideology and the Horatio Alger myth.

[68] Marrow, *The Practical Theorist*, 200.

[69] See Kurt Lewin, "The Research Center for Group Dynamics at Massachusetts Institute of Technology," *Sociometry* 8, no. 2 (May 1945):126–36.

[70] Dorwin Cartwright, "Some Things Learned," *Journal of Social Issues*, 1958, supplement Series No. 12, quoted in Marrow, *The Practical Theorist*, 182.

In the same vein, Lewin's group was also interested in democratic leadership training. One of the more famous studies to come out of the group dynamics perspective was Lippitt and White's experiment with leadership styles, which was designed to ascertain the effects of different management styles on group behavior.[71] The researchers divided middle-class schoolboys into three groups, which were headed by leaders exhibiting, respectively, a laissez-faire style of leadership, a democratic style, and an autocratic style. Not surprisingly (given the researcher's views), the democratic style of leadership was most successful. It motivated group members and fostered friendliness, efficiency, and cooperation. The laissez-faire and autocratic styles did not. Rather they created cynicism and hostility. In a later version of the same type of experiment, the researchers concluded that the experiments showed that "laissez-faire is not the same as democracy," and "democracy can be efficient," refuting common assumptions held by businessmen, as well as Americans in general.[72] This experiment provided data for the participative management movement, a continuation of earlier calls for "industrial democracy," and premised on the idea that an informed, empowered workforce is ultimately more productive.

While launching the Center for Group Dynamics, Lewin also headed the Commission on Community Interrelations (CCI) for the American Jewish Congress. The ostensible purpose of the CCI was to fight racial and religious bigotry, which it did, but under Lewin's leadership, it also became a vehicle for what he termed "action research." The idea was to use the community as a laboratory – to involve the community in a study of itself – and thereby learn about the problem at hand (racial and religious prejudice) while at the same time developing research techniques and effecting change. The CCI conducted studies on the effectiveness of intergroup education programs, the acceptance of Negro salesclerks, racial harmony in newly integrated housing projects, and the best ways to respond to a bigot.[73] The CCI was also responsible for developing one of the most widely used postwar antiracist tools: the Community Self-Survey.

The Community Self-Survey exemplified the philosophy and mission of the CCI, as well as the Center for Group Dynamics. Using guidelines provided

---

[71] Ronald K. Lippitt and Ralph White, "An Experimental Study of Leadership and Group Life," in T. H. Newcomb and E. L. Hartley, *Readings in Social Psychology* (New York: Henry Holt, 1947): 315–30.

[72] Ralph White and Ronald K. Lippitt, "Leadership Behavior and Member Reaction in Three Social Climates," in *Group Dynamics: Research and Theory*, ed. Dorwin Cartwright and Alvin Zander, 2nd ed. (Evanston, IL: Row, Peterson, 1960), 527–53, p. 552.

[73] Marrow, *The Practical Theorist*, 201–18. On the CCI, see also Frances Cherry and Catherine Borshuk, "Social Action Research and the Commission on Community Interrelations," *Journal of Social Issues* 54, no. 1 (1998): 119–42.

by the CCI, local community groups would assemble research teams made up of community members to collect data on racial and religious discrimination and prejudice in their communities. Whereas other antiracist programs would lecture citizens about discrimination, this program had citizens go out and discover it for themselves. Because they had to do this in a group, they were forced to discuss and confront racial inequity with their peers – not just see it but talk about it, and come up with a plan to fix it. The self-survey typically consisted of a broad cross section of the community, bringing together activist types with business leaders, homemakers, unionists, Jews, whites, Protestants, Catholics, and blacks. In Minneapolis, the survey was instigated by then Mayor Hubert Humphrey and headed by Pillsbury executive Bradshaw Mintener, and it forced a normally contentious group of unionists, business leaders, Democrats, Republicans, Jews, Lutherans, blacks, and Irish-Catholics to cooperate. At the end of the experience, community members had not only learned something about discrimination in their communities but had participated in creating a strategy to deal with it. And because they had participated in developing a strategy, it was hoped that they would be more accepting of it than if it had been a decree from above. You see in the self-survey Lewin's hallmark innovations: participatory management, intergroup cooperation, and social action.[74]

The CCI exemplifies the intersection between race relations and industrial relations. Some of the major race-relations researchers who were involved with the CCI included Charles S. Johnson of Fisk University; Margaret Mead; Gordon Allport of Harvard; psychologist Kenneth B. Clark, who had contributed to Myrdal's *An American Dilemma*, and whose research on black children helped convince the Supreme Court to end segregation in the schools; and W. Lloyd Warner of the University of Chicago. The management experts included the same people who were involved in group dynamics, including Douglas McGregor of MIT's Sloan School of Management, Ronald Lippitt, Rensis Likert, Alex Bavelas, and Alfred J. Marrow. Marrow, who became the CEO of Harwood Manufacturing Company and a specialist in executive training, remained active in race relations as well. His 1962 book, *Changing Patterns of Prejudice*, drew heavily from his experiences on the New York City Commission on Intergroup Relations.

The CCI's most significant experiment led to the creation of the National Training Laboratory (NTL) in Bethel, Maine, and the development of the

---

[74] On the self-survey movement, see John Harding, "Community Self-Surveys: A Form of Combating Discrimination," *Congress Weekly: A Review of Jewish Interests*, March 5, 1948; Marrow, *The Practical Theorist*, 214–16; Jennifer Delton, *Making Minnesota Liberal* (Minneapolis: University of Minnesota Press, 2002), 102–3.

so-called T-group, the basis for sensitivity training. We associate sensitivity training with inculcating racial sensitivity, but in practice, it had much broader applications in the business world. Indeed, it was primarily directed at teaching executives how to be sensitive to their interactions with others in any type of group situation. Its purpose was to create more effective management groups. During the 1960s, thousands of executives found themselves in Bethel, Maine, deep in the psychologically intense, sometimes troubling experience of the T-group. But the point for our purposes is, again, how experiments designed to help race relations found larger applications in the business world and were thus already available to firms when they decided to integrate.

In 1946, the director of the Connecticut State Inter-Racial Commission contacted the ICC because he was uncertain whether the efforts of the commission were actually effective in overcoming religious and racial prejudice and discrimination. Could the ICC send some representatives to tell them the latest educational techniques? At the same time, the Research Center for Group Dynamics was dissatisfied with traditional laboratories for human relations research, especially in terms of assessing resistance to change and how to bring about change in group life. So Lewin decided to treat the assignment as an experiment, a chance to test various hypotheses about group behavior, training, and change, as well as contribute to social progress. Lewin's team designed a workshop that would train community leaders (from the commission) on how to train interested citizens in antiracist activities, while at the same time measuring and assessing resistance to change and the effectiveness of certain training techniques in overcoming change. In other words, both the trainers and the trainees were also guinea pigs.[75] The workshop would create data – or produce behavior – that researchers would then analyze and draw conclusions from.

The two-week workshop took place at Teachers College, New Britain, Connecticut, in June 1946. In addition to the research and training teams, there were forty-one recruits who were the objects of the training program. Of the forty-one trainees, 44 percent were educators, 34 percent social workers, and 22 percent community volunteers; 29 percent were black, 25 percent Jewish, 23 percent English American, 13 percent Irish, 5 percent Canadian American, and 5 percent Italian; and 15 percent were Catholic, 60 percent Protestant, and 25 percent Jewish. The workshop encouraged a relaxed atmosphere of equals,

---

[75] On the workshop, see Ronald Lippitt, *Training in Community Relations: A Research Exploration toward New Group Skills* (New York: Harper, 1949), a publication of both the Research Center for Group Dynamics and the ICC of the American Jewish Commission; and Marrow, *The Practical Theorist*, 210–14.

with plenty of discussion, participation, and reflection. It had participants engage in role-playing exercises that enacted difficult racial situations. Ronald Lippitt, who headed the research team, wrote a detailed account of the workshop, identifying the content of the sessions, the process by which the training groups set their goals and strategies, the methods used, and the process by which researchers drew conclusions and measured results.[76]

The reason the workshop became so significant occurred one night when several of the trainees wandered into a research staff meeting. The researchers were discussing how the various training groups had performed that day. As reported by Marrow, most of the research staff was reluctant to have the trainees sit in on these meetings where their behavior was being discussed. But Lewin waved them in. Marrow writes: "The result – in the words of Bradford [a research team member] – was like 'a tremendous electric charge . . . as people reacted to data about their own behavior.' Thus, the role of feedback in a T (training) group was discovered."[77] This story became almost as widely repeated in management literature as the inexplicably perky workers in Hawthorne's wiring room. It is the creation story for how feedback, and the constant, therapeutic reflection on and assessment of one's own performance in group sessions, became a hallmark of sensitivity training.

The workshop apparently was successful also in motivating and preparing community members to take on racial and religious bias in their own communities. Participants said that the workshop gave them a broadened view of the problem, the motivation to become more active, specific human relations skills, new confidence in their own abilities, a basis of personal authority with co-workers, and more tolerant attitudes. Researchers found that 72 percent of participants were using the new methods they had learned in their own communities.[78] Lippitt, however, presents some data that indicate that, while participants came in with concrete goals focused on improving conditions and opportunities for minorities (such as FEPC and housing integration), they left the workshop persuaded to pursue goals of education and attitudinal change. Lippitt puts a positive spin on this, noting that they had a more sophisticated notion of education when they left, but then he states that "there was considerably less fixation on the single goals of 'doing something about' housing and employment," as if that were a good thing.[79] This suggests that antiracist training may have made participants less activist and more interested in education

---

[76] Lippitt, *Training in Community Relations.*
[77] Marrow, *The Practical Theorist* (New York: Basic Books, 1969), 212.
[78] Lippitt, *Training in Community Relations*, 184.
[79] Ibid., 194.

as a means of resolving racial problems. This did not reflect an intentional goal. Lewin believed, and ICC studies had found, that legislation and activism were more effective than education, discussion, and endless preparation for change.

Before his death in 1947, Lewin had secured a grant from the Office of Naval Research, which in combination with funds from the Carnegie Corporation and the National Educational Association, established the NTL in Bethel, Maine. The NTL continued research and training in group behavior by means of the T-group. But the NTL was only one institution of many that had adopted and offered T-groups to industry during the 1960s. The American Management Association developed, with Marrow's help, a three-week executive action course.[80] Some of the larger corporations sponsored laboratories of their own. Graduate programs in business administration held sensitivity training sessions for businessmen, as well as their own students.[81] Although the technique was widely questioned, criticized, and mocked, American corporations continued to send their executives to sensitivity training sessions in the belief that executives who were more sensitive to their interpersonal relations would be more effective and hence more productive.

If race-relations research contributed to executive training techniques, it also, more predictably, contributed to companies' attempts to prepare their workforces for integration. The National Conference of Christians and Jews developed a ten-week-long group-discussion program called Teamwork in Industry, designed to allay prejudice and help whites and minorities work together. True to the human relations philosophy, the program treated the problems of prejudice and discrimination as problems in management, not as one story put it, "conditions to be protested against or denounced."[82] Western Electric, Ford Motor Company, American Smelting Company, and the General Cable Company of Perth Amboy, New Jersey, all adopted this program in the early 1950s. Western Electric's training program featured such race-relations luminaries as Dr. Kenneth Clark and writer James Baldwin. The National Association of Manufacturers recommended for its members such familiar names in race relations as Robert Weaver, Herbert Northrup, Ruth Benedict, Charles Johnson, and Horace Cayton. The Office of Economic Opportunity, created in 1964 as part of the Great Society, developed an awareness sensitivity program,

[80] On which, see Alfred Marrow, *Behind the Executive Mask* (New York: American Management Association, 1964).

[81] See Mary Ann Coghill, "Sensitivity Training," New York State School of Industrial and Labor Relations, *Key Issues*, no. 1 (1967).

[82] "Hiring Minorities," *Modern Industry* (January 15, 1952): 59–62, p. 60.

which was adopted by many employers in the late 1960s.[83] International Harvester and Pitney-Bowes had long included similar interracial classes in their management training programs as part of their fair employment program (see Chapter 5).

After integration began in earnest in the mid-1960s, companies used sensitivity training and group counseling techniques to help both white and black workers adjust to their new workplace environments.[84] Although the effectiveness of these methods was subject to great debate in the 1970s, they have been revived and adapted for what is now called diversity training. Elsie Y. Cross, the founder of one of the leading diversity consulting firms of the 1980s, was trained at the NTL.[85]

Conclusion

Arising in large part out of race-relations research, the techniques of human relations were originally designed to help management control fractious employees and create more harmonious labor relations. As historians Sanford Jacoby, Elizabeth Fones-Wolf, and others have shown, these techniques helped contain the expansion of unionism in the postwar years. They also helped lay the groundwork for racial integration. In his 1966 study of Negro employment, researcher Stephen Habbe found that those companies that had hired blacks into "breakthrough" positions had done so using human relations innovations such as job specifications, recruiting programs, training and education programs, worker counseling, sensitivity training, and community

---

[83] Ibid., 59–62; R. G. Lawrence, "Western Electric's Commitment to Fair Employment," in *The Negro and Employment Opportunity*, ed. Herbert Northrup (Ann Arbor: University of Michigan, Bureau of Industrial Relations, Graduate School of Business Administration, 1965), 137–45; "Personnel Practices for Enhancement of Individual Opportunity and Advancement," June 21, 1947, in NAM Records, Series 7, Box 135, HML; G. E. Morse, "How Honeywell Took the JOBS Program to Heart," *Manpower* (February–March 1969): 22–25.

[84] See, for example, Morse, "How Honeywell Took the JOBS Program to Heart," 54–59; Charles Luce, "Consolidated Edison and the Hard-Core," *Training in Business and Industry* 66 (March 1969): 46–53.

[85] On the effectiveness of group counseling, see Hjalmar Rosen, *A Group Orientation Approach for Facilitating the Work Adjustment of the Hard-Core Unemployed*, final report to the U.S. Department of Labor, Manpower Development and Training Administration (Detroit: Wayne State University, 1969); and Aaron Rutledge and Gertrude Zemon Gass, *Nineteen Negro Men: Personality and Manpower Retraining* (San Francisco: Jossey-Bass, 1967). On diversity training, see Elsie Y. Cross, *The Diversity Factor: Capturing the Competitive Advantage of a Changing Workforce* (Chicago: Irwin Professional, 1996).

relations programs.[86] Researcher Louis Ferman likewise found that companies that had strong bureaucratic controls, where personnel policies were centralized and where promotability was tied to supervisor and managers' administration of company policies and procedures, were more likely to institute successful Equal Employment Opportunity programs. Ferman contrasts the "entrepreneurial norm" of a company with an unsuccessful record of racial integration to a company that had a "bureaucratic norm" and a successful policy of integration.[87] Consider this statement from a management training program used by MCI Communications Corporation in 1980: "Violations [of EEO laws] are usually the result of inefficient management of people. For this reason, positive efforts to comply with EEO laws will produce more effective management practices and increase the management skills of all who take their EEO responsibilities seriously."[88] Good management and integration went hand in hand. Chapters 8 and 9 will demonstrate in more detail how human relations techniques were used to integrate firms in the 1960s and 1970s.

After the 1964 Civil Rights Act was passed, companies complained that they were unprepared to meet the "sudden" pressure to integrate. In fact, however, those companies that had strong industrial relations departments and had adopted human relations techniques already had the infrastructure necessary for successful integration.

---

[86] Norgren et al., *Employing the Negro in American Industry*, and Habbe, *Company Experience with Negro Employment*.

[87] Ferman, *The Negro and Equal Employment Opportunities*, 79.

[88] *Boomerang II: A Management Training Program in Equal Employment Opportunity* (1980), found in MCI Communications Corporation, Human Resources Records, 1973–1996, Accession no. 2225, Box 461, HML.

5   Human Relations at International Harvester and Pitney-Bowes

> But industrial relations – like international relations – happen to be much less a problem of setting up a smoothly functioning organization than a problem of accommodating diverse and conflicting interests.
>
> Daniel Bell[1]

Central to the human relations perspective was the belief that workplace environments and interactions could be influenced and changed, that good management had the power to engineer good human relations between and among groups. Racial integration would challenge this belief, and as it turned out, few industrial relations officers were up to the challenge. But in those "pioneering" companies committed to a fair employment policy, committed industrial relations officers made it happen. This chapter will examine the fair employment policies of two corporations: International Harvester, a Chicago-based manufacturer of farm equipment and trucks, and Pitney-Bowes, a medium-sized manufacturer of postage machines. By the mid-1950s, these two companies were well known as pioneers in fair employment and integration, in large part because their respective vice-presidents of industrial relations, Ivan L. Willis and Joseph Morrow, had publicized their company's success with fair employment in order that others might emulate it. Both companies also had highly developed human relations philosophies and programs, which went hand in hand with their struggles to contain unionism. In addition to demonstrating the mutually reinforcing relationship between fair employment and labor-stabilizing human relations programs, an examination of these companies also reveals the degree to which effective fair employment policies paid attention to race and color. In an era of color-blind ascendancy, these companies understood that it was not enough to simply remove exclusionary policies; real fair employment required extra effort that accounted for race.

[1] Daniel Bell, "Adjusting Men to Machines," *Commentary* 3 (January 1947): 79–88.

International Harvester

International Harvester Company was incorporated in a 1902 merger of the McCormick Company, several other agricultural equipment companies, and a steel concern. Born as a monopoly and afflicted with chronic labor trouble, the company strove for most of its history to show that it was an enlightened, socially responsible corporate citizen. On the eve of World War II, the company employed sixty thousand workers in twenty-three plants. By the mid-1950s, the company had built six new plants, expanded its workforce to its peak of ninety thousand, and was reorganized into six product divisions: farm tractor, motor truck, industrial power, refrigeration, steel, and twine. Harvester's mechanical pickers replaced black agricultural workers in southern cotton fields after World War II, so it was appropriate that the company had an active antidiscrimination program. The company remained the leading manufacturer of agricultural equipment until the late 1950s, when it was surpassed by its main competitors, John Deere and Caterpillar.

In an attempt to better its reputation and stave off unions (which it successfully did until 1941), the company turned to "welfare work" and "human relations." The McCormick family, which maintained a controlling interest in the Harvester Company in the early twentieth century, was especially committed to welfare work and involved in organizations that encouraged harmonious employer-employee relations, such as the National Civic Federation and the Special Committee Conference, which later became Industrial Relations Counselors, Inc. Even though the purpose of the welfare departments was in part to avert unionism, many of the people hired to run them were genuine reformers. As a result, there was always a rivalry between "welfare workers" and managers, and each successive welfare officer negotiated anew the reach of his or her authority in the company. The authority of the various welfare departments' waxed and waned between 1901 and 1944. In 1944, the Industrial Relations Department was raised to vice-presidential status and given more authority, which reflected the new union presence at Harvester, as well as the changing reputation of human relations techniques during the war.[2]

Harvester's postwar Industrial Relations Department was steeped in the philosophy of human relations. It instituted training programs for its foremen and supervisors to, as one training manual put it: develop the skill of

---

[2] Robert Ozanne, *A Century of Labor-Management Relations at McCormick and International Harvester* (Madison: University of Wisconsin Press, 1967), 163–64; See also Roland Marchand, *Creating the Corporate Soul: The Rise of Public Relations and Corporate Imagery in American Big Business* (Berkeley: University of California Press, 1998), 22–25.

"working well with people – of getting along with them and getting their willing cooperation."[3] It conducted attitude surveys of its employees, trying to discern managers' job satisfaction and relationships to other groups. Its officers crossed the country speaking on behalf of their approach to labor relations. Its employee handbooks expressed the proper concern for communication, opportunity, and training that had become hallmarks of the human relations approach.[4] It cultivated relationships in the various communities in which its plants were located.

Just as Harvester had a long history of welfare work, it also had a long history of antidiscrimination policies. Harvester adopted its first statement prohibiting discrimination on the basis of "race, sex, political or religious affiliation" in 1919, in the constitution of the new Harvester Industrial Council Plan. Harvester historian Robert Ozanne argues that this really can't be seen as an "equal opportunity policy" because its purpose was clearly to maintain an open shop and prevent the establishment of unions, which were notoriously all white.[5] But maintaining an open shop did not contradict equal opportunity and antidiscrimination policies, as black leaders well understood. The presence of an open shop was often the only way for blacks to secure employment. It is true, however, that the nondiscrimination policy helped fulfill the main purpose of the early welfare departments: to keep out unions.

Under this early antidiscrimination policy, the employment of blacks and other racial minorities varied according to labor shortages and plant managers. Some plant managers hired large numbers of black workers; others hired none. Fully 24 percent of the workers at McCormick Twine Mills in 1924 were African American, with one department hiring 50 percent black women. McCormick Works was at 18 percent, and the Webber works 21 percent, "generally distributed through the various departments."[6] The Tractor foundry was 35 percent African American. Wisconsin Steel, however, hired no blacks but imported Mexicans from Kansas City. Industrial Relations Director Arthur Young worried about the preponderant number of Negro employees and tried to enforce a quota of 20 percent. This indicates that the antidiscrimination policy was not followed and that Young sought to orchestrate the numbers of different racial and nationality groups (not unlike what was later required

---

[3] "The Man and His Job: An Approach to Human Relations," by Education and Personnel, International Harvester company, n.d., in International Harvester Company, Corporate Archives Central File, McCormick Mss 6Z, Box 534, Folder 02669, at Wisconsin Historical Society, Madison (hereafter WHS).

[4] "Welcome to Harvester Sales Operations" [1947], Management Attitude Survey, and "What's on Your Mind?" May 1953, in International Harvester Company, Corporate Archives Central File, McCormick Mss 6Z, boxes 931 and 787, WHS.

[5] Ozanne, *A Century of Labor-Management Relations*, 184.

[6] Ibid., 185.

under affirmative action). Nonetheless, the company was still a major employer of black labor. Superintendents who had hired black workers and found them satisfactory refused to replace them with whites just to meet a quota. The Industrial Relations Department kept records of the different ethnic and racial groups and conducted surveys that indicated that Negro and Mexican labor was as efficient as white labor and sometimes more so.[7]

During World War II, the Harvester Company reasserted its policy of nondiscrimination, making it company policy to hire, train, and upgrade Negroes according to the same rules that applied to all other workers. The policy was in part prompted by the wartime Fair Employment Practices Committee, but it was retained and strengthened after the war when Harvester opened three new plants in Memphis, Tennessee; Evanston, Indiana; and Louisville, Kentucky, and decided to make them experiments in biracial industrialism. The hope was that operating integrated plants from the start would avert the solidification of "custom," which was so hard to overcome. If white southerners wanted jobs at the new plants, they would have to work alongside and on an equal basis with black workers.[8]

Two people were responsible for developing and implementing Harvester's revived fair employment policy: Harvester president Fowler McCormick and Sara Southall, then supervisor of Employment and Service. The grandson of two robber barons (Cyrus McCormick and John D. Rockefeller), Fowler McCormick carried within him the presumed sins of American capitalism. After a prolonged youth in which he studied and traveled with Carl Jung, was graduated from Princeton, and drifted about, he began work at Harvester in 1928, at almost thirty years of age. McCormick strove to be an enlightened manager of human relations. He believed that corporations had to serve the interests of employees, the community, and consumers, as well as the stockholders. During his years as Harvester's president, he modernized, or decentralized, its corporate structure and instituted new professional training programs that instilled in aspiring executives objective, rational behavior based on the precepts of human relations. He was recognized for developing one of the most progressive racial policies in American industry. Yet he continued the McCormick family's war against unions.[9] Harvester's history of paternalism,

---

[7] Ibid., 185–87.

[8] Ozanne, *A Century of Labor-Management Relations*, 189, and John Hope II, *Selected Studies of the Negro Employment in the South: 3 Southern Plants of International Harvester Company*, Prepared by the NPA Committee of the South (Washington, DC: National Planning Association, 1953).

[9] Barbara Marsh, *A Corporate Tragedy: The Agony of International Harvester Company* (Garden City, NY: Doubleday, 1985), 60–67, 75. See also "Fowler McCormick: Self-Made Man," *Fortune*, September 1946, 111–14, 213–18; Fowler McCormick Papers, 1878–1972, Box 1, Wisconsin

welfare work, and antiunionism in many ways validates the critique of human relations as a technique to thwart unionization and at some level democracy itself. Fowler McCormick, however, seems to have been so genuinely committed to the ideals of democratic human relations that one almost gets the sense that he opposed unions not as unions per se, but because they hindered his democratic vision of human relations.

Fowler McCormick became president and chief operating officer of International Harvester in 1941. That was the same year that the National Labor Relations Board (NLRB) finally ruled that Harvester's "independent" unions were illegal, which sparked a competition among the UAW-CIO, the new left-wing Farm Equipment Workers Organizing Committee, and AFL unions for the right to organize Harvester's sixty-thousand-member workforce. It was also the year that the company readopted its nondiscrimination policy. McCormick strongly endorsed the fair employment policy, required managers and supervisors to conform to it, and authorized the changes necessary to enforce it, and in these ways, he was necessary to the policy's success. There is no reason to think that he did not believe in it, but it was, one supposes, Sara E. Southall who initiated the idea in the first place.

This is how Sara Southall explains how she ended up at International Harvester:

> When I was a young woman living at Hull House, I asked Jane Addams whether I should work in a large corporation. She answered: "I would, if I were you. With America's productive genius, I think the strongest forces of the future will be labor and management. If those forces are intelligent enough to work together for the satisfaction of human goals and needs, America can make a contribution far beyond mere production and distribution."[10]

While one suspects those were not Addams' exact words, it is clear that Southall's career was informed by the Progressive impulse to better the human condition. It is after all a certain type of woman who finds herself "living at Hull House." Southall spent twenty-eight years in industrial relations at International Harvester, from 1920 to 1948, becoming an expert on women workers, industrial relations, and African Americans in industry. She represented International Harvester on the Chicago Urban League's board of directors. She served on President Roosevelt's Fair Employment Practices Committee.

State Historical Society, for personal letters indicating his connections to Jung and his desire to be a progressive employer; and Fowler McCormick, foreword to *Industry's Unfinished Business: Achieving Sound Industrial Relations and Fair Employment*, by Sara Southall (New York: Harper, 1950), xi–xiii.

[10] Southall, *Industry's Unfinished Business*, xv.

Her influence at Harvester was pervasive, and while historians of labor and industry tend toward material and structural explanations of corporate policy, Southall's career is testimony to the power individuals can wield in an organization. Southall is an example of what some of today's diversity experts call "champions," individuals within an organization who take the lead in promoting minority representation.

Southall took Addams' words to heart. Her allegiance was to the field of industrial relations as a way to build harmonious labor-management relations. She was in every way a believer in and practitioner of human relations, but not as a technique to prevent unionism. Indeed, she rejected paternalism and saw unions not only as inevitable but probably a good thing for workers. Unions gave workers autonomy and a sense of dignity in a way that employee representation plans and "rec" rooms never could. She recognized the lie embedded in management's insistence that employees and employers were "one family."[11] Although loyal to management, she saw unions as a progressive force in society. While employers typically blamed labor unions for impeding fair employment, for instance, Southall believed that unions were more vocal in their support for fair employment legislation than management. She observed, "Employers are usually satisfied with the status quo and confine their legislative activities to maintaining and protecting it."[12] True to the aims of human relations (in a way perhaps that Fowler McCormick was not), Southall was sympathetic to both labor and management and saw her mission as helping the two to reconcile their differences, or as she put it, "integrate their commonalities."[13]

The key to integrating the interests of labor and management was a professional industrial relations department. Southall retired just as Harvester was decentralizing, and she was eager to define a new role for industrial relations departments as they became more clearly part of centralized staff divisions. According to Southall's definition, staff divisions set standards, while line divisions produced goods according to those standards. Making industrial relations purely a staff function had its pros and cons. On the one hand, as staff, industrial relations officers could not implement their own policies but had to rely on those in charge of the operating functions, who were sometimes lackadaisical if not resistant to their policies. On the other hand, however, a more centralized industrial relations division could be more professional, more autonomous, and more connected and responsive to the developing field and research in industrial relations. A more professional industrial relations staff could more

[11] Ibid., 12–22.
[12] Ibid., 120.
[13] Ibid., 38.

effectively train line supervisors and managers to implement modern human relations policies.[14]

Southall believed that industrial relations officers needed to be broadly knowledgeable about not only the company but also the labor movement, the community in which the business operated, and the profession of industrial relations. The profession of industrial relations was one of constant learning – preferably outside the company. It is here where one can see the intersection of business and the academic field of human relations (discussed in the previous chapter). Harvester's contract with the University of Chicago, whereby the university would provide faculty for Harvester's Central Training School, was the type of arrangement that human relations researchers sought: an opportunity to inculcate supervisors, managers, and executives with human relations ideology, while at the same time gaining access to the "laboratory" of an actual company. Southall called for companies to invest more resources in researching human relations: "Industry has been doing research in product development for years; there is no reason why research in human relations should not follow a similar pattern."[15]

Harvester's Central Training School ensured the dissemination of human relations ideas into the factory. Whereas previously foremen and supervisors had been trained on a purely local basis, the Central Training School brought them to Chicago, away from their plants, for two to three weeks of classes with University of Chicago faculty in human relations. Like other line operators, foremen and supervisors tended to be parochial in their outlook, focused on their own particular departments. Bringing them to Chicago helped them to see themselves and their responsibilities in the broader context of the entire company and the larger world. There was no technical training; the emphasis was, rather, "on broadening the general knowledge and personality of the individual supervisor."[16] Much like in politics at this time, the fight was against the local, the parochial, the narrow. "Education" meant teaching people to recognize their interdependent relationship to others.

Nowhere was a broadened outlook more important than in the implementation of a fair employment policy. Southall did not dwell on why fair employment was necessary; rather, she framed it as a potential source of industrial conflict – one that might draw the government into private enterprise – and therefore of concern to the industrial relations officer. It was up to industrial relations officers to educate themselves on the issue and to present a plan for

[14] Ibid., 40–46; also discussed in Marsh, *A Corporate Tragedy*, 75.
[15] Southall, *Industry's Unfinished Business*, 48.
[16] Ibid., 47.

action – regardless of top management's interest or noninterest in the issue. If top management rejected the plan, the industrial relations officer should develop new ideas and more convincing arguments. She chided industrial relations officers who did not pursue fair employment and wrote, "if industrial relations executives are to gain status, keep up with the times, and discharge one of their most important functions, they must come to grips with the task of eliminating discriminatory employment policies."[17] As always, it is hard to discern whether this is merely an argument designed to convince readers (in this case industrial relations officers) to support fair employment or if it reflects the author's true convictions on the matter. Either way, the statement does definitively tie fair employment to the bureaucratic ascent of industrial relations. Southall continually stressed the importance of a strong, centralized industrial relations department as the key to a successful fair employment policy.[18]

Southall retired in 1944, but Ivan L. Willis, continued her mission. Vice-president of Industrial Relations from 1947 to 1960, Willis spoke often and forthrightly about fair employment and equal opportunity in testimony before Senate subcommittees and speeches before Harvester personnel, civic organizations, and government contractors. Like Southall, Willis saw fair employment as part of good management, but he also saw voluntary fair employment as necessary to avert federal legislation (see Chapter 2). Or at least that was how he justified the policy to his peers.

Implementing the Fair Employment Policy

Southall and International Harvester representatives always and strenuously insisted that Harvester's policy was one of nondiscrimination only. The company would not hire a man simply because he was a Negro, nor would it engage in what Southall saw as "ineffective policies based on hiring a percentage of Negroes equal to their proportional representation in their communities."[19] During the 1940s and 1950s, those in charge of implementing fair employment policies always tried to make them seem "natural," as if there was nothing significant or unusual about nondiscrimination, as if it were merely in keeping with traditional American principles. Yet the elaborate, proactive policies that

---

[17] Ibid., 65.
[18] Ibid., 62–63, 87.
[19] "Harvester Plants Push Democracy," *New York Times*, July 20, 1947.

Harvester developed to integrate its plants were at odds with the color-blind rhetoric of company officials.

The company devised a three-step program of integration: (1) study and analysis of the local situation; (2) careful selection of qualified Negroes; and (3) cooperation with employees and union officials.[20] Although Southall retired in 1944, she helped the company implement this plan in the three new southern plants it acquired after the war. This was a large, carefully planned undertaking, which involved many meetings with white community leaders and the people who would be likely employees. The company explained the economic necessity of having integrated plants, assuring southern whites that they were not crusaders and that they were not promoting "social equality" in any way. They would hire only fully qualified Negroes and would not discriminate against whites, but they would offer Negroes the same opportunities for advancement as whites. In Memphis, the company would adhere to state segregation laws with regard to the facilities and cafeterias, but the workplace and all training programs would be integrated. The promise of high-wage production jobs led the communities in question to allow Harvester to operate the integrated plants.[21] Following FEP guidelines, the company worked with the local Urban League to hire the "best" Negroes in the area and placed many of them into traditionally white jobs.[22]

During the initial hiring process, all white applicants for positions were informed that the plant practiced fair employment and that they would be working side by side with blacks. It was hoped that this would keep away the most racist whites, since employees had to agree to the policy to be employed at the plant. In Louisville, the company had hired black personnel officers in part to indicate that the plant would be operating on an integrated basis. The orientation for new employees was conducted on an integrated basis. White workers knew what they were getting into from the start. Despite this groundwork, white employees in these plants still rebelled when blacks were upgraded into skilled positions. Harvester officials always downplayed these

---

[20] Southall, *Industry's Unfinished Business*, 142–54; "The Negro Employe at Harvester" (n.d.), found in International Harvester Company, Corporate Archives Central File, McCormick Mss 6Z, Box 545, WHS

[21] This offers support to the thesis developed in Elizabeth Jacoway and David Colburn, eds., *Southern Businessmen and Desegregation* (Baton Rouge: Louisiana State University, 1982), that economic incentive paved the way for desegregation.

[22] This story is told in Hope, *Selected Studies of the Negro Employment in the South*; and "Statement of Ivan L. Willis," before the Senate Subcommittee on Labor and Labor-Management Relations, Washington DC, April 16, 1952, found in International Harvester Company, Corporate Archives Central File (documented series), 1819–1998, McCormick Mss 6Z, Box 758, folder 09131, WHS.

occurrences. It is true that there were only four unauthorized strikes because of Negro upgrading between 1948 and 1953, but the threat of such walkouts continued to make white supervisors wary of advancing blacks into new positions. As labor historian Michael Honey demonstrates, segregation of the labor market was the norm in Memphis; white workers at Harvester constantly harassed black workers and even sabotaged their machines.[23]

Company officials attributed the relative success of the policy to the careful preparation and communication described earlier. In hindsight, however, one can see that other steps that were less color-blind and more affirmative were actually responsible. After the fear of white resistance, on which much of the early how-to literature was focused, the largest impediments to black employment and advancement were intentional discrimination on the part of plant supervisors in charge of hiring and promotion, seniority agreements that confined blacks to the department in which they had been hired, and black workers' lack of access to training programs. These impediments continued to be a problem into the late 1960s (and even after) and received relatively little attention until then. Unlike other companies that professed interest in fair employment, Harvester was one of the very few companies that tried to overcome these impediments beginning in the 1940s.

Hiring and Promotion: The Supervisor Problem

Although personnel departments were very much involved in hiring and promotion, especially in terms of collecting applications, recruitment, and overseeing contract provisions, the decision concerning which individuals would be hired and promoted remained in the hands of departmental supervisors. If a supervisor was opposed to hiring or promoting blacks into white positions, a company's statement of fair employment practices was worthless. Harvester's policy addressed this problem in two ways: (1) it made individual supervisors accountable to the company's executive committee and (2) it instituted intensive training programs.

The president required plant managers and division heads to submit an annual report on, as one memo put it, "the number of colored persons hired and the progress made in furthering the advancement of employment of colored

---

[23] Hope, *Selected Studies of the Negro Employment in the South*. Hope downplayed the incidents of resistance, but noted that the threat of resistance inhibited black promotion. On sabotage, see Michael Honey, *Going Down Jericho Road: The Memphis Strike, Martin Luther King's Last Campaign* (New York: Norton, 2007), 38.

persons."[24] While this would become standard practice in the late 1960s, it was extremely rare in the late 1940s to find top management involved in supervising company policies at this level. For supervisors to comply with this request, they would have to keep statistics on the racial identities of their employees. This too was rarely done, in part because state fair employment laws actually prohibited it. Recognizing the paradox, Southall said that with proper safeguards to prevent the discriminatory use of racial information, "there is no reason why creed, race, national origin, and color could not be coded and punched on internal confidential records, both to help a large corporation follow the progress of its organization and supply information requested by state or federal agencies."[25] Southall recommended that industrial relations staff keep track of this information so that they may identify which departments hire no Negroes, which upgrade them, and so on. With this information, the industrial relations staff could better target problem areas. The company also took particular pride in noting that in some plants a minority of colored employees held unskilled positions, while the majority occupied semiskilled and skilled positions.[26] This suggests there was a special, centralized effort to get blacks out of unskilled positions. With both the president and industrial relations staff monitoring their hiring practices, supervisors were more likely to pay attention to the policy. This did not eliminate discrimination, but it did put pressure on supervisors in a way that other companies did not.[27]

In addition, the company used its extensive training program to educate supervisors and managers about the reasons for and importance of the policy. Harvester officials knew that "education" alone would not change discriminatory practices, but it was nonetheless a necessary, if imperfect, component

[24] Memo, J. L. McCaffrey [president] to [divisions heads and supervisors], January 20, 1947, in H. Fowler McCormick Papers, McC Mss Box 4, WHS. See also "Statement of Ivan L. Willis, Vice President, before the Senate Committee on Labor and Labor-Management Relations, Washington DC, April 16, 1952," in International Harvester Company, Corporate Archives Central File (documented series), 1819–1998, McCormick Mss 6Z, Box 758, folder 09131, WHS and Robert Ozanne, *The Negro in the Farm Equipment and Construction Machinery Industries, "The Racial Policies of American Industry,"* Report No. 26 (Philadelphia: Industrial Research Unit, Department of Industry, Wharton School of Finance and Commerce, University of Pennsylvania, 1972), 29.

[25] Southall, *Industry's Unfinished Business*, 143. On the debate among civil rights activists, see Hugh Davis Graham, *The Civil Rights Era: Origins and Development of National Policy, 1960–1972* (New York: Oxford University Press, 1990), 197–201.

[26] "Integration: It Works in Business," *Management Methods* (May 1956): 33.

[27] Robert Ozanne writes, "The company's initial response [to wartime FEPC] was to terminate the plant superintendent's traditional autonomy in hiring." Ozanne, *A Century of Labor-Management Relations*, 188. I have been unable to confirm this statement, or determine whether it continued in the postwar years. It may that he is referring to the executive monitoring. If true, however, it is a radical change.

for getting employees – especially supervisors – to accept new practices. Given that supervisors could always find some objective reason for refusing to hire or promote a particular black individual and still claim to be complying with company policy, it was essential that the company actually change its attitude about discrimination and black workers. But while some kind of interracial training was necessary, the company was careful not to overemphasize it, lest it, in Southall's words, "make it [fair employment] a problem of special significance rather than a policy to be accepted as naturally as all the others."[28] Southall's comment illustrates the common belief at this time that better race relations depended on the "low visibility" of change. According to this view, the development of new and better patterns in biracial employment depended on preventing self-consciousness and tension and avoiding "making a big deal about it."[29]

Still, Harvester experimented with a special fair employment training session for eighteen months after the war. Supervisors who were sent to the Central Training School attended a special session on fair employment. For the session, they were required to read a company-prepared manual about the Harvester Company's fair employment policy and its various interactions with people of many different races and creeds. The session's instructor further explained the reason for the policy, avoiding any kind of moral or ethical reasoning – nothing was said about racial brotherhood or neighborly love. Rather, the instructor emphasized the hard-nosed economic, practical, and patriotic realities that necessitated the policy: the need for the most qualified people, the expense of segregation, the right of all Americans to earn a living so they were not a burden on taxpayers.[30] Then the class discussed several case studies about how they might deal with resistant white employees, how they might fill an opening for a drill press operator, how they would introduce a Negro into an all-white department. The discussion allowed supervisors to discuss their concerns and opinions about the policy and their experiences thus far with it.[31]

Southall was reluctant to claim that the experimental training session resulted in overall progress in the company, since only a small number of supervisors could attend the Central School. But she had anecdotal evidence that it had some effect on some supervisors and for that reason advocated that all supervisors be trained in all company policies at the plant or sales-branch

---

[28] Southall, *Industry's Unfinished Business*, 107.

[29] Hope, *Selected Studies of the Negro Employment in the South*, iii.

[30] Southall, *Industry's Unfinished Business*, 108–18, "The Negro Employe at Harvester" (International Harvester, n.d.) in International Harvester Company, Corporate Archives Central File (documented series), 1819–1998, McCormick Mss 6Z, Box 881, Folder 13908, WHS.

[31] Southall, *Industry's Unfinished Business*, 116.

level. Why wait until supervisors attended the Central School to teach them company policies? They should already have a clear sense of company policy, and particularly fair employment, before arriving at the Central School for management training. She proposed that, at the plant level, they would be taught the basic methods of introducing black employees, objective evaluation, and how to deal with white resistance. When they attended the Central School, Southall wrote, "they could be brought to understand their own prejudices, to overcome them, and to take for granted the presence of qualified Negroes in any position."[32] What she proposed was some version of sensitivity training along the lines of what Kurt Lewin and Ronald Lippitt were developing at the time. Attitudinal change, the kind of change that could get someone to "take for granted" that which he had rejected, was the challenge – and promise – of human relations training. But notice that while Southall believed attitudinal change was necessary, it was not the first step. The first step was teaching managers how to follow company policy. The inculcation of attitudes came later.

Harvester incorporated Southall's suggestions on training. Fair employment training was decentralized and enfolded into the regular training agenda at the plant level.[33] This was done so that all foremen and supervisors would receive the training and so that it could be adjusted to specific plant situations. In 1956, *Management Methods* noted that a key phase of implementation at Harvester involved the "program of changing attitudes," conducted by the training department.[34] Harvester employees spent a lot of time in training programs. There was a weeklong orientation program. There was a management training program and a separate leadership training course. There were special training programs for specific production or personnel problems. Finally, the company sponsored after-hours courses, "to meet the personal desire of employees," such as arts and crafts classes. As public relations officer R. L. Siegel explained to the refrigeration engineers at the Evansville plant, "We are thinking in terms of long range success, and we think the principal ingredient in achieving that success is education and training."[35]

In his study of Harvester's three southern plants, John Hope II was impressed with the extent to which the Industrial Relations Department had

[32] Ibid., 118.
[33] Hope, *Selected Studies of the Negro Employment in the South*, 86.
[34] "Integration: It Works in Business," 30.
[35] "An Address Delivered by R. L. Siegel before the Evansville Session of the American Society of Refrigeration Engineering," n.d. [circa 1948], p. 6, in International Harvester Company, Corporate Archives Central File (documented series), 1819–1998, McCormick Mss 6Z, Box 715, Folder 07688, WHS; on training, see also Hope, *Selected Studies of the Negro Employment in the South*, 83–96.

secured the cooperation of local and divisional heads in the integration program. Such cooperation was cultivated not only in training programs but also in company-wide conferences, such as the one held in French Lick, Indiana, in November 1948, where vice-president of Industrial Relations Ivan Willis gathered his personnel staff together for five days of fun, seminars, and safety lessons. Photographs show men drinking cocktails, shooting pool, and playing ping-pong, but the agenda was so packed with presentations that one wonders when the fun was had. One of the first presentations was on the nondiscrimination policy. Since Southall's retirement earlier that year, R. L. Siegel of the Public Relations Department was helping to teach interracial understanding to foremen and managers at Harvester's Central Training School. From this experience, he shared three observations. First, he said that few people at any level of management understood or implemented the nondiscrimination policy. There was a tendency for upper management specifically to say "let Sara do it." Siegel expressed disappointment and spoke about why this was a problem. Second, he observed that once properly educated about the nondiscrimination policy, most men sincerely attempted to apply it. Third, he used the foremen's embarrassing questions about the policy ("If Harvester doesn't discriminate, how come all the Negroes work in laboring positions?") to emphasize again that "there has been a breakdown in assuming administrative responsibility for this policy at some level above the foreman."[36] The presentation was a bit of a scold to those in the room, as well as an acknowledgment that their nondiscrimination policy wasn't being implemented. Siegel went on to give a speech that could have been given by any NAACP activist on how racial fairness was essential to democracy and how too often people opposed legislation but offered no educational or voluntary steps to solve the race problem.

Discussion of the nondiscrimination policy did not end with this presentation. The last day was an open session with Willis allotted to participants' questions, which they had been instructed previously to write down on cards provided at each table. One question was why other nationalities were not covered by the nondiscrimination policy. This led to a lengthy discussion about the difficulties of actually implementing the nondiscrimination policy. Mr. Gruener acknowledged that the promotion of Negroes into supervisory and managerial positions was "a problem."[37] Miss McRae reported that her plant had had four Negro assistant foremen, but that they had been recently relieved

---

[36] "Minutes of the Industrial Relations Managers Conference, French Lick, Indiana, Nov. 8–12, 1948," in International Harvester Company, Corporate Archives Central File (documented series), 1819–1998, McCormick Mss 6Z, M2001-125, Box 7, Folder 25, WHS.

[37] Ibid., 182.

of these positions because of a reduction in the workforce and their length of service in the positions.[38] Mr. Almgren of the Louisville works, however, reported great success with a Negro interviewer in the employment office, who worked closely with the Louisville Urban League to set up fair employment procedures in the company and with the union. Mr. Graham reported his plant had success with Mexicans and Filipinos, but was unsure whether those groups were included in the survey. This return to the original question brought forth many opinions about whether Mexicans should be a special concern, which led in turn to a Mr. Hill suggesting that the Harvester Company discriminated as much against Catholics, Jews, and Mexicans as it did against Negroes. At which point Mr. Gruener said that if that sort of thing was in fact going on, and this was the first he had heard of it, it must be reported to Personnel.

Mr. Willis closed the session by asking how many managers experienced resistance when they attempted to implement the policy. The show of hands led him to conclude they had a large problem.[39] But conferences like this one were an essential first step in familiarizing managers with what had never previously been a problem.

Seniority

One of the most persistent impediments to black advancement was departmental, or unit, seniority, which had the effect of limiting workers' advancement to the departments or units in which they were hired. Since blacks were often hired into low-status departments with few advancement opportunities, any seniority they accrued did not help them advance. With equal opportunity programs, blacks gained access to traditionally white departments but found that their seniority did not transfer and that they had to start over at entry level. Thus many blacks chose not to transfer.[40] In some cases, departmental seniority was designed to keep blacks out of white jobs, but departmental seniority made sense in its own right. It ensured that experience in a particular kind of work, not just length of time, was built into the promotion ladder, and

---

[38] Ibid.

[39] Ibid., 185.

[40] On blacks and seniority, see Judith Stein, *Running Steel, Running America: Race, Economic Policy and the Decline of Liberalism* (Chapel Hill: University of North Carolina, 1998); William B. Gould, *Black Workers in White Unions: Job Discrimination in the United States* (Ithaca, NY: Cornell University Press, 1977); Herbert Hill, *Black Labor and the American Legal System: Race, Work and Law* (Madison: University of Wisconsin Press, 1985), originally published by the Bureau of National Affairs, Inc., (1977); and Ozanne, *The Negro in the Farm and Construction Machinery Industries*, 95–103.

it lessened the competition and scrambling for open positions. Nonetheless, in the late 1960s, courts would find departmental seniority in violation of antidiscrimination laws, forcing companies and unions to adopt the less-efficient, but fairer, policy of plantwide seniority.[41]

Harvester and its unions had early on instituted plantwide seniority in its production units as part of a comprehensive fair employment policy.[42] Thus, for example, when a black worker in the Memphis Works foundry, who had had experience as a welder at another company, applied for an opening in the welding department in 1953, he was awarded the job. Normally, in most companies at this time, a foundry worker would not have been able to transfer his seniority out of the foundry, let alone into a skilled position. The company tried to avert the expected walkout by reminding employees that this man was not only fully qualified to be a welder but that he had seniority ("more seniority in fact than 13 welders in the department"), and that according to the company-union contract, job assignments were to be determined by qualification and seniority.[43] The walkout happened anyway, but after being threatened with the loss of their seniority, the strikers returned to their positions after one week. This policy did not ensure complete fairness with regard to advancement, nor did it help blacks who were not qualified for advanced positions, nor did it prevent workers from harassing the man, but it is an example of the type of structural change that Harvester made to implement its fair employment policy.[44]

The seniority policy was never publicized in any of the articles written about Harvester's fair employment policy. If mentioned by Harvester representatives, seniority was cast as a policy that ensured fair employment. If seniority was practiced fairly and without regard to race, it was assumed to help blacks get ahead. There were examples in which this was the case, including Harvester's three southern plants, where blacks had been integrated into

---

[41] *Quarles v. Philip Morris, Inc.* (E.D. Va., 1968); *United States v. Local 189, United Paperworkers, et al* (E.D. La., 1968).

[42] Ozanne, *A Century of Labor-Management Relations*, 190; and Ozanne, *The Negro in the Farm and Construction Machinery Industries*, 95–102, citing UAW union agreements.

[43] "To All Employees," memo from International Harvester Company, General Office, Chicago, April 23, 1953, in International Harvester Company, Corporate Archives Central File (documented series), 1819-1998, 6Z M2001-125 IH Relationship with African Americans (Materials), 1939–1972, WHS.

[44] Memphis Works Managerial newsletter, April 29, 1953, in International Harvester Company, Corporate Archives Central File (documented series), 1819–1998, 6Z M2001-125 IH Relationship with African Americans (Materials), 1939–1972. The welder's name was George Holloway; see Honey, *Southern Labor and Black Civil Rights*, 275–76.

most (not all) departments from the start and thus were, if qualified, theoretically promotable. It is not difficult to see why this policy would not have been publicized. For one thing, one of the main benefits for employers of hiring and promoting blacks was to promote the idea of merit, especially in contrast to seniority. Although merit could be a factor in instituting a policy of plantwide seniority, the policy validated the worst kind of seniority. This was perhaps the main reason Harvester did not promote this idea: it was not cost effective and thus belied the rhetoric that fair employment was good business. By 1979, International Harvester, which had once been the industry leader, was a shadow of its former self. In explaining part of the company's fall from glory, Judith Marsh writes:

> One top issue, believed by management to be the most costly, concerned a worker's seniority right to transfer from one factory job to another. Though seniority rights differed from plant to plant at Harvester, company workers in general enjoyed more transfer options than their counterparts at [John] Deere or Cat [Caterpillar]. When management made production line changes, turmoil ensued as one employee after another exercised the seniority right to change jobs, bumping other employees with each move. [Personnel officer Warren] Mortonson says: "At Deere and Cat, when you had an open job, you'd made one move and the process was over. At Harvester where he has all these options under the seniority system, you might move a hundred people to get the one job that's vacated to another that's open."[45]

Marsh does not mention that this system had anything to do with Harvester's policy of fair employment, but it did.

Training for Black Workers

If blacks did not have the skills and qualifications for higher-level jobs, the plantwide seniority system could not help them. And few did, especially in the South. John Hope II conducted a random survey of workers at the Louisville works one day in the summer of 1951 and found that while 52 percent of whites had completed high school, only 35.4 percent of blacks had. This general educational deficit often impeded blacks' ability to learn and to qualify for jobs to which their seniority granted them access. The rules of progression required that one had to master the job in a limited time or forfeit the opportunity.[46] In

---

[45] Marsh, *A Corporate Tragedy*, 211.
[46] Hope, *Selected Studies of the Negro Employment in the South*, 114; Ozanne, *The Negro in the Farm and Construction Machinery Industries*, 98–100.

addition, blacks were denied access to southern vocational schools where they might have learned job skills and almost universally excluded from apprenticeship programs that controlled access to skilled trade union jobs.[47]

Harvester offered a variety of on-the-job training courses designed to improve the skills and qualifications of all employees. This was part of its long-term investment in employee training, but it particularly benefited blacks. As John Hope II wrote: "The Harvester plants in the cities studied [Memphis, Louisville, and Evanston] are virtually the only places where Negroes can obtain even the basic machine-shop training necessary for semi-skilled jobs."[48] Harvester training programs did a good job of getting blacks into semiskilled positions. In 1959, black workers in semiskilled positions made up 72.4 percent of the black workers at the Memphis plant and 65.7 percent in the Louisville plant.[49] But the company did less well when it came to training blacks for skilled positions. Only 207 blacks in the entire company were in skilled apprenticeable positions in 1959. The company had its own apprenticeship program, which it encouraged qualified blacks to enter, but as late as 1969, the general educational requirements were too restrictive for most blacks. In 1969, Harvester began a program to prepare black workers for the apprenticeship program.[50]

Together, the centralized record keeping, black recruitment, plantwide seniority, and training programs added up to what we now recognize as "affirmative action," positive actions designed to increase the number of black employees in traditionally white positions. Despite the insistence that fair employment was simply practicing the color-blind principles of democracy, Harvester's pioneering policies confirmed what we now know: that racial integration required more than just the cessation of racial discrimination. It required fundamental changes in personnel management.

Human Relations and Fair Employment

The implementation policies discussed earlier exhibited the hallmarks of a human relations management style. They emphasized objective evaluative

---

[47] Much has been written about the exclusionary policies of apprenticeship programs. See Herbert Hill, "Racial Discrimination in the Nation's Apprenticeship Training Programs," 215–17; Hill, "Racial Inequality in Employment," *Annals of the American Academy of Political and Social Science* 357 (January 1965): 30–47.

[48] Hope, *Selected Studies of the Negro Employment in the South*, 28.

[49] Ozanne, *A Century of Labor-Management Relations*, 190.

[50] Ozanne, *The Negro in the Farm and Construction Machinery Industries*, 63.

criteria, attitude training, community relations, and open communication between different groups. There were two other ways in which fair employment policies reinforced human relations ideas and vice versa. These were the contributions to industrial relations research and the fostering of good union-management relations.

Human relations advocates, whether they were in academia or industrial relations departments, valued, many of them, the idea of using the factory or firm as a "human laboratory" to expand human knowledge. This appealed to the pragmatic sensibility of the social scientist – the study of the "here and now," the real, over the theoretical and the abstract. For industrial relations officers it was a chance to align their profession and the company's reputation with human progress, to transcend the parochial Babbittry with which business was associated. Harvester officials always referred to their fair employment policy as "an experiment" or an "experiment in democracy," as indeed it was. As an experiment, it was the subject of research.

In 1951–52, sociologist John Hope II of Fisk University's Race Relations Department conducted a detailed study of biracial relations in Harvester's southern plants. Published in 1953, the study had been initiated by Will Alexander of the National Planning Association's Committee of the South. *Selected Studies of the Negro Employment in the South: 3 Southern Plants of International Harvester Company* detailed the promises and pitfalls of integrating and training a biracial workforce in southern industry. In conducting the study, Hope worked closely with the Harvester Company's Industrial Relations Department, as well as Sara Southall, who, though retired from Harvester, was able to provide information about the company's history and policies. This was human relations research at its best. Harvester opened its factories to professional researchers for the purpose of attaining "scientific" data that, in this case, would help improve its fair employment policy and race relations. The researchers, in turn, would gain valuable sociological information about industrial race relations from which other researchers could also benefit. Hope was impressed with the way Harvester officials freely admitted where their policy was lacking, as if they really wanted to learn how to make it more effective. They tracked their failures as well as successes. Hope noted the key role that the Industrial Relations Department played not only in implementation but also in terms of research: "The Industrial Relations Department, by providing comprehensive knowledge of the situation, is able to indicate how far the practices of the individual units diverge from policy."[51]

---

[51] Hope, *Selected Studies of the Negro Employment in the South*, 14–15.

Another area of human relations that was reinforced by fair employment policies was labor-management relations. By 1956, the recently merged AFL-CIO officially opposed racial segregation and discrimination. But many of its locals, especially in the South, were divided about the issue. The Memphis Harvester plant's UAW Local 988 was a little less than a third black, but it had an active segregationist faction that repeatedly challenged the UAW's integration policy and Walter Reuther's authority to enforce it. In 1956, this faction staged a wildcat strike when Negro workers were upgraded into "white" positions. As it had in previous situations like this in 1948 and 1953, the UAW fully supported Harvester management's efforts to break up the strike and punish those responsible. In this instance, representatives arrived from Detroit to help Harvester management. Similarly, when Local 988 built a new segregated union hall, UAW vice-president Pat Greenhouse came to Memphis personally to remove the Jim Crow signs. After he left, the union put the signs back up, whereupon Greenhouse and his men returned late one evening, took down the signs, changed the locks, and took over the building.[52]

During all of these internecine battles, UAW leaders worked closely with Harvester officials to protect black workers' contract rights and the principle of equal opportunity. Indeed, vice-president of Industrial Relations Ivan Willis often credited the UAW for its work in upholding Harvester's antidiscrimination policy.[53] This cooperation was all the more remarkable because Harvester officials actually had a very difficult relationship with the UAW during these same years. While collective bargaining disagreements led to several strikes, UAW and Harvester officials were able to find common ground on equal opportunity. Such cooperation, while scarce at Harvester, was the aim of the human relations movement.

Results

Ivan Willis frequently said that talk was cheap, and what mattered in terms of racial progress and good management were the results. The results at Harvester were mixed to disappointing, as Harvester officials readily admitted and puzzled over. The high point of black employment at Harvester was actually in the

[52] Recounted in Ozanne, *A Century of Labor-Management Relations*, 191.

[53] For example, see statement of Ivan L. Willis ... before the Senate Subcommittee on Labor and Labor-Management Relations, April 16, 1952, p. 2, in International Harvester Company, Corporate Archives Central File (documented series), 1819-1998, McCormick Mss 6Z, Box 758, folder 09131, WHS. See Chapter 2: There was a struggle between the communist-led FE and the anticommunist UAW.

Table 5.1. *Percentage of Employees Who Were African American at International Harvester*

	1940	1945	1950	1953	1955	1960
West Pullman	na	7.4	8.9	5.5	12.0	9.4
Wisconsin Steel	na	13.3	17.0	14.4	19.1	13.4
McCormick	10.3	25.3	28.5	13.6	33.0	28.7
Tractor	6.5	17.5	22.4	16.2	19.3	13.3
McCormick Twine	18.8	63.6	64.8	*	*	*
Melrose Park	*	*	12.8	11.8	16.6	9.3
Louisville	*	*	14.1	11.2	20.9	11.9
Memphis	*	*	23.1	26.1	23.0	19.3
Company Total	**4.5**	**11.7**	**12.8**	**9.8**	**14.5**	**9.3**

Note: The asterisk indicates that a plant is not yet opened or closed. That these statistics were even available is due to the company's nondiscrimination policy.
Source: From Robert Ozanne, *A Century of Labor-Management Relations at McCormick and International Harvester* (Madison: University of Wisconsin Press, 1967), 192.

mid-1950s, which were peak years of production for Harvester, as well as the years in which Ivan Willis was the head of Industrial Relations. His successors were less interested in minority employment. In 1955, black employees made up 14.5 percent of Harvester's workforce. At the McCormick plant just outside Chicago's downtown Loop, 33 percent of the workers were black.

In 1951, 5,497 out of International Harvester's 9,494 Negro employees were in semiskilled positions, while 485 were in skilled positions. In 1951, 1,708 had been upgraded to better jobs, while another 102 were classified as "other," which included clerical and supervisory positions.[54] In 1959, there were 207 black workers in skilled apprenticeable occupations throughout the company. These numbers have the feeling of "tokenism," but they become more impressive when compared with other companies in the same industry. The workforce of the Milwaukee-based Allis-Chalmers Manufacturing Company, for instance, was 5.9 percent black in 1959. Its Pittsburgh plant was 3 percent African American. Out of 74 black employees at Pittsburgh, one was in a skilled position.[55] Caterpillar, based in rural Illinois, had a total workforce that was 1.5 percent African American. Still, despite the proactive policies, there were

[54] Statement of Ivan L. Willis... before the Senate Subcommittee on Labor and Labor-Management Relations, April 16, 1952, pp. 4–5, in International Harvester Company, Corporate Archives Central File (documented series), 1819-1998, McCormick Mss 6Z, Box 758, folder 09131, WHS.

[55] Ozanne, *The Negro in the Farm and Construction Machinery Industries*, 27, 38.

Harvester plants and offices in Atlanta, Boston, Philadelphia, St. Louis, and Kansas City that would not be described as "integrated."[56]

Harvester's rate of black employment and advancement slowed in the 1960s and 1970s, despite the civil rights movement and the company's exuberant commitment to Plans for Progress. Harvester employed 6,729 black employees in 1964 (compared with 9,494 in 1951), which was 9.7 percent of the total employment. Of these, 191 were in salaried positions, only 30 in apprenticeable skilled trades (journeymen), 8 in skilled trades, and 8 in managerial positions.[57] The decline in black employment was due to automation, plant closings, and the company's declining profitability. The plant closings had an adverse effect on black employment because the company closed the older, less-efficient Chicago plants, which had employed the highest numbers of African Americans. McCormick Twine, where blacks represented more than half of the total workforce, was closed in 1953. The historic McCormick plant, built in 1871 and 37 percent black in 1960, closed in 1961. The Tractor plant, 35 percent black, was closed in 1971. Some historians have suggested that companies moved to new suburban facilities in the 1960s to find cheaper, whiter, nonunionized labor.[58] In Harvester's case, it seems more accurately described as a quest for newer, more efficient facilities. As Judith Marsh indicates, Harvester held on to the old McCormick plant much longer than it should have, in part because of its sentimental place in company history.[59]

Harvester gave workers from the closed plants preferential treatment over new hires at other plants and allowed them to take nine years of seniority with them, but there were instances when the company and the UAW violated the spirit of the historic fair employment policy. One of the newer Harvester plants to which workers from the closed Tractor plant might transfer was Hough, located in the western, all-white suburbs of Chicago. The UAW was trying to unionize the workers at Hough. Hough workers were reluctant to accept the union because they did not want to have to accept Tractor transferees who had more seniority under UAW contracts than they did. Ozanne explains what happened: "After the loss of two NLRB elections, the UAW requested

[56] Memo, March 12 1964, in International Harvester Company, Corporate Archives Central File (documented series), 1819–1998, McCormick Mss 6Z, Box 981, Folder 18494, WHS. Robert Ozanne's study ignored these offices and focused solely on the four Chicago-area plants and three new southern plants.

[57] Ibid.

[58] Jefferson Cowie, *Capital Moves: RCA's Seventy Year Quest for Cheap Labor* (New York: New Press, 2001; originally published in 1999).

[59] Marsh, *A Corporate Tragedy*, 111–12. Marsh quotes one McCormick veteran: "Five story buildings just don't lend themselves to efficient production methods. A lot of our floors wouldn't support forklift trucks."

that Harvester suspend the policy permitting employees to carry seniority if offered a job at Hough. Harvester consented."[60] Harvester might reasonably have declined the UAW's request and prevented unionization, but it did not.

Despite the high hopes for "biracial industrialism" that had accompanied the opening of the Memphis plant in 1948, that plant was largely segregated by 1969. The site of several wildcat strikes and a segregationist faction in the UAW local, this plant had always resisted the company's fair employment policy of the company and its parent union. Of three hundred skilled tradesmen in 1969, only one was black. Out of one hundred welders, three were black. There were six black machine operators and only three black foremen. There were no black apprentices, and a majority of the foundry workers were black.[61] Thus, Harvester's experiment in biracial industrialism in a southern city bears all of the earmarks of a failure. Similarly, in 1982 researchers found that International Harvester had done a poor job recruiting blacks (or women) into professional positions.[62]

In the end, International Harvester's pioneering fair employment policy failed to achieve full integration. Without McCormick, Southall, and Ivan K. Willis, the historic fair employment policy seemed to peter out. In the 1960s, Harvester's leadership chose to ride on the reputation for racial fairness Southall and Willis had built, rather than striving to live up to it. The value of Harvester's experiment for us resides less in its ultimate results than in its early efforts. The industrial relations officers at Harvester identified structural barriers to black employment and advancement and developed concrete measures to overcome them. These measures became standard practices in the era of affirmative action. Their training and personnel development programs introduced thousands of white workers, supervisors, and managers to the idea that discrimination was wrong, that whites did not always recognize it, and that blacks were capable and reliable co-workers. The discussions that occurred in these programs were a necessary, first component of the process of racial integration in a historically segregated nation. Each discussion familiarized managers and supervisors with the reasons for and obstacles to integration. Each discussion further solidified the idea that discrimination was a problem, until the problem was normalized, named, and in the process of being resolved, which was a far cry from the nonacknowledgment of discrimination that had existed earlier, when discrimination was not even an agenda item.

---

[60] Ozanne, *The Negro in the Farm and Construction Machinery Industries,* 69.

[61] Ibid., 85.

[62] "Synopsis International Harvester," in Wharton School Industrial Research Unit Records, Series IV, Box 20, Hagley Museum and Library, Wilmington, Delaware (hereafter HML).

Pitney-Bowes

Another, smaller company that actively pursued integration was the Stamford, Connecticut–based Pitney-Bowes Company, a manufacturer of postage meters. In 1963, the company employed 2,300 employees in Stamford and another 2,500 in sales and service branches across the country. It too was a company steeped in the human relations philosophy. Stuart Chase, the great popularizer of "human relations" in the mainstream press, wrote the foreword to William Cahn's fawning book about the company, comparing its experiments in human relations to those of the Hawthorne Plant.[63] In addition to familiar welfare capitalism programs such as pension plans, health insurance, profit sharing, paid vacation, sick leave, and competitive wages, the company implemented a full roster of human relations programs. It had a communications program, whereby top management informed employees of all decisions. Speaking before the American Management Association in 1950, President Walter H. Wheeler, Jr., explained, "The more we trust employees with the facts of our business, the more they are inclined to accept our judgment and decisions concerning those facts ... by consulting with employees on all our problems we don't risk losing management's prerogatives, but actually restore their faith in them."[64] The company held annual "jobholder meetings," modeled after stockholder meetings, in which employees were able to question company officials about policies, product design, training, or whatever was on their minds. The company rewarded the best employee suggestions for more efficient production methods. The Council of Personnel Relations, which consisted of representatives from management and employees, had as its aim "to build a spirit of mutual confidence between employees and management, in order that both may benefit from maximum organization efficiency and job satisfaction."[65] It was not a company union, Wheeler insisted, but rather a system to guarantee communications between management and employees. In 1950, Wheeler began distributing a monthly bulletin called *The Management Newsletter* to the Pitney-Bowes management staff – executives, foremen, and supervisors. The purpose of the bulletin was to keep managers apprised of company activities and occurrences. It was also a way to disseminate the

---

[63] William Cahn, *The Story of Pitney-Bowes* (New York: Harper, 1961); see also Stuart Chase, "Communication – Up, Down, and Sideways," *Reader's Digest* (September 1952).

[64] Quoted in Cahn, *The Pitney-Bowes Story*, 169.

[65] Ibid., 174; see also "Case history #1, Pitney-Bowes, Inc. Teamwork through Two-Way Communications," in Communications File, Pitney-Bowes, Collection 5583/2, Box 51, Kheel Center for Labor-Management Documentation and Archives, Cornell University, Ithaca, New York (hereafter Kheel Center)

teachings of Elton Mayo and other human relations experts, as the first bulletin indicates.[66]

Unlike Harvester and most other industrial firms in the Stamford area, Pitney-Bowes was not unionized, and many critics attributed its nonunionized state to its excessively generous employee benefits and human relations tricks. Wheeler, who was variously president, CEO, and chairman of the board from 1938 to 1971, took a mildly jocular attitude toward these critics, insisting his company was not antiunion, that the employee policies were simply "good business," that he personally had nothing against unions but that unions were not appropriate in all cases. If Pitney-Bowes employees wanted a union, then he would follow the necessary procedures to ensure that organized labor had a fair hearing. In 1946, the International Association of Machinists (AFL) took Wheeler up on his challenge and began a campaign to organize Pitney-Bowes. As recounted in William Cahn's *The Story of Pitney-Bowes*, Wheeler accommodated the organizers' attempts to reach employees, allegedly protecting their freedom of speech and even offering to debate a union representative (who declined).[67] He used his vast communication apparatus to combat rumors, even antiunion rumors, which lent an air of objectivity to the endeavor. He agreed to an election to determine whether the IAM would represent Pitney-Bowes employees, portraying his actions as generous and open when in fact he was merely following the law. The employees voted against the union. Wheeler had suffocated the organizers with openness, fairness, and communication. These techniques would later be associated with General Electric's Lemuel Boulware, who would claim them as his own.[68] A 1949 opinion poll of Pitney-Bowes employees conducted with the help of the Tuck School of Business Administration found that 90 percent of the employees said "yes" to the question, "Do you believe that the security of your job depends on the company's ability to operate at a fair profit?" As authors sympathetic to the company's human relations program commented, "attitudes like this don't just happen; they have to be built by continual effort."[69]

---

[66] *The Management Newsletter*, June 1950, p. 2, in Communications File, Pitney-Bowes, Collection 5583/2, Box 51, Kheel Center.

[67] Cahn, *The Pitney-Bowes Story*, 184–87.

[68] See Elizabeth Fones-Wolf, *Selling Free Enterprise: The Business Assault on Labor and Liberalism, 1945–1960* (Urbana: University of Illinois Press, 1994), and Herbert R. Northrup, *Boulwarism: The Labor Relations Policies of the General Electric Company* (Ann Arbor: Bureau of Industrial Relations, Graduate School of Business Administration, University of Michigan, 1964).

[69] "Case history #1, Pitney-Bowes, Inc. Teamwork through Two-Way Communications," in Communications File, Pitney-Bowes, Collection 5583/2, Box 51, at Kheel Center.

Walter Wheeler was perhaps the only executive to embrace "proportional hiring" openly during an era of color-blind ascendancy and quota fear. Wheeler had become acquainted with the problem of black employment during World War II when he was the regional director of the War Production Board. Part of his responsibility in that position was to break down prejudice and convince manufacturers to make full use of all labor. When he noticed that his own company wasn't hiring minorities, he recalled that he left an "impatient memo," instructing the executive vice-president to "determine the proportion of all minorities in Stamford to the total population of Stamford, and begin hiring minority group members until we could at least match the same minority ratio within the ranks of our employees."[70] When he did not hear back, he sent another memo, "Are we carrying our quota of colored people at the plant?"[71] The executive vice-president gathered the necessary statistics and pointed out the problems in hiring what would have been sixty-one Negroes and eighty-two Jews, not the least was having to release current employees to accommodate the new ones. Wheeler agreed that the process would have to be gradual but still insisted on a concrete target objective, "and the apportionment of the population is about as good an index as I think can be found."[72] This frankness about quotas, this refusal to partake of the ascendant color-blind norm of the time, was unusual, but it is unclear whether it made the policy any more effective.

Like Harvester, the Pitney-Bowes' "merit employment" policy (as it was called) emphasized indoctrination of the supervisors and a close relationship to the local Urban League. Charged with implementing the policy, vice-president of Personnel Joseph J. Morrow followed the available stock of human relations literature, strategically placing overqualified black employees in visible, traditionally white positions. This would later become known as "tokenism," but in the 1950s, it was called "pioneering." Despite Wheeler's openness to quotas, the company's general "merit employment" policy emphasized qualifications and merit.[73] Unlike Harvester, Pitney-Bowes was not unionized and thus did not have to worry about seniority policies. Also unlike Harvester, the company apparently did not keep statistics on its employees' race and ethnicity (or at

---

[70] U.S. Congress, Senate, Committee on Labor and Public Welfare, Subcommittee on Employment and Manpower, Hearings *Equal Employment*, 88 Congress, 1st sess., July 24–August 20, 1963, p. 209; the story is also told in Cahn, *The Story of Pitney-Bowes*, 204–5.

[71] Cahn, *The Story of Pitney-Bowes*, 204. Cahn provides no citation. The material seems to have come from interviews with Wheeler and other Pitney-Bowes personnel. Presumably Pitney-Bowes approved the book's publication.

[72] Ibid., 205.

[73] Described in ibid., 191.

least did not publicly admit to it).[74] According to Morrow and Wheeler, white resistance to the policy had been minimal and manageable. By August 1963, Morrow was able to report to the U.S. Senate Subcommittee on Employment and Manpower, the company had "employed skilled Negroes in practically every area of our business: in the plant, in engineering, in accounting, in public relations, and in secretarial positions."[75] Morrow estimated that 5 percent of its 2,300 employees at the Stamford plant were black, noting also that blacks actually made up 9 percent of Stamford's population.

As we saw in Chapter 2, Joseph J. Morrow was a vocal proponent of fair employment. Morrow had the same sort of missionary zeal that Ivan Willis had, but while Willis opposed fair employment legislation, Morrow did not. Both Morrow and Wheeler testified in support of what would become Title VII of the 1964 Civil Rights Act. Wheeler explained to Congress that he had previously thought that voluntary measures would be enough but that turned out not to be the case: "Only a Federal law, I am convinced, can accomplish in the field of fair employment what must be done, and done now, for all American Negroes, and other minorities."[76] His company was one of the few that openly regarded African Americans as a group needing special attention rather than individuals to be treated the same as others.

In all of the voluminous materials the company's public relations department produced for employees, however, there is actually very little about the company's fair employment policy. The company "opened its books" to employees, reporting sales, profits, liabilities, and projections to its employees. It explained in great detail its communications program and human relations policies. But no mention of the fair employment policy was made until December 1963, when Pitney-Bowes president John O. Nicklis explained his preferential hiring policy (to be discussed later). This is noteworthy because Pitney-Bowes's fair employment policy was the subject of many articles and studies in the 1950s. The silence could reflect the human relations dictum to treat fair employment as "natural" and unnoteworthy, "the way things were." And yet photographs from company picnics, art shows, farewell parties, baseball clubs, charity dinners, which were regularly featured in the company

---

[74] See Morrow's testimony in U.S. Congress, Senate, Committee on Labor and Public Welfare, Subcommittee on Employment and Manpower, Hearings *Equal Employment*, 88 Congress, 1st sess., July 24–August 20, 1963, p. 215.

[75] U.S. Congress, Senate, Committee on Labor and Public Welfare, Subcommittee on Employment and Manpower, Hearings *Equal Employment*, 88 Congress, 1st sess., July 24–August 20, 1963, p. 213.

[76] United States. Congress, Senate, Committee on Labor and Public Welfare, Subcommittee on Employment and Manpower, Hearings *Equal Employment*, 88 Congress, 1st sess., July 24–August 20, 1963, p. 211. Morrow repeated the support in his testimony on p. 214.

magazine, show what appear to be white people having fun with other white people. Pitney-Bowes's black employees are scattered in photos of the workplace – workplace meetings, office operations, election teams – but do not appear in photographs of social events.[77] Of course, no one had ever promised social integration. The promise was economic integration. In September 1963, the employee newsletter *PB News* featured a short article on the two dozen PB employees who participated in the March on Washington. The lead sentence was, "The spirit of the marchers was very good; there was much singing and things were always in control."[78]

Shortly thereafter, in December 1963, Pitney-Bowes president Nicklis announced that the company would adopt a preferential hiring plan in favor of Negroes. The stepped-up plan was a response to President Kennedy's assassination. The announcement was made not at the Pitney-Bowes factory in Stamford but at the National Social Welfare Assembly. In the speech, Nicklis linked "two hundred years of outright slavery and another hundred years of discrimination" with the "dark horror" of Kennedy's assassination and called for a purge of the nation's soul: "Now is the time to do the purging, and the Negro and his struggle for justice and opportunity should be the place to begin."[79] A week later, Nicklis was forced to clarify what he had meant, in a statement that was published in both the *New York Times* and the *PB News*. The company would not choose a candidate because of his color, he said, but rather it would actively "find and employ more Negroes." Nonetheless, he maintained that "equal opportunity" was not enough. Discrimination in employment and education meant that blacks were unable to compete on equal terms with whites, even if given the opportunity. Thus, Pitney-Bowes would relax test and experience requirements for blacks and give them special training.[80] While Harvester continued to emphasize individual opportunity and color-blind policies, Pitney-Bowes began to justify its policy in terms of black disadvantage. In an interview with *Business Management*, Nicklis tried again to defend the policy, likening blacks to the handicapped, "For years ... we have employed and trained physically handicapped workers. No one considers this discrimination or preferential hiring. It is just good corporate citizenship. The Negro is handicapped by his color. If he is to compete equally he

---

[77] See Pitney-Bowes publications in Communications File, Pitney-Bowes, Collection 5583/2, Box 51, at Kheel Center.

[78] "Marchers Recall Serenity, Discipline," *PB News*, September 16, 1963, in Communications File, Pitney-Bowes, Collection 5583/2, Box 51, at Kheel Center.

[79] "Company Is Giving Negroes Priority," *New York Times*, December 4, 1963; "Pitney-Bowes Announces New Negro Preferential Hiring Plan," *Chicago Defender*, December 5, 1963, p. 3.

[80] "Negro Job Policy Tied to Training," *New York Times*, December 13, 1963, 28.

needs special consideration, at least for a time."[81] It was a frankly paternalistic approach to the problem, from a frankly paternalistic company, but it would eventually be the way corporations came to understand the magnitude of what they needed to do.

Analysis and Conclusion

The important point to take from these two case studies is not how effective the fair employment policies actually were but rather how proactive and systemic they were. These were not merely color-blind policies of nondiscrimination. The companies' industrial relations staff identified barriers to black employment and advancement, changed standard procedures, adopted new ones, and attempted to convince the workplace community to accept it. Even though some presidents and chief executives liked to believe that they could single-handedly change the way things were done, the human relations experts were right: change had to be engineered. And if the field of human relations was about anything, it was about social engineering. In this sense, the structural position of industrial relations was conducive to its mission. As Willis constantly reminded his staff, they acted only in an advisory capacity. This put a premium on methods that could persuade and convince. In persuading supervisors to implement policies, they hoped to engineer a change in attitudes, to get supervisors to internalize the thinking behind the policies. It is difficult to measure the extent to which they succeeded. Southall was fond of reporting instances of foremen who had changed their minds about discrimination, but she understood that this was purely anecdotal.

International Harvester and Pitney-Bowes were pioneers in the area of interracial education; their training programs provided models for other companies that integrated their firms in the 1960s and 1970s. Workplace training sessions became one of the few places where white Americans were forced to think and talk about race, discrimination, and prejudice with their peers. They were places where white people in positions of authority introduced, justified, and championed a new social norm of racial tolerance and fairness.

Industrial relations personnel at Harvester and Pitney-Bowes never placed "education" above concrete policies. The policies came first; the education was necessary to convince supervisors and employees to comply with the policies. As state fair employment agencies were learning, legislation was necessary to

---

[81] "One Company's Answer to the Negro Job Problem," *Business Management* (February 1964): 42–45.

effect change, but because intentional discrimination was almost impossible to prove in court, the law would only really work if those responsible for ensuring compliance believed in it.[82] To the extent that neither Harvester nor Pitney-Bowes were as successful as they had aspired to be in promoting blacks into traditionally white positions, it was the educational part of their endeavor that failed them. The policies after all became the standard policies by which workplaces were eventually integrated. Workable policies were in place. Convincing supervisors and managers to follow them was the difficult part.

Could it be the case that the emphasis placed on human relations, cooperation, and workplace harmony prevented industrial relations officers from advocating a more strong-armed, top-down approach to enforcing company policies? After all, in the face of urban riots, boycotts, and the Equal Employment Opportunity Commission in the late 1960s, employers were able to use their authority to increase the number of black employees and promotions. But that was precisely because the problem in the 1960s was urgent and horrifying for whites in a way that it simply was not in the 1950s. Moreover, by the time the riots began to seem epidemic, by the time the boycotts became more regular, industrial relations staffs, compliance committees, and state fair employment agencies had in varying degrees already primed employers and employees for the changes that were being demanded of them.

Another observation to be taken from these two cases is how utterly they fail to conform to our assumptions about sincerity, effectiveness, and political stance. The Pitney-Bowes executives openly embraced proportional representation and what became known as "targets." They supported fair employment legislation. They were active in race relations organizations. And yet their rate of black employment remained at 5 percent. Harvester executives, however, opposed proportional representation and publicly touted a color-blind vision of integration. They opposed fair employment legislation. Yet their policies, particularly the centralized hiring, maintenance of racial statistics, and plantwide seniority – none of which were used by Pitney-Bowes – were more sweeping in terms of on-the-ground change than Pitney-Bowes's policies. During its peak years, Harvester's rate of black employment stood at 14 percent; in particular plants, it averaged 25–30 percent.

Both companies had an uneasy relationship to the labor movement. One would not call either company "union friendly." Both used human relations

---

[82] On the difficulties of proving violations of state fair employment legislation, see Paul Moreno, *From Direct Action to Affirmative Action: Fair Employment Law and Policy in America, 1933–72* (Baton Rouge: Louisiana State University Press, 1997), and Michael Sovern, *Legal Restraints on Racial Discrimination in Employment* (New York: Twentieth Century Fund, 1966).

programs to create more harmonious labor relations and weaken workers' reliance on the labor movement. Harvester's attempt to stave off unionism failed, but Pitney-Bowes seems to have succeeded at the endeavor. Not surprisingly, given their labor trouble, Harvester's executives were active in the National Association of Manufacturers. But so too was Walter Wheeler. Enlightened racial employment policies did not correspond to enlightened positions on unions or government intervention. Indeed, in the 1950s, those companies that practiced fair employment had problematic labor relations from the labor movement's perspective.

Finally, it has been made clear that these two companies had particularly strong industrial relations departments. These were companies that for whatever reason (labor trouble or personal conviction on the part of executives) had invested in the work of industrial relations officers. Again, it is no accident that the people who pioneered workplace integration – Fowler McCormick, Sara Southall, Ivan Willis, Walter Wheeler, and Joseph Morrow – were advocates and practitioners of human relations style of management. McCormick and Wheeler were particularly important in this regard, since their presidential leadership legitimated the work of industrial relations staff in their companies.

PART II: COLOR-CONSCIOUS ASCENDANCY, 1961–1990

6   How Compliance Became Voluntarism

Our experience in the recent hearings on equal pay for equal work legislation has convinced us that the only way to approach issues of this kind is to improve management performance to the point where it can be defended on the basis of factual accomplishment.

National Association of Manufacturers memo, 1948[1]

There is something about the threat of prosecution that seems to make voluntary programs work much better.

Ray Marshall, 1965[2]

As pressure from civil rights groups and the federal government increased in the late 1950s and early 1960s, executives at the largest corporations began integrating their firms. But they insisted that their actions were voluntary. "Our action was not dictated by government pressure or by a desire to be well-regarded, but simply as recognition of an obligation to do what is right," said General Electric president Frank L. Borch about GE's nondiscrimination policy.[3] Civil rights activists and their allies, as well as historians, mocked the business community's pretensions of voluntarism. To do what laws required

---

[1] Carrol E. French to Noel Sargent, April 5, 1948, in National Association of Manufacturers, Records, 1895–1990 (hereafter NAM Records), Series 7, Box 135, Hagley Museum and Library, Wilmington, Delaware (hereafter HML).

[2] Quoted in Stephen M. Gelber, *Black Men and Businessmen: The Growing Awareness of a Social Responsibility* (Port Washington, NY: Kennicat Press, 1974), 181.

[3] *Community and Government Relations Bulletin*, for Circulation among General Electric Managers, April 17, 1964, quote on p. 2, in NAM Records, Series 7, Box 135, HML.

one to do anyway could hardly be regarded as voluntary.[4] There was, however, an element of truth in businessmen's claim of voluntarism.

The various state agencies charged with enforcing state antidiscrimination laws were notoriously weak and uncertain of their authority. Constitutional concerns constrained the presidential contract compliance committees. In addition, both the state agencies and the compliance committees had difficulty defining or even identifying discrimination. It turned out that discrimination was not always the result of individual discriminatory acts that could be indicted, punished, and ended but rather was the manifestation of long-standing employment traditions and practices that had (often) little to do with race and for which no one person or action was responsible. There were of course industries and unions (especially in the South) whose policies and practices were explicitly exclusionary, but these were relatively easy to prosecute under antidiscrimination laws compared with those firms outside the South that had antidiscrimination policies on the books but few blacks on salary. Even if state agencies had had more power, they still would have had difficulty proving when discrimination had occurred in most industries. Moreover, state agencies had found that accusations of "discrimination" insulted executives and made them less willing to work with the agency. The agencies found it more useful to work with the company to "adjust" its hiring and promotion practices to attain the desired result: the hiring and promotion of black employees into traditionally white positions. Although charged with ending discrimination, state agencies and compliance committees instead sought to persuade companies to take positive actions "voluntarily" to recruit and train black employees.

As more companies cooperated with state Fair Employment Practices Committees (FEPCs) and later the new President's Committee on Equal Employment Opportunity (PCEEO), the business community came to regard its efforts as "voluntary." This chapter will demonstrate that in the face of weak laws, corporations played a significant role in defining compliance and integration. What civil rights activists had long believed was to some degree true: the cooperative, voluntary, approach to contract compliance allowed large employers to negotiate their own compliance standards.[5] But while this has normally been

---

[4] See, for instance, Hugh Davis Graham, *The Civil Rights Era: Origins and Development of National Policy, 1960–1972* (New York: Oxford University Press, 1990), 52–53; Michael Sovern, *Legal Restraints on Racial Discrimination in Employment* (New York: Twentieth Century Fund, 1966); Gelber, *Black Men and Businessmen,* 141–42; and Nancy MacLean, *Freedom Is Not Enough: The Opening of the American Workplace* (New York: Russell Sage Foundation; Cambridge, MA: Harvard University Press, 2006), 44, 97–98.

[5] Sociologists Frank Dobbin and John Sutton have made a similar argument with regard to post-1964 enforcement. Dobbin and Sutton, "The Strength of the Weak State: The Rights Revolution

presented as a negative, I will argue that it indicates employers' role in devising, using, and testing wide-ranging tools for integration that became known as "affirmative action."

The State FEPCs

By 1964, twenty-eight states and fifty municipalities had passed laws prohibiting racial and religious employment discrimination and created some kind of FEPC to enforce them. The first and eventually the most successful of these state committees was the New York State Commission Against Discrimination (NYSCAD), created in 1945. Because the NYSCAD became the model not only for other state FEPCs but also the Equal Employment Opportunity Commission (EEOC), we will use it as a case study, keeping in mind that variations existed among the various state and municipal FEPCs.[6]

The NYSCAD consisted of five salaried members and had the power to create rules and policies, to investigate discrimination complaints, to conduct public hearings, to secure legal testimony, and to order offenders to cease and desist.[7] Complaints were initiated by individuals. If investigation yielded evidence of probable cause, the commissioner attempted to persuade the delinquent company to eliminate discrimination through a process called conciliation. This provision was designed to alleviate businesses' fears of police-state tactics, but it was also in keeping with interracial education theories that most people were unaware of discrimination, and if it was shown to them, they would stop such behavior, especially when it was made clear that it was punishable by law.[8] If the company was uncooperative, the commissioner could

and the Rise of Human Resources Management Divisions," *American Journal of Sociology* 104, no. 2 (September 1998): 441–76.

[6] On the creation of state FEPCs, see the still relevant Paul Norgren and Samuel Hill, *Toward Fair Employment* (New York: Columbia University Press, 1964); Herbert Garfinkel, *When Negroes March: The March on Washington Movement in the Organizational Politics for FEPC* (Glencoe, IL: Free Press, 1959); and Louis Ruchames, *Race, Jobs and Politics: The Story of FEPC* (New York: Columbia University Press, 1953). See also Graham, *The Civil Rights Era,* 19–24. On the creation of the NYSCAD, see Paul Moreno, *From Direct Action to Affirmative Action: Fair Employment Law and Policy in America, 1933–72* (Baton Rouge: Louisiana State University Press, 1997), and Anthony Chen, "The Hitlerian Rule of Quotas: Racial Conservatism and the Politics of Fair Employment in New York State, 1941–45," *Journal of American History* (March 2006): 1238–64.

[7] Moreno, *From Direct Action to Affirmative Action,* 109, and Sovern, *Legal Restraints on Racial Discrimination in Employment,* 20.

[8] Moreno, *From Direct Action to Affirmative Action,* 109–10. See also John P. Dean and Alex Rosen, *A Manual for Inter-Group Relations* (Chicago: University of Chicago Press, 1955), and George B. DeHuzzer, comp., *Anatomy of Racial Intolerance* (New York: H. W. Wilson, 1946).

hold a public hearing in which it presented its case against the company and ordered it to cease and desist, hire, reinstate, or promote the complainant, possibly with back pay. Commission rulings were subject to judicial review, but the courts were directed to construe the findings liberally and usually deferred to the commission.[9]

Like all of the state FEPCs, the New York commission disappointed the groups that had supported it. From 1945 to 1961 the commission handled 6,616 cases. Probable cause for the complaint was found in only 20 percent of these. Out of these 1,365, only 5 respondents were brought to public hearings, and 2 were settled before the hearings.[10] The NYSCAD preferred conciliation to confrontation, even if conciliation processes took several years to complete. The settlements reached in the 1,365 cases where probable cause was found required only that the company hang the commission's poster in a visible place, inform its personnel staff of the law, and uphold the law in the future. Sometimes the company had to consider the complainant for another position or change its recruitment sources. Researcher Michael Sovern sarcastically concluded, "Others will lightly assume the risk that one day they too will have to post posters, issue instructions, and promise to do what the law requires them to do anyway."[11]

By 1956, even the courts were questioning whether the NYSCAD was fully enforcing the antidiscrimination law. The NYSCAD had dismissed a case brought by a black pilot against Pan Am. Pan Am said it had refused to hire the complainant because of his erratic work record; the complainant felt it was because of his race.[12] The complainant appealed to the New York Supreme Court to compel the NYSCAD to take his case. The judge ruled that the court had no jurisdiction until the NYSCAD issued an order for a public hearing. The appellate division upheld the judge's decision, but there were two dissenters, who thought that the NYSCAD should have taken the case on the basis of Pan Am's lack of black pilots. Writes historian Paul Moreno, "In dismissing the complaint the commission had discarded its 'teeth,' and the dissenters regarded this as 'an improvident exercise of discretion and was arbitrary, capricious, and unreasonable.'"[13] Critics recognized the real difficulties the

---

[9] Moreno, *From Direct Action to Affirmative Action*, 110, 133–34.

[10] Sovern, *Legal Restraints on Racial Discrimination in Employment*, 48. On civil rights groups' disappointment with NYSCAD, see also Moreno, *From Direct Action to Affirmative Action*, 117, 156–57; and Martha Biondi, *To Stand and Fight: The Struggle for Civil Rights in New York City* (Cambridge, MA: Harvard University Press, 2003).

[11] Sovern, *Legal Restraints on Racial Discrimination in Employment*, 15.

[12] This story is recounted in Moreno, *From Direct Action to Affirmative Action*, 132–34.

[13] Moreno, *From Direct Action to Affirmative Action*, 133, citing *Jeanpierre v. Arbury*, 1 R.R.L.R. 685 (1956); 162 N.Y.S. 2d 506 (1957).

commissioners faced in carrying out their mission, but given the power the law actually gave them, it was hard not to criticize their apparent unwillingness to use it.

But NYSCAD officials knew what they were doing. The law gave them power, true, but the epistemological and legal murkiness of "discrimination" made it almost impossible to prove in court. Employers could always find some reason other than race for an apparent act of discrimination. Most people had so internalized racial stereotypes that they could truthfully deny they had acted on account of someone's race. In most cases, moreover, standard employment practices that begot discriminatory patterns were not considered discrimination. It was, for instance, legal to recruit from existing employees' families and friends if the intent were to save time and money but illegal if the intent were to maintain an all-white labor force.[14] But how could the commissioners prove the thoughts in a respondent's head? The law was futile in proving something that could not even be objectively recognized. The concept of discrimination was troublesome even within the agency. To stem "tokenism," commissioners told companies that hiring minorities was not evidence of nondiscrimination and indeed may even constitute discrimination, but in their own notes, they counted minorities as evidence of a company's compliance. The agency was flummoxed about how to encourage companies to keep track of applicants' race without noting it on the application or in the interview, which violated the law it was supposed to enforce.[15] Thus while NYSCAD was endowed with great powers, those powers were inadequate for charting the new legal and psychological territory that was necessary for integration to occur smoothly and beneficially.

Instead, NYSCAD officials focused their efforts on adjusting attitudes without rousing resistance. They sought to persuade rather than confront, which is why critics believed they were soft, timid, afraid of management. Such was not the case. They sought something more than mere compliance with the law. It was not enough for managers to comply with an ill-defined law. If they did not agree with it, compliance would be ineffective in the long-term goal of integrating America's workforce. Given the problems of adjustment and

---

[14] Sovern, *Legal Restraints on Racial Discrimination in Employment*, 43.

[15] For instance, Commissioner Simon notes that American Tobacco had hired six Negro girls in the steno pool and two Negro men in maintenance as evidence of its "cooperation." *John A. Williams v. American Tobacco Co.* (1951) in New York Division of Human Rights, Master Case Files for 1951–1968, New York State Archives, Albany. Whether to allow the maintenance of racial statistics was a contested issue in the civil rights community, and the prohibition on statistics collecting was detrimental to enforcement. See Graham, *The Civil Rights Era*, 60–62, 199.

capacity for misunderstanding that integration brought with it, it was essential that this law be followed in spirit, not just in letter. Studies had found that mere compliance with the law led to unsatisfactory experiences because employers hired a minimum number of "tokens" and did nothing to help their workforces adjust to a new reality of integration.[16] Like enlightened industrial relations officers, NYSCAD officials wanted managers who understood the ambiguities of racial readjustment, who would consult experts and take the extra time and effort to ensure that the experience of integration would be smooth. They sought to compel company managers to internalize the spirit of the law, to see the world as they did, to use their authority to convince others. NYSCAD officials used their access to company officials not to berate but rather to collect data, listen to employers' concerns, persuade, and counsel. Requiring company officials to hang the FEPC poster seems laughably mild. But employers hung the posters – to show their cooperation – and little by little the idea that racial discrimination was somehow wrong was disseminated throughout the workplace. Posters, pamphlets, and visits from state agents all drew attention to discrimination as a phenomenon, thereby lifting it out of the unexamined, assumed status it had long held in American life.

Theirs was not a puny exercise in interracial education, which they themselves dismissed, but rather a grand scheme of social engineering. In a 1956 article, "Social Science and the Desegregation Process," sociologist Herbert Blumer criticized those who felt that to end segregation and discrimination, one first had to change the conditions and attitudes that created it.[17] Blumer said that could take forever. He suggested instead that society needed to exert a strong countervailing influence or pressure on those people whose decisions upheld segregation.[18] Such pressure, in the form of laws or regulations, detached white people – employers, for instance – from their own peer group and forced them to consider the pressures of the "transcending group," represented by the civil rights community and its government allies. The benefit of this, in Blumer's eyes, was that it took the argument away from the emotional issue of race and made it about "the validity of *applying* the transcending legal or moral standard" or, in other words, following the law. The emphasis on the law short-circuited disruptive conflicts over the irrational, phantom phenomenon of race. Researcher Paul Norgren found that complying with the law was a primary reason, second only to labor shortages, in companies' decisions

[16] Paul Norgren et al., *Employing the Negro in American Industry: A Study of Management Practices* (New York: Industrial Relations Counselors, 1959), 49.

[17] Herbert Blumer, "Social Science and Desegregation," *Annals of the Academy of Political and Social Science* (March 1956): 137–43.

[18] Ibid., 140.

to hire blacks. He quoted one executive, "American companies are basically law-abiding; they may seek favorable interpretations of the law, but essentially executives want their companies to be good citizens."[19] Blumer was essentially making the social science case for legislation in social/moral matters. But the useful point for our purposes is his idea of a countervailing, "transcending group." In order for this strategy to work, employers had to first accept the validity of the so-called transcending group, in this case, the state antidiscrimination agencies. The validity and authority of the state agencies, however, were under constant challenge and scrutiny.

What appeared to be weakness and ineffectiveness was in fact an attempt by the NYSCAD to make itself a legitimate countervailing force or, in Blumer's words, the "transcending group." This is why NYSCAD commissioner Elmer Carter counted success in terms of winning businessmen's acceptance and cooperation. A former editor of the Urban League's *Opportunity*, Carter understood both the legal limitations of the Law Against Discrimination and the suspicion with which his agency was regarded. Given such circumstances, he wrote, conciliation was the most feasible method to attain the commission's goal: "Any other approach, emphasis on compulsion, swift citation to public hearing, would unquestionably have inspired renewed opposition and the search for vexatious legal barriers to hamper its administration."[20]

Critics were outraged by the NYSCAD's small number of "probable cause" rulings, but the commission had at least two reasons for not pursuing "probable cause." First, there was always a "legitimate" reason, usually lack of qualification or seniority, for an individual's failure to be hired or promoted. By acknowledging this, the commission showed employers that it was reasonable and objective and not overstepping its charge or rewriting the law. Second, more often than not, commission members treated individual complaints as a pretext for collecting comprehensive data about employment patterns at a particular plant, as this note from a 1956 NYSCAD conference with Urban League officials indicates:

> Commissioner Carter stated that there is a possibility that they will not be able to find in the complainants' favor in these series of complaints. He stated, however, that by filing the complaints, the complainants enabled the Commission

[19] Ibid., 143. Blumer writes, "Since such standards carry implicitly the dictates of obedience, one is provided with a line along which to press the case which can largely avoid the issue of racial dispute." Norgren et al., *Employing the Negro in American Industry*, 37.

[20] Elmer Carter, "Policies and Practices of Discrimination Commissions," *Annals of the American Academy of Political and Social Science* 304 (March 1956): 62–77, p. 65.

to begin a study of the overall employment patterns of the General Motors Corp. at the Tarrytown plants.[21]

While individual cases were easily dismissed, statistics told a more damning story. The lack of black employees in a particular position, such as supervisory or clerical work, was not proof of discriminatory practices and therefore not by itself punishable, but the statistics allowed the commission to talk to the employer's representatives about how to take affirmative steps to change practices that led to the situation. In the previous case, for instance, the commission ruled that there was "no probable cause" for the individual complaints but that, on the basis of the statistical imbalances, the commission suggested that General Motors stop its "inbreeding method of employment," reconsider the applications of the complainants, and, most significantly, join with NYSCAD in issuing a statement of GM's cooperation with (i.e., validation of) the NYSCAD.[22] Although GM's reps agreed only to the second suggestion, the requests give us some idea of what NYSCAD officials actually desired. The NYSCAD did not pursue individual cases, which were difficult to prove, but rather focused on changing corporate hiring practices and winning acceptance for their existence. This explains the obsession with making sure the commission's poster was hung in a visible place, a detail mentioned in almost every case.

In its bid for legitimacy, the commission also tried to position itself as a neutral mediator between activist organizations and the employer. In the case mentioned above, for instance, the complainants were connected to activist organizations that were protesting the company. The commission tried to persuade GM officials to issue a public statement of GM's cooperation with the commission by arguing that it would indicate to "the various committees which have recently organized in the general area of Tarrytown to protest discrimination,"

[21] Inter-office Memorandum to Commissioner Elmer Carter from Field Representative Harry Anderson, April 27, 1956, p. 4, found in File 0-4160-56, *Wesley Buckner v. Fisher Body, Div. of General Motors Corp.* (1956) in New York Division of Human Rights, Master Case Files for 1951–1968, New York State Archives, Albany. Even if the complaint was about anti-Semitism, the commissioners made a count of black workers. See Valentine to Simon, March 26, 1951, in *Janet Salston v. Previews, Inc.* (1951) in New York Division of Human Rights, Master Case Files for 1951–1968, New York State Archives, Albany.

[22] Inter-office Memorandum to Commissioner Elmer Carter from Field Representative Harry Anderson, November 8, 1956, found in File 0-4160-56, *Wesley Buckner v. Fisher Body, Div. of General Motors Corp.* (1956) in New York Division of Human Rights, Master Case Files for 1951–1968, New York State Archives, Albany. See also other cases therein.

that GM was in accordance with the Law Against Discrimination.[23] By recognizing the commission's legitimacy, the commission intimated, an employer could mollify activist critics.

Winning the cooperation of employers went hand in hand with effective investigation. Employers facing a visit from a NYSCAD official were adept at masking discrimination. The investigator had to win the respondent's good will and get him to relax his guarded behavior so that the investigator would better be able to assess his "real" attitude. Regional director Peter Libassi instructed investigators:

> Your effort should be directed at gathering information and soliciting the point of view of the persons interviewed. "We want to understand your point of view" went over effectively with persons already interviewed . . . the point is that your contact with these people will be the first contact in a long range program and should leave them in the most cooperative frame of mind possible.[24]

Like the best industrial relations staff, NYSCAD agents understood that plant managers and corporate executives, like all human beings, resented being scolded and punished. Race magnified the resentment. Despite their acceptance of discriminatory patterns of employment, executives and managers bridled at the insinuation that they or their company might be racist. NYSCAD researchers became adept at dealing with defensive executives and posed questions in such a way that assumed an executive's own good intentions. Instead of lecturing an executive about how he might increase the number of black hires in his company, for instance, the investigators asked, "How do you think an employer contemplating the recruitment of Negroes for the first time should go about his task? How, in other words, can Mr. X, who is far behind you, achieve the same results you claim long ago to have achieved?"[25] This is exactly how human relations advocates advised employers to deal with troublesome employees. Not punishment, but understanding and manipulation changed behavior.

---

[23] Inter-office Memorandum to Commissioner Elmer Carter from Field Representative Harry Anderson, November 8, 1956, p. 2, found in File 0-4160-56, *Wesley Buckner v. Fisher Body, Div. of General Motors Corp.* (1956) in New York Division of Human Rights, Master Case Files for 1951–1968, New York State Archives, Albany.

[24] Memo from F. Peter Libassi to George and Eunice Grier, August 4, 1958, in *American Jewish Congress v. [various resorts]*, "Churches Nearby" Survey files (1958), in New York Division of Human Rights, Master Case Files for 1951–1968, New York State Archives, Albany.

[25] Bernard Rosenberg and Penney Chapin, "Management and Minority Groups: A Study of Attitudes and Practices in Hiring and Upgrading," in *Discrimination and Low Incomes . . . Studies under the Direction of the New York State Commission Against Discrimination by the New School for Social Research*, ed. Aaron Antonovsky and Lewis Lorwin (Albany, NY: New York Interdepartmental Committee on Low Incomes, 1959), 147–94, p. 192.

In practice NYSCAD's emphasis on cooperation meant that discrimination was defined in terms of how cooperative a company was. If the manager had a cooperative attitude, opened company files, application procedures, and employee lists to the investigator, listened attentively while the investigator explained the law and its intent, asked substantive questions, then the investigator's interactions with the company were concluded relatively quickly. She left some pamphlets, made sure the poster was hanging in a visible place, and was on her way. If the company representative was uncooperative or had a "bad attitude," investigators worked more zealously to uncover proof of discriminatory practices. Commissioners returned daily sometimes to conduct interviews with supervisors, union leaders, employees, and recruitment sources. They demanded appointments to go over the findings and kept at it for months until the company representative capitulated and cooperated.[26] It is hard to discern who is playing whom. On the one hand, one can imagine a manager thinking he has dealt smartly with a too-earnest commissioner woman. On the other hand, all that the investigator wanted was to make the NYSCAD's presence a felt, natural part of everyday life and economic practices, something an employer has to consider, that is, Blumer's transcending group.

The commission's tendency to seek corporate approval angered activists and complainants alike. In a 1951 case involving the American Tobacco Company, the commission had found "no probable cause" but had given the company nine suggestions to ensure its compliance with the Law Against Discrimination in the future, to which the company readily assented. The complainant, however, strongly disagreed with the finding and tried to appeal it. Commissioner Caroline Simon met with the disappointed job seeker and tried to convince him that though he had lost his case, "definite gains for the Negro" would be the likely result. Not satisfied, the complainant wrote a sarcastic article about his experiences with the commission, which mocked the commission's pretense of "objectivity." Horrified, NYSCAD officials tried to dissuade the man from publishing the article, insisting that the law worked, that American Tobacco had changed its policy, and that NYSCAD was not protecting a corporation.[27]

---

[26] These practices are evident in NYSCAD's investigation of African American John Williams of Syracuse, New York, who charged the American Tobacco Company with refusing to hire him as a salesman because of his color. See File C-2681-51, *John A. Williams v. American Tobacco Co.* (1951) in New York Division of Human Rights, Master Case Files for 1951–1968, New York State Archives, Albany.

[27] Simon to Walsh, March 6, 1952, in File C-2681-51, *John Williams v. American Tobacco Company* (1951) in New York Division of Human Rights, Master Case Files for 1951–1968, New York State Archives, Albany.

If one measures the effectiveness of state FEPCs in the 1950s by the number of companies confronted or the number of African Americans upgraded it is unimpressive (although there was some progress). But if one understands effectiveness in terms of increasing employers' knowledge about black employment, or creating what the American Friends Service Committee called "a climate of receptivity," then the achievements of state FEPCs are more apparent.[28] A 1959 New York state study found that most New York state employers had discarded old excuses like "workers (or customers) oppose integration" and believed that integration could work if top management was resolute and monitored supervisors' practices. The researchers concluded, "The whole weight of social science research would support this general orientation. Whether and to what extent businessmen apply these precepts is another matter. That they know them, subscribe to them in the abstract, and advise others to do likewise is quite clear."[29] That they knew the precepts was due in large part to the state commission's constant proselytizing.

Another indication of the state committees' success was, as Elmer Carter had foreseen, the decrease in opposition to their existence and to legislation in general. Although they bridled when their own companies were investigated, businessmen found that they could live with the committees and, indeed, even the legislation. Pitney-Bowes president Walter Wheeler had always opposed federal legislation and urged employers to practice fair employment voluntarily to avert such an occurrence. But by 1963, he was testifying in support of what would be Title VII of the Civil Rights Act for two reasons: (1) too few businessmen were changing their behavior and (2) Connecticut's Fair Employment Practices Committee had shown that it was not detrimental to efficient business practices.[30]

In their zeal to create cooperative employers, state FEPCs may have left businessmen with the impression that somehow they had cooperated voluntarily, rather than being urged to do so by servants of the state because the state agencies were careful to "suggest" reforms, rather than dictate them. In the American Tobacco case, for instance, the NYSCAD had no authority to force American Tobacco to do anything since they had found "no probable cause" for the complaint. But they did have nine suggestions for American

---

[28] "A climate of receptivity" was the modest goal of the American Friends Service Committee. See Barbara Moffett and Jean Fairfax, "A Private Agency Report on Merit Employment," *Social Action* 29, no. 4 (December 1962): 18–22.

[29] Rosenberg and Chapin, "Management and Minority Groups," 147–194, p. 194.

[30] U.S. Congress, Senate, Committee on Labor and Public Welfare, Subcommittee on Employment and Manpower, Hearings *Equal Employment*, 88 Congress, 1st sess., July 24–August 20, 1963.

Tobacco, including putting a nondiscrimination statement in the employee handbook, distributing the commission's pamphlets to its workforce, and, of course, hanging the poster in a visible place. And within a year of the investigation, the American Tobacco Company had hired five African American women in the steno pool (there had been one at the time of the investigation).[31] Similarly, although General Motors refused to issue a joint public statement about its cooperation with NYSCAD, it did upgrade seventeen black workers during the year and a half-long investigation.[32] Since no one forced General Motors to upgrade these men, the action could be construed as "voluntary." Such face-saving agreements allowed companies to change their behavior without admitting wrongdoing. The FEPCs considered it "cooperation," and as a result, it was never counted in their statistics. Businessmen could plausibly believe they had acted voluntarily.

Moreover, in the early 1960s, the suggestion that a company take "positive steps," or "affirmative action," to increase its nonwhite workforce was expansive and unspecific, implying that the measures taken would be at the company's initiative and discretion. As early as the 1950s, many companies had voluntarily made connections to black community organizations and colleges, changed their recruiting practices, held race-relations workshops, sent their executives to "merit employment" conferences, introduced blacks into traditionally white positions, and identified potential leaders among black employees for promotion.[33] All of these were considered affirmative actions, and historian Nancy MacLean even identifies some of these strategies as "creative," "innovative," and "new," although she attributes their origin to grassroots activists, rather than social scientists and employers' groups.[34]

---

[31] Harry Anderson to Caroline Simon, April 16, 1951, and Memo, January 15, 1952, in File C-2681-51, *John A. Williams v. American Tobacco Co.* (1951) in New York Division of Human Rights, Master Case Files for 1951–1968, New York State Archives, Albany.

[32] "Determination after Investigation and Conference," p. 16, in File 0-4160-56, *Wesley Buckner v. Fisher Body, Div. of General Motors Corp.* (1956) in New York Division of Human Rights, Master Case Files for 1951–1968, New York State Archives, Albany.

[33] See case studies in Stephen Habbe, *Company Experience with Negro Employment*, 2 vols., Studies in Personnel Policy No. 201 (New York: National Industrial Conference Board, 1966); Aaron Antonovsky and Lewis Lorwin, eds., *Discrimination and Low Incomes . . . Studies under the Direction of the New York State Commission Against Discrimination by the New School for Social Research* (NY: New York Interdepartmental Committee on Low Incomes, 1959); Lewis Ferman, *The Negro and Equal Employment Opportunities: A Review of Management Experiences in Twenty Companies* (New York: Praeger, 1968); and Jack Gourlay, *The Negro Salaried Worker*, AMA Research Study 70 (New York: American Management Association, 1965).

[34] MacLean, *Freedom Is Not Enough*, 9–10, 107.

Government Contract Compliance Committees

Beginning with World War II, the U.S. government's international obligations and military spending brought American industry into a close working relationship with the federal government. Each president during the era of our concern issued an executive order prohibiting defense contractors from discriminating on the basis of race, religion, or national origin and created a contract compliance committee to receive complaints (the contracting agency was responsible for monitoring compliance). Like the state FEPCs, the government committees were uncertain of their power and authority. While the first presidential FEPC (1941–45) held twenty-two hearings and investigated 127 employers and unions, the subsequent compliance committees held one private hearing between 1952 and 1963.[35] The compliance committees met infrequently. Their funding and power were minimal. They had no systematic program for eliminating discrimination. They dealt with complaints in a slow, piecemeal process.

Like the state FEPCs, the committees avoided coercive measures, preferring instead a "cooperative approach of education and persuasion" to enforce the executive orders.[36] Education, mediation, and conciliation were the way to convince a reluctant contractor to comply and to neutralize fears of coercive government.[37] The emphasis was on voluntarism, or what Eisenhower's Committee on Government Contracts (PCGC) called "voluntary compliance."[38] Chaired by Vice-President Richard Nixon and consisting of representatives from industry (including the ubiquitous Ivan L. Willis) and labor, the PCGC raised awareness about racial discrimination and publicized the achievements and strategies of those employers who had tried to end it. It produced newsletters, films, and pamphlets. It held conferences on equal opportunity, which brought together government representatives and the heads of major contractors. It collected data about hiring practices from

[35] See chart in Norgren and Hill, *Toward Fair Employment*, 161.

[36] Quote from Deputy Secretary of Defense Reuben Robertson, Jr., in *The President's Committee on Government Contracts Newsletter*, December 1955, p. 2, found in McCormick International Harvester Collection, Folder "IH Relationship with African Americans (Materials), 1939–1972."

[37] Deputy Secretary of Defense Reuben Robertson, Jr., in *The President's Committee on Government Contracts Newsletter*, December 1955, p. 2, found in McCormick International Harvester Collection, Folder "IH Relationship with African Americans (Materials), 1939–1972."

[38] Graham, *The Civil Rights Era*, 55; the phrase was repeated in "The Negro Drive for Jobs," *BusinessWeek*, August 17, 1963, 55–56.

contractors. Its message was that discrimination was un-American, that discrimination weakened the U.S. position vis-à-vis the Soviets, that employee resistance was weaker than previously assumed, and that greater interracial contact would further erode resistance. Moreover, its researchers developed a fairly sophisticated understanding of the structural impediments to black employment.[39]

An expression of a new, more cooperative relationship between industry and government, these techniques of education and persuasion helped change the atmosphere in which contractors operated. The combined authority of the state and one's peers made it difficult – although by no means impossible – to flout committee recommendations openly. Let us look, for example, at the Committee on Government Contracts' attempt to persuade contractors to include an "Equal Job Opportunity" emblem on job advertisements. The request was posed in a letter to the contractor's president or chief executive officer. The letter assured the reader that other "industrial leaders" were supporting the program. It explained that studies had shown that minorities did not apply to companies because they knew they would not be hired and that the emblem was designed to alert them to new policies.[40] The letter was signed by Fred Lazarus, Jr., of Federated Department Stores, John Roosevelt, Allied Industrial Research Consultants, and Ivan L. Willis, of International Harvester.

This simple request caused quite a tumult at Du Pont. When Du Pont President C. H. Greenewalt received the letter, he sent it to E. F. Du Pont, the director of the Employee Relations Department, for advice on how to proceed. Greenewalt did not like the idea (although he professed support in "the principle"), but understood that, as he put it, "the matter is a somewhat delicate one in view of the make up of the committee."[41] It is unclear which members of the committee were of concern, but it is clear that this was not just another Urban League request. In a wordy, belabored reply, Greenewalt explained why Du Pont would not be using the emblem (even though it fully supported the principle of equal job opportunity). Although Du Pont refused this small request, the request itself required presidential consideration and

---

[39] Timothy Thurber, "Racial Liberalism, Affirmative Action, and the Troubled History of the President's Committee on Government Contracts," *Journal of Policy History* 18, no. 4 (2006): 446–75.

[40] Fred Lazarus, Jr. (President's Committee on Government Contracts), to C. H. Greenewalt, June 13, 1957, in Papers of Crawford E. Greenewalt, President and Chairman of the Board of E.I. Du Pont de Nemours & Co., 1947–67 (1928–68), Box 11, Series II, Employee Relations Department, File: Personnel – employment, 1954–57, HML.

[41] Greenewalt to E. F. Du Pont, June 17, 1957, in Papers of Crawford E. Greenewalt, President and Chairman of the Board of E.I. Du Pont de Nemours & Co., 1947–67 (1928–68), Box 11, Series II, Employee Relations Department, File: Personnel – employment, 1954–57, HML.

represented one of many changes proposed by the federal government that, over time, made attention to equal opportunity part of the corporate landscape. And had Du Pont assented, as, for instance, RCA, McDonnell Aircraft, Honeywell, Motorola, and Polaroid had, the action would have been regarded as voluntary.

Like state FEPCs, government compliance committees normalized the existence of nondiscrimination policies. By 1959, classes at business schools were using case studies about how to overcome the problems of complying with federal nondiscrimination mandates.[42] Activists and historians have always eschewed attitudinal change (or "education") as a distraction from the rigor of real regulations, but attitudinal changes were an essential part of preparing executives, managers, and workers alike for an integrated workplace. Measures that seemed ineffectual in forcing employers to integrate (such as the compliance committees) created an atmosphere that made it harder for them to ignore racial discrimination.

As the pressure from civil rights groups and the federal government increased at the beginning of the 1960s, businessmen and employers were ever more insistent that voluntary programs were the most effective way to accomplish what was now called equal employment opportunity. Voluntarism hit its apogee with the Plans for Progress program, begun in 1961.

Plans for Progress

In March 1961, President John F. Kennedy changed the accepted pattern of government compliance committees with Executive Order 10925, which not only made mandatory the EEO emblem that Du Pont had rejected but also required companies to take "affirmative action" to ensure that applicants and employees were treated without regard to race, religion, or national origin. The PCEEO was given a larger staff and the power to initiate review, to collect relevant statistics, to publicize the names of discriminators, to terminate contracts, and to prohibit a company from receiving future contracts.[43] It was the strictest and most comprehensive executive order to date, and the new committee seemed more energetic, more attentive to activists' concerns, and more committed to its authority than had previous committees.

---

[42] See Robert Nixon to International Harvester, August 13, 1959. Nixon enclosed his assignment, which asked students how a company could reconcile federal antidiscrimination mandates with local laws. In McCormick International Harvester Collection, Folder "IH Relationship with African Americans (Materials), 1939–1972."

[43] Sovern, *Legal Restraints on Racial Discrimination in Employment*, 104–16.

As the PCEEO began its work in April 1961, the NAACP's Herbert Hill filed discrimination charges with the new committee against Lockheed Aircraft Corporation, which had just been awarded a billion-dollar defense contract to manufacture jet planes at its plant in Marietta, Georgia. In operation since 1951, Lockheed's Marietta plant had segregated facilities, segregated unions, an exclusionary apprenticeship program, and hiring patterns that confined blacks in unskilled and semiskilled job categories. Charges had been filed against it with previous compliance committees but to no avail. Hill's suit was as much a challenge to the new PCEEO as it was to Lockheed. The committee indicated that if the company were found in violation of the executive order then the contract would be cancelled.[44]

Here is how Lockheed's Industrial Relations director, Howard Lockwood, described what happened next: "While integration, under the Executive Order could be forced upon the company, it was believed that ultimately greater progress would be made if the company undertook a voluntary program to improve conditions."[45] According to Lockwood, a plan of action was then drawn up by the company in cooperation with the PCEEO. The plan – named a Plan for Progress – was similar to what state FEPCs had long been recommending: an end to overt segregation, the recruitment of qualified minority-group applicants, a review of eligible minority personnel for possible promotion, the encouragement of minority candidates to attain training for advancement, the maintenance of statistics, and the monitoring of personnel to make sure divisions complied with the plan. Although historians and researchers dismiss Lockheed's presumption of voluntarism (the events were, after all, prompted by the NAACP and the PCEEO), they largely agree that Lockheed swiftly ended segregation and transformed its hiring and upgrading practices, proving that it was possible to change long-standing habits quickly.[46]

Other major defense contractors – fifty-two by February 1962 – signed similar Plans for Progress with the PCEEO, promising to review their current hiring and upgrading procedures, expand employment and training opportunities for minorities, and submit an annual progress report to the PCEEO. What became the Plans for Progress program was the creation Georgia lawyer Robert Troutman, Jr., who had attached himself to the Kennedy administration. Troutman ascribed to the same philosophy as Elmer Carter and others

[44] This account drawn from ibid., 108–12; Gelber, *Black Men and Businessmen*, 202–6; and Graham, *The Civil Rights Era*, 40–43, 47–49.

[45] *The Selection and Training of Negroes for Managerial Positions: Proceedings of the Executive Study Conference*, held November 10–11, 1964 (Princeton, NJ: Educational Testing Service, 1965), 2.

[46] See Sovern, *Legal Restraints on Racial Discrimination in Employment*, 108–12; Gelber, *Black Men and Businessmen*, 202–6; and Graham, *The Civil Rights Era*, 40–43, 47–49.

that "compliance" in this delicate area could not be forced and that force in fact would be counterproductive.[47] Much to the chagrin of those who favored a hard-line, more coercive approach, businessmen flocked to the voluntary Plans for Progress program headed by Troutman. That businessmen favored Plans for Progress burdened the program with a credibility problem, as it suggested to activists like Herbert Hill that businessmen thought that the program would protect them from investigation, that it was "an easy way out," that it allowed them to write their own standards of compliance.[48] Indeed, as I discuss later, the National Association of Manufacturers (NAM) promoted Plans for Progress as "protection" from boycotts. Notwithstanding these suspicions, it is easy to see why businessmen would have signed on to the program quite apart from whatever "out" it gave them. Plans for Progress set forth a vision of black employment opportunity that was entirely compatible with businessmen's view of the world. It affirmed the rightness of American democracy; it invested in manpower for the future; it encouraged private solutions to public problems – all pitches that civil rights activists were still making to convince businessmen to expand economic opportunities for minorities.

If Plans for Progress was an "out" for businesses, it was also an "out" for a liberal administration that wanted to appear tougher than it was or could actually be. In June 1961, the legal department of the NAM sent a twenty-six-page statement to the PCEEO detailing the burden Executive Order 10925 placed on corporations, as well as its ambiguous legal authority. It is easy to dismiss the NAM's objections to employment regulations as obstructionist. But the burdens and legal ambiguities it described were real. "Discrimination" constituted a violation of the contract and subjected the company to grave consequences, yet the term was never defined, nor were there any guidelines or standards by which reasonable people could identify and agree that a violation had or had not occurred. Without such standards, discrimination, and whether or not a company had engaged in it, was a question of interpretation and opinion. The complaint and hearing procedures provided no due process for the contractor. Just as it was always possible for an employer to explain why a given situation was not discrimination, it was also possible, the NAM feared, for "an energetic investigator" to find discrimination, "if he set his mind to it."[49] With no standards for discrimination, and no procedures in place for the contractor to cross-examine its accusers, provide its own witnesses, or defend

---

[47] On Troutman, see Graham, *The Civil Rights Era*, 50–53.

[48] See MacLean, *Freedom Is Not Enough*, 44.

[49] "Statement of the Law Department of the National Association of Manufacturers to the President's Committee on Equal Employment Opportunity Regarding Executive Order No. 10925...," June 30, 1961, in NAM Records, Series 7, Box 135, HML

itself from the charges, the contractor was vulnerable to the biases of zealous committee members.

The PCEEO's response to such complaints offered little comfort. This is how Theodore Kheel, consultant to the PCEEO, addressed the charge that the determination of "discrimination" was subjective:

> Discrimination is indeed difficult to define. It can be practiced openly or subtly.... Hiring 10 Negroes where none had been previously employed might be substantial compliance with the Executive Order in one area of the country but fall short of the desired goal in another area.... On the other hand, hiring one or two Negroes with outstanding professional or technical skills in "visible" jobs might be regarded as token compliance and such "window dressing" would be judged unacceptable.... The trend now is for civil rights groups and government agencies to insist on even more: Their view is that meaningful equal employment policies require seeking out Negroes who are not likely to have the same access to job openings as whites.[50]

These statements do nothing to allay the fear that judgments about discrimination were subjective. If anything, the references to "the trend now" and "token compliance" illustrate just how subjective the definition of "discrimination" really was.

The NAM had other complaints as well. It was unclear why the PCEEO wanted compliance reports from corporate plants and offices that were not directly involved in producing goods for the government. Surely, the executive order had no jurisdiction over the company's noncontracted work. There was also confusion about whether the committee finding a contractor in noncompliance with the nondiscrimination clause would cancel a contract for default or terminate it on behalf of the government, as defined by the Armed Services Procurement Regulations. The contractor after all could fail to comply through no fault of its own, for instance, if a union or subcontractor failed to comply. The contractor was dependent on its ability to force its various unions and numerous subcontractors into compliance, and yet it had no power or authority to do so; indeed, its attempts to force a subcontractor into compliance might result in its own inability to fulfill the contract. Compliance reports were difficult to file, moreover, not only because of the increased paperwork but also because state antidiscrimination laws prohibited the maintenance of such information in employment records.[51]

---

[50] Theodore Kheel, *Guide to Fair Employment Practices* (Englewood Cliffs, NJ: Prentice Hall, 1964), 28.

[51] "Statement of the Law Department of the National Association of Manufacturers to the President's Committee on Equal Employment Opportunity Regarding Executive Order No. 10925...," June 30, 1961, in NAM Records, Series 7, Box 135, HML

Finally, the NAM legal team reminded the committee that while the government had the authority to fix the terms and conditions of its contracts, the separation of powers spelled out in the Constitution vested the power to define such terms and conditions in the legislative branch. Except for this one issue, Congress had exercised this power in many acts that defined the terms and conditions of government contracts. The language of the executive order was legislative in nature, involving sanctions and penalties, and replicating state legislation on the same issue. Setting aside differences in constitutional interpretation, the NAM's point affirmed what many activists understood at the time and historians have since confirmed: the executive order allowed the government to fulfill its obligation to black Americans and American democracy in the face of the special "circumstances" (southern Democrats and congressional rules) that prevented the legislative branch from acting on this issue, as dictated by the Constitution.

Throughout the document, the NAM legal team suggested that cancellation of contracts would jeopardize U.S. national security. The document almost dares the PCEEO to use its claimed authority. Would the PCEEO really take "unilateral action" and cancel contracts vital to U.S. military interests? Were these really the terms by which the government wanted to defend such drastic and potentially damaging actions? Was the committee willing to risk turning public opinion against itself? Although the government officials on the PCEEO no doubt regarded the NAM as an extremist and ineffective organization, there is reason to believe that they understood the NAM's implied threats and recognized their own limited authority. Although it was bolder than its predecessors, the PCEEO essentially followed the same pattern of conciliation and recommendations that previous committees had. In two highly publicized cases, the PCEEO had suspended contracts with Comet Rice Mills, a southern company, and Danly Machine Specialties of Cicero, Illinois, until they submitted compliance reports and promised to pursue the standard list of affirmative actions, which they both did within a month. The example of these two relatively small companies probably prompted other companies to comply, but as Michael Sovern observed, such actions had been few: "for the most part, the Committee relied on conciliation."[52] While the PCEEO sought to limit exemptions for subcontractors of standard commercial supplies and raw materials, the issue became so complicated that the committee was forced to rewrite its initial guidelines, leading the legal counsel of one company to write: "Thus, it appears that the Committee [PCEEO] may not act for some

---

[52] Sovern, *Legal Restraints on Racial Discrimination in Employment*, 113.

time and that . . . each contractor is more or less free to proceed under his own definition using the former regulations as a guide."[53]

The actual authority of the PCEEO was no greater than its predecessors. The cancellation of contracts was sheer madness; it would harm not only the contractors but also the government, its military interests, and its economic development programs, which were tied to defense spending.[54] Given the government's limited ability to enforce the executive order, it is not that outlandish to have believed that the Plans for Progress program was voluntary. Plans for Progress companies promised to expand their minority workforces, not because the government had the power to make them do so but because the companies were willing to find a workable compromise that would threaten neither the government's interests nor their own. Plans for Progress corporations saw themselves as working with the government, as partners, to expand opportunities for minorities, and, as the NAM legal team put it, "to find solutions which will not endanger or deter in any manner the national defense effort."[55] The program was especially popular among the largest contractors – General Electric, Boeing, RCA, Douglas, General Motors, Goodyear – with which the majority of the government's business was conducted and whose executives were members of the NAM. Even as liberal members of the PCEEO sought to limit and de-emphasize Plans for Progress, then, the Kennedy and Johnson administrations retained the program.

The business community, and particularly the large defense contractors, threw themselves into making the Plans for Progress program their own, an endeavor helped by the PCEEO's backing away from the program after liberal criticism of it (Troutman had been eased out in 1962). In 1963, the major defense contractors created and financed the Plans for Progress Advisory Council, composed of nineteen of their own executives.[56] The Advisory Council remained in the PCEEO. Again, it is not surprising that businessmen would have thought this was voluntary, given that it was a renegade organization of corporate representatives lodged within a government body that

[53] Walter Lyman to Lambert Miller, NAM, November 9, 1961, in NAM Records, Series 5, Box 65, HML

[54] On the connection between economic development and military spending, see Bruce J. Schulman, *From Cotton Belt to Sunbelt: Federal Policy, Economic Development, and the Transformation of the South, 1938–1980*, rev. ed. (Durham, NC: Duke University Press, 1994).

[55] "Statement of the Law Department of the National Association of Manufacturers to the President's Committee on Equal Employment Opportunity Regarding Executive Order No. 10925 . . . ," June 30, 1961, p. 26, in NAM Records, Series 7, Box 135, HML.

[56] Sovern, *Legal Restraints on Racial Discrimination in Employment*, 120, and *The Selection and Training of Negroes for Managerial Positions*, 3; and Kheel, *Guide to Fair Employment Practices*, 22.

ignored it. By 1965, 308 companies with 8.6 million employees were enrolled in the program.[57] Although historians have paid little attention to Plans for Progress in the years following the adoption of Title VII in 1964, the program actually continued until 1969, even making the transition to the Labor Department in 1966 after President Johnson disbanded the PCEEO.[58]

In July 1964, Congress finally passed federal legislation that prohibited employers from practicing racial discrimination. While individual businessmen had opposed Title VII, the business community as a whole did little to stop it. The NAM took no position on the bill. The major corporations whose leaders dominated the NAM were already monitored by the PCEEO.[59] And the trade journals began publishing articles about how to comply with the impending legislation before it was even passed. Title VII of the 1964 Civil Rights Act was modeled on the state laws against discrimination, although its enforcing body, the EEOC, did not have the power to order companies to cease and desist as some state agencies, including the NYSCAD, did. The law went into effect in July 1965 for employers of 100 or more employees and was phased in over three years for smaller companies. Employers who were covered under the PCEEO or state fair employment laws were not initially bound to the enforcement measures of the EEOC. Title VI of the Civil Rights Act gave the president the statutory authority to cut off government funds that the NAM legal staff had complained was missing from Kennedy's executive order. The effect that the new EEOC would have on business practices was unknown, and it would take some time for the Johnson administration to coordinate its many far-flung and competing equal opportunity ventures.[60] In the meantime, the business community continued its own voluntary efforts.

In December 1963, the NAM had helped the White House organize an informational session about Plans for Progress for sixty-four companies, with the hope of inducing them to sign on. After this meeting, the NAM organized a separate, second meeting for the sixty-four companies that had attended the White House meeting. The purpose of this meeting was to provide a forum for the companies to discuss the pros and cons of joining Plans for Progress.[61] The

---

[57] "Information from the President's Committee on Equal Employment Opportunity," June 11, 1965, in NAM Records, Series 5, Box 64, Plans for Progress Folder, HML; and Kheel, *Guide to Fair Employment Practices*, 22.

[58] George Schermer, *Employer's Guide to Economic Opportunity* (Washington, DC: Potomac Institute, 1966), 71.

[59] Small manufacturers and NAM members opposed Title VII and wrote to the NAM demanding why it was not opposing the bill. See Chapter 7 for more detailed discussion.

[60] Graham, *The Civil Rights Era*, 153–62.

[61] A series of memos from Charles Kothe to Sam Berry, Bennett Kline, headed Employment of Minorities, dated January 20, 1964, in NAM Records, Series 7, Box 135, HML.

NAM had long felt that manufacturers and management needed to take a leading role in integrating American workplaces. To convince individual companies to join, the NAM emphasized the benefits. Being known as a participating member of Plans for Progress was "protection against pressure from the more militant minority organizations," and the government itself advertised a company's participation therein.[62] Belonging to the plan gave the member company the benefit of the plan's Advisory Council, which consisted of the executives of powerful defense contractors who could mediate if there was trouble. Companies belonging to the plan experienced less frequent and bothersome compliance inspections than those that did not.[63] These arguments give credence to the idea that businesses signed on to "hide" from the PCEEO and later the EEOC, but these arguments were mainly rhetorical, intended to persuade the balkers. For the NAM, anyway, the idea was to maintain the credibility of voluntarism and to increase businesses' leadership role in equal employment opportunity. As the Advisory Council chair wrote to Plans for Progress companies in an invitation urging them to attend the five-year anniversary of Plans for Progress, "if the concept of voluntary action by industry is to maintain its credibility and if Plans for Progress is to build on the respect it has gained in government and among minority groups, there must be constant public demonstration by our companies of their commitment and continued support."[64]

Lukens Steel Company, with a workforce of about five thousand, enlisted in Plans for Progress in June 1964. For the conservative Lukens executives, joining Plans for Progress may have been a way to put their company in compliance with the impending legislation (although, as contractors, they were already under the jurisdiction of Executive Order 10925). But once signed up, the Lukens executives took seriously their commitment to the plan; that is, they began doing voluntarily what would later be required and still later would become common corporate practice. Before signing onto the program, there is no existing evidence that the company made any effort to ensure equal opportunity for all races. After signing the plan, the company formed a committee in the Industrial Relations Department to administer the plan, to collect and maintain statistics, and to develop and implement affirmative action policies to increase the employment and upgrading of nonwhite workers. For the

---

[62] Quote from Memo, Charles A. Kothe to Bennett E. Kline, "Study of the Employment of Minorities," January 20, 1964, in NAM Records, Series 7, Box 135, HML.

[63] Memo, Charles A. Kothe to Bennett E. Kline, "Study of the Employment of Minorities," January 20, 1964, in NAM Records, Series 7, Box 135, HML.

[64] Charles E. Spahr to Charles L. Huston, Jr., May 11, 1966, in Lukens Steel Company, Executive Officers Files, 1903–1979, Box 2020, HML.

first time, "advancing equal employment opportunities" became a top goal of the Industrial Relations Department. Managers and supervisors submitted progress reports and statistics to the Industrial Relations director. Like today's affirmative action reports, the company listed specific goals (i.e., "recruit one or more qualified Negroes for salaried positions in the professional and technical job categories"), what steps it had taken to fulfill the goals, and the extent to which each goal was fulfilled.[65] The affirmative actions they took resembled those of other companies: recruiting at black colleges, reviewing/revising tests for advancement, outreach to black community organizations, desegregating locker facilities, and identifying and selecting nonwhite workers for advancement into supervisory positions. They used the nonwhite population of Coatesville (17 percent) as a rough "target," even as their results in most categories fell far short of it. The majority of their nonwhite workforce continued to be found in the unskilled and semiskilled categories, but the number of nonwhite skilled craftsmen increased from nineteen (2.3 percent of the workforce) in 1963 to sixty-six (5.8 percent) in 1966. The number of nonwhite managers increased from twelve (2.7 percent of the workforce) to nineteen (3.6 percent) for the same period.[66] Actual progress in terms of numbers of minorities hired and upgraded into traditionally white jobs would take time, but the company's membership in Plans for Progress meant that it had put in place the institutional structures for integration.

Lukens president Charles Huston, Jr., sent his brother and vice-president Stewart Huston to several conferences and workshops on equal employment opportunity. Stewart took meticulous notes on the conferences for his brother, noting speakers and delineating major themes and recommendations. Conservative in his outlook, Stewart nonetheless respectfully highlighted the parts of a speech by a "militant" NAACP officer that struck him as useful and sensible.[67] He responded well to those speakers who emphasized the moral component of the problem, Negro responsibility, business's affirmative action strategies (which he considered voluntary), and job creation as a solution to juvenile delinquency and racial conflict. At certain points, he seems almost excited about the new venture, gushing about the good talks, noting specific

[65] See Industrial Relations Annual Report, 1964; Industrial Relations Annual Report, 1965; in Lukens Steel Company, Corporate Records, Box 2163, HML.

[66] "1966 Plans for Progress Report," in the Industrial Relations Annual Report for 1966, in Lukens Steel Company, Corporate Records, Box 2163, HML,.

[67] "Report on Workshop Panels, Regional Conference on Equal Opportunity and Economic Growth, [PCEEO]," Philadelphia, Pennsylvania, June 10, 1964; and Stewart Huston to C.L.H., Jr. (Pres.), June 9, 1966, in Lukens Steel Company, Executive Officers Files, 1903–1979, Boxes 2018 and 2020, respectively, HML

comments he found wise or useful.[68] There is genuine interest here. This is not a man scoffing, but one seeking to learn. To what extent he applied what he learned to his company is another question and, for our purposes, less important than his attitude to the endeavor, which was not disingenuous but rather sincere – or, at least, no less sincere than his attitude toward safety procedures, wage and salary structuring, and the maintenance of the firm's IBM equipment, other subjects he discussed in correspondence to his brother.

The sudden appearance of equal opportunity goals in its 1964 records suggests that the company was simply complying with Title VII. But Lukens officials themselves, like so many businessmen at this time, believed that their actions were "voluntary." This was because Title VII did not require that companies take the affirmative steps that were part of the Plans for Progress program. In its emphasis on upgrading, training, and outreach, Plans for Progress went far beyond Title VII. Sounding rather like an affirmative action activist, Plans for Progress chairman Howard Lockwood explained:

> What many people don't realize is that action under Title VII of the Act dealing with employment relies on complaints filed by individual aggrieved employees. A company might discriminate for years and unless an employee or applicant complained, no action would be taken. The action, then, would primarily be directed at the adjudication of the individual grievance, which might be a very extended legal process.[69]

Lockwood judiciously acknowledged the value of Title VII, but felt that the voluntary affirmative actions initiated by Plans for Progress companies to change attitudes and behavior were still necessary. It may be true that Title VII prodded companies to adopt affirmative action policies, but this was because it provided no standard for determining compliance. Companies adopted affirmative action plans to hedge their bets, to show cooperation, to try to find some way to indicate nondiscrimination. A company's adoption of affirmative action policies can thus appear to be involuntary (a response to the new law) or voluntary: because the law failed to state firm guidelines, businessmen concocted their own.

The business leaders who directed Plans for Progress touted the program's relevance to both the Johnson administration and the civil rights struggle. As president, Johnson continued the PCEEO until September 1965, when he issued Executive Order 11246, which replaced the PCEEO with the Office of Federal Contract Compliance Programs (OFCC), which was placed in the

---

[68] Stewart Huston to C.L.H., Jr. (Pres.), June 12, 1964, in Lukens Steel Company, Executive Officers Files, 1903–1979, Box 2018, "Equal Employment Opportunity 1964" file, HML.
[69] *The Selection and Training of Negroes for Managerial Positions*, 14.

Department of Labor. While some historians have regarded Plans for Progress as largely symbolic and even an embarrassment to Johnson, businessmen presented Plans for Progress as a vibrant, pioneering, and important part of the Johnson administration's social agenda. Howard Lockwood, released from his duties at Lockheed to chair the Plans for Progress Advisory Council, credited President Johnson's leadership in recruiting corporations into Plans for Progress, implying Johnson's support for the program.[70] Whatever Johnson was telling his liberal supporters about Plans for Progress, he was, at the same time, cultivating the support of the business community for the program. Johnson may have eased Robert Troutman from the PCEEO, but he also replaced the activist John Feild with loyal aide Hobart Taylor, Jr., who continued to support and strengthen Plans for Progress. Taylor's conciliatory relationship to business leaders led Lockwood to observe, "Mr. Taylor's confidence in the ability and willingness of business and industry to contribute significantly to the solution of this national problem through voluntary action has been justified."[71] And Johnson himself lauded the voluntary achievements of Plans for Progress companies: "Through the volunteer actions of these government contractors the President's Committee on Equal Employment Opportunity is well on the way to successfully achieving equal employment opportunity for all people."[72] The Johnson administration later went out of its way to gain the support of business executives, and they returned the favor, granting their executives paid leaves to serve on the Plans for Progress Advisory Council, for instance.[73]

In many ways, the Plans for Progress Advisory Council resembled groups like the Business Advisory Council (later the Business Council) or the Committee on Economic Development (CED), semiofficial policy-making bodies made up of industrial and financial leaders, which were, in historian Kim McQuaid's words, "in the government, but not of it."[74] A 1963 NAM publication, *A Study of the Employment of Minorities*, listed the Plans for Progress Advisory Council as the "President's Committee on Equal Employment Opportunity's Advisory Council," completely conflating the business-led group with the governmental body.[75] One reason business leaders were interested in government-industry

[70] Ibid., 4.

[71] Ibid., 4.

[72] Quoted in the NAM, "A Study of the Employment of Minorities," November 14, 1963, from a 1962 PCEEO Study, in NAM Records, Series 7, Box 135, HML.

[73] See Theodore Leavitt, "The Johnson Treatment," *Harvard Business Review* (January–February 1967): 114–28; this topic will be developed further in the following chapter.

[74] Kim McQuaid, *Uneasy Partners: Big Business in American Politics, 1945–1990* (Baltimore: Johns Hopkins University Press, 1994), 19.

[75] The NAM, "A Study of the Employment of Minorities," November 14, 1963, in NAM Records, Series 7, Box 135, HML

cooperation was to gain influence in and hence some control over the agencies and policies that would regulate their businesses. This was an old ruse, which had once led Woodrow Wilson to observe that "cooperation" between government and industry was like asking the fox into the henhouse. But Theodore Roosevelt, mirroring the human relations philosophy, had understood that the goals of the state were more efficiently met through cooperation with industry rather than conflict, even if cooperation meant self-regulation.

If we consider Plans for Progress not in the context of civil rights struggles, but rather as another government-industry partnership, then, we can see more clearly the role business leaders played in shaping affirmative action policies. Just as the CED formulated economic and trade policies, so too did Plans for Progress formulate affirmative action policies. Its "Guidelines for Affirmative Action," written to aid companies that were voluntarily seeking to integrate, became the basis for the OFCC's infamous Order no. 4, issued in 1969, which made such policies mandatory.[76] In the same way that CED officials hoped to gain influence in the discussions about trade and economics, so too did Plans for Progress officials seek influence in the policy-making conversation about integration. Plans for Progress and the NAM co-sponsored many conferences and workshops to help employers begin integration. Summarizing the results of one of these conferences, a NAM staffer commented: "The Conference was extremely well received; ... it has already increased NAM acceptance at OFCC and EEOC and should help us in getting our voice heard in the future."[77] What sounds like bald machination on the part of the NAM to gain influence in regulatory agencies was exactly that, but it required a great degree of real research, action, and results for it to work. While Plans for Progress may have been self-serving for some companies, it was more significantly a genuine attempt on the part of corporations to prove their commitment to a positive program for minority employment. It collected and analyzed statistics on minority employment patterns. It sponsored hundreds of conferences and workshops to help companies begin integration. It developed scholarship and training programs. It sponsored vocational guidance seminars at high schools with predominantly black populations.[78]

---

[76] "The Unhappy Parent of New Hiring Rules," *Business Week*, January 24, 1970, and "Summary Analysis of revised Order No. 4 regarding Affirmative Action under Government Contracts," NAM Law Department Memo, February 12, 1970, in NAM Records, Series 5, Box 64, Philadelphia Plan Folder, HML.

[77] National Association of Manufacturers Inter-office Memo, R. D. Godown to L. H. Miller, October 4, 1968, NAM Records, Series 5, Box 64, Plans for Progress Folder, HML ,.

[78] Kheel, *Guide to Fair Employment Practices*, 22, and Howard Lockwood, "Critical Problems in Achieving Equal Employment Opportunity," *Personnel Psychology* (Spring 1966): 3–10.

The conferences that Plans for Progress executives planned, sponsored, and participated in were designed to help businessmen identify and overcome the structural, built-in obstructions to minority employment opportunity. No longer about prejudice and racism, these conferences focused on biases in and alternatives to testing, the cultural disadvantages of minorities, and the structural inequities that had resulted from 200 years of slavery and injustice. Speakers explained to attendees why simply ignoring color did not expand opportunity, as businessmen had once thought. Some special acknowledgment of the disadvantages black people labored under was necessary. [79] Even when black professionals testified that they had no special problems as Negroes, and that there should be no difference between the training of white managers and black, as three panelists did at a 1964 Executive Study Conference, conferees reminded themselves that these were three exceptional people whose experiences did not necessarily reflect those of "the other 22 million Negroes," and that there was evidence to suggest that Africans American applicants' different experiences require different considerations from those used for whites.[80] Conferences such as these indicate that executives were trying to wean themselves from a color-blind perspective that prevented proactive solutions.

The effectiveness of the Plans for Progress program has been the subject of great debate, in part because its performance or lack thereof fueled arguments about the need for federal legislation. Plans for Progress representatives claimed progress of course. Their reports indicated that between 1961 and 1964 the number of nonwhite salaried workers at the first hundred PFP companies grew from 28,143 (1.5 percent of the total number of employees) to 47,134 (2.5 percent of the total number of employees). Their statistics showed that the number of nonwhite employees in supervisory, professional, and sales positions was increasing at a higher rate than total employee increases in those categories, while the rate of nonwhites in service and labor positions had declined or at least not grown.[81] The impressive growth rate for nonwhites in salaried positions was due to the small number who initially inhabited those positions. Still, as PFP

---

[79] See, for example, *The Selection and Training of Negroes for Managerial Positions*; see Eli Ginzberg, ed., *The Negro Challenge to the Business Community* (New York: McGraw-Hill, 1964), and Ginzberg, *Business Leadership and the Negro Crisis* (New York: McGraw-Hill, 1968), which present the highlights of conferences held under the auspices of the Executive Program of the Graduate School of Business, Columbia University. A large number of corporations sent representatives; papers by Charles Silberman, Whitney Young, Kenneth C. Clark, Daniel Patrick Moynihan. The NAM was particularly active in organizing conferences; see, for instance, the Plans for Progress folder in NAM Records, Series 5, Box 64, HML.

[80] *The Selection and Training of Negroes for Managerial Positions*, 146–53.

[81] "Tentative Report on 1964 EEO-10 Statistics," in Information from the PCEEO, for release June 11, 1965; and *The Selection and Training of Negroes for Managerial Positions*, 7.

executives pointed out, the increase indicated a purposeful recruitment effort. Stephen Gelber observes that since the southern PFP companies "virtually ignored" their commitments, the actual gains made in those PFP companies that fulfilled their commitments were even higher than the national statistics indicate.[82] In 1962, an antisegregationist organization called the Southern Regional Council conducted a survey of PFP companies in the Atlanta area and found widespread noncompliance with Executive Order 10925 and little evidence that any effort was being made to enact the agreements (except in the three largest firms, Lockheed, Goodyear, and Western Electric). This study was widely cited as evidence of the program's ineffectiveness.[83] Subsequent studies found that those employers with the largest number of employees were in compliance, however, and that it was the smaller companies that were a problem.

Focusing on the "results" as a measure of effectiveness, however, obscures the real achievement of Plans for Progress. Regardless of the number of black employees, who were hired or upgraded as a result of the program, the program was significant because it presented a business model for how employers might begin the process of integration. The program's "voluntary" status ensured that it was neither an insult nor a threat to employers and kept open the possibility that if companies took affirmative steps to integrate, perhaps more drastic legislative and enforcement methods could be avoided. Knowing that employers were suspicious of government programs, proponents of integration pointed them to Plans for Progress as an example of industry's voluntary support for and efforts toward equal employment opportunity. When the feared legislation finally came, the large Plans for Progress corporations had few adjustments to make. Title VII required less of them than Executive Order 11246 or the Plans for Progress program. Other companies tried to put themselves in compliance by practicing the familiar list of affirmative actions recommended by Plans for Progress (and still used today): recruitment at black colleges; outreach to black community organizations; reviewing black employees for possible advancement; evaluating and revising job and training program criteria; collecting and maintaining statistics about race and ethnicity; communicating policy to all employees, supervisors, and managers via orientation sessions, handbook, or memo; review of union agreements; review of grievance procedures; and, most important, the establishment of institutional structures to carry out what had become not merely a nondiscrimination program but actual integration. By themselves, without "results," these affirmative actions would not save a

---

[82] Gelber, *Black Men and Businessmen*, 207.
[83] Norgren and Hill, *Toward Fair Employment*, 166–67; Graham, *The Civil Rights Era*, 68.

company from legal suits or citation, but these were the techniques companies used to get "results," that is, to integrate.[84]

Conclusion

Equal employment opportunity was a jungle of mixed messages and competing authorities. To a businessman of the late 1950s and early 1960s, everything about antidiscrimination legislation and enforcement must have seemed bewildering and uncertain. Those state agencies that had the power to enforce antidiscrimination laws preferred to use persuasion and conciliation. The compliance committees that monitored defense contractors' hiring and upgrading practices were either passive (Eisenhower's) or overreaching (Kennedy's). Companies were, on the one hand, prohibited from maintaining statistics about their employees' race and ethnicity but, on the other hand, required to furnish such information to the PCEEO. Companies were told to upgrade black employees into previously white positions but also told that doing so would not be proof of nondiscrimination and could in fact be regarded as "tokenism." The many definitions of discrimination were fluid, contingent on local and regional hiring patterns, the number of minority employees at a particular firm, union agreements, and the occupational class of the position in question. Black professionals wanted to be treated like white professionals, without regard to race, but equal opportunity experts told executives that they had to consider racial, or "cultural," differences in evaluating and training blacks for advancement. The new EEOC seemed to have both more and less authority than the old PCEEO: it was more constitutionally sound, but its scope was less expansive.

In such a situation, with no clear lines of authority, no firm definitions, it is understandable that business leaders believed their own actions to be voluntary, autonomous, another part of the overall solution to the unsettled problem of minority employment. Critics sneered that they were doing what the law required that they do anyway, but the law was hardly clear about what they were supposed to be doing. Then, too, the state agencies and the Johnson administration seemed to welcome their cooperation, even praising their efforts with Plans for Progress. Business leaders did not oppose equal employment opportunity or the affirmative steps that were necessary to achieve it. They did not see

---

[84] See, for instance, Ferman, *The Negro and Equal Employment Opportunities*, 131–47; Schermer, *Employer's Guide to Economic Opportunity*; and Habbe, *Company Experience with Negro Employment*.

themselves in opposition to the government or civil rights groups but rather as cooperators, representing industry's solution to a complicated but urgent social problem. There were businessmen who opposed integration, but by the early 1960s, the social atmosphere and public opinion had changed (due in part to the cooperative and educational tactics of the state agencies and compliance committees) to the point that they were, to use Herbert Blumer's language, part of the "descending group," on the verge of irrelevance. The executives of the largest corporations generally embraced the use of voluntary affirmative action and the larger goal of equal opportunity, even as they disagreed with liberals, activists, and government officials about the best methods to secure equal opportunity. One sign that this was the case was the relative absence of opposition or outrage to Title VII in the business community. As researcher Herbert Northrup noted, "Unlike the analogous case of the Wagner Act in 1935, large employers are not fighting the law. Rather they are moving to comply with it before it becomes effective."[85] What Northrup saw as "compliance," the large employers saw as voluntary, but the end point was the same: better employment and advancement opportunities for minorities.

While the terms of compliance remained vague and contested, the means by which a corporation could achieve integration were widely agreed on and originated with the corporations themselves. The lists of standard "positive steps," or "affirmative actions," that a firm might take to increase minority employment opportunities were distributed by state fair employment committees, the Urban League, or the American Friends Service Committee, but the techniques themselves were based on the experiences of companies that had successfully experimented with integrating their firms, such as International Harvester, Pitney-Bowes, Western Electric, and the many unnamed companies that provided the data for innumerable studies and surveys. The experiences of these pioneering companies taught experts that fears of white employee or customer resistance were exaggerated, that a firm command from the top could deter resistance, and that evaluating hiring and testing procedures might reveal unexpected discrimination. Corporations were the laboratories for integration. They bore the cost and burden of the various "experiments" and shared their experiences with others. Without their successful example, without the endorsement of actual businessmen, there would be little reason for other companies to believe the techniques peddled by equal employment experts were feasible, cost-effective, or useful.

[85] Herbert Northrup, "Equal Opportunity and Equal Pay," in *The Negro and Employment Opportunity*, ed. Herbert Northrup and Richard Rowan (Ann Arbor: Bureau of Industrial Relations, Graduate School of Business Administration, University of Michigan, 1965).

Historians' focus on grassroots activism and the state, and the accompanying emphasis on coercion and pressure, has ignored the role played by persuasion, compromise, and negotiation in convincing employers to change their practices. Activists and state agents at the time understood the limits of coercion in a way that historians seem to have forgotten. NYSCAD researchers recognized that the law alone was not enough to attain the goal of democratic employment. It was merely a first step. Getting people to follow the law was the key, and what was needed for this to occur was its endorsement by the powers that be – industry, labor, and public bodies: "As authorities, they can convince others; as power-wielders, they can translate belief into action."[86] In the end, integration was as much the result of persuasion and negotiation as coercion and pressure.

[86] Aaron Antonovsky, "The Social Meaning of Discrimination," in *Discrimination and Low Incomes ... Studies under the Direction of the New York State Commission Against Discrimination by the New School for Social Research*, ed. Aaron Antonovsky and Lewis Lorwin, eds., (NY: New York Interdepartmental Committee on Low Incomes, 1959): 307–324, p. 322.

7   The National Association of Manufacturers Helps Out

The National Association of Manufacturers (NAM) has long been a paragon of American business conservatism. Since its founding in 1895, the NAM has fought against unions, taxes, labor legislation, and the encroachment of the federal government into private enterprise. It opposed the New Deal and did everything in its power to subvert the prounion Wagner Act (1935). Its battle against the Wagner Act helped secure the passage of the Taft-Hartley Act (1947), which limited unions' power and signified a rightward shift in postwar domestic policy. In the 1950s, it continued its war against "creeping socialism," standing athwart history, becoming in the eyes of the liberal establishment a bitter, extremist organization with little relevance in mainstream life.

Yet the NAM endorsed fair employment with regard to racial minorities and women beginning in 1941, restated its commitment to equal opportunity in the 1950s, and helped implement the equal opportunity legislation of the 1960s. The NAM facilitated and encouraged compliance with civil rights legislation and worked closely with government agencies such as the President's Committee on Equal Employment Opportunity (PCEEO), the Office of Contract Compliance (OFCC), and the Equal Employment Opportunity Commission (EEOC) to publicize the new regulations among small and medium-sized businesses. The NAM generally opposed federal legislation, but it did not officially oppose Title VII of the 1964 Civil Rights Act nor did it try to stop its passage. It did however prefer voluntary approaches to legislation and encouraged its members to take affirmative actions to integrate their companies. It is true that the NAM opposed the imposition of quotas and the OFCC's preferential hiring schemes, but after failing to stop them, the NAM urged compliance with them.

In its efforts on behalf of equal employment opportunity, the organization made itself relevant to American businesses in a way that it hadn't been for more than a decade. The NAM's activities on behalf of EEO enforcement were part of a larger organizational transformation carried out by Werner "Gully"

Gullander, a former General Dynamics executive and NAM president from 1962 to 1973. Gullander purged the extremists and, like so many NAM leaders before him, attempted to make the NAM (and conservatism) relevant in a changing world. The moral authority of equal opportunity helped rehabilitate the NAM's image in the corporate establishment, while NAM's authority among conservative businessmen and small employers helped legitimate Title VII and affirmative action in the workplace. This chapter will examine the NAM's crucial and, heretofore, unrecognized, role in the integration of the workplace.

About the NAM

The NAM was founded in 1895 to protect high tariffs, fight unionization, and provide manufacturers with useful information. Although historians regularly refer to the NAM to illustrate antilabor activism and extremism, little has actually been written about the organization. There is, for instance, no book-length history of the NAM. Nonetheless, what emerges from assorted articles and references is a story of an organization that has struggled, not always successfully, to balance a conservative ideology with a pragmatic flexibility. Since its inception, the NAM has claimed to be the voice of American business and industry, and yet American business and industry has not always been comfortable with the NAM's ideological rigidity. When historians refer to the NAM it is often to identify a rift in the business community between conservatives (represented by NAM) and more enlightened, pragmatic corporate liberals (represented variously by Progressive-era reformers, the Business Advisory Council [BAC], the Committee for Economic Development [CED], and even the post–World War II Chamber of Commerce).[1] Several articles have argued that NAM's ideological "backwardness" made it an ineffective lobby and unrepresentative of the business community.[2] Malcolm Forbes called the NAM's endorsement "the kiss of death." But neither the NAM's ineffectiveness nor its membership was a constant over its hundred-year history.

[1] See, for example, James Weinstein, *The Corporate Ideal in the Liberal State, 1900–1918* (Boston, 1968); Kim McQuaid, *Uneasy Partners: Big Business in American Politics, 1945–1990* (Baltimore: Johns Hopkins University Press, 1994); Andrew Workman, "Manufacturing Power: The Organizational Revival of the National Association of Manufacturers, 1941–45," *Business History Review* 72, no. 2 (Summer 1998): 279–317. Labor historians have also made mention of the NAM, see Julie Greene, *Pure and Simple Politics: The American Federation of Labor and Political Activism, 1881–1917* (New York: Cambridge University Press, 1998).

[2] Philip H. Burch, Jr., "The NAM as an Interest Group," *Politics and Society* 4, no.1 (1973): 97–130; Richard Gable, "NAM: Influential Lobby or Kiss of Death?" *Journal of Politics* (May 1953); and less adamantly, Alfred Cleveland, "NAM: Spokesman for Industry?" *Harvard Business Review* 26, no. 3 (May 1948): 353–71.

From 1895 until 1932, the NAM represented and was dominated by small to medium-sized firms. It was conservative but so too was much of the nation. During the Depression, the organization's membership shrank. At the same time, its leadership structure changed, as anti–New Deal corporate executives took refuge – and leadership positions – in the NAM. From 1935 through the late 1940s, large corporations dominated the NAM leadership. By 1935, close to 60 percent of the board of directors membership came from the upper ranks of major manufacturing firms, including Colgate-Palmolive, General Mills, Eastman Kodak, and Standard Oil of Ohio. Sixty to 75 percent of the executive committee consisted of representatives from large corporate concerns.[3] The most prominent of these, during the 1930s, were active in right-wing organizations such as the Liberty League. They included executives from General Foods, Colgate-Palmolive, Du Pont, General Motors, Lambert Pharmaceuticals, and General Mills. Under their leadership, the NAM opposed almost all of the New Deal legislation and gained a reputation as an ineffective, churlish lobby. *Fortune* magazine wrote of these years: "all industry has suffered from N.A.M.'s maladroit presentation of industry's case."[4]

During the war years and immediately thereafter, the NAM remained dominated by large corporations, but there emerged a small group of men who were interested in making NAM more effective. Alarmed at the rising tide of corporate liberalism – signified by Eric Johnston's leadership of the Chamber of Commerce and the creation of the CED (both in 1942) – these men sought to make the NAM a relevant voice in postwar economic planning, which meant offering a more positive program, creating unity within the association, and acknowledging the right of workers to organize. Much of this work was done through public relations campaigns, but it also involved reorganizing the association and infiltrating liberal business organizations.[5] By the summer of 1945, NAM activists occupied six of the eight spots on the BAC's labor relations committee.[6] By 1946, the NAM had respun its antiunionism into a stance of labor-management cooperation and economic productivity. Even *Fortune* noted the change: "Industry's intransigent spokesman now says 'yes' as well as 'no.'"[7] The NAM had softened its cantankerous rhetoric, but its unlikely

[3] Burch, "The NAM as an Interest Group," 97–130; Burch defines "big business" as worth more than $50 million.
[4] "Renovation in the NAM," *Fortune*, July 1948, 72–75, 165 ff., quote on p. 72.
[5] See Elizabeth Fones-Wolf, *Selling Free Enterprise: The Business Assault on Labor and Liberalism, 1945–1960* (Urbana: University of Illinois Press, 1994), and Workman, "Manufacturing Power," 279–317.
[6] Workman, "Manufacturing Power," 308.
[7] "Renovation in the NAM," 72–75, 165 ff.

resurrection was due mainly to a general postwar reaction against the perceived excesses of the New Deal. The NAM's stock rose during conservative periods. With its newfound relevance, the NAM was able to play an indeterminate but apparently substantial role in the passage of the Taft-Hartley Act in 1947, which in the eyes of conservatives and Republicans put some much-needed legal restraints on the actions of unions.[8]

During the 1950s, the association's leadership reverted to the executives of small and mid-sized family-owned companies. By 1955, large corporate representation on the board of directors had fallen to a low of 29 percent.[9] The new leadership marked a return to arch-conservatism. In 1953, fifteen out of the twenty-five members of the executive committee were involved in one or more rightist movements of the 1950s. The NAM of these years was an incubator for John Birch Society leadership. Founded in 1958, the John Birch Society became the epitome of cranky right-wing extremism – *Fortune* called it "bizarre" – in part because its founder, Robert Welch, Jr., charged President Eisenhower and Secretary of State John Foster Dulles with being communist agents. Robert Welch, an executive at his brother's small Connecticut candy-making firm, sat on the NAM executive committee throughout the 1950s. Historian Philip Burch argues that "the bulk of the economic leadership of the John Birch Society seems to have emerged out of a set of corporate executives who had been associated with the upper echelons of the NAM in the post-World War II period."[10] This number included three NAM presidents: Cola Parker, president of Kimberly-Clark Corporation, a Wisconsin corporation; William Grede, president of Grede Foundries, a mid-sized Wisconsin firm; and Ernest Swigert, president of the Hyster Company, a medium-sized manufacturer of heavy equipment in Oregon.[11] The rancor of the Birch Society and other right-wing organizations in the 1950s was directed against communism and the liberal economists, internationalists, and intellectuals who seemed to tolerate it. During this era, the NAM again lost its relevance in the mainstream business community and was widely dismissed as an extremist organization.

Despite the extremism of the NAM leadership during the fifties, its Industrial Relations Department endorsed the "human relations" approach to management. Based on the idea of "social interdependence," the human relations

[8] Gable, "NAM."

[9] Burch, "The NAM as an Interest Group," 106.

[10] Ibid., 122.

[11] "The N.A.M. and the J.B.S.," *Fortune*, May 1961, 74. It is worth noting that many of these manufacturers were from Wisconsin, Senator McCarthy's state, or other parts of the Midwest. For details, see Burch, "The NAM as an Interest Group."

philosophy was fundamentally at odds with the traditional conservative values that the NAM represented. Human relations experts de-emphasized the authority of the boss, valued teamwork over the individual, and used sociology and psychology to control employees rather than coercion. There are two ways to understand this incongruence. On the one hand, the NAM's promotion of human relations can be seen as evidence that human relations techniques were fundamentally a way to subvert unionism.[12] On the other hand, it can also be an indication that not all parts of the NAM were as ideologically rigid and homogeneous as has been assumed. Perhaps there were NAM members who were less ideologically extreme than those who have been the focus of study.[13]

During the 1960s, a new leadership regime once again tried to refashion the association into a useful, pragmatic organization that would be able to represent industry's interests. In the face of declining membership, money, and clout, concerned NAM members made efforts to recruit larger corporations, which were often, as historian Jonathan Soffer points out, defense contractors with close ties to the government.[14] As more contractors became part of the NAM, the association's traditional antipathy to the government and government largesse receded. In 1961, President John F. Kennedy, oddly, became the first U.S. president to speak before the NAM. After the president's speech, longtime NAM member and management consultant Murray Shields wrote to Walter Heller, the very liberal chairman of the very liberal Council of Economic Advisors, about the speech's success among NAM members: "I heard many individuals of competence (Republican as well as Democrat) say that his arguments were exceedingly hard to disagree with and that it is high time that the business interests in this country worked closer and more cooperatively with whatever Administration happened to be in power."[15] Shields's views represented long-buried, pragmatic elements in the NAM, which in 1962 appointed

[12] See Sanford Jacoby, *Modern Manors: Welfare Capitalism since the New Deal* (Princeton, NJ: Princeton University Press, 1997).

[13] See especially "The New Challenge in Industrial Relations," an Address by Earl Bunting, June 21, 1948, as well as other materials in National Association of Manufacturers, Records, 1895–1990 (hereafter NAM Records), Series 7, Boxes 136 and 143, "Human Relations" and "Employee Relations" folders, at Hagley Museum and Library (hereafter HML). For a critique of the teamwork and social liberalism of the human relations approach, see William H. Whyte, *The Organization Man* (Garden City, NY: Doubleday-Anchor, 1957).

[14] Jonathan Soffer, "The National Association of Manufacturers and the Militarization of American Conservatism," *Business History Review* 75 (Winter 2001): 775–805. Soffer's excellent article on the militarization of the NAM is the only historical work on the NAM during this crucial period (Burch, "The NAM as an Interest Group," covers the 1960s in one paragraph).

[15] Murray Shields to Walter Heller, December 22, 1961, in Presidential Office File, Box 73, Counsel of Economic Advisors folder, at the John F. Kennedy Presidential Library. My thanks to Aaron Minor for pointing this out to me.

a new president, Werner Gullander, a vice-president from a major government contractor, General Dynamics. Gullander purged the Birchers from leadership positions and set out to create a more tolerant, open, and cosmopolitan NAM, one that understood the modern realities (and opportunities) of government contracts, one that took seriously businesses' social responsibility.[16] It remained antiunion, of course, but otherwise seemed to accept the so-called liberal consensus of the postwar decades. NAM speakers professed an interest in working with the government, not against it, and, in December 1963 the organization pledged to cooperate with the new Johnson administration.[17] By the late 1960s, the NAM seemed amenable to the Johnson administration's social welfare initiatives, even as it sought what it termed "private solutions to public problems." Gullander hired government officials to help develop business solutions to inner-city problems and began new programs like MIND (Methods of Intellectual Development) to train inner-city youth for white-collar jobs, and STEP (Solutions to Employment Problems).[18] Once again, the NAM had shed its crankiness and pragmatically adapted to the realities of American political life.

The NAM and Fair Employment, 1941–61

The NAM's softening attitude toward government contracts provides some context for understanding its position on civil rights in the 1960s, but it is not the whole story. Long before its moderate turn, the NAM had supported equal opportunity for minorities and women (as well as older workers and the physically handicapped). In June 1941, the organization officially adopted an antidiscrimination position, pledging its support to President Roosevelt's policy of nondiscrimination in the war industries. In August 1941, NAM President Walter D. Fuller of Curtis Publishing Company reiterated the policy at the historically black Lincoln College, exhorting as if he were a fair employment activist, "The right to work is one of the most sacred rights of every individual." Also in August, Howard Coonley, chairman of the executive committee and board chairman of the Walworth Company, spoke before the Improved

[16] Soffer, "The National Association of Manufacturers," 786–88; see also "The Surging Tide of Change," an Address by J. Stanford Smith, December 1, 1964, in NAM Records, Series 7, Box 135, HML.

[17] "N.A.M. Pledges Aid to Johnson," *New York Times*, December 5, 1963.

[18] See Soffer, "The National Association of Manufacturers," 788, Theodore Leavitt, "The Johnson Treatment," *Harvard Business Review* (January–February 1967): 114–28; and NAM Records, Series 7, Boxes 136 and 143, "Human Relations" and "Employee Relations" folders, HML.

Benevolent and Protective Order of Elks, an African American fraternal organization, about breaking down the color line in industry and "full equality of
employment opportunity."[19]

Nor was the policy limited to speech making before black audiences. The
NAM's Industrial Relations Department began commissioning and collecting
research about the "color-line" in industry during World War II. Its researchers
summarized for NAM members Urban League reports and corporate "experiments" with integration. They reported on the operation of state Fair Employment Practices Committees (FEPCs). They prepared arguments for "the full
utilization of minority groups" that drew from the human relations idea that
fair employment was just good management.[20] The impetus behind these
activities seems to have been President Roosevelt's ban on racial discrimination in the war industries. But there was nothing insincere or disingenuous
about their support of what NAM officials called "individual opportunity."
Indeed, as we saw in Chapter 2, it comported perfectly with the NAM philosophy of individualism, business responsibility, antiunionism, and the free
market.

Even the most conservative NAM members, those associated with the
Birch Society, and those least capable of being pragmatic, spoke out for equal
opportunity during the 1950s. In 1953, William Grede, president of Grede
Foundries, Inc., NAM chairman, and allegedly one of the secret founders of
the Birch Society, gave an address at the historically black Lincoln College in
Jefferson City, Missouri, entitled "NAM Speaks out for Equal Opportunity."
The address emphasized how equal opportunity supported the principles of
American individualism and opportunity but that restating principles was
not enough; action was necessary. After listing the NAM's actions, which
included educational workshops, reaching out to minority group leaders, and
distributing fair employment pamphlets, he offered what is still a common
refrain, "but still more remains to be done." Grede emphasized "merit" and
competition, ideas that fair employment activists also emphasized. Echoing
Booker T. Washington, Grede reminded his black audience of the wisdom
of starting at the bottom and working harder than anyone else. The punch
line was that Negro Americans' best chance of success was the competitive

[19] "Fuller on Job Discrimination," *NAM Newsletter*, August 9, 1941; and NAM Press Release,
    dated August 26, 1941; both in NAM Records, Series 7, Box 135,HML.
[20] Opinion Research Corporation, "The Color Line in Industry," April 1944; "Problems of Racial
    Discrimination," memo, August 5, 1942; "Office of Production Management," memo, May 10,
    1941; "Suggested Outline for Booklet Implementing NAM's Position against Discrimination,"
    and "Report on Operation of New York Anti-Discrimination Law," in NAM Records, Series
    7, Boxes 135 and 136, HML.

system, unhampered by government control and union power.[21] A conservative message, certainly, but it was also an invitation to blacks to participate in the workforce. It is evidence that even the most conservative industrialists recognized minority employment as an important issue. Another John Bircher, NAM vice-president Charles R. Sligh, Jr., addressed the National Conference of Christians and Jews on the importance of tolerance. In an address entitled, "Intolerance Is a Heart Disease," Sligh condemned bigotry and xenophobia and gave examples of what American industry was doing to stem their prevalence. Speeches like these, of course, were self-serving, but at the same time, they contributed to the vilification of racism and the development of a new antiracist consensus. Moreover, other organizations, such as the liberal BAC, were not giving public addresses on racism.

We know from earlier chapters that a large part of the NAM's support for equal employment opportunity grew out of its desire to avert legislative solutions. There are at least two other, not unrelated, ways of understanding it. The first is that the NAM leadership understood the ways in which equal opportunity undercut union power. NAM antiunionism was couched in a rhetoric of the "right to work," which, it is worth noting, was a slogan for both fair (and full) employment activists of the 1940s and the open-shop "right-to-work" activists of the 1960s.[22] NAM claimed to speak for those many workers who chose not to join unions and those who could not (minority group members). One of the points the NAM indoctrinated in its members was the "need for protecting individual workers and minority groups from practices of majority bargaining representatives."[23] The NAM made sure that the various governmental committees concerned about fair employment understood that the prejudices that prevented minority employment originated with workers and unions, not management. During the war, NAM secretary Noel Sargent requested that the House Committee on Labor Migration collect the names of all unions that refused membership to Negroes and conduct studies to determine the effect of the "closed shop" on Negro employment.[24] This was

[21] "NAM Speaks out for Equal Opportunity," excerpts from a speech by William J. Grede... April 30, 1935," in NAM Records, Series 7, Box 135, HML.

[22] See David Grant testimony: "I feel that the man who deprives me of my right to work makes prostitutes of my daughters and convicts and criminals of my sons." In U.S. Congress, House Committee on Labor, *To Prohibit Discrimination in Employment* (Washington, DC: U.S. Government Printing Office, 1944), 53. On the "Right to Work" movement, see Robert Zieger, *For Jobs and Freedom: Race and Labor in America since 1865* (Lexington: University Press of Kentucky, 2007), 172–73; and George Leff, *Free Choice for Workers: A History of the Right to Work Movement* (Ottawa, IL: Jameson Books, 2005).

[23] Quoted in Workman, "Manufacturing Power," 279–317, p. 301.

[24] *NAM Newsletter*, July 19, 1941.

not just about "passing the buck" but rather reminding government agencies, the public, and particularly the black public that "compulsory unionism" undermined workers' individual rights.

Fearful that newly employed black workers might be attracted to unions, NAM officials reminded African Americans that unions were exclusionary and that their best chance for employment was to work with employers. NAM officials tracked and tried to counter the efforts of the Congress of Industrial Organization (CIO) to recruit African Americans.[25] Black activists themselves were briefly divided on the question of unions, and their new position in the New Deal Democratic coalition put them in a difficult position. On the one hand, blacks stood to gain from the expansion of federal power and the precedent set by prolabor laws, which gave the government license to regulate employment policies. On the other hand, however, prolabor legislation strengthened exclusionary unions' power in the workplace, which worked against black employment. Inasmuch as the Taft-Hartley Act (1947) outlawed the closed shop and prohibited unions from unfair labor practices (such as discrimination), it was potentially a good thing for black employment.[26] By the end of World War II, A. Philip Randolph and the CIO's own efforts had convinced most black leaders that unions could be an ally, but this possibility only spurred the NAM to work harder to convince blacks that industry was their best bet.[27]

Second, the NAM's interest in equal opportunity may have been the result of certain individuals' convictions and energy. Just as Sara Southall goaded executives at International Harvester to embrace integration, a woman named Phyllis Moerhle may have played a similar role at the NAM. Like Southall, Moerhle was an officer in the Industrial Relations Department. Also like Southall, Moerhle seems to have been a woman of convictions, in this case

---

[25] See "Problems of Racial Discrimination" [1942] and [memo] from Office of Production, Labor Division, May 10, 1941, for tracking of CIO efforts, in NAM Records, Series 7, Box 136; "Fuller on Job Discrimination," NAM Press Release, dated August 26, 1941; and "NAM Speaks out for Equal Opportunity," April 30, 1953, for addresses before black colleges, in NAM Records, Series 7, Box 135, HML.

[26] See Paul Moreno, *Black Americans and Organized Labor: A New History* (Baton Rouge: Louisiana State University Press), 167; Robin D. G. Kelley and Earl Lewis, *To Make Our World Anew: A History of African Americans* (New York: Oxford University Press, 2000), 415; and Herbert Hill, *Black Labor and the American Legal System: Race, Work and Law* (Madison: University of Wisconsin Press, 1985), originally published by the Bureau of National Affairs, 1977, p. 102; Moreno, *Black Americans and Organized Labor*, 211.

[27] On this issue, see Eric Arnesen, "The Quicksands of Economic Insecurity': African Americans, Strikebreaking, and Labor Activism in the Industrial Era," in *The Black Worker: Race, Labor, and Civil Rights since Emancipation* ed. Eric Arnesen (Urbana: University of Illinois Press, 2007), 41–71; and Beth Tompkins Bates, "A New Crowd Challenges the Agenda of the Old Guard in the NAACP, 1933–1941," *American Historical Review* 102, no. 2 (April 1997): 340–77.

religious ones. Moerhle was active in the Presbyterian Lay Committee, serving as its director after her retirement from the NAM.[28] During the 1940s and 1950s, Moerhle was the NAM's point person on race and gender issues. She answered inquiries about the NAM's equal opportunity position, crafting somewhat lengthy but informed letters that show an awareness of the latest fair employment literature.[29] She represented the NAM on fair employment panels. During the 1960s, she receded to the background, becoming support staff, even as the NAM devoted more resources and energy to the issue of equal employment opportunity.

In 1950, Moerhle represented the NAM at the National Urban League's annual conference. The tone of her report of the Urban League conference was positive, but in a way that was designed to persuade its recipients (other NAM leaders) of the value of NAM's antidiscrimination activities. She emphasized the benefits accrued by her attendance at the conference. First, there was the public relations advantage: "I was invited to sit at the speaker's table at an official luncheon on Thursday and was introduced to the audience – many of whom I noted expressed visible surprise and pleasure at having an [sic] NAM representative present." Second, there were the valuable contacts she made: "I had the occasion to talk privately with [NUL officers], and feel that considerable benefit should accrue from these contacts, both as to our greater understanding of their efforts and their better acceptance of our Association." Finally, she was able to clear up misconceptions of the NAM's policy, such as the presumption that the organization opposed FEP legislation:

> I was able to win considerable support – as evidenced by audience reaction – with a brief explanation that the NAM has no position on Fair Employment Practice Legislation, either for or against the bill. In contrast, I emphasized that we have a firm policy urging employers to examine their personnel practices to make sure that no arbitrary discrimination exists.

With regard to this last point, Moerhle added: "It is my sincere feeling that we are sound in refraining from taking a position at present on FEPC, but I believe we should be giving serious thought to some further implementation of our policy. Unless some record of accomplishment or achievement results from our leadership action, we are still somewhat vulnerable."[30] This last point suggests

[28] "Moerhle, Husband of Lay Committee Director, Dies," *Presbyterian Layman* 34, no. 1 (Jan. 24, 2001), at www.layman.org/layman/the-layman/2001.

[29] See, for instance, Phyllis Moerhle to Robert Hill, April 19, 1955, and Phyllis Moerhle to John Fallon, November 14, 1949, in NAM Records, Series 7, Box 135, HML.

[30] Quotes from Phyllis Moerhle, "Summary Report of the Annual Conference of the National Urban League – Grand Rapids, September 3rd to 8th, 1950," in NAM Records, Series 7, Box 135, HML,

that there was probably disagreement on the issue among NAM members and that she was here making a case for not opposing FEP legislation and for continuing the nondiscrimination activities. One of her suggestions was for the *NAM News* to review Sara Southall's book.

The NAM and Equal Employment Opportunity Legislation, 1957–65

Throughout the 1950s, liberals had attempted to introduce legislation setting up a permanent, federal FEPC. Individual NAM members testified for or against such legislation, but the NAM neither opposed nor supported an FEP law. Nor was the NAM involved in the maneuvering to prevent civil rights legislation from coming to the Senate floor for debate. For decades, southern Democrats and their Republican allies had been able to thwart civil rights legislation by threatening a filibuster that could only be stopped with a two-thirds majority. The two-thirds majority was required by Senate Rule XXII. Liberals would expend a great deal of energy trying to change this rule by proposing cloture (closure of debate) with a simple majority vote. In July 1957, Georgia Senator Herman Talmadge wrote to the NAM requesting that it record its position on Senate Rule XXII.[31] Calvin Skinner, of NAM's Industrial Problems Committee, responded that the NAM did not have an official position on "this or any related subject," and said that the committee would investigate whether it should have a position on the issue. On October 8, the committee had prepared information on the cloture issue and passed it on to general counsel Lambert Miller with the comment, "You will note that no attempt was made to draw any conclusions or to formulate any recommendations."[32] No real attempt had been made to even research the issue, other than to find the different versions of the proposed changes. It was common to have no position on a controversial issue. What it tells us, however, is that the NAM was not joining southern Democrats' efforts to sink civil rights legislation. It seemed to be sitting on the sidelines in 1957.

The NAM was concerned about the various civil rights bills that Congress was considering in 1963 and 1964, bills that would have significant implications for employers and NAM members. The NAM law department closely tracked the bills' progress through Congress, exchanging dozens of memos featuring

[31] On cloture and the 1957 Civil Rights Bill, see Timothy Thurber, *The Politics of Equality: Hubert H. Humphrey and the African American Freedom Struggle* (New York: Columbia University Press, 1999), 69–70, 102–5.

[32] Calvin Skinner to Ernst Farley, Jr., July 31, 1957, and Memo dated October 8, 1957, in NAM Records, Series 7, Box 136, HML.

accounts of the changes.[33] NAM officials had the same concerns about the new bills that they had had about Executive Order 10925 (1961). The terms "discrimination," "to discriminate," and "race" remained undefined. The bills provided no standards of proof or evidence, and it seemed likely that evidence for noncompliance could consist of the existence of disproportionately low number of minorities. The bills provided no due process to employers accused of discrimination. NAM officials were concerned that the reach of the new law might apply as well to managerial positions and perhaps even corporate boards. They were concerned that suits might be brought not just by individuals but also by organizations acting on behalf of individuals.[34] There were other questions, as well. What was the relationship between the new laws and already existing state and local legislation, NLRB procedures, and executive orders? Who would be responsible for the financial costs of the investigations, hearings, and trials? From the perspective of business owners, these were reasonable concerns. Even liberals were concerned about standards of proof and the redundancy of antidiscrimination agencies.

Despite these misgivings, the NAM did not officially oppose the law. It seems to have retained its position of "no position" with regard to equal employment opportunity legislation. Although NAM officials questioned the constitutionality of the proposed civil rights bills, they seemed resigned to the likelihood that the Supreme Court would uphold the new laws, lamenting in one instance that the Johnson administration was "confident that the broad grant of authority proposed in Title VII of the bill will be upheld [by the court]."[35] NAM members wrote suggesting, urging, the NAM to take some action to stop the civil rights bill or at least certain aspects of it.[36] The NAM indulged its members, responding politely that it was keeping track of the legislation but took no steps to rally the troops against it. The association organized no letter-writing campaigns (as it had, for instance, with regard to the tax-reducing Sadlak-Herlong Bill of 1958). It issued no manifestos

---

[33] See, for example, Memo, Ted Compton to Staff, October 7, 1963, "Background on Civil Rights" and "Memorandum Regarding Civil Rights Bill" (S. 1731) [May 30, 1963] in NAM Records, Series 5, Box 65, and "Outline of Proposed Changes in Civil Rights Bill, H.R. 7152," in NAM Records, Series 7, Box 135, HML.

[34] From "Summary Analysis of Equal Employment Provisions (Title VII) of the Civil Rights Bill, H.R. 7152, as reported by the House Committee Judiciary," November 7, 1963, Prepared by the NAM Law Department, in NAM Records, Series 7, Box 135, HML.

[35] "Memorandum Regarding Civil Rights Bill" (S. 1731) [May 30, 1963], p. 15, in NAM Records, Series 5, Box 65, HML.

[36] C. E. Cunningham to Ted Compton, March 26, 1964; W. Harnischfeger to W. P. Gullander, July 29, 1964; Marshall Diebold to W. P. Gullander, March 31, 1964, and others in NAM Records, Series 5, Box 65, HML.

or calls of alarms, as it had with the Wagner Act. To do so "could be so easily misinterpreted," as one executive put it.[37] Instead, NAM officials helped develop voluntary programs like Plans for Progress and prodded their members to adopt voluntary affirmative action policies to integrate their companies. The NAM's recruitment campaign for Plans for Progress (discussed in the previous chapter) occurred in late 1963 and can be considered part of the NAM's response to Title VII. Also in 1963, the NAM launched what was loosely referred to as the "minority program," which sought "to provide free market solutions to the current Negro employment problem."[38] Working with black cosmetics manufacturer S. B. Fuller, the program aimed to motivate African Americans to take advantage of education and training opportunities.

While NAM members may have once hoped that voluntary actions might avert legislation, by 1963, they understood that federal legislation was inevitable. Their activities on behalf of voluntary programs and "private solutions" were not intended to stop legislation but to gain legitimacy for the NAM among its peers, as well as with the government agencies, so that it might play an informed role in the coming battles over enforcement of the new legislation. There are many indications that this was NAM's strategy, but the Industrial Relations Committee stated it explicitly in an October 1964 meeting at the Hotel Delmonico. The minutes of that meeting show that the Industrial Relations Committee sought to make the NAM "a channel through which [business] leadership flows" to government, educators, clergymen, and industry itself. Singled out was its effort with regard to Title VII: "Dealing with the government offices concerned with this legislation, we will attempt to develop industry's views and problems."[39]

NAM's interest in voluntary initiatives was also part of its efforts to rehabilitate its image and become a real interest group. Werner Gullander had been appointed president of the NAM in 1962 with the expectation that he would remake the NAM into a forward-looking, progressive organization. In a 1964 speech, General Electric's vice-president of Marketing and Public Relations, J. Stanford Smith, described Gullander's mission:

> Two years ago Gully Gullander, with the full backing of the directors of NAM, took on a mighty job – to develop NAM into the kind of association which is vitally needed in this nation – an association in step with the surging tides of change that are sweeping the world – an association that will sound the

[37] C. E. Cunningham to Ted Compton, March 26, 1964, NAM Records, Box 65, Series 5, HML.

[38] "Minority Program," n.d., in NAM Records, Series 7, Box 135, HML.

[39] NAM Industrial Relations Committee, Minutes, October 27, 1964, p. 8, in NAM Records, Series I, Box 26.

alarm to threats that would hamper industry's ability to serve the American people, but even more important, an association that will sound the clarion for national progress.[40]

Smith reminded the audience of public relations men that industry was a progressive, even revolutionary force and that it was essential that its organizations take a leading role in "tackling the problems and opportunities" that change brings. Smith pointed to several examples of what the NAM had done to show its leadership and meet the challenges of human progress. The first two examples were the NAM's initiatives in "hard core unemployment" and "equal employment opportunity," both of which pertained to issues of minority employment (the former with automation and deskilling, the latter with discrimination).[41] Let us look more closely at its initiatives in the area of equal employment opportunity.

After the passage of the Civil Rights Act in July 1964, the NAM began a nationwide series of seminars to help business owners and managers adjust to what it called "the new era in industrial relations." By December 1964, Charles Kothe, NAM's vice-president of industrial relations, had conducted twenty-two seminars attended by more than three thousand businessmen from large and small companies. Featuring officials from state FEP agencies, the federal government, integrated businesses, and the Urban League, the message of the seminars was "get your house in order" now before the Civil Rights Act became active the following July. Given the roster of speakers, it is not surprising that NAM seminars affirmed what state FEP agencies had long been telling employers: do not practice tokenism; do not lower standards; do re-evaluate testing requirements; do consult with union leaders; do maintain a daily log of hiring and recruiting instructions.[42] Even if you think a black salesman will be unable to sell to your white customers, you must hire him if he is otherwise qualified. Quotas are illegal, but they may be appropriate in some situations to remedy unlawful discrimination. While NAM legal analysts had critiqued the ambiguity of such statements, NAM seminars endorsed them. A NAM survey taken of seminar attendees indicated that nearly half of the six hundred respondents who had participated in the seminar had initiated "positive action programs" or broadened already existing programs, including revising testing procedures and working with the Urban League to find qualified candidates

---

[40] "The Surging Tide of Change," an Address by J. Stanford Smith, December 1, 1964, in NAM Records, Series 7, Box 135, HML.

[41] Ibid., 6–7. The fourth example represented a remarkable turnaround in the NAM's program: "the challenge of developing constructive relations with government ... "

[42] Charles Kothe, "Some DOs and DON'Ts for Management under Title VII of the Civil Rights Act of 1964" [n.d., ca. 1965], in NAM Records, Series 7, Box 135, HML.

for new positions. Only 9.8 percent complained of the cost of implementation. And only 3.6 percent indicated any trouble with new job applicants. The survey included both small (fewer than five hundred employees) and large (more than five hundred employees) companies from all regions of the United States.[43] The survey showed businesses in a positive light, as one would expect a NAM survey to do. But it was also a prod to those businesses not yet on board, those that had taken no action. It was form of peer pressure – kudos to those far-seeing leaders who had gone along with the program, a challenge to those who hadn't. Leaders who took steps to integrate their firms became a model of what appropriate behavior was in this new era. In addition to the seminars, the NAM published numerous pamphlets and a compliance guidebook that covered Title VII, the EEOC, federal contract compliance, seniority, testing, sex discrimination, and affirmative action.

Introducing the seminars, NAM president Gullander stated that "no piece of legislation since the Wagner Act of three decades ago will have a more significant bearing on industrial relations procedures than Title VII of the new act."[44] In 1935, the NAM had condemned the Wagner Act (which protected union activities) and sought to subvert it. In contrast, Gullander's NAM endorsed Title VII, cooperated with the government to implement it, and instructed its members how to comply. The seminars then were not merely a sign of NAM's leadership on equal employment opportunity but also, as important, an indication that the NAM (the NAM!) was cooperating with the federal government for the larger social good. And the results were spectacular, not so much in terms of black advancement, but in rehabilitating the NAM's reputation. The executive director of the Baltimore Urban League wrote to Kothe about the program: "NAM and you are to be congratulated .... It is a far-sighted project and should do much to promote equal employment opportunity as called for under Federal law."[45] A NAM member wrote Gullander the following:

> The comments which I have received as a result of these meetings would hearten you and the other directors of NAM. I would hope that further meetings of this caliber could be programmed because they would make real contributions to the industrial life of all the companies and, no doubt, would make the job of increasing membership in NAM much easier.[46]

[43] Press release "News from the National Association of Manufacturers," Friday, January 7th [n.d. 1965], in NAM Records, Series 7, Box 135, HML.

[44] "Seminars to Help Members Deal with Civil Rights Act," *NAM Reports* 9, no. 30 (July 27, 1963 [*sic*]): 1.

[45] Furman Templeton to Charles Kothe, November 5, 1964, in NAM Records, Series 7, Box 135, HML.

[46] Henry Harding to W. P. Gullander, October 2, 1964, in NAM Records, Series 7, Box 135, HML.

In its own report on the seminars, the NAM emphasized its leadership role in the business community, noting that the New York Chamber of Commerce and the University of Pennsylvania's Wharton School were now offering seminars, "essentially similar to our own series."[47]

The NAM further increased its visibility in the business community by positioning itself as a mediator between government agencies and its members. It organized two informational sessions in December 1963 and 1964 to help companies consider the pros and cons of joining Plans for Progress. During these sessions, the NAM claimed neutrality on the question: it neither advocated nor opposed participation. It self-consciously assumed a mediating role, as one report explained: "The Association was credited with performing a unique function by bringing together companies which had decided to join with those who had not. The free exchange of questions and answers, off the record, revealed both advantage and disadvantages of participation."[48] After the Civil Rights Act was passed, the NAM fielded dozens of letters from NAM members across the nation, inquiring about the availability of guidelines, the constitutionality of the law, or the implications of pending or new legislation. Often business owners did not want to wade through all of the material and just wanted an answer to a single question. Which party was responsible for legal costs? Do I follow the guidelines of the existing state FEPC or the new EEOC? This is what our company has done, are we in compliance? To these requests, the NAM sent answers and pamphlets. Many letters complained about problems with the new legislation, such as the conflict between state FEPCs, which prohibited the collection of racial data, and the EEOC, which required it, and, later, the conflict between OFCC requirements and Title VII. They reported that state employment commissions were sending decoys to apply for positions. They groused about the inclusion of women in the legislation.[49] The NAM was a sounding board for these complaints. There were also more positive letters, which expressed appreciation for NAM's help and reported that the new legislation was less burdensome than expected.[50] All of this indicates that NAM was no longer an extremist club for a few irate businessmen but, finally, a useful spokesman for industry.

---

[47] Progress Report Re Seminars on Title VII of the Civil Rights Act, December 1, 1964, in NAM Records, Series 7, Box 135, HML.

[48] NAM, Industrial Relations Division, "Employment of Minorities," February 1964; see also nearby memos from Charles Kothe to Sam Berry, Bennett Kline, headed "Employment of Minorities," dated January 20, 1964, all in NAM Records, Series 7, Box 135, HML.

[49] Scott Seydel to Don Robinson, January 15, 1968; Robert Landon to Lambert Miller, June 19, 1968; Donald Lenarz to Lambert Miller, April 2, 1962, in NAM Records, Series 5, Box 65, HML.

[50] C. L. Irving to Lambert Miller, August 4, 1964, in NAM Records, Series 5, Box 65, HML.

The new NAM, however, found itself in a delicate position. It had successfully shed its older, crippling image of extremism, and this would allow
it to play a larger role in the formulation of policy, as we will see later. But
with cooperation came compromise, and this meant risking the ire of its old
members, who expected the NAM to curb government intervention, not sur-
render to it. The association was bombarded with letters from irate members,
who had less interest than the NAM in equal opportunity, demanding to
know what steps the association was taking to fight the legislation. Mrs. W. R.
McElvey, a businesswoman from Norcross, Georgia, was critical of NAM literature because it seemed "not as concerned about this Senate bill" as it ought to
have been.[51] The head of a small southern switchgear company wrote, "What
is NAM doing to stop this nonsense?"[52] A conservative, former NAM leader
named W. Harnischfeger of Milwaukee wrote urging that NAM find a case to
test the constitutionality of the new law before the Supreme Court.[53] NAM officials' replies to these suggestions were sympathetic but noncommittal, citing
the current political climate as a factor inhibiting action. They vaguely assured
James L. Williams, the personnel director of a Greensboro, North Carolina,
company, that "we are keeping in close touch with developments in this area
[S. 1308] ... we will, of course, move promptly in determining what we can
most effectively do in order to accomplish the desired result."[54] In one instance,
a NAM official reminded an irate letter writer that connecting equal opportunity with government contracts began with the Eisenhower administration –
there was nothing new really about the Johnson administration's efforts.[55]

One gets a sense of the NAM's dilemma from these letters. Its new public
image, its willingness to work with the government, its decision to interpret
legislation rather than fight it were all designed to enhance the organization's
ability to represent its members' interests in the halls of government. But as
the demands of the EEOC and the OFCC on employers became more onerous,
many members were left to wonder whether the NAM was really protecting their interests. By ingratiating itself with the Johnson administration, the
NAM gained some small amount of influence but found itself uncomfort-
ably complicit in one of the most ambitious expansions of federal power in
U.S. history.[56] Previously, the NAM's emphasis on voluntarism had helped

[51] Mrs. W. R. McElvey to Lambert Miller, August 14, 1967, in NAM Records, Series 5, Box 65,
      HML.
[52] M. E. DeNeui to Lambert Miller, March 2, 1970, in NAM Records, Series 5, Box 64, Folder:
      Philadelphia Plan, HML.
[53] W. Harnischfeger to W. P. Gullander, July 29, 1964, in NAM Records, Series 5, Box 65, HML.
[54] General Counsel to James L. Williams, July 13, 1967, in NAM Records, Series 5, Box 65, HML.
[55] [NAM] to Ed C. Burris, November 14, 1968, in NAM Records, Series 5, Box 65, HML.
[56] "N.A.M. Pledges Aid to Johnson," New York Times, December 5, 1963.

it straddle these competing tensions. Voluntarism had indicated cooperation with state ends, while upholding private means. By the late 1960s, however, with northern cities engulfed by rioting, the rise of increasingly militant black leaders, and a black unemployment rate double that of whites, voluntarism was not enough, and the NAM had to get down to the real work of lobbying.

The Struggle over Enforcement: EEOC and OFCC

By 1967, a typical large corporation, likely to be a defense contractor or subcontractor, had to comply with the EEO guidelines of, and report to, the following government agencies: the EEOC, which enforced Title VII; the OFCC, charged with enforcing Executive Order 11246 (which had replaced and superseded President Kennedy's Executive Order 10925, requiring contractors to take affirmative steps toward nondiscrimination under threat of contract cessation); the Department of Defense; various state and municipal antidiscrimination committees; and the Civil Rights Division of the Justice Department.[57] Of these, the EEOC and OFCC were most actively seeking to expand and redefine the scope of their powers, through new legislation where possible, otherwise through increasingly radical regulations, which were tested and upheld in the courts.

From 1965 to 1972, the fight over enforcement engulfed the civil rights community, the various government agencies charged with enforcing new EEO legislation, Congress, and the courts. The struggle spanned the administrations of two presidents and found a shaky resolution under the Nixon administration. Through it all, the NAM continued to prove its efficacy as an interest group for industry and was able to work with and through government agencies to weaken the more stringent requirements, especially with regard to "quotas." At the same time, however, it helped its membership adjust to the new regulations and in doing so helped make both the EEOC and OFCC more effective as government agencies.

The EEOC

The EEOC that emerged after the congressional debates over Title VII of the 1964 Civil Rights Act was, in the much-quoted words of one disappointed

---

[57] See, for instance, letter from Warren Shaver, U.S. Steel Corporation, to William Zimke, October 26, 1967, in NAM Records, Series 5, Box 64, HML,; Hugh Davis Graham has an even lengthier list, which includes the National Labor Relations Board and the U.S. Attorney General, on p. 156, Hugh Davis Graham, *The Civil Rights Era: Origins and Development of National Policy, 1960–1972* (New York: Oxford University Press, 1990).

activist, "a poor, enfeebled thing." It could receive and investigate complaints of discrimination, but it had no enforcement powers. It could not prosecute companies nor could it order them to cease and desist discriminatory behavior. It had to defer to state and local FEPCs. Moreover, to ensure passage, liberals had added amendments to the bill that limited its scope. Thus, Title VII specifically stated that accidental or inadvertent discrimination (of the sort that resulted from seniority, testing, and educational level) did not violate the law; that nothing in the law required an employer to maintain a racial balance in his workforce; that, in fact, any deliberate attempt to maintain a racial balance would violate the law; and that nothing in the law required employers to abandon bona fide qualification tests, even if, because of cultural or educational differences, members of some groups did not perform well on the tests. Moreover, the new EEOC, with its vague mandate and structural position, would be competing for resources and jurisdictional power against older, established equal employment bureaucracies.[58] These weaknesses were compounded by underfunding and the labor-intensive process of fielding and investigating individual complaints. As a result, there was a backlog of cases, which by 1968 exceeded thirty thousand.[59]

To correct these deficiencies, liberals and civil rights activists wanted to make the EEOC into a proper regulatory agency with cease-and-desist powers, modeled after the National Labor Relations Board. Among other things, such a model shifted the burden of enforcement from individual victims of discrimination to the federal government. Not all liberals believed this was the best strategy. Afred Blumrosen, a Rutgers law professor who had briefly worked for the EEOC in its first year, believed that a regulatory agency modeled after the NLRB was susceptible to co-optation by those it was supposed to regulate. Nor had state FEPC agencies with cease-and-desist powers proved that successful. The judicial impartiality required of a regulatory agency interfered with its ability to be an advocate for a particular group or cause – as the experience of the NYSCAD demonstrated (see previous chapter). Blumrosen thought a "weak" EEOC could be an effective advocate and prosecutor, bringing cases before the courts, rather than judging them itself. The courts were friendlier to civil rights than they had been previously. But the liberal community, still close to its New Deal heritage, and the civil rights community, still seeking the legitimacy of its own agency, held on to the ideal of a regulatory agency with cease-and-desist powers.[60]

---

[58] The best discussion of the details of the compromise remains, Graham, *The Civil Rights Era*, 125–176, 233–54.

[59] Graham, *The Civil Rights Era*, 422.

[60] Blumrosen believed, in 1969, that the weak EEOC "enabled civil rights groups to use the federal courts which are favorable to their demands." Quoted in Graham, *The Civil Rights*

What appeared like a weak, enfeebled agency to liberals and civil rights activists was a scourge to employers and the NAM. As the members of the EEOC grew more militant and activist, employers felt harassed. Contractors had been used to working with the Department of Defense (DOD) and the old Presidential Compliance Committees in a spirit of cooperation. They experienced the EEOC (and the new OFCC) as upstart organizations and resented their requests for information, which had already been given to DOD, the contracting agency, or state FEPCs.[61] They saw the EEOC as overreaching its mandate by *requiring* "affirmative action plans" or working with the state antidiscrimination committee to target certain employers.[62]

Employers' biggest complaint was the lack of coordination among government agencies, which seemed to be competing against one another, rather than working together. Companies found themselves the target of several separate investigations at once, sometimes with different outcomes. In 1965, U.S. Steel was investigated by both the EEOC and OFCC, neither of which seemed to acknowledge the efforts the company was making.[63] Increasingly the regulations of one agency contradicted those of another. In 1968, the OFCC's infamous Philadelphia Plan required construction contractors to correct racial imbalances in each craft category through the use of quotas, which violated EEOC regulations against taking race into account in hiring.[64] In the face of the EEOC's activist tendencies, the NAM quietly opposed liberal attempts to increase EEOC power.

In January 1969, the Democratic Congress took up several EEO enforcement bills, which proposed to grant cease-and-desist powers to the EEOC and considered shifting the OFCC's compliance duties to the EEOC. (Like employers, liberals were concerned about the effectiveness of redundant and

Era, 431. For full discussion of the merits of regulator versus advocate-and-authority means of enforcement, see Graham, *The Civil Rights Era*, 429–31.

[61] See, for instance, Warren Shaver, U.S. Steel Corporation, to William Zimke, October 26, 1967, in NAM Records, Series 5, Box 64, HML. See also "Where Civil Rights Law Is Going Wrong," *Nation's Business* 53, no. 11 (November 1965): 60–67.

[62] Richard Noyes to Lambert Miller, April 16, 1969, in NAM Records, Series 5, Box 64; and Scott Seydel to Don Robinson, January 15, 1968, in NAM Records, Series 5, Box 63, HML.

[63] See "Concern of EEOC," *NAM Reports*, November 20, 1967; Warren Shaver, U.S. Steel Corporation, to William Zimke, October 26, 1967; W. K. Zimke to A. W. Elliot Memo, Nixon Proposal on EEOC, April 23, 1969, in NAM Records, Series 5, Box 64, Folder: 1969 Civil Rights, HML; Rohm and Haas Co. to Lambert Miller, June 19, 1969, in NAM Records, Series 5, Box 63, HML. On the issue of redundancy and bureaucratic competition, see Graham, *The Civil Rights Era*, 177–204; Judith Stein, *Running Steel, Running America: Race, Economic Policy and the Decline of Liberalism* (Chapel Hill: University of North Carolina Press, 1998), 103–18.

[64] See NAM Law Department Memo, dated April 25, 1969, regarding "authority of the Office of Federal Contract Compliance pursuant to E.O. 11246" in NAM Records, Series 5, Box 64, HML, and Graham, *The Civil Rights Era*, 322–45.

overlapping compliance structures.) Together with the ongoing urban crisis, growing black unemployment, and racial violence, the bills ensured that the incoming Nixon administration would be forced to deal with the civil rights issue.

Although Richard Nixon's presidential campaign had successfully cultivated and benefited from white resentment of civil rights (the so-called southern strategy), Nixon had long shared the moderate Republican position in support of racial progress. He had been the head of Eisenhower's Committee of Government Contracts, and thus was familiar with the obstacles to minority employment. In an early campaign speech before the NAM, where one might have expected him to denounce civil rights excesses, Nixon instead said that racial injustice was the most urgent issue facing the nation and had to be corrected if the United States hoped to win in Vietnam. The answer to the racial crisis was not to repress the militants but, rather, exhorted Nixon, "to seize the initiative ourselves; to forge new alliances among the forces of progressive change, to accept the challenges that the disinherited have flung both at our conscience and to our ingenuity."[65] The audience showered Nixon with hearty, approving applause. Although the dominant historical interpretation of Nixon remains that he paid little attention to domestic affairs, there is a growing body of work that emphasizes his civil rights achievements.[66] By April 1969, the new Republican administration was able to offer several alternatives to the Democrats' civil rights bills.[67]

The NAM's Manpower and Personnel Committee met in May 1969 to discuss the Nixon administration's two alternatives to the Democratic bills.[68] The first option would integrate the OFCC into the EEOC; grant cease-and-desist powers to the new EEOC, with enforcement in the U.S. district courts; and create an Office of General Counsel in the EEOC, appointed by the president. This option gave the EEOC cease-and-desist powers, which NAM opposed, but on the plus side, it offered to streamline compliance organizations and guarantee the employer a trial, both reforms the NAM supported. The second approach would cast the EEOC as "a huge conciliation agency," with no cease-and-desist powers "but with the power through its own attorneys to go into a District

---

[65] "Nixon Puts Rights Ahead of Vietnam," *New York Times*, December 9, 1967, 1.

[66] See Dean Kotlowski, *Nixon's Civil Rights: Politics, Principle, and Policy* (Cambridge, MA: Harvard University Press, 2001), and Joan Hoff, *Nixon Reconsidered* (New York: Basic Books, 1994), for instance.

[67] Graham, *The Civil Rights Era*, 421.

[68] The Manpower and Personnel Committee consisted of NAM Industrial Relations staff and executives from First National City Bank (New York), the Bogart & Carlough Company (New Jersey), Sybron Corporation (Rochester, NY), Eastman Kodak Company, ESB Corporation (Philadelphia), Trans World Airlines (New York), and ACF Industries (New York).

Court for a trial de novo on the merits where conciliation fails." This second approach was very similar to what Alfred Blumrosen had proposed, an EEOC that was advocate and prosecutor, using its own lawyers to sue companies for whom conciliation had been unsuccessful. At this point, the NAM's focus was on curbing the power of the OFCC, whose hated Philadelphia Plan, it felt, was wreaking havoc in the construction industry. Thus, the committee favored the plan that would merge the EEOC and OFCC.[69]

The Nixon administration went with the second approach, backing a bill in August 1969 that granted the EEOC authority to bring suit in federal district court. The OFCC would stay in the Labor Department. Although the NAM admitted privately that "we can live with the Administration's approach," it was reluctant to publicly support it, because, in the words of an internal memo, "taken alone, it amounts to a substantial additional grant of power to the EEOC."[70] By 1971, however, with Congress still trying to pass a bill granting enforcement powers to the EEOC, the NAM came out in support of the administration's position and urged its members to do so as well. A NAM analyst noted that "business generally does support the court approach contained in H.R. 9247 as under this legislation, the EEOC is the prosecutor and the court is the judge – thus assuring to some extent the separation of powers and due process concepts."[71] Indeed, the NAM and businessmen had been complaining about the lack of due process since the days of the PCEEO. Thus, when this version of the bill finally passed as the Equal Employment Opportunity Act of 1972, the NAM's interests were not unrepresented.

Still, neither the NAM's Industrial Relations Department nor its Legal Department seemed to have been overly concerned about the liberal direction of recent court decisions, such as the 1971 *Griggs* decision that replaced Title VII's original standard of discriminatory intent with a standard of discriminatory effect, thereby making incidental discrimination unlawful.[72] Given conservatives' later critique of the liberal strategy of using the courts to legislate reform, it is somewhat ironic that the conservative NAM supported the bill that validated the courts as the proper arena for civil rights disputes. Historian Hugh Graham Davis notes this irony in his discussion of how each

---

[69] To Members of the Manpower and Personnel Subcommittee, June 9, 1969, in NAM Records, Series 5, Box 64, Folder: 1969 Civil Rights, HML.

[70] "Notes on the EEOC Hearings, August 11 and 12, 1969," in NAM Records, Series 5, Box 64, Folder: 1969 Civil Rights, HML.

[71] "NAM Legislative Proposal – An Analysis," August 20, 1971, in NAM Records, Series 5, Box 64, Folder: 1969 Civil Rights, HML.

[72] Paul Moreno, *From Direct Action to Affirmative Action: Fair Employment Law and Policy in America, 1933–72* (Baton Rouge: Louisiana State University Press, 1997).

party's proposed bill contradicted its desired outcome. The Democrats and liberals favored the NLRB cease-and-desist model, which they hoped would confer legitimacy on the EEOC. But large employers had adjusted to regulatory agencies, which had, as Woodrow Wilson had once feared, proved vulnerable to their influence. The Republicans and employers for their part endorsed a judicial strategy that gave employers due process in the courts and avoided the dreaded cease-and-desist solution. But during this era of unrest and protest, the courts were no longer protectors of the status quo but had become instigators of reform. In fact, they tended to be more liberal than the regulatory agencies. As Graham notes, "both sides seemed to be betting on the wrong horse."[73] Given the political ambiguities of the proposed solutions, and given that the NAM actually supported the Equal Employment Opportunity Act of 1972, it can hardly be said that the NAM opposed civil rights. It is more accurate to say that the organization opposed the dominant liberal version of civil rights.

The OFCC

Like the EEOC, the OFCC was a new bureaucracy with a vague mandate whose purported duties put it in competition with more established, powerful bureaucracies. Created with President Johnson's Executive Order 11246 in September 1965, the OFCC replaced the old PCEEO and was housed in the Department of Labor. It was charged with ensuring that federal contractors practiced the principles of nondiscrimination. Unlike President Kennedy's Executive Order 10925, which it had replaced, Executive Order 11246 had constitutional legitimacy by virtue of Title VI of the 1964 Civil Rights Act, which stipulated that federal funds could be cut off if companies were not in compliance with nondiscrimination laws. Staffed by black activists and white liberals, the OFCC adopted a more confrontational attitude than its predecessors had; its policies were designed to overcome the structural impediments to integration, such as hiring criteria, seniority practices, and testing.

The relationship between the NAM and the OFCC was cordial and professional, as both organizations sought to further their constituents' goals. Perhaps reflecting the role of contractors in the NAM, NAM officials communicated more regularly with OFCC officials than they did with EEOC administrators. Underneath this veneer of professionalism, however, there was a real struggle. The NAM sought to protect employers from what it saw as an

---

[73] Graham, *The Civil Rights Era*, 430.

overreaching, capricious agency with little understanding of the constraints within which employers operated. Concerned business owners and employers wrote to the NAM with their complaints about the OFCC, its cavalier tactics, and its impractical solutions.[74] The NAM's legal department tracked the OFCC's initiatives, plotted to curb its power, and supported legislation that would have subsumed the OFCC under the EEOC.[75] In addition to protecting employers' interests, the NAM was trying to preserve business's ownership of the concept of affirmative action. Affirmative action was at the center of the NAM's voluntary initiatives to integrate American firms. As part of its EEO seminars, the NAM had advised companies how to take affirmative action to put themselves in compliance with the new legislation and regulations. For the NAM, affirmative actions were voluntary suggestions. Companies chose which suggestions made sense for their particular situation, whether it was recruitment reforms, re-evaluating job qualifications, or creating a new office to oversee EEO actions.

The OFCC had its own ideas about what affirmative action meant. Seeking to end the structural barriers to integration, OFCC regulations redefined "affirmative action" as "results," which meant minority hires and promotions.[76] This was the idea behind the Philadelphia Plan, first floated in November 1967. The plan applied to construction contractors only and required them to submit, as part of their bid for the job, an affirmative action plan specifying the number of minorities it would hire in each craft category, with the idea of attaining a racial balance in proportion to the number of minorities in the local population. "Results," then, could mean a racial balance, something very close to quotas, which of course were illegal. The first version of the Philadelphia Plan was successfully stymied by the Associated General Contractors and the U.S. comptroller general, who declared it invalid in November 1968.

The OFCC's version of affirmative action was exhibited also in its new regulations, which it posted in the *Federal Register* on May 28, 1968. The NAM had received a draft of the regulations and offered its comments to the OFCC in hopes of softening some of the more stringent requirements. The NAM's comments were about details, not principles. Conceding the right of the OFCC to propose regulations, it asked only that the regulations "reflect on the part of the government an understanding of employer ability and capacity to deal

[74] See March 25, 1969, memos about the Timken Company; Warren Shaver, U.S. Steel Corporation, to William Zimke, October 26, 1967, in NAM Records, Series 5, Box 64, HML.

[75] See January 25, 1968, memo marked Office of Federal Contract Compliance, Confidential, in NAM Records, Series 5, Box 63, HML.

[76] "OFCC Equal Employment Opportunity Commission Compliance Efforts" [n.d., presumed 1968], in NAM Records, Series 5, Box 64, Folder: Philadelphia Plan, HML.

effectively in this area [EEO policy]."[77] In its concise ten-page memo, the NAM sought to secure for employers due process and judicial review and tried to convey to the OFCC the practical difficulties of particular regulations. For instance, the regulations required the contractor to impose regulations on subcontractors, failed to define the standard of compliance, and contradicted Title VII.

OFCC officials Ward McCreedy and Len Bierman met with the NAM to discuss the NAM's concerns and fears. According to the NAM notes of the meeting, McCreedy and Bierman told them to focus on "results," not trying to reach a standard, just more "results." Employers must concentrate not on whether a recruit *can* do a particular job, but whether he or she *is capable of doing* that job. In other words, employers' recruitment efforts must shift "from developed ability to apparent potential." Employers must determine whether the number of minority job applicants is close to the percentage of the total population of minorities in the area, and if it is not, employers must take all steps to make it so. Employers would not have to end testing but would have to demonstrate a significant relationship between test performance and job behavior. Government representatives would also be looking to see whether cut-off scores were "so high as to impede a realistic affirmative action program." In addition, employers must eliminate departmental seniority and find a way to "determine where each Negro employee would be today in terms of position etc., but for the discrimination worked against them through segregated seniority practices." The OFCC suggested that this could be done by finding "a presently employed white, hired at about the same time as the Negro, whose abilities at the time of employment appear comparable to the Negro in question" and training that Negro.[78] If there was trouble with the union as a result of these changes, the OFCC assured employers that the government would assist companies in quelling union objections, either by enjoining a union from striking or helping an employer file a charge against the union under Title VII. Government officials would be looking for a list of all hires, by race and by position, as well as a list of those not hired. OFCC demands made on the pulp and paper industry included the employment, with back pay, of Negro applicants who would have passed the tests had the revised standards been in place when they had originally applied for the job, and the placement of black employees into white departments at a rate no less than the number of white employees. If these efforts failed to yield "results," the contractor would

---

[77] "Comments by the National Association of Manufacturers on Proposed Regulations of Office of Federal Contract Compliance Issued Pursuant to Executive Order 11246" [n.d., presumed March 1968], in NAM Records, Series 5, Box 64, Folder: Philadelphia Plan, HML.

[78] "OFCC Equal Employment Opportunity Commission Compliance Efforts" [n.d., presumed 1968], p. 3, in NAM Records, Series 5, Box 64, Folder: Philadelphia Plan, HML.

not necessarily be found in noncompliance as long as it could give evidence that it had tried these "suggestions."

The OFCC's version of affirmative action, then, sought to undo the discriminatory effects of past practices. Its demands were far more detailed and disruptive than what the NAM recommended, and seemed to rely on a standard of racial proportionalism that contradicted Title VII. Despite the impracticable nature of some of the suggestions and the legal ambiguity of the standard, the NAM minutes of the meeting recorded no disgruntlement or objection, in part because there appeared to be room for negotiation: "It was clear that all demands made by OFCC or contracting agencies are made for the purpose of negotiating equitable solutions."[79] In addition, the OFCC offered assurances that evidence of effort was enough to keep a company in compliance. As long as there was room for negotiation and the recognition of a good-faith effort, the NAM was able to work with the OFCC and interpret its regulations to its members.[80]

While the OFCC's plan for what amounted to quotas was meeting resistance from unions, construction contractors, and the comptroller general in the summer of 1968, the NAM, in conjunction with the still operating Plans for Progress program, organized a series of four regional conferences on "Equal Employment Opportunity and Affirmative Action," to be held in October 1968. In some ways, the conference series was an attempt to retain business ownership over the concept of affirmative action. Featuring representatives from the EEOC, OFCC, and industry, the conferences aimed to hold a two-way conversation in which government officials could learn from industry and vice versa. After some deliberation, the conference organizers decided to include the phrase "affirmative action" in the conference title in order to, as the organizers put it, "make it clear by 'affirmative action' that we mean industry action and not compulsory and arbitrary action as imposed by the government."[81] The conferences were successful in terms of conveying to government agents the practical problems and contradictions created by the new regulations, and NAM officials even believed that they had increased acceptance of the NAM by the EEOC and OFCC.[82] But subsequent events would show that their efforts to retain control of the meaning of affirmative action had failed.

---

[79] Ibid., p. 10.

[80] "Summary Analysis of Revised Regulations of the Office of Federal Contract Compliance," in NAM Records, Series 5, Box 64, Folder: Philadelphia Plan, HML.

[81] NAM Memo, August 21, 1968, to W. K. Zimke, from H. C. Williams, in Series 5, Box 64, Folder: Plans for Progress, HML.

[82] NAM Memo, R. D. Godown to L. H. Miller, October 4, 1968, in NAM Records, Series 5, Box 64.

In June 1969, the OFCC introduced a revised Philadelphia Plan. Unlike the previous version, this one would specify the number of minorities needed in each craft category for bidders to be successful. Because exact numbers would have been considered a quota, technically prohibited by Title VII, the new plan specified a target "range," expressed in percentages, within which contractors could determine their own minority "goals." So that, for instance, Philadelphia contractors promised that between 5 percent and 8 percent of the plumbers and pipe fitters they hired in 1970 would be minorities.[83] The new plan had the backing of Secretary of Labor George Shultz and the Nixon administration, who saw it as a way to break the craft unions' grip on the labor market and thereby lower skyrocketing construction costs.[84] In addition, the plan had the effect of pitting two Democratic constituencies (labor and blacks) against each other. It was in many ways an antilabor measure more than a civil rights initiative, and yet even this did not persuade conservatives in the NAM, who viewed the plan as a gross abuse of power on the part of the OFCC. The NAM joined organized labor and Democrats in opposing the Republican plan, which received the implied approval of Congress in a vote against a rider to an appropriations bill that would have barred federal funding to agencies that were in violation of federal statutes.[85]

In subsequent months, federal courts would uphold the constitutionality of the Philadelphia Plan and, moreover, equate it with affirmative action. In March 1970, in what was regarded as the Philadelphia Plan's first court test, Judge Weiner of the U.S. District Court in the Eastern District of Pennsylvania explained part of his rationale for upholding the legality of the Philadelphia Plan:

> The heartbeat of "affirmative action" is the policy of developing programs which shall provide in detail for specific steps to guarantee equal employment opportunity keyed to the problems and needs of members of minority groups, including when there are deficiencies, the development of specific goals and timetables for the prompt achievement of full and equal employment opportunity. The Philadelphia Plan is no more or less than a means for implementation of the affirmative action obligations of Executive Order 11246.[86]

[83] Graham, *The Civil Rights Era*, 327.
[84] Ibid., 322–329; Stein, *Running Steel, Running America*, 148–53; John David Skrentny, *The Ironies of Affirmative Action: Politics, Culture and Justice in America* (Chicago: University of Chicago, 1996), 215.
[85] Graham, *The Civil Rights Era*, 339–40.
[86] "Philadelphia Plan Survives its First Court Test," *Washington Outlook, a Staff Report to NAM Members*, March 30, 1970, in NAM Records, Series 5, Box 64, Folder: Philadelphia Plan, HML.

The NAM's attempt to control the meaning of affirmative action had failed. But that wasn't the worst of it.

As bad as it was from the NAM's perspective, the Philadelphia Plan applied only to the construction industry. In November 1969, however, OFCC head John Wilks issued a new order that applied the Philadelphia Plan's version of affirmative action to all government contracts. Order no. 4, as it was called, required all government contractors to hire minority applicants at a rate approximating the ratio of minorities to the applicant population in each location.[87] It appeared to make quotas mandatory, although it did not set specific goals and targets as the Philadelphia Plan had. In a painful twist for NAM leaders, John Wilks explained that Order no. 4 simply made mandatory the affirmative action guidelines of the old Plans for Progress program. (The Nixon Administration had merged Plans for Progress into another Johnson era program, the National Alliance of Businessmen.[88]) The guidelines Wilks had chosen to make mandatory were the very ones that the NAM had written to accompany the PFP/NAM-sponsored conferences on "Equal Employment Opportunity and Affirmative Action" in the fall of 1968, the purpose of which had been to preserve the voluntary component of affirmative action. Indeed, when *BusinessWeek* chortled that the NAM was the "unhappy parent of new hiring rules," the NAM's legal counsel quickly responded that such a claim was "not consistent with the facts" since the NAM had intended the guidelines to be voluntary. Making them mandatory changed their meaning and placed "an extremely heavy burden on those seeking to do business with the government."[89] One gets the sense that the letter was directed in part to outraged NAM members who were already suspicious of the NAM's acquiescence to the OFCC.

In the wake of the controversy, the Labor Department revised Order no. 4 and re-presented it to the public on February 3, 1970. Although historian Hugh Graham described the new Order no. 4 as "largely unchanged," the NAM found it much more acceptable and tried to persuade its membership that the OFCC had been forced to "tone it down." The NAM reported that the revised version did not call for "rigid and inflexible quotas" but rather "goals." "Underutilization" was no longer defined as a strict racial proportionalism but

---

[87] Graham, *The Civil Rights Era*, 342.

[88] Richard Nixon, Statement on the Merger of the National Alliance of Businessmen and Plans for Progress, June 13, 1969, on John T. Woolley and Gerhard Peters, *The American Presidency Project* [online]. Santa Barbara, CA: University of California (hosted), Gerhard Peters (database). Http:/www.presidency.ucsb.edu/ws/?pid=2099.

[89] Harding Williams to The Editor, Draft, January 26, 1970, in Box 64, Series 5, Folder: Philadelphia Plan; "The Unhappy Parent of New Hiring Rules," *BusinessWeek*, January 24, 1970.

rather the softer "having fewer minorities in a particular job category than would be reasonably expected by their availability." And finally, the revised Order no. 4 recognized a "good faith effort" as compliance even if the company failed to achieve the desired results.[90] The time and effort required by a company to be in compliance were still enormous – requiring studies of area labor demographics and recalculations of seniority placement – but at least employers could be assured that having made the effort they would not be denied a contract if they failed to achieve all of their numerical goals. Having had a hand in tempering the OFCC's affirmative action policy, the NAM then convinced its members to comply with it.

After receiving the NAM's Law Department memo about the revised order, M. E. DeNeui, a small switchgear manufacturer from Fulton, Missouri, wanted to know what the NAM was doing "to stop this nonsense." DeNeui wrote, "Small companies like ourselves will be helpless without an aggressive counterattack by NAM. Let's get to work!"[91] Unfortunately for Mr. DeNeui, NAM had already done its best. After acknowledging the problems with Order no. 4, the NAM law department responded:

> In truth, however, it must be stated that the order, which bears an effective date of January 30, 1970, is a much modified and softer approach than the original version of Order No. 4 which bore the date of November 20, 1969. We feel that the softer line taken by the Labor Department was the result of a number of actions taken inside and outside government. Throughout the controversy, which began with the proposed "Philadelphia Plan" and ran through the final publication of Order No. 4, NAM was foremost in drawing public attention to the various considerations involved through the publication of a series of articles in "NAM Reports."[92]

One can imagine that this reply did not help Mr. DeNeui, the head of a small company with twenty-five to thirty employees, muster the resources and know-how to conduct the demographic surveys required by the new regulations.

How then might we assess the NAM's influence on the evolution of affirmative action policy? Given its inability to thwart the OFCC's power, to stop the use of racial proportionalism as a legal standard, or to retain its own voluntary version of affirmative action, its influence seems weak at best. And yet the NAM

[90] NAM Law Department Memo, Summary Analysis of Revised Order No. 4 Regarding Affirmative Action Programs Under Government Contracts, February 12, 1970, in NAM Records, Series 5, Box 64, Folder: Philadelphia Plan, HML.

[91] M. E. DeNeui to Lambert Miller, March 2, 1970, in NAM Records, Series 5, Box 64, Folder: Philadelphia Plan.

[92] Assistant Counsel to Mr. M. E. DeNeui, March 10, 1970, in NAM Records, Series 5, Box 64, Folder: Philadelphia Plan, HML.

was there for the whole process, communicating with the OFCC, commenting, objecting, mediating, cooperating. Although shorn of their original intent, the NAM guidelines for affirmative action became the basis of OFCC affirmative action regulations. Most important, the NAM helped its membership accept and adjust to the new legislation. The NAM's memos were straightforward, with no sly editorial comments. They simply instructed executives on how to put their companies in compliance. Their matter-of-factness made outrageous requests (such as recalculating where black workers would be in seniority had they been white when they were hired) normal and necessary.

Conclusion

Fair employment activists always understood that the effort to integrate American workplaces would require a high level of cooperation among government agencies, businesses, and unions. It could not be a top-down effort on the part of government alone. The law was too precise an instrument to eradicate the deep, pervasive patterns of exclusion and discrimination in U.S. economic structures. Laws were necessary, of course, but their implementation would depend on the good-faith efforts of businesses and unions. While many individual business owners balked, NAM officials made the decision to cooperate with government and, using the human relations techniques it recommended to companies to manage labor, helped its members adapt to the new realities and onerous, contradictory policies. So well had the NAM acclimated its members to the new situation that large corporations overwhelmingly opposed the Reagan administration's 1985 attempt to revoke the goals and timetables requirements of Executive Order 11246.[93]

Without mediating conservative organizations like the NAM, which spoke in a language business owners and employers could understand, compliance would have been a nightmare or nonexistent. Given the vagueness of the new laws, the disruptions inherent in the new regulations, integration required, in the end, real cooperation, which is by definition voluntary. Some might argue that had the EEOC been stronger, had the NAM not worked to weaken its powers of enforcement, it could have more effectively implemented the law. To believe that underestimates the pervasiveness and extent of racial exclusion and discrimination and the degree to which following the letter of the law

[93] Anne B. Fisher, "Businessmen Like to Hire by the Numbers," *Fortune* 112 (September 16, 1985): 26, 28-30. See also "A New Drive to Reaganize Equal Opportunity," *BusinessWeek*, March 11, 1985, 42 and Herman Schwartz, "The 1986 and 1987 Affirmative Action Cases: It's All over but the Shouting," *Michigan Law Review* 86, no. 3 (December 1987): 524–576.

was not enough to dismantle the structures of discrimination. Even today, the diversity experts who are carrying on the struggle for integration, understand that following the law is not enough to "diversify" institutions, which continue to be largely white. Key people in leadership positions have to cooperate, believe, and persuade others.

In playing this role, the NAM resembles its rival, the CIO. Like their counterparts in the CIO, NAM officials tried to persuade a recalcitrant and, in some cases, perhaps, racist membership of the importance of integration. They used arguments that would appeal to businesspeople, just as CIO leaders used arguments that would appeal to unionists. Like the CIO, the NAM was not entirely successful in its efforts, since many businesses, like many unions, continued to practice discrimination and exclusion. But unlike the CIO, the NAM has received no recognition for its efforts. Those who have credited business's role in integration tend to focus on the more liberal members of the business community, but the NAM's activities had a much deeper reach among individual business owners than those of the enlightened executives.

8   Changing Hiring Criteria

We have a growing conviction that we should not restrict our hiring entirely to qualified applicants, even if the supply of qualified applicants permitted us to do so.
Charles Luce, Chairman of the Board, Consolidated Edison, 1969[1]

Finally, we just tore up the regular [application] form and devised a very simple one. You want a job, describe why you want it.
William Norris, founder and CEO of Control Data Corporation[2]

In the late 1960s, American cities were in a state of crisis marked by racial unrest, high unemployment, and urban decay. The Kerner Commission on Civil Disorders blamed the crisis on white racism and recommended the creation of 2 million new jobs, comprehensive school desegregation, a massive job-training program, and a guaranteed income. The heads of major corporations tried to rally their peers to regain control over the situation, to assert the leadership of the so-called private sector. In the words of a senior vice-president of First National City Bank of New York, "Government has demonstrated its inability to deal with many of these problems effectively and it is imperative that the talents and experience of business be brought to bear upon them."[3] Although many within the business community rejected the idea that businesses should become agents of reform, others embraced the role. In a short-lived burst of social responsibility, employers took on the job of training what were termed variously "the hard-core unemployed," the "unemployable," or "the disadvantaged," the majority of whom were imagined as black.

---

[1] Charles Luce, "Consolidated Edison and the Hard Core," *Training in Business and Industry* 66 (March 1969): 46–53.

[2] "Corporate Do-Gooder Bill Norris," *Inc.*, May 1988, 37–52, quote on p. 37.

[3] E. Sherman Adams, "The Public Role of Private Enterprise," in *Business and the Cities*, ed. Neil W. Chamberlain (New York: Basic Books, 1970), 13–18, quote on p. 14.

The project of turning disadvantaged black people into tax-paying employ-ees entailed dropping traditional hiring criteria and qualifications. Employers threw out tests, references, and demands for previous work experience and even waived such basic requirements as a high school diploma and the ability to read and write. A prison record? Not a problem. Traditional hiring criteria, experts said, had been designed to screen people out – not necessarily black people per se, but rather all people who did not have what were deemed "basic qualifications." The new mission, subsidized in some cases by government funds, was to find ways to pull people into jobs and to develop their potential to be productive employees. By 1970, at least twenty-five thousand large firms were part of this mission. Massive advertising campaigns to enlist businesses in the endeavor further disseminated the idea that traditional hiring criteria kept good people out of jobs.

It is the argument of this chapter that corporate experiences with the hard-core unemployed helped white managers overcome their traditional hiring biases and thus sped up workplace integration in the early 1970s. This seems counterintuitive – one would assume that the special efforts that had to be made would confirm stereotypes rather than allay them. But race riots and disproportionately high rates of black unemployment had already convinced many employers that special efforts had to be made to get young black men off the streets and into society. What the hard-core programs showed was that traditional hiring criteria could and indeed should be re-evaluated if business was going to be part of the solution. It is true that the Equal Employment Opportunity Commission (EEOC), encouraged by the Motorola case (1966) in Illinois and later the Supreme Court's *Griggs v. Duke Power Co.* (1975), demanded that employers reassess their testing procedures and hiring criteria. But many employers had begun to do that anyway in their voluntary efforts to hire the disadvantaged, which, as it turns out, were closely linked to their attempts to meet contract compliance and EEOC requirements.

Hiring the hard-core unemployed was different from the integration of middle-class African Americans into all levels of the workforce. The former was a voluntary manpower development program aimed at helping lower-class blacks; the latter was (after 1964) required by law. Yet the techniques developed to hire the hard-core unemployed – the dropping of traditional hiring criteria, the acknowledgment of special racial considerations, sensitivity training – were deployed as well in the implementation of affirmative action plans. The language of disadvantage, which was used to justify special efforts to hire the "unemployables," was used as well to justify affirmative action for middle-class, professional blacks. Both the hard-core unemployed project and affirmative action programs resurrected old human relations ideas, such as recognizing the potential of individual workers, understanding the workplace as a social community, and rationalizing employee relations. The relationship between the hard-core project and racial integration went beyond techniques, moreover. Employers used the government-subsidized training programs to meet EEOC and Defense Department compliance requirements. At their most successful, the hard-core jobs programs cultivated minorities who could be promoted and advanced within the company, helping to meet affirmative action goals.[4]

White managers had long complained about the dearth of "qualified" blacks, but researchers found that their definitions of "qualified" were informed by traditional assumptions about black work and white work. It took something like the hard-core training programs, which completely eviscerated traditional hiring criteria, to get white managers to relinquish those assumptions and just start hiring minorities – not regardless of race, but regardless of their qualifications. It is at this point that color-blind ideals gave way to recognition of black employees' special circumstances.

Unemployment, Urban Crisis, and State Solutions

Racism (in the form of educational, economic, and residential discrimination) was a major long-term factor in the urban crisis, but the immediate causes of the crisis were less racial than economic. Beginning in the late 1950s, automation, the growth of high-technology industries, and plant relocations had decreased the number of well-paying production jobs in the urban centers in which the majority of blacks resided. In Detroit, for instance, there had been 3,453 manufacturing firms in 1954, supplying 232,300 production jobs, whereas by 1967 there were 2,947 manufacturing firms, with 149,600 production jobs. In 1972, there were 2,398 firms with 125,000 production jobs.[5] Between 1954 and 1972, Detroit had lost 46 percent of its production jobs. In Cleveland, the number of production jobs declined from 354,200 in 1948 to 283,200 in 1967.[6]

---

[4] Jobs programs were also key to integrating craft unions. According to sociologist Jill Quadagno, jobs programs "became the vehicle for implementing equal employment opportunity as federal officials used the programs to integrate the skilled trades." Quadagno, "Social Movements and State Transformation: Labor Unions and Racial Conflict in the War on Poverty," *American Sociological Review* 57 (October 1992): 616–34.

[5] Thomas Sugrue, *The Origins of the Urban Crisis: Race and Inequality in Postwar Detroit* (Princeton, NJ: Princeton University Press, 1997), chart on p. 144. See also Nicholas Lemann, *The Promised Land: The Great Black Migration and How It Changed America* (New York: Vintage, 1991).

[6] Judith Stein, *Running Steel, Running America: Race, Economic Policy and the Decline of Liberalism* (Chapel Hill: University of North Carolina Press, 1998), 125. See also Philip Scranton,

The deindustrialization of the cities had a devastating effect on black economic life. Whereas the national unemployment rate in 1966 stood at 3.8 percent, black unemployment was at 7.3 percent, and the unemployment rate of black teenagers was 25.4 percent.[7] While whites were experiencing "full employment," certain segments of black America were experiencing Depression-era rates of unemployment. Black unemployment rates had been twice as high as whites' only since 1955, suggesting the effect of automation and plant relocation on black unemployment. Despite the increasing number of blacks in stable white-collar and skilled positions, most black workers remained in positions vulnerable to automation and cutbacks. Although whites at the lower end of the job scale experienced the same sorts of job loss as blacks, more whites found jobs in the emerging areas of aerospace technology, electronics, and the computer industry.[8]

The Johnson administration had tried to avert disaster. Johnson's War on Poverty was in large part designed to address the problems of the black ghettoes. Despite the color-blind rhetoric that surrounded the Economic Opportunity Act (1964), many understood it to be "an anti-riot bill."[9] The majority of trainees in the urban Office of Economic Opportunity (OEO) programs were black. The new OEO programs included the Neighborhood Youth Corps, the Job Corps, and the New Careers program, which joined the already existing programs created under the Manpower Development and Training Act (1962) as part of the federal government's efforts to address the manpower crisis. The programs suffered from a lack of funding and coordination, and, in the case of the Job Corps, bad administration and publicity. Critics felt the programs were too small and too expensive to have a substantial effect on the problem, enrolling seventeen thousand here and thirty thousand there, when the number of unemployed African Americans was approaching millions.[10] In addition, there was no standard against which to measure their effectiveness, so there was no way of telling how many trainees went on to productive, tax-paying jobs. IBM president Thomas Watson, Jr., recalled that IBM ended up hiring

"Large Firms and Industrial Restructuring: The Philadelphia Region, 1900–1980," *Pennsylvania Magazine of History and Biography* 116, no. 4 (October 1992): 419-465.

[7] Statistics in Charles Killingsworth, *Jobs and Income for Negroes* (Ann Arbor: Institute of Labor and Industrial Relations and the National Manpower Policy Task Force, 1968), 1. One of the reasons Killingsworth gives for the high employment rate is the draft for the Vietnam War.

[8] Ibid., 37.

[9] Quote from *New York Times*, Aug. 4, 1964, in Gareth Davies, *From Opportunity to Entitlement: The Transformation and Decline of Great Society Liberalism* (Lawrence: University Press of Kansas, 1996), 65.

[10] Killingsworth, *Jobs and Income for Negroes*, 72; See also Davies, 75–104; and Lemann, *The Promised Land*, 111–221.

very few of the "graduates" from the Job Corps center it had sponsored, having failed to anticipate the level of drug and alcohol abuse among trainees.[11] In the face of increased rioting, the OEO programs were perceived as failures, a perception abetted by the Kerner Commission, which condemned federal efforts as inadequate.

In 1968, President Johnson tried a new tack. He created the National Alliance of Businessmen (NAB), headed by Henry Ford II, president of Ford Motor Company, to encourage leading employers and businessmen to hire and train the most disadvantaged citizens, known as the hard-core unemployed. The program was called Job Opportunities in Business Sector (JOBS), and it would subsidize the extra costs associated with hiring someone from the hard-core population. These costs included intensive training, loss in productivity, job creation, and transportation from the slums to the industrial site. The government would pay the employer an average of $3,500 for each disadvantaged man trained and hired. Johnson budgeted $350 million for the program with the expectation that the group would find and create one hundred thousand new jobs for the disadvantaged by July 1969.[12] Johnson sold the program as an alternative to a large-scale, New Deal–style public works program. The fifteen-member NAB board included top executives from Ford Motor Company, Coca-Cola, ITT, Aluminum Company of America, McDonnell-Douglas, Levi-Straus and Company, and Mobil Oil. Despite the subsidy, which was, after all, merely compensation for basic costs, businessmen regarded the program as voluntary, and therefore not really, or at least not wholly, a government program but rather a chance to show what the private sector could do.

"Social Responsibility" in the Private Sector

Businessmen had long debated the degree to which their enterprises should help in resolving social problems. Stalwarts held tight to the idea that businesses existed for the sole purpose of making a profit. Profitable corporations contributed to society in the form of jobs, taxes, and goods and services. As Texas

[11] Thomas Watson, Jr., with Peter Petre, *Father Son & Co.: My Life at IBM and Beyond* (New York: Bantam Books, 1990), 370. IBM subsequently helped fund inner-city drug treatment centers.

[12] Max Frankel, "President Offers Project to Spur Hiring of Jobless," *New York Times*, January 24, 1968, p. 1; on LBJ and creation of the NAB, see Cathie Jo Martin, *Stuck in Neutral: Business and the Politics of Human Capital Investment Policy* (Princeton, NJ: Princeton University Press, 2000), 150–53. On the NAB, see U.S. Congress Senate Committee on Labor and Public Welfare, Subcommittee on Employment, Manpower and Poverty, *The JOBS Program*, background information, April 1970.

millionaire H. L. Hunt put it: "The most philanthropic thing a man can do is provide gainful employment for as many people as possible."[13] Even with government subsidies, hiring the disadvantaged was uneconomical and difficult to explain to both stockholders and unions. Suddenly, the most conservative businessmen were reminding the federal government of its responsibility to provide social welfare.[14]

Inasmuch as the rioting and unemployment represented a national emergency, however, there were businessmen eager to do their part. Johnson's formation of the NAB-JOBS program appealed to this sense of service. Ignoring the crisis was simply too costly.[15] As Henry Ford II reminded his peers, "Whatever seriously threatens the stability or progress of the country and its cities, also threatens the growth of its economy and your company."[16] Surveys showed that a majority of corporations were willing to initiate and support programs to help high school dropouts, retrain workers laid off due to automation, and improve work/career opportunities for minority groups.[17] Businesses offered financial support to black community efforts to train and prepare minority youth for employment, such as the Reverend Leon Sullivan's Opportunities Industrialization Center (OIC) or the Urban Coalition, nongovernment organizations that promoted self-help and individual enterprise.[18] Despite the lack of consensus about what business should be doing to address the urban crisis, there was a definite trend of experimentation and for a little while in 1968–1969 the phrase "hard-core unemployed" was ubiquitous at business conferences, in publications, and in research studies. The Committee for Economic Development (CED), the NAM, and the National Industrial Conference Board all endorsed the idea of some business intervention in the inner cities. Let us examine two cases of business leaders' efforts to deal with the explosive racial

---

[13] Quoted in Stephen M. Gelber, *Black Men and Businessmen: The Growing Awareness of a Social Responsibility* (Port Washington, NY: Kennicat Press, 1974), 15.

[14] A view described by Theodore Leavitt, "The Dangers of Social Responsibility," *Harvard Business Review* 36, no. 5 (September–October 1958): 41–50, which argued for business and government to return to their proper roles. See also John Iacobelli, "A Survey of Employer Attitudes toward Training the Disadvantaged," *Monthly Labor Review* 93, no. 6 (June 1970): 51–55, and Martin, *Stuck in Neutral*, 141–55.

[15] For a discussion of these viewpoints, see National Industrial Conference Board, "The Role of Business in Public Affairs," in *Business and the Cities*, ed. Neil W. Chamberlain (New York: Basic Books, 1970), 5–12; Gelber, *Black Men and Businessmen*, 7–22; and Neil H. Jacoby, *Corporate Power and Social Responsibility: A Blueprint for the Future* (New York: MacMillan, 1973).

[16] Both quoted in Gelber, *Black Men and Businessmen*, 18, 20, respectively.

[17] See National Industrial Conference Board, "The Role of Business in Public Affairs," 5–12.

[18] On the OIC, see Arnold Nemore, "The Transferability of Manpower Programs," in *Business and the Cities*, ed. Neil W. Chamberlain (New York: Basic Books, 1970): 268–97.

situations of the late 1960s and early 1970s, paying special attention to the interconnections between the experimental programs on the one hand and integration on the other.

The National Alliance of Businessmen

Within a year after President Johnson created the NAB-JOBS program, twelve thousand companies had pledged to create 172,153 jobs for the hard-core unemployed. By December 1968, some 118,411 people had been hired and 80,460 were still on the job.[19] The 67 percent retention rate was a feat of sorts, considering the many disadvantages that burdened the so-called unemployable, although it would decrease substantially in the years ahead. The companies provided trainees with on-the-job training, remedial education, life skills, and counseling. The Nixon administration bolstered the JOBS program, budgeting $200 million for it in 1970–71, while at the same time slashing funds for the troubled Job Corps program. Nixon also merged the old Plans for Progress program with the NAB, stating that the purposes of the two organizations "have been related if not identical."[20] This was not altogether true. The Plans for Progress program, founded in 1961, was intended to integrate the workforces of defense contractors and pertained to African Americans of all economic classes, while the NAB, begun in 1968, was founded to help "the disadvantaged," which included poor blacks but also included other minorities, ex-convicts, Vietnam veterans, the mentally ill, and the physically handicapped. Both programs were voluntary, however, and both represented the business sector's attempts to address urgent social issues.

Despite the JOBS program's focus on economic disadvantage, NAB officials sold it as a "race" program, playing on businessmen's racial guilt. They were not afraid to blame the economic system for the extreme racial inequality seen in the inner cities. But they offered a way out. The Ford Motor Company's Leo Beebe, the executive vice-president of the NAB, spent the summer of 1968 trying to convince businessmen that they had a stake in making sure black Americans were part of the system, not opposed to it. He was trying to sell the JOBS program, but what he was really selling was a vision of an integrated America.

[19] Robert A. Wright, "From Overalls to the Attaché Case," *New York Times*, January 6, 1969, 71–72.

[20] Richard Nixon, Statement on the Merger of the National Alliance of Businessmen and Plans for Progress, June 13, 1969 in John T. Woolley and Gerhard Peters, *The American Presidency Project* [online]. Santa Barbara, CA: University of California (hosted) Gerhard Peters (database). On Job Corps, see "The Program Is Reshaped – and Curtailed," *New York Times*, April 13, 1969.

A master salesman, he used a folksy vernacular to tell what was essentially a conversion tale of how he, a tough-thinking, hard-talking, practical white man, came to recognize racial discrimination as an injustice and a problem.

Beebe went out of his way to assure his audience he was no do-gooder. He took this job for NAB because Henry Ford [II] asked him to and he had learned to get ahead at Ford by doing what Henry Ford asked him to do. But having taken on the job, he started to realize some things, just like how a fellow who goes to church because "it's a good thing to do" starts to get something out of it. He remembered how he had grown up in Detroit, in what was now called a ghetto. He had played with the Negro boys in the neighborhood. They were good kids. Not all of them, but then not all of the white kids were either. Today, he knew that his old white playmates were working at Ford or were proprietors of small businesses. But he had no idea what had happened to his black friends, who, after all, had seemed back then to be smart, aggressive, and full of hustle. He went on like this, concluding finally that there was a flaw in a system that rewarded "the breaks" to people of one race and not the other. He reminded the audience that he wasn't preaching, but then, as if he were a student radical, asked the audience members to consider their own role in this flawed system.

Beebe continued. He, like many of them probably, had always ignored the memos from headquarters reminding him to "think about employing some Negroes." He recalled, "I used to take the memorandum and say, 'the hell with that,' and throw it in the basket." He held "a very simple concept" of equal opportunity, he noted, which was that he wasn't going to hire anyone "except on the basis of their qualification to do the job."[21] He now understood that his conception of "qualification" and "merit" was too limited. This rejection of the color-blind ideal is remarkable and indicates that by 1968 some businessmen had moved beyond a simple color-blind, merit-based conception of minority hiring and were beginning to understand the structural impediments that kept minorities out of jobs. Beebe's challenge to the color-blind way of thinking was subtle – more a dismissal than a critique, which further normalized the idea that race had to be taken into account. White managers who could never see blacks as qualified, could and did understand the mandate to hire minorities regardless of their qualifications. Beebe threw in a lot of one-liners to soften the blow, but he was asking the audience to consider their own culpability in the racial crisis. In return, he offered them a way to make amends. The speech

---

[21] National Industrial Conference Board, Working Conference on Basic Education and Industrial Employment of the Hard Core Unemployed, Luncheon session, June 27, 1968, in National Industrial Conference Board, Records (hereafter NICB records), Box 143, Hagley Museum and Library, Wilmington, Delaware (hereafter HML).

was a rhetorical masterpiece. Beebe understood his audience, their skepticism of reformers, their secret guilt, their belief in free enterprise, their desire to correct problems, and he played on these emotions to sell the program.

For little while, businessmen bought it and the pledges came in. General Motors hired 21,706 hard-core unemployed, which made up nearly one-fifth of the jobless hired in the program in 1968. RCA pledged to train 400 in the growing electronics field. In May 1969, the Chrysler Corporation signed a $13.8 million training pact with the government to train 4,450 hard-core unemployed over two years. Western Electric, Xerox, and Du Pont also participated as did innumerable banks, department stores, insurance companies, and utilities in those cities hard hit by riots.[22] Only one-quarter of participating companies accepted the federal subsidy, which entailed audits, restrictions, and heavy documentation.[23] The government subsidy turned out to be less of an incentive than the large numbers of minority workers the program brought into a company. When companies hired the disadvantaged, they increased the percentage of minority workers in their workforce and thus satisfied the demands of the EEOC, the Defense Department, CORE, and the NAACP.[24]

Beebe made his quota. But the inspiration to act rarely survived the many problems that came with hiring the disadvantaged. In surveys, employers listed government red tape, low productivity/motivation of disadvantaged trainees, no jobs available, and union problems as deterrents to their participation in the manpower training programs.[25] Employers needed people in entry-level jobs who could be moved up the line and be trained to take on additional

[22] See "21,706 Jobless Hired by GM in 8 Months," *New York Times*, January 7, 1969, 1; "%13.8 Million Job Training Pact, Signed by Chrysler," *New York Times*, May 15, 1969, 53; "120 Jobless to Be Trained Here by RCA," *Chicago Daily Defender*, September 9, 1968; "Chrysler Hires, Trains Hard-Core Jobless," *Chicago Daily Defender*, February 10, 1968, 31; Pamela Walker Laird, *Pull: Networking and Success since Benjamin Franklin* (Cambridge, MA: Harvard University Press, 2006), 214–16; Stein, *Running Steel, Running America*, 124–25; National Industrial Conference Board, Working Conference on Basic Education and Industrial Employment of the Hard Core Unemployed, June 27, 1968, in NICB records, Box 143, HML.

[23] Paul Delaney, "Dissidence Mounts in Job Aid Alliance," *New York Times*, October 27, 1969, 1; See also U.S. Congress, Senate Committee on Labor and Public Welfare, Subcommittee on Employment, Manpower and Poverty, *The JOBS Program, Background Information*, April 1970, pp. 111–12, and Statement of Secretary of Labor George Shultz, May 11, 1970, in U.S. Congress, Senate Committee on Labor and Public Welfare, Subcommittee on Employment, Manpower and Poverty, *Manpower Development and Training Legislation*, p. 2402.

[24] Jerry Flint, "G.M. Reports a Rise in Hiring of Workers in Minority Groups," *New York Times*, February 7, 1970, and Avril Adams, Joseph Krislov, and David Lairson, "Plantwide Seniority, Black Employment, and Employer Affirmative Action," *Industrial and Labor Relations Review* 26, no. 1 (Oct. 1972): 686–90.

[25] Iacobelli, "A Survey of Employer Attitudes toward Training the Disadvantaged," 51–55, and Myron Fottler, John Drotning, and David Lipsky, "Reasons for Employer Non-participation

responsibility. Ideally, the disadvantaged would be those people – indeed the whole point of the program was to get the disadvantaged into those higher-level jobs – but in practice, only a few had the ability to move up. Researchers always referred to the inadequacies of the trainees as "perceived," the product perhaps of employers' biases, but from an employer's perspective it made very little sense to hire people who lacked motivation, literacy, and the ability to show up to work on time when there were people available who were motivated, literate, and reliable. While employers were willing to drop basic qualifications, which had kept people out of the workforce, such as high school diplomas and previous job experience, few were willing to take on trainees who needed remedial classes in reading, math, and life skills. As one employer clarified, "We are not concerned with getting a federal subsidy. We are concerned with getting people who will report to work on time, stay on the job, and be willing to take on responsibility."[26]

Researchers' descriptions of the disadvantaged hardly inspired confidence. At a Michigan State University Management Conference on Effectively Utilizing the Disadvantaged, Dr. Aaron Rutledge pointed out that the typical Negro inner-city dropout will have a police record, no experience meeting time schedules, and will be angry, suspicious, distrustful, and apathetic, especially when pressed to deal with new situations. The co-author of the much-cited 1968 study *Nineteen Negro Men: Personality and Manpower Training*, Dr. Rutledge explained that these characteristics were psychological defense mechanisms, the result of disadvantage, and that employers had to anticipate and accommodate them if the program were to work. Dr. Rutledge believed that "personality repair was vital," and recommended that employers hire highly skilled psychological consultants to train the supervisors, foremen, and managers, who would be dealing with the disadvantaged.[27] Unlike the middle-class blacks who had first broken the workplace color-line, lower-class blacks were not as interested in putting whites at ease. That integration had gone as smoothly as it had was a tribute to black pioneers' tolerance of white insensitivities.[28] But the new trainees were not as patient with whites, and employers had to deal with the fallout.

in Manpower Training Programs for the Disadvantaged," *Labor Law Journal* 22, no. 11 (November 1971): 708–12.

[26] Fottler et al., 711.

[27] Virginia Baird, "Employing the Disadvantaged Fraught with Challenges," *Training and Development Journal* 23, no. 7 (July 1969): 44–51.

[28] On middle-class black experiences in the newly integrated workplace, see George Davis and Glegg Watson, *Black Life in Corporate America: Swimming in the Mainstream* (New York: Anchor Books, 1985; originally published by Doubleday in 1982); Dan Cordiz, "The Negro Middle Class Is Right in the Middle," *Fortune*, November 1966, 174–80 ff.

Craft unions generally disliked programs designed to train the hard-core unemployed. They feared such programs expanded the pool of available skilled labor, undercut union wages, and deprived unions of their control over training and the labor supply.[29] If the government (OEO programs) or employers (JOBS program) worked within the union apprenticeship system, they necessarily impinged on union control over jobs, but if they worked outside the apprenticeship system, they subsidized a nonunion source of labor that competed against union labor. Either way, craft unions were hurt by efforts to train and integrate minorities into the skilled trades. Unions believed that government training programs were ineffective and hence dangerous. The Carpenters and Painters Internationals, for instance, opposed a Job Corps program at the Armstrong Cork Company, alleging that the program did not meet union standards and that "the injection of poorly trained workers into the contemplated field (would) destroy training standards, wages and working conditions."[30] The unions wanted to administer the new training programs, but this would have negated the purpose of the programs, which was to train and hire the black workers whom unions would not train. Indeed, the point of the Manpower Development Training Act, the OEO, and the JOBS program was in large part to get minorities the skills and training that exclusionary craft unions had denied to them.

Union antipathy is one reason that the new, nonunionized computer industry took the lead in hiring the disadvantaged.[31] Employers in unionized industries who chose to participate in a hard-core training program had to negotiate wages and conditions of the hard-core trainees with resentful unions. While these programs had the potential to weaken unions, they also strained union-management relations, which may have discouraged some employers from pursuing the program.[32] The introduction of hard-core labor also alienated a company's existing workforce – both whites and blacks – who resented the lowering of standards, especially when qualified people existed to do the jobs

[29] See Quadagno, "Social Movements and State Transformation," 616–34. Quadagno's article is based on sources from the George Meany Memorial Archives and the National Archives. See also Paul Moreno, *Black Americans and Organized Labor: A New History* (Baton Rouge: Louisiana State University Press, 2006).

[30] Quoted in Quadagno, "Social Movements and State Transformation," 616–34, on p. 622.

[31] As will be discussed later, IBM, Xerox, Sperry-Rand, and Control Data took the lead in hiring the disadvantaged and opening plants in ghetto areas.

[32] See, for instance, explanations and discussion about unions in National Industrial Conference Board, "Basic Education and Industrial Employment of the Hard Core Unemployed," Panel Discussion on Job Training, June 27, 1968, in NICB records, Box 143, HML, and U.S. Congress, Senate Committee on Labor and Public Welfare, Subcommittee on Employment, Manpower and Poverty, *JOBS Program, Background Information*, April 1970.

in question. White and black workers at New York Bell Telephone Company, for instance, felt that the new trainees could not do the job and that regular employees ended up working harder to compensate for their inefficiencies.[33]

The additional work and headaches that came with training and hiring the disadvantaged – the psychologists, the remedial classes, the sensitivity training, the readjustment of expectations, the racial tension, the union trouble, the resentment of the existing workforce – were costly and time consuming, and certainly outside the normal economic calculus of most businessmen. This was why Beebe had been correct to emphasize moral motivation in his speeches, rather than economic benefits. That some employers actually took on the challenge is testimony to their commitment to the mission of integrating American society.[34] That the effort was short-lived, that so many smaller and medium-sized companies chose not to participate, is understandable, given the disincentives.

While NAB officials tried to convince skeptical businessmen to hire the disadvantaged, the people whose recognition and affirmation they sought, indeed, the intended "audience" for the whole endeavor – white liberals and African Americans – became ever more critical of the program. A 1970 Senate subcommittee investigation of the efficacy of the JOBS program found that there was no monitoring system in place that could confirm the program's claims of the numbers of people hired and retained.[35] Turnover rates were high; almost half of the trainees had left the program by 1969. Democrats did not believe the program stemmed rising unemployment and thought the money would be better spent in other areas.[36] Even the program's government sponsor, the Labor Department, found deficiencies in its reporting system and its fulfillment of contracts.[37] In the face of deteriorating economic conditions, some companies reneged on their pledges or, it was alleged, trained people, received money, but then did not provide the promised jobs. By March

[33] Venus Green, *Race on the Line: Gender, Labor, and Technology in the Bell System, 1880–1980* (Durham, NC: Duke University Press, 2001), 229–30.

[34] For accounts of extra measures taken to retain the disadvantaged see, "How Honeywell Took the JOBS Program to Heart," *Manpower*, February/March 1969; "21,706 Jobless Hired by GM in 8 Months," *New York Times*, January 7, 1969,1; James C. Worthy, *William C. Norris: Portrait of a Maverick* (Cambridge: Ballenger, 1987); and executive accounts in National Industrial Conference Board, Working Conference on Basic Education and Industrial Employment of the Hard Core Unemployed, June 27, 1968, in NICB records, Box 143, HML.

[35] U.S. Congress, Senate Committee on Labor and Public Welfare, Subcommittee on Employment, Manpower and Poverty, *JOBS Program, Background Information*, April 1970.

[36] Paul Delaney, "Job Training Policy Questioned in Light of Unemployment Rise," *New York Times*, May 25, 1970, 23.

[37] Paul Delaney, "Defects Charged in JOBS Program," *New York Times*, May 30, 1972.

1970, only 39,000 of the 99,000 hired through the contract program still remained.[38]

Black activists felt the NAB program was too removed from the communities it sought to help. Used to the community participation that was the hallmark of OEO job programs, they felt that the program could have profited from hiring blacks as staffers or consultants. (The program was staffed by unpaid white executives, on loan from their companies.) Critics also complained that trainees were assigned to unskilled, dead-end jobs that hardly required "training." The government should not be subsidizing training for such jobs as busboy, porter, and housekeeper.[39] Even if companies offered training in specific skills, they were often skills in jobs slated to be automated or exported. The auto companies, for instance, offered training in welding, assembling, and drill press operating, but these were not the job skills of the future. Historian Venus Green argues that the Bell System's hard-core training programs trained operators and low-level clerical workers, jobs that Bell managers knew were "dead-end" and soon to be eliminated.[40]

Given the multitude of criticisms from employers, workers, and activists one might well ask what the net benefits of the program were. Secretary of Labor George Shultz believed that the NAB's achievements were positive. The program had offered jobs to 432,000 disadvantaged persons in two years, and found summer employment for 300,000 young people. Seventy-three percent of JOBS participants were African American, and an additional 16 percent Mexican American or Puerto Rican. Most important, for our purposes, Shultz said that the letters from participating employers indicated that the program induced companies to revise their personnel practices and to at least consider how ostensibly unqualified people might be trained to become productive members of society.[41] Despite its criticisms, the Subcommittee on Manpower,

---

[38] Statement of Secretary of Labor George Shultz, May 11, 1970, in U.S. Congress, Senate Committee on Labor and Public Welfare, Subcommittee on Employment, Manpower and Poverty, *Manpower Development and Training Legislation*, p. 2402; Shultz was actually defending the program and went on to explain that this retention rate was not unusual in American industry.

[39] Delaney, "Dissidence Mounts in Job Aid Alliance," 1; "Report to Senators Chides Job Project," *New York Times*, May 4, 1970, 44; "Dick Clark Criticizes NAB Job Program," *Chicago Daily Defender*, July 1, 1968, 6; and U.S. Congress, Senate Committee on Labor and Public Welfare, Subcommittee on Employment, Manpower and Poverty, *JOBS Program, Background Information* (1970).

[40] "Job Training Policy Question in Light of Unemployment Rise," *New York Times*, March 25, 1970, 23; "Auto Industry Lay-Offs Set Back Drive to Train Hard-Core Jobless," *New York Times*, April 11, 1970, and Green, *Race on the Line*, 234.

[41] Statement of Secretary of Labor George Shultz, May 11, 1970, in U.S. Congress, Senate Committee on Labor and Public Welfare, Subcommittee on Employment, Manpower and Poverty, *Manpower Development and Training Legislation*, pp. 2402–6.

Employment, and Poverty likewise acknowledged that the NAB-JOBS program increased executives' understanding of the problems of racial minorities and the disadvantaged in seeking and retaining employment. Between its mammoth advertising campaign with the Ad Council and its training seminars for executives, the NAB conveyed to American employers the idea that hiring was not about keeping people out (with tests and unnecessary qualifications), but pulling people in (with training and encouragement).[42]

Historian Pamela Walker Laird confirms the NAB's role in broadening employers' definitions of "employable." In her history of networking and social capital in the workplace, Laird shows that by 1968 most explicitly discriminatory policies had been ended but that the mere removal of discriminatory policies was not in itself enough to ensure blacks' employment and advancement. Without policies that could "pull" blacks into jobs, gainful employment remained out of reach. Laird credits the NAB with helping employers understand that they would have to reach out and pull people – specifically minorities – into their companies by re-evaluating hiring criteria, overcoming biases, making a special effort to train and retain those people who did not have anyone else pulling them into jobs. Laird notes that the NAB's buddy system, whereby the trainee was assigned an experienced worker for guidance and mentorship, can be seen as a form of "synthetic mentorship," of the sort that would be necessary not just for the disadvantaged but also for educated blacks and white women, who were, like the disadvantaged, strangers in the corporate workplace.[43] Drawing from human relations insights, the NAB strategies recognized the importance of the entire workplace community in the development and retention of new kinds of workers. Despite its failure to achieve its job-creation goals, then, the NAB helped employers readjust their practices to meet new social realities.

Moreover, the NAB's efforts complemented and supported other community-based efforts. Sperry Rand Corporation's Univac division joined the JOBS program in 1968, instituting an ambitious program of re-education and minority recruitment in Minneapolis that specifically intersected with local programs run by the Urban League, churches, and black community organizations. Univac re-evaluated and dropped certain testing and job requirements,

---

[42] In 1972, the seminars were held at the Joseph Curran Memorial in the National Maritime Union Building, which was ironic since the NMU was one of the most radical labor unions, and not all of the unions were happy with jobs programs that promised to increase the labor supply. See "Executives on Sabbatical Learn to Direct On-the-Job Training," *New York Times*, May 7, 1972, 54. On the Ad Council campaign, see materials in Ad Council Archives, University of Illinois at Urbana-Champaign or http://www.library.uiuc.edu/archives/adcouncil/.

[43] Laird, *Pull*, 214. On "push" and "pull" factors, see pp. 2–8.

offered on-the-job training for the disadvantaged, and instituted a new review program for minority employees that ensured that they were progressing at a normal rate. It required all of its employees to participate in a six-session course, "Understanding Minority Group Problems," which explained the new hiring policies to employees and imparted to them "awareness and appreciation for Negro attitudes today." It also donated equipment and supplies to job programs run by the Urban League and Opportunity Industrialization Center (OIC) and participated in local community events and programs.[44] Local black newspapers publicized the JOBS program, positioning it as just another outreach program, part of the new "opportunity" landscape. At the ground level, it did not necessarily matter whether the resources for programs came from the federal government, the city, or the private sector.

Part of the Solution: The Case of Control Data Corporation

The computer industry, which was nonunionized and subsidized in large part by the federal government, played an active role in developing experimental programs to hire the disadvantaged, including building plants in the inner city. Although only a small number of corporations participated in these experiments, their experiences are worth considering. Not only are they examples of enlightened corporate responses to social crisis, they also illustrate the connection between changing hiring criteria, integration, and the advancement of human relations ideas.

The early computer industry produced large mainframe supercomputers and was dependent for its success on the support of the U.S. government and the military. In 1953, 75 percent of all new computer installations were in government organizations or government-subsidized research centers and universities.[45] Thanks to its punch card tabulating machines, which administered the New Deal and World War II, IBM had become the U.S. government's leading supplier of computers and computer systems after the war. But other computer companies – dubbed "the dwarves" – soon rose to compete for the

---

[44] "Univac Began Ambitious Program for Improvement of Jobs for Minorities," *St. Paul Recorder,* February 27, 1969, 7.

[45] David M. Hart, "From 'Ward of the State' to 'Revolutionary without a Movement': The Political Development of William C. Norris and Control Data Corporation, 1957–1986," *Enterprise and Society* 6, no. 2 (June 2005): 197–223. On the development of the computer industry in the United States, see Alfred Chandler, Jr., *Inventing the Electronic Century: The Epic Story of the Consumer Electronics and Computer Industries* (Cambridge, MA: Harvard University Press, 2005).

government's business. One of these was the Control Data Corporation, based in Minneapolis, Minnesota.

Founded in 1957 by former Sperry-Rand executive William Norris, Control Data initially produced custom-built, large-frame supercomputers for research and engineering concerns. But Norris quickly turned to government agencies and was able to win major contracts with the U.S. Navy, the Atomic Energy Commission, and the Defense Department.[46] Control Data also developed overseas markets and diversified its product lines and consulting services, so that by 1964, it was the third largest computer company in the United States, behind IBM and Sperry-Univac. In 1968 Control Data filed an antitrust suit against IBM, and compiled a computerized index of incriminating IBM documents, which it threatened to make available to other companies. IBM settled the suit out of court in 1973, selling Control Data its successful Service Bureau Corporation subsidiary for a fraction of its worth in exchange for the index, which, as Thomas Watson, Jr., admitted, held the key to the other antitrust suits against IBM. The acquisition of IBM's Service Bureau Corporation made Control Data the largest supplier of computer services.[47] At its height in the late 1970s, Control Data employed 60,000 people and was generating $5 billion in revenue. And then, as quickly as it rose, it fell. By 1985, it was in financial trouble and its stock price plunged. Norris was forced out of his position as CEO in 1986. In 1992, the company was divided into the Ceridian Corporation and Control Data Systems, Inc., which was bought by Syntegra in 1999.[48]

The rapid decline of Control Data's fortunes can be attributed to the rise of microcomputers and personal computers in the 1980s, which shrank the market for the big mainframe computers that were Control Data's specialty. But another popular explanation for the company's downfall has been that the company's leadership dragged it into unprofitable, offbeat social schemes that subsumed its resources and distracted its management.[49] And herein lies our interest in the Control Data Corporation. William C. Norris, the company's founder and president, invested a substantial portion of Control Data's resources into the idea that unmet social needs could be transformed into

---

[46] Worthy, *William C. Norris*, 33–57, and Hart, "From 'Ward of the State' to 'Revolutionary without a Movement,'" 205–6.

[47] See Watson, *Father Son & Co*, 384–85, 387.

[48] Steve Alexander, "Gone, but Not Forgotten," *Minneapolis Star-Tribune*, October 12, 2007, D1.

[49] Discussed and refuted in Worthy, *William C. Norris*, 203–4; "Corporate Do-Gooder Bill Norris," *Inc.*, May 1988, 37–52; and David M. Hart, From 'Ward of the State' to 'Revolutionary without a Movement': The Political Development of William C. Norris and Control Data Corporation, 1957–1986," *Enterprise and Society*, vol. 6, no. 2 (June 2005): 197–223.

business opportunities.[50] Norris was critical of government and philanthropic efforts, which he felt were little better than charity. Such efforts consumed resources. He believed that businesses, in cooperation with government, could solve the problems in such a way that created resources.[51] Norris was interested in capitalizing on a variety of social issues, including pollution control, alternative energy sources, South Africa, and education, but for our purposes, we will focus on his interest in employing the disadvantaged and affirmative action.

In November 1967, Norris announced that Control Data Corporation would begin manufacturing computer controllers in a North Minneapolis facility as soon as December of that year. The site of race riots the summer before, North Minneapolis had the highest concentration of nonwhites in the city and the highest unemployment rates. Working with the Hennepin County Office of Economic Opportunity, Control Data promised to build a new 85,000-square-foot plant in the area.[52] According to Norbert Berg, Control Data vice president for Administration and Personnel, Norris had gotten the idea for an inner-city plant after a visit with the Urban League's Whitney Young, who told him that only one thing was necessary to avoid race riots in the future: jobs. Berg recalled, "All of a sudden, Norris was different. It was like he'd had his eyes opened. He had become aware of problems and of his ability to do something about them. I always believed Whitney Young did that."[53]

Norris often referred to Whitney Young's ideas, especially when trying to convince someone of the need to hire African Americans, but the motivations behind his decision to open the North Minneapolis plant were at once more complicated and more basic. At the most basic level, Norris needed black employees in order to comply with new guidelines at the Defense Department, with which he conducted much of his business. In a letter to an old friend and skeptical stockholder, Norris explained that he was under great pressure to hire minorities: "The government is seeing to it that there is a certain percentage of

[50] Worthy, *William C. Norris*, 3–4. Management consultant and professor James C. Worthy, a longtime advocate of human relations and a close associate of Norris, regarded William Norris's social initiatives as examples of good management in the private sector.

[51] Worthy, *William C. Norris*, 133.

[52] "Northside to Get Control Data Manufacturing Plant," *Minneapolis Spokesman*, November 30, 1967, 1, and "Control Data Corporation: Minneapolis, Minnesota and Washington, D.C.," a company report in Control Data Corporation, Executive Papers (hereafter CDC Executive Papers), Series 8, Box 7, Folder 4, in Charles Babbage Institute collections, University of Minnesota, Minneapolis (hereafter CBI).

[53] Quoted Worthy, *William C. Norris*, 108. Norris recalled that he had met Young at a senior executive course in April 1968, after Norris had decided to open the plant. See Norris to Mrs. Whitney Young, March 17, 1981, Control Data Corporation, William C. Norris Executive Papers, 1946–1995 (Hereafter WCN Papers), Series 9, Box 29, Folder 20, CBI.

any company's employees of the right color. If this is not the case, then there is retaliation through difficulties in getting new government business."[54] Based in Minneapolis – a city not then known for its racial diversity – Control Data had been having difficulty finding minority workers to meet the demands of the Office of Federal Contract Compliance. It had advertised in black newspapers and offered free transportation to its suburban plants but to no avail.[55] The inner-city plant was a way to ensure a steady supply of minority employees. This suggests that compliance was the main factor behind Norris's decision, but it was actually more interesting than that.

In the same letter, Norris explained: "The government is going to spend a large amount of money to try to educate minority groups. It is Control Data's plan to get at the right end of the funnel when this money starts flowing, as it will eventually."[56] As a government entrepreneur, Norris had spent his adult life, as he put it in the letter, "finding funnels and getting at the right end." He was at home in the world of government red tape and looked forward to taking advantage of government subsidies to train the minorities he needed to hire. He had close associations with liberal politicians and lobbyists like Hubert Humphrey, Walter Mondale, and James Rowe to help him navigate government channels.[57] For Norris there was no rigid line between the public and private sectors. His profits came from doing business with government agencies, and if government was going to start offering incentives for training minorities, he wanted in on it. This was what he meant when he said that there were economic opportunities in solving social problems. Businesses could work with the government, not against it, to develop programs that would address social needs.[58]

Norris's justifications for what he called the "ghetto plant" varied, depending on whom he was talking to. To stockholders, Norris predictably emphasized economic pragmatism, arguing that the plant was part of the company's long-term solution to the tight labor market, which required that it develop and use all available forms of manpower.[59] To interested administrators and human

---

[54] Letter, Norris to Barrett, October 18, 1967, in WCN Papers, Series 9, Box 29, Folder 12, CBI.

[55] "Control Data Corporation: Minneapolis, Minnesota and Washington, D.C.," a report in CDC Executive Papers, Series 8, Box 7, Folder 4, CBI.

[56] Letter, Norris to Barrett, October 18, 1967, in WCN Papers, Series 9, Box 29, Folder 12, CBI.

[57] See correspondence in WCN Papers, Series 9, CBI.

[58] At times, this could seem exploitative, as when Norris explored the possibility of developing "war rooms" and computer systems for riot-torn cities and states: "The implementation of war rooms could mean both the actual sale of computational equipment and possibly service from a data center." See Norris to R. D. Schmidt, May 31, 1968, WCN Papers, Series 9, Box 29, Folder 13, CBI.

[59] "Control Data Corporation: Minneapolis, Minnesota and Washington, D.C.," a report in CDC Executive Papers, Series 8, Box 7, Folder 4, CBI.

resources professionals, he emphasized the social benefits of moving businesses back into urban areas and providing opportunities for Negroes in a "glamour industry" and growth area.[60] To segregationists like Georgia governor Lester Maddox, he emphasized how free enterprise could replace federal government in solving social problems.[61] To skeptical white employees, he emphasized the plant as a guard against anarchy and riots.[62] None of these explanations contradicted Norris's basic idea that there was money to be made in working with the government to solve social problems.

As it turned out, the government – in the form of the Commerce Department – contacted Norris after seeing the news reports of his plans for a Northside plant. In a letter to liberal lobbyist James Rowe, Norris wrote, "The Commerce Dept. contacted us and suggested that we might want to put in a proposal for some financial assistance for training, etc. This was pleasing, because while we did plan to contact Commerce later, Commerce took the initiative."[63] Senator Walter Mondale stepped in as an intermediary and was able to arrange for Control Data to get the financial support being made available as part of the Target City program. In December 1967, Mondale phoned Norris to say that it wasn't possible to get Minneapolis designated a Target City, but because of the significance of Control Data's program, Commerce Secretary Sandy Trowbridge was willing to guarantee Control Data the same level of support without the classification. Norris reported to Norbert Berg that all they needed to do was send someone to Mondale's office and "he would make arrangements to get the money flowing."[64] The official company account tells a slightly different story, one that indicates that the money came from the Labor Department. According to the company account, William Zisch, vice chairman of the Aerojet Corporation and head of President Johnson's Test Program for Job Development (which would soon become the NAB-JOBS program), contacted Norris in 1967 when he learned about the Northside venture and invited Control Data to be part of the government's test program. Norris was interested and after an unexpectedly difficult negotiating session, Control Data signed a $1,077,000 contract with the Labor Department. The government monies were to cover training and counseling costs. In return,

[60] Norris to H. D. Barnard, May 13, 1968; Norris to Spring, Wellesley College, October 22, 1968, in WCN Papers, Series 9, Box 29, Folder 13, CBI.

[61] Norris to Lester Maddox, October 27, 1969, in WCN Papers, Series 9, Box 29, Folder 16, CBI.

[62] Norris to Clemmer Wait, May 21, 1968, in WCN Papers, Series 9, Box 29, Folder 13, CBI.

[63] Norris to James Rowe, November 30, 1967, in WCN Papers, Series 9, Box 29, Folder 12, CBI.

[64] Norris reports the phone call from Mondale to Berg in Norris to Norbert Berg, December 8, 1967, in WCN Papers, Series 9, Box 29, Folder 12, CBI.

Control Data promised to train 270 hard-core unemployed.[65] There is corroborating evidence of this deal in Norris's correspondence with Secretary of Labor Willard Wirtz.[66] Whether the money came from the Commerce Department or Labor, or both, it was clear that Norris had found the funnel. Senator Walter Mondale announced the agreement in February 1968, extolling it as a classic example of government-business cooperation.

Like International Harvester's earlier decision to open plants in Memphis and Louisville, the Northside plant required a great degree of coordination between manufacturing needs, community expectations, and training capabilities. It was decided that the new plant would produce computer controllers, refrigerator-sized units that transmitted information between the computer and peripheral equipment. These units had been produced at the Arden Hills plant, which meant that the personnel who would be responsible for training were already in the area. Next, the company sought the advice of the community into which the new plant would be built. They contacted the head of Minneapolis's OEO, an African American named Edgar Pillow, who arranged for company officials to meet North Side community leaders and the heads of Minneapolis minority organizations, including the Phyllis Wheatley Settlement House, the Minneapolis Urban League, the North Side Youth Opportunity Center, and the Twin Cities Opportunity Industrialization Center. These leaders would help the company develop appropriate policies for the so-called ghetto plant. Together (according to the company account) they decided that the plant would employ the most economically disadvantaged, black or white, including ex-felons.[67] The company also consulted nationally renowned human relations and manpower expert Eli Ginzberg, whom Norris had met at Columbia University's Senior Executive Seminar in early 1968.[68]

Given the charge of the new plant – to hire the disadvantaged – the company was forced to change the established ways of hiring people. As James Worthy noted, "The traditional purpose of the hiring interview is to screen people out; Control Data undertook the more difficult task of finding ways to bring people in."[69] After consultation with community leaders, the company shortened

[65] "Control Data Corporation: Minneapolis, Minnesota and Washington, D.C.," a report in CDC Executive Papers, Series 8, Box 7, Folder 4, p. 16, CBI.

[66] Norris to Willard Wirtz, February 29, 1968, in WCN Papers, Series 9, Box 29, Folder 12, CBI.

[67] "Control Data Corporation: Minneapolis, Minnesota and Washington, D.C.," a report in CDC Executive Papers, Series 8, Box 7, Folder 4, CBI; see also "Northside area to Get Control Data Manufacturing Plant," Minneapolis Spokesman, November 30, 1967, 1.

[68] Norris to Strichman, Colt Industries, April 11, 1968; Norris to Eli Ginzberg, Columbia University, April 17, 1968; Norris memo to [top executives], Dinner with Eli Ginzberg, May 10, 1968; all in WCN Papers, Series 9, Box 29, Folder 13, CBI.

[69] Worthy, William C. Norris, 112.

the application to one page, threw out aptitude testing, and, to avoid the appearance of white managers standing in judgment of blacks, essentially hired people according to the order in which they applied. It turned out that qualifications that had always been thought to be essential weren't.[70] In a 1988 interview with *Inc.* magazine, the changed application form was the first thing Norris recalled about the Northside venture.[71]

Training the disadvantaged required extensive use of two human relations chestnuts: sensitivity training for managerial staff and counseling for employees. At first, supervisors and managers were mainly white, imported from the Arden Hills plant. To avoid undue tension, they underwent a special two-week course in "leadership training," where they were apprised of the special conditions of the hard-core workforce. They also participated in several eight-hour-long sensitivity sessions called "Minority Group Dynamics," which had been developed by the Control Data Institute (the company's technical school). At the same time, the company invested in counselors to help the new employees adjust to the discipline of work life. It hired counselors who had experience working with the disadvantaged and put a premium on professionalism. In this area, the company adhered to stringent qualifications. It wanted counselors with a genuine awareness of the problems of the poor, a degree in psychology or sociology, and with the capacity to inspire trust and confidence in the workers. Each employee was assigned a counselor, and there were strict procedures about the role of the counselors to prevent a conflict between them and the supervisors.[72] Here we can see how the innovations designed to help minorities adjust to the workplace heightened everyone's awareness of the underlying structure of employee relations, which again was a longtime goal of the human relations movement. If employees and supervisors understood the interdependent relationship between themselves and others who made up the workplace community, then workplace tensions would evaporate.

Control Data provided not just training for its Northside employees but also an entire social-welfare network, including medical care, daycare, banking, and legal services. Company managers often interceded with neighborhood landlords or law enforcement on their employees' behalf, as if they were manor lords. For instance, the company found that absenteeism on Mondays was particularly high because weekend hijinks often landed workers in jail. So the plant manager visited the city jail on Monday mornings to bail out Control Data

[70] "Control Data Corporation: Minneapolis, Minnesota and Washington, D.C.," a report in CDC Executive Papers, Series 8, Box 7, folder 4, CBI.
[71] "Corporate Do-Gooder Bill Norris," *Inc.*, May 1988, 37–52.
[72] "Control Data Corporation: Minneapolis, Minnesota and Washington, D.C.," p. 30, in CDC Executive Papers, Series 8, Box 7, Folder 4, CBI.

employees who had run afoul of the law. Eventually the court authorized Control Data to print its own bail bond forms, which allowed errant employees to automatically be released into Control Data's custody.[73] Although excessively paternalistic, these services were essential to the success of the endeavor and represented the company's enlightened acknowledgment that personal problems could not always be left at home.

By the end of 1969, the Northside facility employed 412 people. Of these, 56 percent were nonwhite (52 percent black, 4 percent American Indian). The company aimed to match the racial composition of north Minneapolis, which was 60 percent black. Sixty percent of the employees were female. Company officials in 1969 were not yet as sensitive to the shape of gender discrimination and assumed, like so many other firms, that women were particularly suited to electronics assembly.[74] The plant eventually proved itself to be productive and even survived the firm's 1985 financial crisis. There was a high degree of turnover, but according to James Worthy, this was the result of promotions of Northside people to other Control Data plants. The plant was perhaps most successful in ensuring a supply of minority employees to other areas of the company.[75]

Despite the company's best efforts to be sensitive to the black community's concerns, to adapt "to the special character of the ghetto situation," there were criticisms of the plant and others like it. As the company noted in its report, there were blacks who felt that Control Data was segregating all of its black employees in the Northside plant. This was untrue, since a major purpose of the plant was to supply Control Data with minority employees for its other plants and offices, but it is easy to see how it appeared that way. In an effort to win the trust of black trainees, the company had installed black managers and counselors in the plant. In an effort to conform to affirmative action guidelines, it sought to have the number of minority employees match the

[73] Story told in Worthy, *William C. Norris*, 116. See also Memo to Committee on Social Responsibility, from G. H. Lohn, January 7, 1974, in Control Data Corporation Records, Corporate Administration (hereafter CDC Corporate Administration), Series 6, Box 3, Folder 32.

[74] See p. 38 of "Control Data Corporation: Minneapolis, Minnesota and Washington, D.C.," a report in CDC Executive Papers, Series 8, Box 7, Folder 4. By 1975, the company was conducting gender sensitivity training, which pointed out the errors of this and similar assumptions. See "CDC Executive Management Awareness Program in CDC Corporate Administration," Series 6, Box 5, Folder, 2. On gender and the electronics industry, see Green, *Race on the Line*, and Jefferson Cowie, *Capital Moves: RCA's Seventy Year Quest for Cheap Labor* (New York: New Press, 2001; originally published in 1999).

[75] Worthy, *William C. Norris*, 114; see also Norris to James Woodbury, Dir. of Professional Resources, Perkin-Elmer Corp., March 8, 1968, in WCN Papers, Series 9, Box 29, Folder 13, CBI.

population in the area, which was 60 percent black. These efforts created an ostensibly segregated workplace, but this segregation also enabled success. One of the main problems the hard-core trainees encountered in regular plants was the hostility and unhelpfulness of white workers. Here was a plant where whites were a minority and, except for the managers, at an equal level of disadvantage with the black workers.

Another more serious criticism was directed at Control Data's use of government funding. Some members of the black community and historians have been critical of companies that have enjoyed good public relations and lauded the efforts of the "private sector," while at the same time receiving government subsidies. Reflecting a common sentiment, historian Venus Green characterizes the Bell System's acceptance of subsidies as dishonest and exploitative.[76] Norris's eagerness to exploit the subsidies (shown earlier) does little to dispel criticism. There were local black militants at the time who saw the Control Data plant as an attempt to exploit poor people and who even threatened to torch the new plant once it was built.[77] But Norris rightly regarded them as a minority faction; he had done his homework and cultivated black community support. The Twin Cities' black newspaper at the time, *The St. Paul Recorder*, never mentioned the government subsidies, one way or the other, even though it regularly (and positively) reported on government-funded OEO and JOBS programs.

Norris's frank and unrelenting pursuit of government subsidies and incentives – his attempt to be "at the right end of the funnel" – can come across as little more than exploitation of government funds, but it is important to remember that few of his peers were similarly willing to exploit the same government opportunities. Only a handful of corporate heads opened inner-city plants designed to provide employment for the poorest Americans.[78] Members of the business community regularly criticized Norris for his social philosophizing and his failure to "maximize shareholder wealth." In a negative

[76] Writes Green: "Publicity obscured the fact that integration not only supplied the industry with an inexpensive labor force for whose training the company received government funds, but that it also made possible a favorable public image that expedited rate increases." Green, *Race on the Line*, 228, 231–32.

[77] See Norris to Berg, December 19, 1967, Report on Militant North Side Group Meeting with Urban Coalition, in WCN Papers, Series 9, Box 29, Folder 13; and "Control Data Corporation: Minneapolis, Minnesota and Washington, D.C.," a report in CDC Executive Papers, Series 8, Box 7, Folder 4, p. 19, CBI.

[78] See Alex Beam, "Why Few Ghetto Factories Are Making It," *BusinessWeek*, February 16, 1987. The corporations were Aerojet General (Watts); Avco (Roxbury); Control Data (Minneapolis, Toledo, Washington, and San Antonio); Digital Equipment (Roxbury and Springfield, MA); EG&G (Roxbury); General Electric (Philadelphia); IBM (Brooklyn); Lockheed (Watts); Xerox (Rochester, NY); and Westinghouse (Baltimore and Pittsburgh).

review of Norris's 1983 *New Frontiers for Business Leadership*, *Fortune* contributor Daniel Seligman noted that most entrepreneurs derive from their success an affirmation of capitalism and rugged individualism: "We haven't had too many entrepreneurs who build 5 billion dollar companies and then proceed to sound like Naderites."[79] Derided by free-market conservatives on the one hand and militant radicals on the other, Norris relished his ideological independence.

The Northside experience led to a vigorous equal employment and affirmative action plan for all of the corporation's plants and offices. In a 1969 memo about the company's new affirmative action plan, Norris reminded all Control Data managers of their responsibility to hire, train, and advance minority employees at every level. While proud of the success of the Northside and Capital (Washington, DC) plants in terms of hiring minorities, it was time for all managers at all plants to become involved in retaining and advancing minorities. In true human relations fashion, Norris wrote, "For all of us it means cooperating to the fullest with administrative and personnel people who will be making unique efforts to obtain and qualify minority individuals for the fullest range of jobs."[80] Notice that the responsibility of providing qualifications for minority individuals resided with the administrators, not the applicants. Notice also that Norris was asking his managers and supervisors to defer to human relations experts. Managers were of course also expected to partake of the company's myriad sensitivity training programs.[81] In addition, the company started a minority purchasing program, which committed $766,000 to minority firms in 1973.[82]

Both affirmative action and minority purchasing initiatives were required by the Office of Federal Contract Compliance. But Norris preferred to see his efforts as good management. He insisted, for instance, that the affirmative action goals were to become, as Worthy put it, "integral parts of efficiently managing the business; they were not to be additions to normal costs of operations but means in themselves to increase productivity and lower costs."[83] In other words, the company had adopted affirmative action and minority purchasing plans not because they were required to by the government, but because they made good business sense. Like so many businessmen, he wanted to

[79] Daniel Seligman, "The Norris Enigma," *Fortune*, January 23, 1984.
[80] Control Data Corporation Inter-office Memo, To: Control Data Management, From: WC Norris, October 16, 1969, in WCN Papers, Series 9, Box 29, Folder 16, CBI.
[81] Memo to Committee on Social Responsibility, from G. H. Lohn, March 5, 1974, in CDC Corporate Administration, Series 6, Box 3, Folder 32, CBI.
[82] Ibid.
[83] Worthy, *William C. Norris*, 127.

frame affirmative action as a part of good management and sound business, not another (costly) government regulation. Observers have usually construed this as a self-serving public relations bid, but it is better understood as an attempt on the part of executives to sell the policy to themselves and their managers, supervisors, and workers.[84]

Affirmative action was just one part of the company's focus on employee relations and social responsibility. The company's Committee on Corporate Social Responsibility (CCSR) oversaw and helped developed programs and policies concerning minority and EEO issues, gender equity, pollution control, energy conservation, recycling, employee career development, consumer education, Vietnamese refugees, OSHA regulations, scholarships, American Indians, urban redevelopment, affirmative action in South Africa,[85] alcohol and drug addiction, the handicapped, the mentally ill, the aged, and the ethics of defense contracts. Headed by top company executives, the committee met monthly to discuss policy and instigate new initiatives. The CCSR supplemented and backed the company's EEO office, affirming its mission in the company at large. The CCSR was the apotheosis of human relations management. From its focus on employee career development to its concern about Control Data's role in the community and the world to its insistence on clear policies, records, and procedures, it fulfilled in every way human relations experts' dreams of transforming American industry from a chaotic, insensitive, greed-driven enterprise into one that was highly rationalized and caring.

The eighty-page 1974 affirmative action plan of Control Data's Star-100 Development Division exhibits the kind of explicit, highly rationalized organizational clarity desired by human relations experts and required by government compliance agencies.[86] It very carefully laid out the responsibilities of the EEO coordinator, the line manager, and the divisional personnel manager and their relationship to each other. It explained how the policy was disseminated within and outside the plant. It contained a "division utilization analysis" for both minorities and females, which included demographic statistics from the Twin Cities area, identified the number of promotable minorities and nonminority females in a variety of job categories, and identified problem areas. In light of

[84] Frank Dobbin and John Sutton, "The Strength of the Weak State: The Rights Revolution and the Rise of Human Resources Management Divisions," *American Journal of Sociology* 104, no. 2 (September 1998): 441–76, makes a similar argument.

[85] CDC participated in debates about whether to boycott South Africa or reform it. CDC stayed in South Africa, but practiced affirmative action. See policy statements in CDC Corporate Administrative, Series 6, Box 3, Folder 30, CBI.

[86] STAR-100 Development Division 1974 Affirmative Action Plan, in CDC Engineering, Research, and Development, Series 7, Box 35, Folder 26, CBI.

the identified deficiencies, it listed numerical goals and then a "plan of execution" for achieving them. To help create a welcoming environment, the plan required executives and managers to undergo sensitivity training in "Minority Group Dynamics," designed to provide understanding between black and white Americans, and the Control Data Executive Management Awareness Program, which dealt with gender.

Despite Norris's intention to make affirmative action just another normal and profitable company policy, its context within the company was in the realm of corporate social responsibility. It was part of good management, yes, but it was also part of an enlightened, pioneering program of corporate social responsibility. Structurally and philosophically, the affirmative action program was associated with hiring the unemployable, recycling, and South Africa, rather than more traditional profit-oriented divisions such as technological research and marketing. Its status as a "special" program, however, may have contributed to its success. Norris's philosophy notwithstanding, it was difficult to argue that affirmative action was profitable and "normal" in the early 1970s. The *Workforce 2000* report would make a case for the profitability of diversity, but that would be in 1987, after minority scholarships and the effects of new immigration rules had succeeded in creating a larger and more qualified pool of minority employees.[87] But in the early 1970s, affirmative action was still regarded as a burden, a chore, an extra effort required by government regulations and new political realities, but hardly a normal part of business. It required extra paperwork, extra training, and extra resources. Hence, even as Norris tried to normalize it, affirmative action was most successful when it was justified in terms of black disadvantage and social responsibility. This made it easier for managers to accept and deliver. It was precisely because it was so out of the norm that managers were able to reimagine qualifications, merit, and other traditional hiring criteria. By 1974, Control Data had increased the number of minority employees from 4 percent of its U.S. computer operations in 1968 to 10.1 percent. It had tripled the number of minority officials and managers in the same period and showed a significant increase of minorities in all of its occupational categories.[88] (See Table 8.1.)

There was one way in which Control Data's affirmative action programs had proven profitable. In keeping with Norris's philosophy that social needs could be potential markets, Control Data packaged and marketed the

---

[87] See Hugh Davis Graham, *Collision Course: The Strange Convergence of Affirmative Action and Immigration Policy in America* (New York: Oxford University Press, 2002).

[88] From Report on Social Responsibility, prepared by the Control Data Corporate Social Responsibility and Concerns Committee, [1975], in CDC Corporate Administration, Series 6, Box 3, Folder 33.

Table 8.1. *Control Data Corporation, U.S.-Based Computer Business, Increase in Minority and Women Employees, 1968–1974*

Job category	Year	Total employment	Minority	Percent minority	Nonminority women	Percent nonminority women
Officials and	1968	3,075	40	1.3	61	1.9
managers	1974	3,909	150	3.8	117	2.9
Professional	1968	4,832	176	3.6	285	5.8
	1974	6,321	425	6.7	528	8.3
Technical	1968	3,855	122	3.1	101	2.6
	1974	4,594	416	9.0	120	2.6
Sales	1968	424	4	0.9	1	0.2
	1974	1,044	61	5.8	98	9.3
Clerical	1968	5,008	269	5.3	3,343	66.7
	1974	5,193	692	13.3	3,373	64.9
Craft	1968	969	29	2.9	296	19.5
	1974	1,055	152	14.4	159	15.0
Operatives	1968	4,136	251	6.0	2,830	68.4
	1974	3,766	716	19.0	2,562	68.0
Services	1968	240	22	9.1	6	2.5
	1974	186	41	22.0	13	6.9
Totals	1968	22,539	913	4.0	6,913	30.6
	1974	26,068	2,653	10.0	6,970	26.7

Source: From *Report on Social Responsibility,* prepared by the Control Data Corporate Social Responsibility and Concerns Committee, (1975), in CDC Corporate Administration files, CBI#80:6, Box 3, Folder 33.

corporation's various employee training programs to other businesses and government agencies seeking to hire the hard-core unemployed, minorities, or women.[89] The company developed and marketed its "Minority Group Dynamics" program, the Fair Break Program, Advanced Career Employment Training, PLATO (a computer system designed to teach remedial skills to the disadvantaged), and Career Outreach to state agencies grappling with unemployment and urban unrest. The firm also marketed the highly successful Employee Advisory Resource (EAR), an ombudsman program for all employees that is still in use. Eventually, the corporation created Control Data Business Advisors, incorporated in 1979 as a subsidiary of Control Data.

---

[89] Worthy, *William C. Norris*, 127; and Gary Lohn to Committee on Corporate Social Responsibility, March 6, 1973, in CDC Corporate Administrative, Series 6, Box 3, Folder 31, CBI.

Nor was Norris content to fill the need for such programs passively. Rather, he lobbied extensively for state and federal legislation that would encourage or require municipalities and states to offer training to the unemployed. He supported Minnesota state legislation that would have provided tax credits for small businesses to buy technology, tax credits for large companies that made their technology available to small companies, and tax credits for investments in technology centers that furnished services to new businesses.[90] He was exalted when President Carter proposed to spend $2 billion on programs for the unemployed and disadvantaged youth, writing, "Control Data presently has or can assembly [sic] in a reasonable time all of the components for a holistic program to provide unemployed youth with basic skills, vocational training and so forth – the whole fair break concept which is essentially what is needed to implement the president's total program."[91] He testified on behalf of the Humphrey-Hawkins full employment bill of 1978, right before which Senator Humphrey had written him a note that Norris's proposal to establish a "nationwide technology information transfer system and promote the development of new technology" would be key to carrying out the purposes of the Humphrey-Hawkins bill.[92] When liberals were finally voted out of office, Norris adjusted his strategies accordingly and latched on to the opportunities presented by President Reagan's Enterprise Zone initiatives.[93]

To critics who would accuse Control Data's calculated performance of "corporate social responsibility" as self-interested, Norris would nod in agreement. It was his mission to make corporate social responsibility profitable, or at least convince other businesspeople that doing business with the government was good business, even if it didn't involve weapons systems, napalm, and arms manufacturing. While not wanting to appear exploitative of social crises, he did hope to set a lucrative example that other businesses would want to follow. There were many reasons for Control Data's eventual failure, but it is not unreasonable to suspect, as many did at the time, that the company's heavy investment in what turned out to be unprofitable social initiatives contributed

[90] Draft August 24, 1981, Potential [Minnesota State] Legislative Actions Supporting Small Enterprise, in WCN Papers, Series 9, Box 2, Folder 29, CBI.
[91] January 24, 1980, National Fair Break Program, WCN Draft, in WCN Papers, Series 9, Box 2, Folder 37, CBI.
[92] Hubert Humphrey to W. C. Norris, January 5, 1978, in WCN Papers, Series 9, Box 2, Folder 37, CBI.
[93] See materials in WCN Papers, Series 9, Box 2, Folders 28–29 (Enterprise Zone legislation), CBI.

in some way. In which case, perhaps, Norris's social responsibility wasn't as self-serving as either he or his critics imagined.

Control Data Corporation was just one of several computer companies that actively sought to recruit – pull in – minority employees. Computer companies had always worked closely with the government, and when the government pressured them to do so, they changed their hiring criteria in order to hire more minorities. Black newspapers regularly reported that IBM, Honeywell, Univac, and others were looking for talented African Americans and constantly announcing those individuals who had been appointed to management positions. IBM had a renowned management training program, into which it recruited minorities.[94] IBM also opened a plant in the Bedford-Stuyvesant section of Brooklyn, which hired the hard-core unemployed and eventually employed 404 people. IBM's Brooklyn plant provided on-the-job training, remedial education, and technical classes for the disadvantaged. Like Control Data, IBM used the facility to train and develop black managers for positions in other parts of the company. At one point, three-quarters of the Brooklyn plant managers were black, which, in addition to training and development purposes, had the added benefit of providing role models for the minority workforce.[95]

Conclusion

Control Data and IBM were representative of the new economy. They were high-tech, multinational, service-oriented, and nonunion. Their experiments with inner-city plants tested theories about the trainability of the hard-core population and thus provided concrete data for a project that was the topic of much speculation and innumerable articles and conferences. In combination with the efforts of the National Alliance of Businessmen and government agencies like the EEOC, these companies helped transform employers' conception of hiring criteria and qualifications for advancement. Their recognition that black workers' needs and experiences differed from white workers weaned

---

[94] See the *Chicago Defender* and *the St. Paul Recorder* during 1967–1970 for examples of black appointments to managerial positions in these companies. See Davis and Watson, *Black Life in Corporate America.*

[95] Steven Roberts, "The Slums: Private Capital Takes a Chance," *New York Times*, April 28, 1968, E4; Thomas Lueck, "New Yorkers & Company; Save the Business Keep it in Brooklyn," *New York Times*, July 17, 1994; and Watson, *Father Son & Co.*

white managers from their color-blind nostrums. Their use of special counselors and sensitivity training further normalized the idea that "extra steps"
were necessary for integration, while at the same time promoting the human
relations in management movement. Employers' complaints that there were
no "qualified blacks" to hire or advance could no longer explain the dearth
of minorities in certain areas of their firms. Moreover, companies that experimented with inner-city plants and training the hard-core unemployed created a
supply of minority labor that they could cultivate and develop for the purposes
of meeting affirmative action goals.

9   The Du Pont Company's Affirmative Action Efforts

Business, at least big business, accepts not only the overall concept of affirmative action by now, but knows that goals and timetables provide a way of showing that they are meeting the law.

A former director of the Office of Federal Contract Compliance Programs, 1981[1]

The E.I. Du Pont de Nemours & Company had never shown much interest in equal employment opportunity, the black community, or affirmative action until 1963, when it joined Plans for Progress. Even then its efforts to hire and promote minorities can best be described as lackluster. While the other companies we have thus far considered were at the forefront of integrating American business and industry, the Du Pont Company wasn't. Yet by the early 1970s, like so many other companies, it was forced to respond to racial unrest, government demands, business leadership, and public opinion, and make a concerted attempt to hire and promote minorities. The Du Pont Company's efforts to adjust to the new social and racial realities of the 1960s and 1970s were at once ambivalent and ambitious, and bring together the major themes of the previous chapters: the role of business leaders in changing attitudes and practices, the full acceptance of color-conscious hiring policies, the way integration strengthened human relations managerial techniques, and the adverse relationship between racial integration and labor union activity.

---

[1] Lawrence Z. Lorber, quoted in "The New Bias on Hiring Rules," *BusinessWeek*, May 25, 1981, 123.

255

The Du Pont Company

Begun in 1802 as a manufacturer of black powder, the Du Pont Company was reorganized into a centrally administered modern corporation in 1902 when it was acquired by three young du Pont cousins. The new E.I. Du Pont de Nemours Powder Company quickly bought up and consolidated the smaller explosive companies and then moved into the burgeoning chemical industry after World War I. The target of antitrust suits, the company shifted its focus in the 1930s from acquiring new companies to creating new products for developing markets. Du Pont was able to recruit talented scientists and chemical engineers whose research led to the development of products like neoprene, a synthetic rubber product used in adhesives, paints, and rocket fuels, and nylon, a synthetic resin fiber with innumerable commercial uses. The post–World War II market for chemicals, plastics, and synthetic fibers like Dacron and Orlon was enormous, and Du Pont continued its upward trajectory, with annual sales in 1968 of three and a half billion dollars.[2] In 1965, Du Pont employed 106,013 people and had twelve industrial departments, thirteen staff departments, and eighty manufacturing plants in twenty-eight states. The majority of its employees were highly skilled scientists, engineers, technicians, and managers. Unlike the auto, farm equipment, and steel industries, the chemical industry did not go into decline in the 1970s. Du Pont's workforce had expanded to 135,900 by 1980.[3]

During the 1930s, Du Pont executives had been vehemently opposed to unions, the New Deal, and Franklin D. Roosevelt. While other corporate heads were wheedling their way into New Deal agencies and tentatively accommodating the idea of unionism, Du Pont head Pierre S. du Pont and John Raskob, his chief aid, were financing the anti-New Deal Liberty League.[4] Du Pont executives were also active in the National Association of Manufacturers' war against the pro-labor Wagner Act of 1935.

After the war, Du Pont executives adopted a more moderate stance and refrained from overt political activism. But they continued their battle against

---

[2] See Herbert Northrup, *Negro Employment in Basic Industry* (Philadelphia: Industrial Research Unit, Wharton School of Finance and Commerce, 1970), 612. On Du Pont's rise, see Alfred D. Chandler, Jr., and Stephen Salsbury, *Pierre S. Du Pont and the Making of the Modern Corporation* (New York: Harper & Row, 1971).

[3] See Appendix 1 in David Hounshell and John Kenly Smith, Jr., *Science and Corporate Strategy: Du Pont R&D, 1902–1980* (New York: Cambridge University Press, 1988), 602, and Stephen Habbe, *Company Experience with Negro Employment*, 2 vols., Studies in Personnel Policy No. 201 (New York: National Industrial Conference Board, 1966), 125.

[4] See Robert Burk, *The Corporate State and the Broker State: The Du Ponts and American National Politics, 1935–1940* (Cambridge, MA: Harvard University Press, 1990).

unions, instituting the HOBSO ("How our Business System Operates") program to dissuade employees from organizing. The company funded its own research program in human relations, "derived from the best thinking in the social sciences," with the aim of improving employee relations.[5] It created an in-house Labor Relations Institute to instruct plant managers on "the relationship of good employee relations to the maintenance of a no-union status."[6] Its Employee Relations Department kept careful track of union membership, charting the gains and losses of the national unions in NLRB elections. But unlike other companies that had instituted such programs to deter unionism (International Harvester and Pitney-Bowes), Du Pont did not institute a corresponding program of fair employment.

Du Pont's EEO Efforts before 1968

As a major government contractor, the E.I. Du Pont de Nemours & Company was required to meet government nondiscrimination requirements beginning during World War II, but there is little surviving evidence of its efforts to do so before 1963. It was never one of the companies that made racial integration a priority. Its executives were not on presidential compliance committees. Its Research Department had a history of anti-Semitism. Its president balked at adding the Equal Employment Opportunity (EEO) emblem on its job advertisements in 1957.[7] Wilmington, Delaware, its headquarters and home to its considerable managerial, technical, and scientific staff, was a segregated city until the late fifties. The first Employee Relations Department Annual Report to mention minority employment was from 1963; it described the company's efforts to implement its "Plans for Progress" contract in compliance with Executive Order 10925. Thereafter, Du Pont actively tried to recruit minority

---

[5] Employee Relations Department Annual Report, 1954, February 11, 1955, in Du Pont Human Resources, Accession 1615, Series I, Box 1, at Hagley Museum and Library, Wilmington, Delaware (hereafter HML).

[6] Du Pont's Employee Relations Department instituted HOBSO at the first company-wide Conference of Training Supervisors. See Employee Relations Annual Report, 1952. On its Labor Relations Institute, see Employee Relations Department, Annual Report, 1955, p. 6, both in Du Pont Human Resources, Accession 1615, Series I, Box 1, HML.

[7] Hounshell and Smith, *Science and Corporate Strategy*, 295–97. On the EEO emblem, see Greenewalt to E. F. Du Pont, June 17, 1957, in Papers of Crawford E. Greenewalt, President and Chairman of the Board of E. I. Du Pont de Nemours & Co., 1947–67 (1928–68), Series II, Box 11, File: Personnel – employment, 1954–57; HML; the company did, however, have an outstanding record with regard to hiring the handicapped. See Employee Relations Department Annual Report, 1955, p. 9, in Du Pont Human Resources, Accession 1615, Series I, Box 1, HML.

Table 9.1 *Du Pont Statistics on Black Employment, 1963–1964*

	1963			1964		
	Total Employees	Blacks	Percent Black	Total Employees	Blacks	Percent Black
Total Company	98,715	4,112	4.17	98,436	4,076	4.14
Eng.-Const. Div.	5,719	558	9.76	3,809	269	7.06
Total (excluding Const. Div.)	92,996	3,554	3.82	94,627	3,807	4.02

Source: Employee Relations Department Annual Report, 1964, p. 6, in Du Pont Human Resources, Accession #1615, Series I, Box 1, Hagley Museum and Library.

workers and scientists, kept track of minority hires, desegregated its southern plants, and began contributing to the National Urban League.[8]

Historically, the chemical industry had not been as welcoming to black workers as industries such as steel, rubber, and automobiles. This was because the chemical industry was less labor intensive, more easily automated, and had a higher percentage of educated, highly skilled, white-collar workers than other industries. Black workers made up 4.7 percent of all chemical industry employees in 1964, almost all of them concentrated in laboring and service positions.[9] African Americans made up 4.17 percent of Du Pont's entire workforce of 98,715 in 1963. The majority of blacks were concentrated in the Engineering Department's Construction Division (see Table 9.1).[10]

In 1964, black employment at Du Pont dropped slightly to 4,076, or 4.14 percent of the total workforce, with the biggest decline occurring in the Construction Division. The company underwent 54 compliance reviews with the Atomic Energy Commission in 1964 (its main government contract was with the Atomic Energy Commission, which was charged with monitoring compliance). Two of these involved complaints to the President's Committee on Equal Employment Opportunity (PCEEO), which were later dismissed. Du

[8] Its southern efforts described in Habbe, *Company Experience with Negro Employment,* and confirmed in Employee Relations Department Annual Reports, 1964–72, in Du Pont Human Resources, Accession 1615, Series I, Box 1. On the UL, see Informational Memo, "National Urban League," May 20, 1974, in Box 31, Charles Brelsford McCoy Papers, 1967–74, Accession 1815, HML.

[9] Compared to the automobile and steel industries where they were 10 and 12 percent, respectively. See Northrup, *Negro Employment in Basic Industry,* 607–713.

[10] Employee Relations Department Annual Report, 1964, p. 6, in Du Pont Human Resources, Accession 1615, Series I, Box 1, HML.

Pont managed to recruit eight black college graduates in 1964 through its new contacts with black colleges.[11]

The main problem that integration presented for Du Pont was in the area of testing. The company had developed rigorous, but decentralized, recruiting programs, designed to secure the best scientists and researchers.[12] In addition to the "old boy's network," the company relied on a battery of tests and strict entrance requirements. As a result, the Employee Relations Department regularly complained about a shortage of qualified candidates, from the 1950s on.[13] The constant shortage of qualified white male candidates could have created a situation that encouraged the hiring of qualified black candidates, or even white women. But Du Pont managers found it increasingly difficult to hire talented black college graduates, who were being snatched up by those corporations who had made minority employment a priority long before Du Pont.[14] Du Pont executives feared that new demands for minority hires meant that the company would have to lower entrance requirements or drop tests. That, certainly, was the direction of the new Equal Employment Opportunity Commission (EEOC), as the Employee Relations Department noted in a 1965 report.[15] There was a complicated process by which a company could validate and prove that its tests were necessary to the jobs in question and that they did not discriminate against racial minorities. Although Du Pont had revised and lowered certain entrance requirements where it seemed appropriate, it chose to validate its tests and prove that they were nondiscriminatory. A 1970 report declared, "Du Pont continues to remain at the forefront of industry in test validation, and work completed in this field is held in high regard by both the [EEOC] and the Atomic Energy Commission."[16] By 1972, however, there was a note of discouragement as the Employee Relations Department reported that the EEOC and compliance officers were repeatedly challenging the company's pre-employment and upgrading procedures. The report indicated that the company had yet to establish the validity of upgrading tests and of "tests for

---

[11] Ibid.

[12] See Hounshell and Smith, *Science and Corporate Strategy*, 286–300.

[13] See "Recruitment" sections in Department of Employee Relations Annual Reports, 1952–72, in Du Pont Human Resources, Accession 1615, Series I, Box 1, HML.

[14] Employee Relations Department Annual Report, 1964, p. 6, in Du Pont Human Resources, Accession 1615, Series I, Box 1.

[15] One EEOC official proposed, "If tests are excluding minorities, the tests should be changed or dropped." To which Du Pont responded, "It will be necessary to insure that our programs are consistent, job-related and validated." Employee Relations Department Annual Report, 1965, p. 7, Du Pont Human Resources, Accession 1615, Series I, Box 1, HML.

[16] Employee Relations Department Annual Report Year Ending June 30, 1970, p. 9, in Du Pont Human Resources, Accession 1615, Series I, Box 1.

minorities at sites which have not had sufficient numbers of such employees to meet validation requirements." Also, the company had yet to demonstrate that the "ratings of minority employees by nonminority supervisors are not inherently biased."[17] But it seemed prepared to work on the problems.

In addition to testing, the 1965 Employee Relations Annual Report identified three other areas on which the company's EEO efforts would be focused. First, the company would establish an affirmative action program in the Wilmington area. Second, the company would use its influence to eliminate discrimination in housing, recreation, and social activities in the communities in which it was a significant employer. And third, to fulfill the EEOC's goal "to get jobs for minorities," the company would participate in local programs "designed to prepare minorities to qualify for industrial jobs."[18] All three of these endeavors involved the Du Pont Company with the black communities of Wilmington, Delaware.

Wilmington, Du Pont, and Race

Since the early twentieth century, when the du Ponts moved the company's headquarters into Wilmington, the Du Pont Company had dominated the economic life of the medium-sized, segregated city. Du Pont family members and executives owned the city's banks, its two newspapers, and its finest hotel (the Hotel Du Pont). John Raskob, Pierre S. du Pont's influential aid, redesigned the city around the Du Pont Building in the 1920s. Pierre S. du Pont built modern, well-equipped schools for the white children. Even the city's other major employers – the Atlas Chemical Company and Hercules Powder Company – had once been part of the Du Pont colossus, before the courts split them off. Du Pont's manufacturing plants were located in other states, and the people Du Pont brought into Wilmington, who worked at its headquarters and research laboratories, were white-collar, middle-class, well-educated people, accountants, managers, scientists, technicians. By the 1920s, the dominant business of the city was corporate management. There was relatively little industrial work.[19]

---

[17] Employee Relations Department Annual Report Year Ending June 30, 1972, p. 9, in Du Pont Human Resources, Accession 1615, Series I, Box 1.

[18] Employee Relations Department Annual Report, 1965, p. 7, Du Pont Human Resources, Accession 1615, Series I, Box 1.

[19] On Du Pont and Wilmington, see Carol Hoffecker, *Corporate Capital: Wilmington in the Twentieth Century* (Philadelphia: Temple University Press, 1983).

From 1950 to 1980, Wilmington's population declined from 110,536 to 70,195. During the same years, its suburban population almost tripled, growing from 158,031 to 453,913.[20] The racial implications of this population shift become clear when one realizes that the suburbs were closed to African Americans. African Americans constituted 10 percent of Wilmington's population in the early twentieth century. By 1968, they made up nearly half of the city's population.[21] Unlike other cities with large African American concentrations, Wilmington had relatively few black business owners. There was no Urban League branch in Wilmington. There was a small middle-class black population, but most educated African Americans left the city. Schools were desegregated in 1954, which accelerated whites' movement out of the city. As in other cities, urban renewal, highway construction, and ongoing residential segregation led to a housing shortage for African Americans, which created tension between remaining ethnic whites and displaced blacks. Those blacks who tried to move into suburban neighborhoods were harassed and terrorized. Blacks and their white allies lobbied for open-housing laws in Delaware, but suburban whites fought residential integration well into the 1970s.[22]

By 1960, poor planning and white flight had left the city in shambles, and a group of prominent citizens and businessmen formed the Greater Wilmington Development Council (GWDC) to correct the situation. The Du Pont Company had removed itself from local politics and civic affairs during the 1920s to avoid "bad publicity."[23] But Wilmington's decline was so disheartening that Henry B. du Pont, president of the Christiana Securities Company (the du Pont family holding company) and member of the Du Pont Company board of directors, became involved with the GWDC in the late 1960s. The GWDC initially focused its efforts on reconstructing the central business district but eventually funded and helped develop experimental neighborhood, job-training, and antigang programs.[24] In 1965, the company began efforts to train and hire the hard-core unemployed. Despite these efforts, however, Wilmington's African Americans continued to live in substandard housing,

---

[20] Hoffecker, *Corporate Capital*, appendix.

[21] Ben A. Franklin, "Armed Guardsmen Still Patrol in Wilmington's Slums, 7 Months after Riot," *New York Times*, November 17, 1968.

[22] Hoffecker, *Corporate Capital*, 94, 158–261. On the struggle to integrate residential areas, see Arnold Hirsch, *Making the Second Ghetto: Race and Housing in Chicago, 1940–1960* (New York: Cambridge University Press, 1983), and Thomas Sugrue, *Sweet Land of Liberty: The Forgotten Struggle for Civil Rights in the North* (New York: Random House, 2008).

[23] See Hoffecker, *Corporate Capital*, 173.

[24] Ibid., 188–192. On Du Pont's contributions, see "Du Pont Summary Community Projects in Greater Wilmington," by Du Pont Public Relations Department, April 1969, in Charles Brelsford McCoy Papers, 1967–74, Accession 1815, Box 12, HML.

the state legislature continued to thwart open-housing legislation, and racial tensions continued to rise.

The two-day riot that occurred after Martin Luther King, Jr.'s assassination was small compared with riots in other cities, but its aftermath highlighted the depth of Wilmington's racial problem. During the riot, which occurred on April 9–10, 1968, the mayor asked for a small number of National Guardsmen to help restore order. Democratic Governor Charles L. Terry (a southern-style Democrat) sent in the entire state National Guard and refused to remove them after the rioting was brought under control. Despite repeated requests from the white mayor, black leaders, the State Human Relations Committee, religious leaders, business leaders, and Republican and Democratic legislators, Governor Terry refused to remove the National Guard, insisting that they were necessary to avert more rioting. Their presence in the streets of Wilmington predictably attracted violence, which validated the governor's position that they were still necessary. In November 1968 – six months after the riots – the National Guard was still patrolling Wilmington over the objections of city leaders, who accused the governor of playing to white fears in an election year. City Supervisor O. Francis Biondi told the *New York Times*, "the National Guard here has become a symbol of white suppression of the black community. That may be a useful way to get elected, but who wants to ... run a city under those circumstances?"[25] If the "law and order" signified by the National Guard had been a bid for votes, it failed. The election went to those who opposed Governor Terry's National Guard policy: two liberal Republicans with Du Pont connections. Republican Russell W. Peterson, a Du Pont research executive and GWDC member, defeated Governor Terry, and Harry Haskell, son and nephew of various du Ponts, became the new mayor. Upon his inauguration in January 1969, Governor Peterson ended the National Guard's nine-and-a-half months of occupation in Wilmington.[26]

Black activist groups around the nation blamed the nine-month occupation of Wilmington on the Du Pont Company. The *Chicago Defender* referred to Wilmington as a "capital of corporate racism."[27] A delegation from the Pittsburgh Area Religion and Race Council visited the Du Pont Offices in Pittsburgh to request that the company use its influence to get the National Guard removed. The National Emergency Committee Against Repression in Wilmington staged demonstrations outside Du Pont offices in New York and

---

[25] Franklin, "Armed Guardsmen Still Patrol in Wilmington's Slums, 7 months after Riot." See also Hoffecker, *Corporate Capital*, 198–205.

[26] "Guard Patrols to Be Ended in Wilmington," *New York Times*, January 20, 1969. See also Hoffecker, *Corporate Capital*, 198–205.

[27] "Relief for Wilmington," *Chicago Defender*, January 28, 1969.

Wilmington in January 1969, featuring people dressed as National Guards-men carrying signs reading "Du Pont" chasing people carrying signs reading "Wilmington Blacks."[28] The committee published an accompanying pamphlet that argued that the Du Pont Company controlled the city of Wilmington, the state of Delaware, and the GWDC on behalf of its own corporate interests, and therefore was responsible for the retention of the National Guard and the persecution of young black militants. The pamphlet contained this critique of private-sector solutions:

> For those who look to the large corporation to save our cities, then, Wilmington should be an object lesson. Despite the pretenses of the Urban Coalition and the theology of Urban Uplift espoused by Nixon's ghetto guru Daniel P. Moynihan, continued paternalism and economic dependency cannot solve the problems of America's black community. Corporate imperialism for America's poor, like imperialism everywhere, leads to military solutions.[29]

The idea that "corporate social responsibility" might really be "corporate impe-rialism" gained currency and momentum through the works of Frances Piven, C. Wright Mills, and Gabriel Kolko.[30] Similar to leftist arguments about human relations in management, arguments about "corporate imperialism" held that "corporate social responsibility" was really a ploy to allow a corporation to exert control over a community while at the same time gaining public relations benefits. This can be a useful concept, but it doesn't explain Du Pont's response to the urban crisis, at least not initially.

Before the National Guard crisis, the Du Pont Company and its executives had taken some steps to ameliorate racial tensions in Wilmington, but they were hesitant, uncoordinated, and can hardly be described as "imperialist." Du Pont chemist and GWDC member Russell Peterson was responsible for the GWDC's experimental Neighborhood program, of which historian Carol Hoffecker observed the following:

> It is not surprising that an experimental program such as this produced admin-istrative confusion; but considering that the people in charge were chief execu-tives of complex business bureaucracies, one must conclude that businessmen

---

28 Memo, John Burchenal to Chairman of the Board, January 16, 1969, re: New York Demon-stration – January 16; "The Wilmington Story"; and Memo re: Pittsburgh Area Religion and Race Council, January 10, 1969, all in Charles Brelsford McCoy Papers, 1967–74, Accession 1815, Box 12, HML.

29 "The Wilmington Story" in Charles Brelsford McCoy Papers, 1967–74, Accession 1815, Box 12, HML.

30 Gabriel Kolko, *The Triumph of Conservatism* (New York: Free Press, 1963), and Frances Fox Piven and Richard Cloward, *Poor People's Movements* (New York: Pantheon, 1997).

must have been very unsure of themselves in their role as social reformers. One cannot help but to compare the self-assured businesslike way in which Pierre S. Du Pont directed his charitable activities during the 1920s with the more tentative approach to social involvement among business leaders in the 1960s.[31]

Back in the 1920s, the du Ponts could usefully be described as "corporate imperialists," which, if it means anything, means control. Contrary to the assumptions of the demonstrators, neither the Du Pont Company nor its executives seemed to have control over the fate of Wilmington in the 1960s.

The company's hesitancy did not arise out of a desire to protect corporate interests, but rather from executives' unfamiliarity with a new and frightening racial situation, combined with their desire to act progressively. It is true that the GWDC was dominated by executives from Du Pont and Atlas Chemical Company (which had at one time been a subsidiary of Du Pont), but it was these executives who constantly steered the organization toward more "experimental," radical programs, such as the Neighborhood program described above, and the Wilmington Youth Emergency Action Council (WYEAC). The WYEAC was an attempt to co-opt gang members by putting them in charge of a well-funded community development project. The youth in charge of the group, many of whom were gang leaders with police records, were black militants who sought ways to subvert the "white power structure." As it turned out, their most loyal supporters were prominent members of the white power structure, such as Atlas Chemical Company president Edward J. Goett, who believed that the gang backgrounds of WYEAC leaders gave them the credibility to reach hundreds of wayward youth and channel their energies into wholesome athletic and social activities. As author Tom Wolfe and others have noted, members of the white elite during these years were quick to accept black militants to prove their open-mindedness and concern, but the terrain was so unfamiliar that they lost the confidence and control that an earlier generation had possessed. There were elite whites, however, who were not afraid to stand by the values of the white power structure. Mrs. Thomas Herlihy, a prominent liberal Republican leader, resigned from the Community Service Council to protest support for the WYEAC, which she believed subsidized gangs at the expense of law-abiding black youths.[32]

The Du Pont Company's defensive and baffling abdication of responsibility during the National Guard crisis cannot be seen as "imperialist" or even self-serving. The company gained nothing from the occupation except bad publicity, and many of its officials had spoken privately to the governor about the matter. But the company took no action. Over the course of the occupation,

[31] Hoffecker, *Corporate Capital*, 182–83.
[32] Ibid., 185–93.

various groups appealed to the Du Pont Company to use its influence to have the National Guard withdrawn. Each time, Du Pont Company representatives explained that the company felt it was inappropriate to involve itself in a matter that was the responsibility of elected officials. The company's official line was that it should not "influence the action of public officials."[33] An earlier generation of du Ponts had openly and boldly influenced the action of public officials, but apparently the company was trying to distance itself from its history of political influence and peddling. It is possible that someone in the company was interested in having the National Guard in Wilmington to protect Du Pont property. Du Pont officials had after all alerted the New York City police and the FBI of impending demonstrations against the company in New York City and Wilmington in early 1969.[34] But there is no evidence that Du Pont was involved in bringing the National Guard into the city.

Du Pont's timid response to the racial tensions and the National Guard crisis is best explained not by corporate imperialism, but by disagreement among its top officials about the proper role of business in social affairs. While some executives like H. P. du Pont and Russell Peterson were actively involved in community programs, others stood aloof. During the height of the crisis, Irenee du Pont, Jr., spoke to plant managers about the dangers of overinvolvement in social affairs. Businessmen, he said, were not social psychologists or city planners. They hadn't been elected. If they reached beyond their talents or authority, they would rouse the resentment of the public. There were specific things they could do, such as hiring more minorities or funding a Head Start program, but they should avoid a generalized commitment to experimental programs.[35] After the crisis, however, the opinions of those in the company who advocated more aggressive intervention into social problems, a return to the activism of an earlier du Pont generation, gained stature.

Du Pont Confronts New Racial Realities

Following the National Guard crisis, the Du Pont Company began to apply its considerable resources and influence to what it called the "social/urban/race" (or SUR) problem. A year after the riots, the Public Relations Department

---

[33] Quotes from Memo re: Pittsburgh Area Religion and Race Council, January 10, 1969, see also other memos in same box, in Charles Brelsford McCoy Papers, 1967–74, Accession 1815, Box 12, HML.

[34] Donald Roney to F.J. Zugehoer, January 13, 1969, re: Picketing Demonstration Against Du Pont [2 memos with same citation] in Charles Brelsford McCoy Papers, Accession 1815, 1967–74, Box 12, HML.

[35] TW Stephenson, Public Relations, to President, etc., and Dept. Heads. December 23, 1968, in Charles Brelsford McCoy Papers, 1967–74, Accession 1815, Box 12, HML.

reported on Du Pont's extensive involvement in the Wilmington community. Cooperating with the new Republican governor and mayor, as well as federal, state, and community organizations, Du Pont had contributed funds to develop and aid local job creation and training, education, housing, and community planning. Two Du Pont executives sat on the Bi-racial Coordinating Committee for Metropolitan Wilmington, which opened a communication network between influential black leaders and white citizens. Du Pont's Employee Relations Department manager was released at full pay for two and a half months to coordinate summer employment programs, which provided employment for more than one thousand youth. Lab technician Milton Olazagasti was released at half-pay to teach at the Delaware Opportunities Industrialization Center, Inc., a black-run organization that trained disadvantaged workers for possible employment at Du Pont. Du Pont also supplied personnel for YMCA job training programs. Two Du Pont executives sat on the GWDC, to which Du Pont was now the largest single financial contributor. Du Pont contributed $330,000 to the United Fund of Delaware, and more than twenty thousand Du Pont employees contributed over $1 million to the same organization. Seventeen Du Pont executives sat on the United Fund's board. Du Pont was an original sponsor of the Upward Bound Program.

To create a larger pool of potential minority hires, Du Pont contributed substantial funding to Delaware State University and the University of Delaware's programs in the hard sciences, secondary science teaching, social science, and Upward Bound.[36] Du Pont also increased its employment of minority workers: 14 percent of the 1,200 employees hired in the last half of 1968 were black, bringing the number of black employees in the company to 6,400. Since 1966, Du Pont had hired 573 minority employees and hired and trained 599 disadvantaged citizens.[37] There was no pretense of color-blind policies; the policy was to hire minorities.

In 1970, Du Pont's Employee Relations Department conducted a "social responsibility" study to propose ways Du Pont could streamline and coordinate its many activities relating to social/urban/racial issues. The study affirmed the need for Du Pont to continue its intervention in the social affairs of its "employment point communities." A company facility and its employees and their families can only prosper if the community is progressive in solving its social problems. At the same time, however, the report conceded (in a nod to Irenee

[36] John Oliver to J. A. Dallas, Dec. 11, 1970, in Charles Brelsford McCoy Papers, 1967–74, Accession 1815, Box 12, HML.

[37] T. W. Stephenson to Management Heads, April 18, 1969, in Charles Brelsford McCoy Papers, 1967–74, Accession 1815, Box 12, HML.

du Pont, Jr.) that the company must remain competitive. To this end, the study proposed that the company adopt a formal statement expressing the company's willingness to contribute leadership and resources to solve social problems "in fields of our expertise and interest."[38] The proposed guidelines for programs Du Pont would support prioritized those programs that would prepare minority citizens for employment and hence help Du Pont achieve its commitment to equal opportunity and affirmative action. Thus, rather than just complaining about the dearth of qualified black candidates or having to lower its standards, Du Pont would use its expertise in training to ameliorate the problem. The company would also commit resources to housing and community improvement (parks, traffic, urban renewal). The report recommended creating a new position, "Director of Community Affairs" to coordinate the "SUR" activities.

This proposal was Du Pont's attempt to accommodate and frame the required changes on its own terms. As we saw in our examination of Control Data Corporation, companies usually tried to explain new EEO/affirmative action measures on their own terms – not as government requirements, but as something that made sense from an economic perspective.[39] This allowed executives to regain control over the issue and convince stockholders, boards, and employees of the need to change, but it also represented an internalization of new expectations and social obligations. When employees complained about the company's new interest in social activism, as they increasingly did, the president took a firm stand. This is how Du Pont president C. B. McCoy explained it to one irate employee:

> I look upon the company's profits as a yardstick of business success, as I am sure you do. However . . . we must acknowledge that profit-making is not the whole of the story. A company such as ours exists by public permission, and unless companies such as Du Pont are seen by the public as responsible organizations, they will be faced with an ever increasing battery of codes and regulations . . . . Thus, I believe, that in the long range, the companies which identify themselves with the economic needs and aspirations of the public will be the ones that are most successful in making profits.[40]

---

[38] John Oliver, "Social Responsibility," January 7, 1970 in Charles Brelsford McCoy Papers, 1967–74, Accession 1815, Box 12, HML.

[39] This was a common observation in the business press beginning during the 1980s; see for instance, "Taking Adversity out of Diversity," *BusinessWeek*, January 31, 1994. It is also an argument made in Frank Dobbin and John Sutton, "The Strength of the Weak State: The Rights Revolution and the Rise of Human Resources Management Divisions," *American Journal of Sociology* 104, no. 2 (September 1998): 441–76.

[40] C. B. McCoy to Mr. Morris, November 5, 1969, in Charles Brelsford McCoy Papers, 1967–74, Accession 1815, Box 19, HML.

This is a classic statement of corporate social responsibility and it is a clear departure from what Irenee du Pont, Jr., had told managers just a year before. In it one can see the balance that executives struck between corporate self-interest and social responsibility, between their obligations to stockholders and their appeasement of activists. Activists regarded any admission of self-interest as evidence of corporate imperialism. But corporate heads had to attribute their actions to self-interest in order to rationalize costly policies and programs to their boards, stockholders, and employees.

There was in Du Pont's heavy-handed policies and programs a sense of control and authority that had been lacking in the years leading up to the Wilmington riot. The project of creating productive workers out of potential rioters, for instance, which is where Du Pont concentrated much of its energy after the riots, carried within it a desire to co-opt the radical elements of black power. That such co-optation occurred is perhaps best illustrated in a thank-you note to the company from one of Du Pont technician Milton Olazagasti's OIC students, who wrote,

> Peace not war; love not hate; don't accept the status quo; revolution, not play acting, down with groups, down with the military-industrial complex, unless it is used to help human beings better themselves with steady employment . . . . down with employment tests, unless I can teach people to pass them; down with welfare mothers, up with lab technicians, down with human spectrograph machines, up with helping people![41]

Down with the military-industrial complex, unless it is used to help human beings better themselves with steady employment . . . . It would be hard to find a better expression of deflated radicalism than that.

Despite the new Community Affairs Committee and the internalization of the new social values by some board members, the company remained conservative in its outlook. In 1970, Employee Relations director John Oliver advised against supporting a local film project about Martin Luther King, Jr. Oliver explained that the project was sponsored by the Southern Christian Leadership Conference (SCLC), which supported Operation Breadbasket and used boycotts and other unreasonable tactics to pressure employers to hire minorities. Oliver explained that Du Pont supported only one national minority organization – the Urban League – because the Urban League helped the company to recruit minorities. To assist the SCLC would bring in similar requests from CORE, the NAACP, and SNCC. The Public Relations Department agreed with Oliver's recommendation but encouraged "individuals in the company" to

---

[41] In Box 12, Charles Brelsford McCoy paper, 1967–74, Hagley.

buy tickets for the film project to avoid offending "the Negro community." The memos indicate the company's wariness of civil rights organizations, its sensitivity to black and employee opinion (a Du Pont researcher had made the request), and its desire to recruit minority employees.[42] Du Pont's conservative outlook did not prevent the company from instituting an affirmative action program to hire minorities.

Management Development and Affirmative Action

There was a close correlation between the human relations goal of management development and the advancement of minorities (and white women). Although Du Pont's Employee Relations Department had always paid attention to personnel development, there was after 1970 more concern for instructing line managers (in plants, labs, sales, and staff units) how to recognize and develop promising employees for management positions.[43] This concern corresponds with the company's EEO efforts to recruit, prepare, and develop minority personnel for advancement, as well as the general recognition that line managers were very often the missing link in this endeavor.[44] The Employee Relations Department reported that department managers were being taught how to get line managers to see the development of personnel as an integral part of management and how to hold them accountable for the development of people reporting to them. The department had found that the focus on formal training seminars and courses had become a substitute for the effective supervision of the line managers. In the coming year, the department would provide instead more direct assistance to unit managers who wanted to strengthen their in-line management development efforts. The report also indicated that members of the Employee Relations Department had been working with managers from five operating departments (Elastomers, Fabrics and Finishes, Film, Organic Chemicals, and Textile Fibers) to improve procedures for selecting first-line supervisors.[45]

---

[42] John Oliver to Community Affairs Committee, March 13, 1970, and T. W. Stephenson to McCoy, March 16, 1970, both in Charles Brelsford McCoy Papers, 1967–74, Accession 1815, Box 12, HML.

[43] See Employee Relations Department Annual Report Year Ending June 30, 1970, p. 3, in Du Pont Human Resources, Accession 1615, Series I, Box 1.

[44] Employee Relations Department Annual Report Year Ending June 30, 1968, p. 7, in Du Pont Human Resources, Accession 1615, Series I, Box 1.

[45] See Employee Relations Department Annual Report Year Ending June 30, 1970, p. 4, in Du Pont Human Resources, Accession 1615, Series I, Box 1. This supports what Frank Dobbin

In 1971, the Executive Committee had requested the Employee Relations Department to discuss with departments plans for advancing minority and female salaried employees. The resulting report summarized the state of the company's efforts and made recommendations.[46] The department reported a definite need for more aggressive affirmative action. Of the 29,542 exempt (salaried) employees, only 241 (0.8 percent) were African American, 312 (1.1 percent) were other minorities (Asian), and 602 (2 percent) were women. Only one minority employee had advanced beyond level 6A. As affirmative action reports were required to do, the report identified the advancement potential of minorities and women within five years. Of the 241 blacks, 103 (43 percent) had the potential to advance one full level or higher, and 199 (64 percent) of the 312 minorities did. Most of these were in research and development. Of the 602 nonminority females, 152 had the potential to advance. In April 1972, the Personnel Department established a group to improve minority-female employee relations by assisting departments in recruitment, advancement, the identification of potential, and the reduction of turnover. The Employee Relations Department made the following recommendations, which were approved by the board in May 1972:

1. All departments were expected to improve corporate performance in the employment, retention, development, and advancement of minorities and women in coordination with Employee Relations Department.
2. For 1971–72, all departments were expected to fill authorized college graduate requisitions at the 12 percent minority hiring rate previously designated and to increase female hiring above the previously designated 5 percent.
3. All departments were to submit forecasts of college graduates to be recruited for 1972–73. From these figures, appropriate hiring goals for the period will be established.
4. All departments were to submit requisitions to fill mid-level management positions.
5. All departments would be evaluated on their performances in advancing and retaining minorities and women and would be required to incorporate the subject into their annual reviews. The Employee

and Sutton have argued: that EEO law was the source of formal promotion mechanisms after 1964. See Dobbin and Sutton, "The Strength of the Weak State."

[46] Memo to Executive Committee from Employee Relations Dept., May 9, 1972, re: Minority and Female Personnel Exempt Salary roll. In E. I. Du Pont de Nemours & Co. Executive Committee, Records, Accession 2091, Box 1, HML.

Relations Department would summarize the promotions and transfers of minorities and females designated as having potential as part of this department's "Equal Opportunity Report Semiannual Report."[47]

By approving the recommendations, the board empowered the Employee Relations Department vis-à-vis the operating and other staff departments, making it something more than an advisory office, which could be ignored. These recommendations were fairly standard at this time as companies tried to increase and retain minorities and women. Many of these recommendations had been pioneered by International Harvester, and all of them fulfilled and advanced the tenets of the human relations movement. During the 1971–72 year, Du Pont concentrated on achieving its affirmative action goals. A minimum of 12 percent of the new hires were to be minorities and 5 percent of them women. The company hired significantly more new college graduates than it had the year before, 387 compared with only 80 the previous year. Of those 387, 40, or 10 percent, were minorities (unspecified), while 27, or 7 percent, were women. Du Pont had a more difficult time meeting its goals for minorities than for women. The Employee Relations Department helped industrial and staff departments improve their assessment procedures for identifying noteworthy (or marginal) performers, a key element of successful affirmative action plans, as well as human relations agendas. In addition, the recruitment advertising budget for 1973 was $155 million to be directed at attracting women and minorities.[48]

Unfortunately, the company's quarterly EEO reports are not available, so it is difficult to track the company's progress. But Herbert Northrup's research team interviewed Du Pont officials about their personnel policies for engineers and other scientific professionals in 1982. Northrup's research team discovered that Du Pont was meeting its affirmative action goals, which required that 50 percent of new recruits were to be minorities or women. However, the company was having a difficult time retaining both minorities and nonminority women. The turnover rate for minorities and women was double that of white males.[49] After studying the problem company officials concluded that

[47] Ibid.

[48] Employee Relations Department Annual Report Year Ending June 30, 1972, p. 4, 5, in Du Pont Human Resources, Accession 1615, Series I, Box 1; on the consequences of inadequate appraisal procedures for minorities see George Davis and Glegg Watson, *Black Life in Corporate America: Swimming in the Mainstream* (New York: Anchor Books, 1985; originally published by Doubleday in 1982).

[49] "Du Pont Synopsis," in Wharton School Industrial Research Unit Records, Accession 2296, Series IV, Box 20, HML.

the problem in retaining minorities was due to the "perception of discrimination," which they (company officials) attributed to unrealistic expectations of corporate life. This was not necessarily incorrect; the adjustment to corporate life, with its petty hierarchies, conformity, and hidden cues of status was a strange and difficult experience for blacks entering the corporate world for the first time, and regular pecking-order slights could be seen as racism.[50] To solve the problem, Du Pont organized special conferences for young black recruits to hear the experiences of minorities who had worked at Du Pont for some time. The company also developed a corporate-wide "Effective Black-White Relationship" program.[51]

By 1982, Du Pont had a centralized recruiting and hiring department and a professional recruitment staff, which operated year-round visiting college and university campuses, sponsoring tours, cultivating contacts, and generally representing the company. All hires for professional positions began in the central recruiting department. This was a significant change from the decentralized way professional recruitment had once occurred, and was in keeping with effective affirmative action strategies.[52] Each site (plant) submitted a requisition containing information about available jobs to the central recruiting department, which matched available applicants to appropriate sites. After a series of interviews, the final offer was extended by the site. Selection criteria varied according to a candidate's university, which indicated the appropriate flexibility required by affirmative action. Although Du Pont did most of its recruiting from universities and colleges, it did hire experienced scientists and professionals, particularly minorities and women, from other companies and research organizations.[53] A return visit from Northrup's team in 1985 concentrated on the advancement of nonminority women, which seemed to be more successful than the firm's record with minorities.

The State of the Unions

The years that saw the integration of minorities and women into the workforce also saw the decline of once powerful unions in the private sector. The percent of union workers in the workforce declined between 1960 and 1980, from

[50] See, for instance, Davis and Watson, *Black Life in Corporate America.*
[51] "Du Pont Synopsis," in Wharton School Industrial Research Unit Records, Accession 2296, Series IV, Box 20, HML.
[52] See Hounshell and Smith, *Science and Corporate Strategy.*
[53] "Du Pont Synopsis," in Wharton School Industrial Research Unit Records, Accession 2296, Series IV, Box 20, HML

31.4 percent of all employed in 1960 to 25.2 percent in 1980. By 2000, only 13.5 of the workforce would belong to unions (see Table 4 in appendix).[54] Many factors contributed to the decline of unionism, including deindustrialization, which reduced the number of union jobs; the movement of industry out of the northeast to southern and western states with "right to work" laws; employers' increased use of human relations practices to deter unionization; and the rise of newer industries like computers and the service industries, where unions never took hold. There is no evidence to suggest that racial integration weakened unions, but whereas once federal oversight of industry had been concerned with safeguarding union rights, by the 1960s, it was focused on minority employment and advancement. Union members' hostility to EEO/affirmative action goals strained the once friendly relationship between the government and unions, and it was regularly observed that the integration and advancement of minorities in the workforce occurred more smoothly in nonunionized parts of industry.[55]

The labor movement played a relatively minor role in the chemical industry, where a smaller percentage of workers were in unions compared to the steel, automobile, rubber, or aluminum industries.[56] But this did not translate into more opportunities for black workers because the reason that unions were less prevalent in chemicals was the same reason that blacks were less prevalent. The chemical industry was research-oriented and capital-intensive; even its blue-collar workforce was more highly educated than in other industries.

Of all the chemical companies, Du Pont had done the best job of deterring national union organizing. Only 4 percent of its hourly workers belonged to one of the three national unions in 1967, although 56 percent belonged to independent local unions (which had grown out of the company's old works councils).[57] Du Pont preferred independent unions to the national unions, in part because separately negotiated contracts with independent unions allowed

[54] From George Thomas Kurian, ed., *Datapedia of the United States: American History in Numbers*, 3rd ed. (Lanham, MD: Bernan Press, 2004), table 8–9, Series D 946–951. "Labor Union Membership as a Percent of Total Employment, 1930–2002," p. 123.

[55] See, for instance, "Acting Affirmatively to End Job Bias," *BusinessWeek*, January 27, 1975, and Jill Quadagno, "Social Movements and State Transformation: Labor Unions and Racial Conflict in the War on Poverty," *American Sociological Review* 57 (October 1992): 616–34. See Judith Stein, *Running Steel, Running America: Race, Economic Policy and the Decline of Liberalism* (Chapel Hill: University of North Carolina Press, 1998), 89–120, for a description of how unions made integration complicated and see the previous chapter for examples of how the nonunionized computer industry proceeded with integration.

[56] Of 1,085,058 persons employed in the chemical industries in 1966, approximately 490,000 belonged to three different national unions. Northrup, *Negro Employment in Basic Industry*, 618–19.

[57] Ibid., 618.

the company to take advantage of regional wage differences rather than paying all of its employees at a national union rate. But by the 1970s, even the
independent unions were trying to form coalitions in an effort to strengthen
their bargaining power, a move Du Pont sought to thwart by expanding the
nonunion segment of its workforce.[58] In response to the challenge posed by
coordination among independent unions, an Employee Relations Department
memo noted comfortingly, "We are now more than 50% nonunion among
wage and nonexempt salary employees and these employees operate more
than half of the total investment in plant, laboratory, and office facilities.
This sector is growing more rapidly than the union represented sector."[59] The
goal of expanding the nonunion sector of the workforce comported well with
EEO/affirmative action goals to hire minorities into white-collar positions.

As the memo quoted above suggests, the company had worked hard to
maintain the no-union status that existed in at least 40 percent of Du Pont
plants. The Employee Relations Department kept careful track of organizing
drives, NLRB elections, and the latest antiunion techniques. Almost every year
during the fifties, the Employee Relations Department anxiously reported that
Du Pont was a target of yet another major organizing campaign. Company
officials were aware that the national unions saw Du Pont as key to effectively organizing the rest of the industry. Thus its resistance was not merely
self-interested, but stood to benefit the entire chemical industry. The same
management development programs that were later used to educate managers
about affirmative action for minority workers were first used to teach managers
how to bargain effectively with unions.[60]

In 1974, the United Steelworkers began a seven-year effort to organize
Du Pont. As it had done since the 1930s, Du Pont responded with human
relations programs that sought worker input, opened lines of communication,
expanded benefits, and raised wages. The company's message was that Du Pont
workers had a pretty good deal and that unions were losing ground nationally.
With a 96 percent turnout of eligible voters, workers overwhelmingly rejected
the United Steelworkers in 1981, preferring, again, the independent unions or

---

[58] See Employee Relations Department Annual Report 1955, p. 4, in Du Pont Human Resources,
Accession 1615, Series I, Box 1; and "Coordinated Bargaining Organizing Activity in Du Pont,"
June 8, 1972, in E. I. Du Pont de Nemours & Co. Executive Committee, Records, Accession
2091, Box 1, HML. See also "An Acid Test for Du Pont," *BusinessWeek*, December 14, 1981,
123, 127.

[59] "Coordinated Bargaining Organizing Activity in Du Pont," June 8, 1972, in E. I. Du Pont de
Nemours & Co. Executive Committee, Records, Accession 2091, Box 1, HML.

[60] See, for instance, description of "collective bargaining institutes" in Employee Relations
Department Annual Report 1955, p. 6, in Du Pont Human Resources, Accession 1615, Series
I, Box 1.

none at all.[61] Coming just four months after the air traffic controllers' defeat and almost a year into the Reagan administration, the loss was devastating for the labor movement, and indicative of renewed antiunion sentiments.

What Du Pont Tells Us

Du Pont was not a typical company, nor was it representative of American corporations in the late twentieth century. It was a giant in its industry. It had mostly escaped unionization. Its executive committee and board were family dominated. But it wasn't exceptional in its efforts to comply with the government's EEO and affirmative action requirements. In this area it followed the lead of other large American corporations at this time. Like them, Du Pont instituted a color-conscious affirmative action plan based on government and civil rights agencies' recommendations for recruiting, retaining, and advancing minorities within the company. It conducted inventories of its workforce, made an effort to hire the "hard-core unemployed" and minorities, reimagined its recruitment and advancement procedures, reassessed its testing programs, invested millions in minority engineering education programs, refocused its management development programs, created EEO/affirmative action offices, and gradually, eventually, recalibrated its policies and procedures to meet the needs of an integrated workforce. Government pressure and public opinion spurred Du Pont and other corporations to take such actions. Nonetheless, the corporate effort represented an unprecedented commitment of resources and leadership to the creation of a fully integrated workplace. If the results have been less than desired, if there are still racial and gender imbalances and inequities in the workplace, the reason cannot be summarily attributed to employers' lack of effort or commitment.

Because the results have been mixed, critics have regularly dismissed corporate commitments to integration as lip service, a public relations gambit. There may be some instances where this criticism is accurate, but it is also the case that corporate human resources departments – the descendants of the old human relations movement – have taken the lead in identifying and removing obstacles to the retention and advancement of minorities and women in the workplace.[62] If we shift our frame of analysis from "results" to historical

---

[61] Ben A. Franklin, "Union Is Beaten by Wide Margin in Du Pont Vote," *New York Times*, December 12, 1981, 1.

[62] This is an argument made and supported by Dobbin and Sutton, "The Strength of the Weak State," 441–76; and John D. Skrentny, *The Minority Rights Revolution* (New York: Cambridge University Press, 2002). Anecdotally, the corporate world has been far ahead of the academy

context, we can better assess the depth of corporations' commitment to racial integration. One way to clarify the level of corporate commitment to racial integration is to compare it to corporations' responses to other types of labor relations regulations, such as, for instance, labor-management legislation.

Despite the many ways in which the Du Pont Company is unique, it is representative of a certain conservative strain in American business, which has typically responded negatively to government attempts to regulate labor relations. We have seen, for instance, that Du Pont executives and family members led the business opposition to Franklin Roosevelt, the New Deal, and most particularly the Wagner Act of 1935. Du Pont executives held leadership positions in the National Association of Manufacturers (NAM). The NAM and Du Pont executives opposed the Wagner Act for reasons of principle and self-interest. The free-market ideology that they espoused held that government regulations and union activity interfered with the laws of economics and the rights of management. In their eyes, decisions about employee relations resided with management alone; any interference from outside parties threatened productivity and hence also the stability of the entire economic system. It wasn't just that the government was attempting to regulate employee-management relations, which was bad enough, but the government was also in effect siding with unions, which conservative business leaders believed engaged in illegal, coercive activity. Even if the NAM and Du Pont executives could have overlooked the means (government regulation), the end of the Wagner Act (the legitimacy of unions) was so heinous that the Wagner Act had to be opposed by all right-thinking Americans. While historians were initially quick to assume that all large corporations accepted unions as part of a new political reality, it turned out that many corporations, Du Pont among them, resisted the trend.[63]

As we have seen in previous chapters, both the NAM and Du Pont had a very different reaction to government attempts to ensure employment opportunities for minorities. In this case, both the NAM and Du Pont professed to support the end of the endeavor – fair employment for minorities – but, initially, opposed the means, federal legislation. They believed that corporations should voluntarily pursue fair employment, but they both allowed that the federal government had a right to require corporations that did business with the government to meet certain (reasonable) conditions as part of their

in the recruitment and advancement of minorities, due mainly to the original requirements of the Defense Department.

[63] This is the argument of Sanford Jacoby, *Modern Manors: Welfare Capitalism since the New Deal* (Princeton, NJ: Princeton University Press, 1997).

government contracts.[64] Unlike unions, which remained undesirable, the integration of minorities into the workplace was a desirable goal for even the most conservative elements of the business community. The initial argument was over the means by which this would happen, not whether it should happen.

Whereas the Wagner Act inspired widespread opposition among businessmen, Title VII of the Civil Rights Act prompted no such opposition among businessmen and indeed was met with widespread efforts to comply. Few members of the business community vocally opposed Title VII of the 1964 Civil Rights Act. In part, this was because Republicans had managed to limit the new EEOC's enforcement powers; in part because they did not want to appear racist. The most powerful members of the business community endorsed the legislation and its goal, the integration of minorities into the workforce. It is true that employers were wary of the legislation because they knew how difficult, costly, and disruptive it was to change embedded patterns and did not want to be punished if their efforts failed, but in principle, they agreed with the goal. As we saw in Chapter 7, government contractors even accepted the OFCC's demands that companies conduct expensive community studies, renegotiate union contracts, and accept what amounted to quotas.

None of this is to suggest that employers and managers did not hold biases against minorities or practice discrimination. They did. But most of them knew that discrimination and racism were wrong. They just did not, could not, recognize their own behavior as discriminatory or racist. Discrimination was something others did. One reason managers and employers may have accepted hours of sensitivity training and affirmative action's "goals and timetables" was because they recognized their own guilt. Even if they could not quite bring themselves to admit it aloud, managers and executives had attended enough sensitivity training sessions to suspect that they might, unintentionally, be engaging in racist behavior. After the civil rights movement, employers regarded antidiscrimination measures with ambivalence and guilt, resenting the federal interference, but suspecting that it was necessary.

It is possible that Du Pont executives and NAM officials understood the changing political and racial climate and, not wanting to be written off as reactionary, tempered or hid their true feelings. That is, their acceptance of fair employment and affirmative action was nothing more than corporate

[64] "Comments by the National Association of Manufacturers on Proposed Regulations of Office of Federal Contract Compliance Issued Pursuant to Executive Order 11246" [n.d. presumed March 1968], in National Association of Manufacturers, Records, 1895–1990, Series 5, Box 64, Folder: Philadelphia Plan HML.

conformity. If so, this would support my contention that within the business community there was widespread acceptance of fair employment and affirmative action, which there was not for pro-labor legislation. While Du Pont and the NAM reined in their bombastic antilabor rhetoric after World War II (to conform to corporate liberal opinion), they continued to pursue antiunion policies. Neither Du Pont nor the NAM continued to pursue discriminatory policies after 1964. In fact, both organizations took concerted steps to encourage the hiring and advancement of minorities. These two conservative organizations supported the goal of minority employment, and were thus willing to accept and comply with government requirements in the hiring and promotion process. The law of course required compliance, but the law had once required fairness in the treatment of unions as well. While business leaders had managed to change, tweak, and amend the Wagner Act over the years, they accepted Title VII and affirmative action even after conservatives regained power in Washington and promised to repeal affirmative action.

Perhaps the best measure of corporate leaders' commitment to racial integration was their endorsement of color-conscious affirmative action policies even in the face of conservative efforts to eliminate such policies. The backlash against affirmative action in the 1980s came from politicians and intellectuals, not the corporate world. Although large employers welcomed the elimination of certain onerous EEOC and OFCC requirements, such as back-pay awards, redundant paperwork, and the monitoring of subcontractors, they opposed the elimination of affirmative action. It is not difficult to see why. As the former director of the OFCC noted, affirmative action programs allowed employers to prove their compliance with a whole series of antidiscrimination laws.[65] Employers had learned that passive, color-blind policies did not lead to the integration and advancement of minorities. They had come to understand that minorities had been handicapped in ways that meant they needed extra training, encouragement, and support to be successful in the business world, all of which required policies that recognized the special conditions of color. By allowing corporations to target racial minorities and plan for their advancement, color-conscious affirmative action plans made integration more efficient. Moreover, laws requiring affirmative action plans ensured that all employers had to commit resources to an affirmative action program, thus removing the competitive disadvantage from those companies that would have chosen to do so voluntarily. Simply put, affirmative action was the most efficient means to comply with legislation and integrate the workforce. Thus in 1985, the NAM's EEO Committee voted against Reagan's proposals to weaken the OFCC

---

[65] "The New Bias on Hiring Rules," *BusinessWeek*, May 25, 1981, 123.

affirmative action requirements. As the Monsanto Company's EEO director put it, "We're accustomed to setting goals."[66] Editors at both *BusinessWeek* and *Fortune* favored preserving affirmative action, noting that government regulators and business leaders had worked out affirmative action guidelines, which had resulted in significant progress in workplace integration. The policies worked, *BusinessWeek* argued, and urged the Reagan administration to leave them alone.[67]

The Du Pont Company bought into the corporate consensus on the benefits of affirmative action. Despite heroic yearnings to "buck the system" on the part of individuals within corporations, corporations themselves are organizations that conform, if only for competitive purposes. Initially the tendency to conform to prevailing corporate practices inhibited racial integration. But after government pressure, social unrest, and the example of a few outspoken corporate executives began to change corporate policies, the corporate tendency to conform facilitated racial integration in the workplace, as corporations competed with each other to have the most effective affirmative action programs. This transformation was not smooth, but neither was it resisted, not like unions were resisted. Although it was difficult to change long-standing attitudes and practices, the end goal of hiring racial minorities and white women was not openly opposed. Du Pont is a useful case study because it illustrates this transformation. A conservative company, Du Pont was slow to change. But then it did. Its many human relations programs, developed to fight unions, were easily refitted to the project of recruiting, advancing, and retaining minorities and women. Adopting affirmative action in no way impeded its long-standing antiunionism; indeed, in some ways the new affirmative action programs complemented Du Pont's fight against unions. Racial integration did not require that businesses give up their fundamentally conservative goals. It required a change in the way things were done, but not the objective and goals of corporations.

---

[66] "A New Drive to Reaganize Equal Opportunity," *BusinessWeek*, March 11, 1985, 42.

[67] "Don't Scuttle Affirmative Action," *BusinessWeek*, April 15, 1985, 174; and "Businessmen Prefer Affirmative Action Goals," *Fortune*, September 16, 1985, 26 ff. Historians and sociologists have likewise concluded that large employers had come to accept affirmative action. See Terry H. Anderson, *The Pursuit of Fairness: A History of Affirmative Action* (New York: Oxford University Press, 2004), 277; Dobbin and Sutton, "The Strength of the Weak State," 441–76; Skrentny, *The Minority Rights Revolution*; and John Skrentny, ed., *Color Lines: Affirmative Action, Immigration, and Civil Rights Options for America* (Chicago: University of Chicago, 2001).

Epilogue: From Affirmative Action to Diversity

By 1985, large corporations were affirmative action's most credible champions. To deter conservatives' attempts to prohibit affirmative action, business leaders had revived the old "fair employment is good business" argument, substituting in the place of fair employment a new concept: "diversity." In its original form, diversity referred to racial and ethnic variety, embraced as a positive social goal. Diversity seemed especially concocted to persuade critics that affirmative action policies were necessary in both education and employment to keep American business competitive in the increasingly global marketplace. The term had made its rhetorical debut in the Supreme Court's *Bakke* decision of 1978, which struck down the University of California at Davis's quota-based affirmative action admissions program, but left open the possibility that university admission policies could take race into consideration as one factor among many to create "a diverse student body."[1] After that, proponents of affirmative action recast arguments about making up for past injustices into new arguments about the benefits of diversity in education and in the workplace, all of which seemed to center around preparing white students and employees for work in a racially and ethnically diverse workforce.[2] In 1987, the Hudson Institute published *Workforce 2000: Work and Workers for the Twenty-First Century*, with its alarming statistics about the decreasing whiteness of the American workforce and its warnings that American employers should prepare

---

[1] On the *Regents of California v. Allan Bakke*, see Terry H. Anderson, *The Pursuit of Fairness: A History of Affirmative Action* (New York: Oxford University Press, 2004), 150–55; Gary Orfield and Edward Miller, eds., *Chilling Admissions: The Affirmative Action Crisis and the Search for Alternatives* (Cambridge, MA: Harvard University Civil Rights Project, 2000).

[2] See Erin Kelly and Frank Dobbin, "How Affirmative Action Became Diversity Management," in *Color Lines: Affirmative Action, Immigration, and Civil Rights Options for America*, ed. John David Skrentny (Chicago: University of Chicago, 2001), 87–117; and Frederick Lynch, *The Diversity Machine* (New York: Transaction Publishers, 1997).

280

for an increasingly diverse employee body by 2000.[3] Employers heeded the warnings. They hired diversity consultants, adopted diversity initiatives, and put employees through a new round of sensitivity seminars, focused not just on minorities and gender but on all "differences," from physical disabilities to ethnicity to "lifestyle choice."

The new focus on diversity gave thousands of new immigrants the benefits of affirmative action programs that were designed in part to make up for historical wrongs against African Americans. This, in turn, helped American employers to more easily meet their affirmative action goals. Critics have argued that the new emphasis on diversity watered down efforts to redress African Americans' specific experiences with white racism and structural inequity. Americans of Hispanic or Asian backgrounds were hired for jobs once reserved for African Americans.[4] In a larger sense, however, the focus on diversity, precisely because it is so much broader and more inclusive, has facilitated a more definitive change in corporate culture. As transformative as affirmative action was in the 1970s, it was still tied to government regulations and compliance. As accepting of affirmative action as companies were, it was not completely their own policy. Diversity, however, is.

Diversity is almost wholly a corporate creation, the product of human resources departments, the accumulated wisdom of intergroup human relations researchers. After decades of "voluntarism" and compliance, corporations had finally succeeded in regaining control and leadership over the social and demographic changes of the twentieth century. Corporations linked "diversity goals" to business objectives – the global marketplace, immigration, manpower – and wove them into personnel management. Although white males were initially resentful and angry, diversity consultants found a way to refine the diversity project to include even them in the mosaic of pluralities. Inclusiveness in all of its forms became a new corporate virtue. Even if true integration in the workplace remains elusive, the corporate culture and personnel structures – with their emphases on inclusion, "difference," and pluralism – are now prepared to accommodate and to encourage it.

None of this was really new. The constituent elements of "diversity" had long existed within the business community, although instead of "diversity"

---

[3] The Hudson Institute, *Workforce 2000: Work and Workers for the Twenty-First Century* (Washington, DC: U.S. Bureau of Labor Statistics, 1987).

[4] On immigration and affirmative action, see Hugh Davis Graham, *Collision Course: The Strange Convergence of Affirmative Action and Immigration Policy in America* (New York: Oxford University Press, 2002); John David Skrentny, ed., *Color Lines: Affirmative Action, Immigration, and Civil Rights Options for America* (Chicago, 2001); and Lynch, *The Diversity Machine*.

they had supported fair employment, equal employment opportunity, or affirmative action. As we have seen, there had always been leaders within the business community who had linked fair employment with business objectives and who had seen integration as a problem of personnel management. These leaders had always insisted that hiring minorities made "good business sense." Employers had long tried to gain control of the issue of integration from the government. And human relations advocates had long tried to convince their peers to create a more welcoming, inclusive, group-oriented workplace. The roots of today's diversity initiatives are planted firmly within the domain of big business.

But there are also parts of the old arguments for fair employment and equal opportunity that have completely disappeared. Whereas fair employment advocates once celebrated merit and individualism, today's diversity experts have little use for either word. Whereas fair employment advocates preached that color was meaningless, today's diversity experts invest color with a multitude of positive meanings. Fair employment advocates once tied fair employment to positive relations with labor unions and the government. But this, too, is largely irrelevant, a distant memory of a time when labor unions and government regulations had actually mattered to corporations.

Despite all of these efforts, charges of discrimination continue to occur in the corporate workplace. As of 2006, African Americans occupied only 6 percent of managerial and executive positions. Only 3.2 percent of chief executives are African American.[5] Despite the very real changes instituted in corporate employment policies, bias, ignorance, and evasion continue to limit blacks' opportunities within corporations. Sometimes white supervisors do not fully train new black workers, leaving them at a disadvantage for promotion. Often blacks are "ghettoized" in personnel divisions and new human resources offices – what had once provided white-collar opportunities now limits advancement. There are companies whose executives genuinely care about diversity and minority opportunities, who make diversity and opportunity priorities. But there are many executives who regard diversity as a public relations gambit, not a serious concern of business.

While it is important to recognize minorities' ongoing problems in corporate America, it is equally important to not let these problems prevent us from seeing that corporations have been a real and powerful force for racial progress in the United States. From Ford's decision to hire and train Negroes in the early

---

[5] U.S. Census Bureau, *Statistical Abstracts of the United States, 2006* (Washington, DC: U.S. Government Printing Office, 2006), table 604.

twentieth century to IBM's efforts to recruit African Americans into its executive training programs in the 1970s, there have been corporations that have not only offered blacks opportunities but have also developed programs and techniques to overcome systemic practices that prohibited black advancement. Corporations gave thousands of black Americans the opportunity to improve their economic and social standing, to move up the ladder of middle-class success, to realize their ambitions. For those of us – both white and black – who had hoped that the civil rights movement and racial progress would deliver us from the sterile materialism and structured inequality embodied in the phrase "corporate America," it has been difficult to acknowledge that there were corporate actors interested in the cause of racial progress. Hence the skepticism, the questioning of motives, the constant reiteration of statistics about racial economic inequality. But it is time to recognize corporations as a source of social progress and give credit to those executives and managers who actually devised and implemented the policies that integrated the workplace and transformed American society.

Statistical Tables

Table 1 *Distribution of African Americans in Particular Occupational Groups, 1950–2000 (percent)*

Occupation	1950	1960	1970	1980	2000
Total	100.0	100.0	100.0	100.0	100.0
White-collar	**9.9**	**16.1**	**27.9**	**39.2**	**52.5**
Professional, technical	3.4	4.8	9.1	12.7	25.2**
Managers	1.8	2.6	3.5	5.2	—
Sales	—	1.5	2.1	2.9	—
Clerical	4.7*	7.3	13.2	18.4	27.3*
Blue-collar	**40.3**	**40.1**	**42.2**	**35.8**	**25.1**
Craft	5.3	6.0	8.2	9.6	—
Operatives	19.0	20.4	23.7	19.4	—
Nonfarm labor	15.9	13.7	10.3	6.9	—
Service	**31.0**	**31.7**	**26.0**	**23.1**	**22.0**
Farmwork	**18.8**	**12.1**	**3.9**	**1.8**	**0.4**

*This number includes salesworkers.

**This number includes managers.

The occupational categories for 2000 are configured differently than for previous years, especially with regard to traditionally blue-collar work, which in 2000 is divided into "Construction, extraction, and maintenance," in which 6.5 percent of blacks worked, and "Production, transportation, and material moving," in which 18.6 of blacks worked.

Source: Compiled from *U.S. Bureau of the Census, Statistical Abstract of the United States, 1955, 1981;* and *U.S. Bureau of the Census, Occupations, 2000,* August 2003, www.census.gov.

Table 2 *Percent of Whites and Blacks below Poverty Level, 1970–1990*

Year	White	Black
1970	9.9	33.5
1975	9.7	31.3
1980	10.2	32.5
1985	11.4	31.3
1990	10.7	31.9
1995	11.2	29.3
2000	9.4	22

Source: From George Thomas Kurian, ed., *Datapedia of the United States: American History in Numbers,* 3rd ed. (Lanham, MD: Bernan Press, 2004), table 9–9. *Persons below Poverty Level . . . , 1960–2001,* p. 161.

Table 3 *Unemployment Rates of Civilian Workers, 1948–1995*

Year	White	Black (and Other)*
1948	3.5	5.9
1955	3.9	8.7
1960	4.9	10.2
1965	4.1	8.1
1970	4.5	8.2
1975	7.8	14.8
1980	6.3	14.3
1985	6.2	15.1
1990	4.8	11.4
1995	4.9	10.4

*Before 1971, this category includes Asians and Native Americans.
Source: From George Thomas Kurian, ed., *Datapedia of the United States: American History in Numbers,* 3rd ed. (Lanham, MD: Bernan Press, 2004), table 8–3 – Series D 87–101. *Unemployment Rates by Sex and Race in the Civilian Labor Force, 1947–2002.*

Table 4 *Labor Union Membership as a Percent of Total Employment, 1930–2002 (numbers in thousands)*

Year	Total Union Membership	Percent of Employed
1930	3,632	11.6
1940	8,944	26.9
1950	15,000	31.5
1960	18,117	31.4
1970	20,752	27.4
1980	22,811	25.2
1991	16,568	16.1
2000	16,258	13.5

Source: From George Thomas Kurian, ed., *Datapedia of the United States: American History in Numbers,* 3rd ed. (Lanham, MD: Bernan Press, 2004), table 8–9 – Series D 946–951. *Labor Union Membership as a Percent of Total Employment, 1930–2002,* p. 123.

Table 5 *Educational Attainment by Race, 1940–1990*

	Completed Four Years of High School (percent)			
Year	White Male	White Female	Black Male	Black Female
1940	24.2	28.1	6.9	8.4
1950	34.6	38.2	12.6	14.7
1960	41.6	44.7	20.	23.1
1970	57.2	57.7	35.4	36.6
1980	72.4	71.5	51.2	51.5
1990	81.6	81.3	65.8	66.5

	Completed Four Years of College (percent)			
Year	White Male	White Female	Black Male	Black Female
1940	5.9	4	1.4	1.2
1950	7.9	5.4	2.1	2.4
1960	10.3	6	3.5	3.6
1970	15	8.6	6.8	5.6
1980	22.8	14.4	7.7	8.1
1990	26.7	19.8	11.9	10.8

Source: From George Thomas Kurian, ed., *Datapedia of the United States: American History in Numbers,* 3rd ed. (Lanham, MD: Bernan Press, 2004).

Table 6 *Median Income of Black Households as a Percent of Median Income of White Households, 1952–1977*

Year	Percent
1952	57
1957	54
1962	53
1967	59
1972	59
1977	57

Source: From Jennifer Hochschild, *What's Fair: American Beliefs about Distributive Justice* (Cambridge, MA: Harvard University Press, 1981), 14.

Table 7 *Median Income of Black and Other Races, Families and Individuals, as Percentage of White Families and Individuals, 1939–1970*

Year	Percent
1939	37
1949	49
1955	56
1960	56
1965	57
1970	65

Source: U.S. Bureau of the Census, *Historical Statistics of the United States: Colonial Times to 1970* (Washington, DC: U.S. Government Printing Office, 1975), 303.

Table 8 *Median Income of Black Households as Percentage of White Household Median Income, 1980–2003*

Year	Percent
1980	57.0
1985	59.4
1990	59.7
1995	62.6
2000	68.6
2003	64.9

Source: U.S. Bureau of the Census, *Statistical Abstract of the United States: 2006* (Washington, DC: U.S. Government Printing Office, 2005), p. 462.

Bibliography

Archival and Manuscript Collections

Archives Organization File, Kheel Center for Labor-Management Documentation and Archives, Cornell University Library, Ithaca, New York

William Goff Caples transcripts of speeches, 1950–1968. Kheel Center for Labor-Management Documentation and Archives, Cornell University Library, Ithaca, New York

Control Data Corporation Records, 1946–1991. Charles Babbage Institute, University of Minnesota, Minneapolis

E. I. Du Pont de Nemours & Company. Advertising Department, General Files, 1807–1971 at Hagley Museum and Library, Wilmington, Delaware

E. I. Du Pont de Nemours & Company. Executive Committee Records, at Hagley Museum and Library, Wilmington, Delaware

E. I. Du Pont de Nemours & Company. Du Pont Human Resources, at Hagley Museum and Library, Wilmington, Delaware

Greenewalt, Crawford E. Papers, 1947–1967, at Hagley Museum and Library, Wilmington, Delaware

International Harvester Company. Corporate Archives Central File (documented series), 1819–1998, at Wisconsin Historical Society, Madison, Wisconsin

Lukens Steel Company. Executive Officers Files, 1903–1979, at Hagley Museum and Library, Wilmington, Delaware

McCormick, Fowler. Papers, 1878–1972, at Wisconsin Historical Society, Madison, Wisconsin

McCoy, Charles Brelsford. Papers, 1967–1974, at Hagley Museum and Library, Wilmington, Delaware

MCI Communications Corporation. Corporate Communications and Public Relations Department. Records, 1967–1996, at Hagley Museum and Library, Wilmington, Delaware

National Association of Manufacturers. Records, 1895–1990, at Hagley Museum and Library, Wilmington, Delaware

National Industrial Conference Board. Records, 1916–1985, at Hagley Museum and Library, Wilmington, Delaware

New York (State). State Division of Human Rights. Discrimination Case Files, 1946–1985, New York State Archives, Albany, New York

President's Papers 1950–1955, Special Collections Research Center, University of Chicago Library, Chicago, Illinois

Reed, Philip D. (1899–1989). Papers, 1927–1989, at Hagley Museum and Library, Wilmington, Delaware

Wharton School of Industrial Research Unit. Records, at Hagley Museum and Library, Wilmington, Delaware

Books and Articles

"An Acid Test for Du Pont." *BusinessWeek*, December 14, 1981.

"Acting Affirmatively to End Job Bias." *BusinessWeek*, January 27, 1975.

Adams, Avril, Joseph Krislov, and David Lairson. "Plantwide Seniority, Black Employment, and Employer Affirmative Action." *Industrial and Labor Relations Review* 26, no. 1 (October 1972): 686–90.

Adams, E. Sherman. "The Public Role of Private Enterprise." In *Business and the Cities*, edited by Neil W. Chamberlain. New York: Basic Books, 1970.

Adams, Stephen B. *Mr. Kaiser Goes to War: The Rise of a Government Entrepreneur.* Chapel Hill: University of North Carolina Press, 1997.

American Management Association. *The Negro Worker: An Analysis of Management Experience and Opinion on the Employment and Integration of the Negro in Industry.* Special Research Report No. 1. New York: American Management Association, 1942.

———. *The Personnel Job in a Changing World.* New York: American Management Association, 1964.

American Presidency Project. John T. Woolley and Gerhard Peters. Santa Barbara, CA: University of California (hosted), Gerhard Peters (database).

Anderson, Terry H. *The Pursuit of Fairness: A History of Affirmative Action.* New York: Oxford University Press, 2004.

Antonovsky, Aaron, and Lewis Lorwin, eds. *Discrimination and Low Incomes . . . Studies under the Direction of the New York State Commission Against Discrimination by the New School for Social Research.* Albany: New York Interdepartmental Committee on Low Incomes, 1959.

Arensberg, Conrad, et al., eds., *Research in Industrial Human Relations: A Critical Appraisal.* Industrial Relations Research Association, Publication No. 17. New York: Harper, 1957.

Arnesen, Eric. *Brotherhoods of Color: Black Railroad Workers and the Struggle for Equality.* Cambridge, MA: Harvard University Press, 2002.

———. "The Quicksands of Economic Insecurity: African Americans, Strikebreaking, and Labor Activism in the Industrial Era." In *The Black Worker: Race, Labor, and Civil Rights since Emancipation*, edited by Eric Arnesen, 41–71. Urbana: University of Illinois Press, 2007.

Ayers, Edward. *The Promise of the New South: Life after Reconstruction.* New York: Oxford University Press, 1992.

Backer, Sally, and Harry Harris. "Progress toward Integration: Four Case Studies." In *Discrimination and Low Incomes*, edited by Aaron Antonovsky and

Lewis Lorwin. Albany: New York Interdepartmental Committee on Low Incomes, 1959.

Baird, Virginia. "Employing the Disadvantaged Fraught with Challenges." *Training and Development Journal* 23, no. 7 (July 1969): 44–51.

Baker, Harry C. "A Voluntary Approach to Equal Opportunity." In *The Negro and Employment Opportunity*, edited by Herbert Northrup and Richard Rowan, 111–122. Ann Arbor: University of Michigan, 1965.

Baldwin, James. "The Image of the Negro." *Commentary* 5 (April 1948): 378–80.

Baritz, Loren. *The Servants of Power: A History of the Use of Social Science in American Industry*. Middletown, CT: Wesleyan University Press, 1960.

Beam, Alex. "Why Few Ghetto Factories Are Making It." *BusinessWeek*, February 16, 1987.

Bell, Daniel. "Adjusting Men to Machines." *Commentary* 4 (January 1947): 79–88

Bendix, Reinhard, and Seymour Martin Lipset. *Class, Status, and Power: A Reader in Social Stratification*. Glencoe, IL: Free Press, 1953.

Benedict, Ruth. *Race: Science and Politics*. New York, 1940.

Benton, William. "The Economics of a Free Society: A Declaration of American Business Policy." *Fortune*, October 1944.

Berman, William. *The Politics of Civil Rights in the Truman Administration*. Columbus: Ohio State University Press, 1970.

Bernays, Edward L. *Biography of an Idea: Memoirs of Public Relations Counsel Edward L. Bernays*. New York: Simon and Schuster, 1965.

———. "Manipulating Public Opinion: The Why and the How." *American Journal of Sociology* 33, no. 6 (May 1928): 958–71.

Biondi, Martha. *To Stand and Fight: The Struggle for Civil Rights in Postwar New York City*. Cambridge, MA: Harvard University Press, 2003.

Bird, Caroline. "More Room at the Top." *Management Review* 52 (March 1963): 4–16.

Blood, Robert O., Jr., *Northern Breakthrough*. Belmont, CA: Wadsworth, 1968.

Blumer, Herbert. "Social Science and Desegregation." *Annals of the Academy of Political and Social Science* 304 (March 1956): 137–43.

———. "Sociological Theory in Industrial Relations." *American Sociological Review*, 12 (June 1947): 271–78.

Borstelmann, Thomas. *Cold War and the Color Line: American Race Relations in the Global Arena*. Cambridge, MA: Harvard University Press, 2001.

Boyle, Kevin. *The UAW and the Heyday of American Liberalism, 1935–1968*. Ithaca, NY: Cornell University Press, 1995.

Brattain, Michelle. "Race, Racism, and Antiracism: UNESCO and the Politics of Presenting Science to the Postwar Public." *American Historical Review* 112, no. 5 (December 2007): 1386–1413.

Breen, William. "Social Science and State Policy in WWII: Human Relations, Pedagogy, and Industrial Training, 1940–1945." *Business History Review* 76 (Summer 2002): 233–66.

Brinkley, Alan. *The End of Reform: New Deal Liberalism in Recession and War*. New York: Vintage, 1996.

Brooks, Maxwell. "American Class and Caste: An Appraisal." *Social Forces*, 25 (December 1946): 207–11.

Brown, Cliff, et al., *Racial Competition and Class Solidarity*. Albany: SUNY Press, 2007.

Bunche, Ralph. "A Critical Analysis of the Tactics and Programs of Minority Groups." *Journal of Negro Education* 4, no. 3 (July 1935): 308–20.

_____. "A Critique of New Deal Social Planning as It Affects Negroes." *Journal of Negro Education* 5, no. 1 (January 1936): 59–65.

Burch, Philip H., Jr. "The NAM as an Interest Group." *Politics and Society* 4, no. 1 (1973): 97–130.

Burk, Robert. *The Corporate State and the Broker State: The Du Ponts and American National Politics, 1935–1940*. Cambridge, MA: Harvard University Press, 1990.

"Businessmen Prefer Affirmative Action Goals." *Fortune*, September 16, 1985.

Cahn, William. *The Story of Pitney-Bowes*. New York: Harper, 1961.

Caro, Robert. *Master of the Senate: The Years of Lyndon Johnson*. New York: Knopf, 2002.

Carter, Elmer. "Policies and Practices of Discrimination Commissions." *Annals of the American Academy of Political and Social Science* 304 (March 1956): 62–77.

Cayton, Horace, and George Mitchell. *Black Workers and the New Unions*. Chapel Hill: University of North Carolina Press, 1939.

Chamberlain, Neil W., ed. *Business and the Cities*. New York: Basic Books, 1970.

Chambers, Jason. *Madison Avenue and the Color Line: African Americans in the Advertising Industry*. Philadelphia: University of Pennsylvania Press, 2007.

Chandler, Alfred D., Jr. *Inventing the Electronic Century: The Epic Story of the Consumer Electronics and Computer Industries*. Cambridge, MA: Harvard University Press, 2005.

Chandler, Alfred D., Jr., and Stephen Salsbury. *Pierre S. Du Point and the Making of the Modern Corporation*. New York: Harper and Row, 1971.

Chapin, F. Stuart. "Social Obstacles to the Acceptance of Existing Social Science Knowledge." *Social Forces* 26, no. 1 (October 1947): 7–12.

Chase, Stuart. "Communication – Up, Down, and Sideways." *Reader's Digest*, September 1952.

_____. *Men at Work: Some Democratic Methods for the Power Age*. (New York: Harcourt, Brace, 1941, 1945.

_____. *The Proper Study of Mankind: An Inquiry into the Science of Human Relations*. New York: Harper and Row, 1948; rev. ed., 1956.

Cheit, Earl, ed., *The Business Establishment*. New York: Wiley, 1964.

Chen, Anthony. "The Hitlerian Rule of Quotas: Racial Conservatism and the Politics of Fair Employment in New York State, 1941–45." *Journal of American History* 92, no. 4 (March 2006): 1238–64.

Cherry, Frances, and Catherine Borshuk. "Social Action Research and the Commission on Community Interrelations." *Journal of Social Issues* 54, no. 1 (1998): 119–42.

Coghill, Mary Ann. "Sensitivity Training." *Key Issues*, no. 1 (1967).

Cohen, Lizabeth. *Making a New Deal*. New York: Cambridge University Press, 1990.

Collins, Orvis. "Ethnic Behavior in Industry: Sponsorship and Rejection in a New England Factory." *American Journal of Sociology*, 51 (January 1946): 293–98; reprinted in Robert Dubin, ed. *Human Relations in Administration*. Englewood Cliffs, NJ: Prentice Hall, 1951.

Collins, William J. "The Labor Market Impact of Anti-Discrimination Laws, 1940–1960." *Industrial and Labor Relations Review* 56, no. 2 (January 2003): 244–72.

_____. "Race, Roosevelt, and Wartime Production: Fair Employment in WWII Labor Markets." *American Economic Review* 91, no. 1 (March 2001): 272–86.

Cordiner, Ralph. *New Frontiers for Professional Managers.* Mckinsey Foundation Lecture Series, Graduate School of Business, Columbia University. New York: McGraw-Hill, 1956.

Cordiz, Dan. "The Negro Middle Class Is Right in the Middle." *Fortune,* November 1966.

"Corporate Do-Gooder Bill Norris." *Inc.,* May 1988.

Cowie, Jefferson. *Capital Moves: RCA's Seventy Year Quest for Cheap Labor.* New York: New Press, 2001. (Originally published in 1999.)

Cox, Oliver C. "An American Dilemma: A Mystical Approach to the Study of Race Relations." *Journal of Negro Education* 14, no. 2 (Spring 1945): 132–48.

_____. "The Modern Caste School of Race Relations." *Social Forces* 21 (December 1942): 218–26.

_____. "Race and Caste: A Distinction." *American Journal of Sociology* 50, no. 5 (March 1945): 360–68.

Cross, Elsie Y. *The Diversity Factor: Capturing the Competitive Advantage of a Changing Workforce.* Chicago: Irwin Professional, 1996.

Dale, Ernest. "Contributions to Administration by Alfred P. Sloan Jr. and GM." *Administrative Science Quarterly* 1 (June 1956): 30–62.

Dalton, Melville, and Oliver C. Cox. "Conflicts between Staff and Line Managerial Officers." *American Sociological Review* 15, no. 3 (June 1950): 342–51.

_____. "Worker Response and Social Background." *Journal of Political Economy* 55, no. 4 (August 1947): 323–32.

Daves, J. H. "TVA and Negro Employment." *Journal of Negro Education* 24, no. 1 (Winter 1955): 87–90.

Davies, Gareth. *From Opportunity to Entitlement: The Transformation and Decline of Great Society Liberalism.* Lawrence: University Press of Kansas, 1996.

Davis, Allison, Burleigh Gardner, and Mary R. Gardner. *Deep South: A Social Anthropological Study of Caste and Class.* Chicago: University of Chicago Press, 1941.

Davis, George, and Glegg Watson. *Black Life in Corporate America: Swimming in the Mainstream.* New York: Anchor Books, 1985. (Originally published by Doubleday in 1982.)

Davis, John A. *How Management Can Integrate Negroes in War Industries.* New York State War Council, Committee on Discrimination in Employment, 1942.

_____. "Negro Employment: A Progress Report." *Fortune,* July 1952.

Davis, John A., and Cornelius Golightly. "Negro Employment in the Federal Government." *Phylon* 6, no. 4 (1945): 337.

Dean, John P., and Alex Rosen. *A Manual for Inter-Group Relations.* Chicago: University of Chicago Press, 1955.

DeHuzzer, George B., comp. *Anatomy of Racial Intolerance.* New York: H. W. Wilson, 1946.

Delton, Jennifer. *Making Minnesota Liberal: Civil Rights and the Transformation of the Democratic Party.* Minneapolis: University of Minnesota Press, 2002.

Dewey, Donald. "Negro Employment in Southern Industry." *Journal of Political Economy,* 60 (1952): 279.

Dittmer, John. *Local People: The Struggle for Civil Rights in Mississippi.* Urbana: University of Illinois Press, 1994.

Dobbin, Frank, and John Sutton. "The Strength of the Weak State: The Rights Revolution and the Rise of Human Resources Management Divisions." *American Journal of Sociology* 104, no. 2 (September 1998): 441–76.

Dobbin, Frank, John Sutton, John W. Meyer, and Richard Scott. "Equal Opportunity Law and the Construction of Internal Labor Markets." *American Journal of Sociology* 99, no. 2 (September 1993): 396–427.

"Does the State FEPC Hamper You?" *BusinessWeek,* February 25, 1950, reprint.

Dollard, John. *Caste and Class in a Southern Town.* New York: Harper, 1937, 1949.

"Don't Scuttle Affirmative Action." *BusinessWeek,* April 15, 1985.

Doyle, Bertram W. *The Etiquette of Race Relations in the South: A Study in Social Control.* Chicago: University of Chicago Press, 1937.

Drake, St. Clair, and Horace Cayton. *Black Metropolis: A Study of Negro Life in a Northern City.* New York: Harcourt Brace, 1945.

Drucker, Peter. *Adventures of a Bystander.* New York: Harper, 1978.

_____. *America's Next Twenty Years.* New York: Harper, 1955, 1957.

_____. *Concept of a Corporation.* New York: John Day, 1946.

_____. *The New Society: The Anatomy of Industrial Order.* New York: Harper, 1949, 1950; paperback ed., 1962.

Dudziak, Mary. *Cold War Civil Rights: Race and the Image of American Democracy.* Princeton, NJ: Princeton University Press, 2000.

Edwards, Richard. *Contested Terrain: The Transformation of the Workplace in the 20th Century.* New York: Basic Books, 1979.

Elliott, Osborn. *Men at the Top.* New York: Harper and Brothers, 1959.

Ellison, Ralph. "An American Dilemma: A Review." Republished in Callahan, John F., ed., *The Collected Essays of Ralph Ellison.* New York, 1995; written in 1944, published in *Shadow and Act* (1964).

Embree, Edwin. "Human Relations: Mid Century." *Journal of Educational Sociology* 23, no. 6 (February 1950): 363–69.

Evans, L. M. "Freedom or Regimentation." *Vital Speeches of the Day* 13, no. 17 (June 15, 1947): 541–44.

Ferguson, Thomas. "Industrial Conflict and the Coming of the New Deal: The Triumph of Multinational Liberalism in America." In *The Rise and Fall of the New Deal Order,* edited by Steve Fraser and Gary Gerstle, 3–31. Princeton, NJ: Princeton University Press, 1989.

Ferman, Lewis. *The Negro and Equal Employment Opportunities: A Review of Management Experiences in Twenty Companies.* New York: Praeger, 1968.

Fones-Wolf, Elizabeth. *Selling Free Enterprise: The Business Assault on Labor and Liberalism, 1945–1960.* Urbana: University of Illinois Press, 1994.

Fottler, Myron, John Drotning, and David Lipsky. "Reasons for Employer Nonparticipation in Manpower Training Programs for the Disadvantaged." *Labor Law Journal* 22, no. 11 (November 1971): 708–12.

"Fowler McCormick: Self-Made Man." *Fortune,* September 1946.

Frank, Thomas. *The Conquest of Cool: Business Culture, Counterculture, and the Rise of Hip Consumerism.* Chicago: University of Chicago Press, 1997.

Frazier, E. Franklin. "Sociological Theory and Race Relations." *American Sociological Review* 12 (June 1947): 265–71.

Gable, Richard. "NAM: Influential Lobby or Kiss of Death?" *Journal of Politics* (May 1953).

Gabor, Andrea. *The Capitalist Philosophers*. New York: Time Business, 2000.

The Gallup Poll: Public Opinion, 1935–1970. 3 vols. New York: Random House, 1972.

Gardner, Burleigh, and David Moore. *Human Relations in Industry*. Chicago: Richard D. Irwin, 1945; rev. ed., 1950.

Garfinkel, Herbert. *When Negroes March: The March on Washington Movement and the Organizational Politics of the FEPC*. Glencoe, IL: Free Press, 1959.

Gelber, Stephen M. *Black Men and Businessmen: The Growing Awareness of a Social Responsibility*. Port Washington, NY: Kennicat Press, 1974.

Gerstle, Gary. *American Crucible: Race and Nation in the Twentieth Century*. Princeton, NJ: Princeton University Press, 2002.

———. "Race and the Myth of the Liberal Consensus." *Journal of American History*, 82 (September 1995): 579–86.

Gillespie, Richard. *Manufacturing Knowledge: A History of the Hawthorne Experiments*. New York: Cambridge University Press, 1991.

Ginzberg, Eli. *Business Leadership and the Negro Crisis*. New York: McGraw-Hill, 1968.

———. *Manpower Agenda for America*. New York: McGraw-Hill, 1968.

———. *The Negro Challenge to the Business Community*. New York: McGraw-Hill, 1964.

———. *The Negro Potential*. New York: Columbia University Press, 1956.

Glick, Clarence. "The Position of Racial Groups in Occupational Structures." *Social Forces* 26, no. 2 (December 1947): 206–11.

Gould, William B. *Black Workers in White Unions: Job Discrimination in the United States*. Ithaca, NY: Cornell University Press, 1977.

Gourlay, Jack. *The Negro Salaried Worker*. AMA Research Study 70. New York: American Management Association, 1965.

Graham, Hugh Davis. *The Civil Rights Era: Origins and Development of National Policy, 1960–1972*. New York: Oxford University Press, 1990.

———. *Collision Course: The Strange Convergence of Affirmative Action and Immigration Policy in America*. New York: Oxford University Press, 2002.

Green, Venus. *Race on the Line: Gender, Labor, and Technology in the Bell System, 1880–1980*. Durham, NC: Duke University Press, 2001.

Greene, Julie. *Pure and Simple Politics: The American Federation of Labor and Political Activism, 1881–1917*. New York: Cambridge University Press, 1998.

Griffith, Robert. "Old Progressives and the Cold War." *Journal of American History* 66 (September 179): 334–47.

Gruenfeld, Elaine. "Promotion: Practices, Policies, and Affirmative Action." *Key Issues*, no. 17 (1975).

Habbe, Stephen. *Company Experience with Negro Employment*. 2 vols. Studies in Personnel Policy No. 201. New York: National Industrial Conference Board, 1966.

Halpern, Rick. *Down on the Killing Floor: Black and White Workers in Chicago's Packinghouses*. Urbana: University of Illinois Press, 1997.

Hammett, Richard, Joel Seidman, and Jack London. "The Slowdown as a Union Tactic." *Journal of Political Economy* 65, no. 2 (April 1957): 126–34.

Harding, John. "Community Self-Surveys: A Form of Combating Discrimination." *Congress Weekly: A Review of Jewish Interests*, March 5, 1948.

Harris, Howell John. *The Right to Manage: Industrial Relations Policies of American Business in the* 1940. Madison: University of Wisconsin Press, 1982.

Harris, William H. *The Harder We Run*. New York: Oxford University Press, 1982.

Hart, David M. "From 'Ward of the State' to 'Revolutionary without a Movement': The Political Development of William C. Norris and Control Data Corporation, 1957–1986." *Enterprise and Society* 6, no. 2 (June 2005): 197–223.

Haynes, George Edmund. "Public Approbation as a Means of Changing Interracial Attitudes and Customs." *Social Forces* 24 (October 1945).

Hefner, James, and Alice Kidder. "Racial Integration in Southern Management Positions." *Phylon* 33, no. 2 (1972): 193–200.

Herberg, Will. *Protestant, Catholic, Jew: An Essay on American Religious Sociology*. Chicago: University of Chicago Press, 1983.

Higgs, Robert. *Competition and Coercion: Blacks in the American Economy, 1865–1914*. Chicago, 1980.

Hill, Herbert. *Black Labor and the American Legal System: Race, Work and Law*. Madison: University of Wisconsin Press, 1985. (Originally published by the Bureau of National Affairs, 1977.)

————. "Racial Discrimination in the Nation's Apprenticeship Training Program." *Phylon* 23, no. 3 (1962): 215–44.

————. "Racial Inequality in Employment." *Annals of the American Academy of Political and Social Science* 357 (January 1965): 30–47.

Hill, Mozell. "Review of *Caste, Class, and Race: A Study in Social Dynamics*, by Oliver Cromwell Cox." *Social Forces* 27 (December 1948): 168–69.

Hill, T. Arnold. "The Plight of the Negro Industrial Worker." *Journal of Negro Education* 5, no. 1 (January 1936): 40–47.

Hirsch, Arnold. *Making the Second Ghetto: Race and Housing in Chicago, 1940–1960*. New York: Cambridge University Press, 1983.

Hodgson, Godfrey. *America in Our Time*. Garden City, NY: Doubleday, 1976.

Hoff, Joan. *Nixon Reconsidered*. New York: Basic Books, 1994.

Hoffecker, Carol. *Corporate Capital: Wilmington in the Twentieth Century*. Philadelphia: Temple University Press, 1983.

Homans, George Caspar. *Coming to My Senses: The Autobiography of a Sociologist*. New Brunswick, NJ: Transaction Books, 1984.

Honey, Michael. *Going Down Jericho Road: The Memphis Strike, Martin Luther King's Last Campaign*. New York: Norton, 2007.

————. *Southern Labor and Black Civil Rights: Organizing Memphis Workers*. Urbana: University of Illinois Press, 1993.

Hope, John, II. *Selected Studies of the Negro Employment in the South: 3 Southern Plants of International Harvester Company*. Prepared by the NPA Committee of the South. Washington, DC: National Planning Association, 1953.

Hounshell, David, and John Kenly Smith, Jr. *Science and Corporate Strategy: Du Pont R&D, 1902–1980*. New York: Cambridge University Press, 1988.

Hudson Institute. *Workforce 2000: Work and Workers for the Twenty-First Century*. Washington, DC: U.S. Bureau of Labor Statistics, 1987.

Hughes, Emmet John. "The Negro's New Economic Life." *Fortune*, September 1956.

Hughes, Everett C. "Caste, Class, and Race: A Study in Social Dynamics." *Phylon* 9, no. 1 (1948): 66–68.

———. "The Knitting of Racial Groups in Industry." *American Sociological Review* 11, no. 5 (October 1946): 512–19.

Hyman, Sidney. *The Lives of William Benton.* Chicago: University of Chicago Press, 1969.

Iacobelli, John. "A Survey of Employer Attitudes toward Training the Disadvantaged." *Monthly Labor Review* 93, no. 6 (June 1970): 51–55.

Industrial Relations Research Association. *Research in Industrial Human Relations: A Critical Appraisal.* New York: Harper, 1957.

"Integration: It Works in Business." *Management Methods* (May 1956).

"The Issues behind Opposition to Reagan." *BusinessWeek,* January 23, 1984.

Jackson, Walter. *Gunnar Myrdal and America's Conscience: Social Engineering and Racial Liberalism, 1938–1987.* Chapel Hill: University of North Carolina Press Press, 1990.

Jacobs, Meg. *Pocketbook Politics: Economic Citizenship in Twentieth Century America.* Princeton, NJ: Princeton University Press, 2005.

Jacobson, Matthew. *Whiteness of a Different Color.* Cambridge, MA: Harvard University Press, 1998.

Jacoby, Neil H. *Corporate Power and Social Responsibility: A Blueprint for the Future.* New York: Macmillan, 1973.

Jacoby, Sanford. *Employing Bureaucracy: Managers, Unions, and the Transformation of Work in American Industry, 1900–1945.* New York: Columbia University Press, 1985.

———. *Modern Manors: Welfare Capitalism since the New Deal.* Princeton, NJ: Princeton University Press, 1997.

Jacoway, Elizabeth, and David Colburn, eds. *Southern Businessmen and Desegregation.* Baton Rouge: Louisiana State University Press, 1982.

James, J. Hagen. "Guidelines for Initiating Fair Employment Practices." *Personnel* (May/June 1963): 53–59.

Johnson, Charles S. "From Race Relations to Human Relations." In *Race Relations: Problems and Theories, Essays in Honor of Robert E. Park,* edited by Jitsuichi Masouka and Preston Valien, 3–12. Chapel Hill: University of North Carolina Press, 1961.

———. "Social Changes and Their Effects on Race Relations in the South." *Social Forces* 23 (March 1943): 343–48.

Johnston, Eric. "Hate Challenges America." *Negro Digest* (March 1946): 3–5.

Kanter, Rosabeth Moss. *Men and Women of the Corporation.* New York: Basic Books 1977, 1984.

Kariel, Henry S. "Democracy Unlimited: Kurt Lewin's Field Theory." *American Journal of Sociology* 62, no. 3 (November 1956): 280–89.

Kelley, Robin D. G. *Race Rebels: Culture, Politics, and the Black Working Class.* New York: Free Press, 1996.

Kelley, Robin D. G., and Earl Lewis. *To Make Our World Anew: A History of African Americans.* New York: Oxford University Press, 2000.

Kelly, Erin, and Frank Dobbin. "How Affirmative Action Became Diversity Management." In *Color Lines: Affirmative Action, Immigration, and Civil Rights Options for America,* edited by John David Skrentny, 87–117. Chicago: University of Chicago, 2001.

Kersten, Andrew. *Race, Jobs, and the War: The FEPC in the Midwest, 1941–1946.* Urbana: University of Illinois Press, 2000.

Kesselman, Louis. *The Social Politics of FEPC: A Study in Reform Pressure Movements.* Chapel Hill: University of North Carolina Press, 1948.

Kheel, Theodore. *Guide to Fair Employment Practices.* Englewood Cliffs, NJ: Prentice Hall, 1964.

Khurana, Rakesh. *From Higher Aims to Hired Hands: The Social Transformation of American Business Schools and the Unfulfilled Promise of Management as a Profession.* Princeton, NJ: Princeton University Press, 2007.

Killingsworth, Charles. *Jobs and Income for Negroes.* Ann Arbor: Institute of Labor and Industrial Relations and the National Manpower Policy Task Force, 1968.

Kirby, John. *Black Americans in the Roosevelt Era: Liberalism and Race.* Knoxville: University of Tennessee Press, 1980.

———. "Ralph J. Bunche and Black Radical Thought in the 1930s." *Phylon* 35, no. 2 (1974): 129–41.

Kolko, Gabriel. *The Triumph of Conservatism.* New York: Free Press, 1963.

Korstad, Robert, and Nelson Lichtenstein. "Opportunities Found and Lost: Labor, Radicals, and the Early Civil Rights Movement." *Journal of American History* 75, no. 3 (December 1988): 786–811.

Kotlowski, Dean. *Nixon's Civil Rights: Politics, Principle, and Policy.* Cambridge, MA: Harvard University Press, 2001.

Kryder, Daniel. *Divided Arsenal: Race and the American State during World War II.* New York: Cambridge University Press, 2000.

Kurian, George Thomas, ed. *Datapedia of the United States: American History in Numbers.* 3rd ed. Lanham, MD: Bernan Press, 2004.

Laird, Pamela Walker. *Pull: Networking and Success since Benjamin Franklin.* Cambridge, MA: Harvard University Press, 2006.

Landsberger, Henry A. *Hawthorne Revisited: Management and the Worker, Its Critics, and Developments in Human Relations in Industry.* Cornell Studies in Industrial and Labor Relations. Vol. 9. Ithaca: New York State School of Industrial and Labor Relations, Cornell University Press, 1958.

Lawrence, R. G. "Western Electric's Commitment to Fair Employment." In *The Negro and Employment Opportunity,* edited by Herbert Northrup, 137–45. Ann Arbor: Bureau of Industrial Relations, Graduate School of Business Administration, University of Michigan, 1965.

Leavitt, Theodore. "The Dangers of Social Responsibility." *Harvard Business Review* 36, no. 5 (September–October 1958): 41–50.

———. "The Johnson Treatment." *Harvard Business Review* 45, no. 1 (January–February 1967): 114–28.

Leff, George. *Free Choice for Workers: A History of the Right to Work Movement.* Ottawa, IL: Jameson Books, 2005.

Lemann, Nicholas. *The Promised Land: The Great Black Migration and How It Changed America.* New York: Vintage, 1991.

Lewin, Kurt. "Action Research and Minority Problems." *Journal of Social Issues* 2, no. 4 (November 1946): 34–46.

———. "The Research Center for Group Dynamics at Massachusetts Institute of Technology." *Sociometry* 8, no. 2 (May 1945): 126–36.

_____. *Resolving Social Conflicts: Selected Papers on Group Dynamics*, edited by Gertrude Weiss Lewin. Foreword by Gordon Allport. A publication for the Research Center for Group Dynamics, Ann Arbor, MI. New York: Harper, 1948.

Lewin, Kurt, and Paul Grabbe. "Conduct, Knowledge, and Acceptance of New Values." *Journal of Social Issues*, 1, no. 3 (Summer 1945): 53–64.

Lewis, Sinclair. *Kingsblood Royal.* New York: Bantam Books, 1949.

Lippitt, Ronald. *Training in Community Relations: A Research Exploration toward New Group Skills.* A publication of the Research Center for Group Dynamics, University of Michigan, and the Commission on Community Interrelations of the American Jewish Congress. New York: Harper, 1948.

Lippitt, Ronald K., and Ralph White. "An Experimental Study of Leadership and Group Life." In *Readings in Social Psychology*, 315–30. New York: Henry Holt, 1947.

Lockwood, Howard. "Critical Problems in Achieving Equal Employment Opportunity." *Personnel Psychology* 19, no. 1 (Spring 1966): 3–10.

Logan, Raymond, ed. *What the Negro Wants.* Chapel Hill: University of North Carolina Press, 1944.

Lorber, Lawrence Z. "The New Bias on Hiring Rules." *BusinessWeek*, May 25, 1981.

Luce, Charles. "Consolidated Edison and the Hard-Core." *Training in Business and Industry* 66 (March 1969): 46–53.

Lynch, Frederick. *The Diversity Machine.* New York: Transaction Publishers, 1997.

Mack, Walter. *No Time Lost.* New York: Atheneum Press, 1982.

MacLean, Nancy. *Freedom Is Not Enough: The Opening of the American Workplace.* New York: Russell Sage Foundation; Cambridge, MA: Harvard University Press, 2006.

Maloney, Thomas N. "Higher Places in the Industrial Machinery? Tight Labor Markets and Occupational Advancement by Black Males in the 1910s." *Social Science History* 26 (2002): 475–502.

_____. "Personnel Policy and Racial Inequality in the Pre-WWII North." *Journal of Interdisciplinary History* 30 (1999): 235–58.

Maloney, Thomas N., and Warren Whatley. "Making the Effort: The Contours of Racial Discrimination in Detroit's Labor Markets, 1920–40." *Journal of Economic History*, 55 (September 1995): 465–93.

The Management of Racial Integration in Business. Prepared under the supervision of Georges Doriot, professor of Industrial Management. New York: McGraw-Hill, 1964.

Marchand, Roland. *Creating the Corporate Soul: The Rise of Public Relations and Corporate Imagery in American Big Business.* Berkeley: University of California Press, 1998.

Marrow, Alfred J. *Behind the Executive Mask.* New York: American Management Association, 1964.

_____. The *Practical Theorist: The Life and Work of Kurt Lewin.* New York: Basic Books, 1969.

Marsh, Barbara *A Corporate Tragedy: The Agony of International Harvester Company.* Garden City, NY: Doubleday, 1985.

Marshall, Ray. "Some Factors Influencing the Upgrading of Negroes in the Southern Petroleum Refining Industry." *Social Forces* 42 (December 1963): 186–95.

Martin, Cathie Jo. *Stuck in Neutral: Business and the Politics of Human Capital Investment Policy.* Princeton, NJ: Princeton University Press, 2000.

Matthews, Fred. *Quest for an American Sociology: Robert E. Park and the Chicago School.* Montreal: McGill-Queen's University Press, 1977.

Mattson, Kevin. *When America Was Great: The Fighting Faith of Postwar Liberalism.* New York: Routledge, 2004.

May, Lary, ed. *Recasting America: Culture and Politics in the Age of the Cold War.* Chicago: University of Chicago Press, 1989.

McDonald, Dwight. *The Ford Foundation: The Men and the Millions.* New York: Reynal, 1956.

McQuaid, Kim. *Uneasy Partners: Big Business in American Politics, 1945–1990.* Baltimore: Johns Hopkins University Press, 1994.

McWilliams, Cary. *Brothers under the Skin.* Boston: Little, Brown and Co., 1951.

Meier, August, and Elliot Rudwick. *CORE: A Study in the Civil Rights Movement, 1942–1968.* New York: Oxford University Press, 1973.

Mills, C. Wright. Afterword by Alan Wolfe, *The Power Elite.* New York: Oxford University Press, 2000.

_____. "Review of Warner's *Social Life of a Modern Community.*" *American Sociological Review* 7 (April 1942): 263–71.

_____. *White Collar.* New York: Oxford University Press, 1951.

Minchin, Timothy. *The Color of Work: The Struggle for Civil Rights in the Southern Paper Industry, 1945–1980.* Chapel Hill: University of North Carolina Press, 2000.

_____. *Hiring the Black Worker: The Racial Integration of the Southern Textile Industry, 1960–1980.* Chapel Hill: University of North Carolina Press, 1999.

Moffett, Barbara, and Jean Fairfax. "A Private Agency Report on Merit Employment." *Social Action* 29, no. 4 (December 1962): 18–22.

Montagu, Ashley. *Man's Most Dangerous Myth: The Fallacy of Race.* New York: Columbia University Press, 1942.

Moon, Bucklin, ed. *Primer for White Folks.* Garden City, NY: Doubleday, Doran, 1945.

Moore, Wilbert E. "Industrial Sociology: Status and Prospects." *American Sociological Review* 13 (August 1948): 382–91.

Moreno, Paul. *Black Americans and Organized Labor: A New History.* Baton Rouge: Louisiana State University Press, 2006.

_____. *From Direct Action to Affirmative Action: Fair Employment Law and Policy in America, 1933–1972.* Baton Rouge: Louisiana State University Press, 1997.

Morrow, Joseph J. "American Negroes – A Wasted Resource." *Harvard Business Review* 35, no. 1 (January–February, 1957): 65–74.

_____. "Employment on Merit: The Continuing Challenge to Business." *Management Review* (February 1957): 10.

Morse, G. E. "How Honeywell Took the JOBS Program to Heart." *Manpower* (February–March 1969): 22–25.

Myrdal, Gunnar. *An American Dilemma.* New York: Harper and Brothers, 1944.

National Industrial Conference Board. "The Role of Business in Public Affairs." In *Business and the Cities,* edited by Neil W. Chamberlain, 5–12. New York: Basic Books, 1970.

"The Negro Drive for Jobs." *BusinessWeek,* August 17, 1963.

Nelson, Bruce. *Divided We Stand: American Workers and the Struggle for Black Equality.* Princeton, NJ: Princeton University Press, 2001.

Nemore, Arnold. "The Transferability of Manpower Programs." In *Business and the Cities*, edited by Neil W. Chamberlain, 268–97. New York: Basic Books, 1970.

"The New Bias on Hiring Rules." *BusinessWeek*, May 25, 1981.

"A New Drive to Reaganize Equal Opportunity." *BusinessWeek*, March 11, 1985.

Newman, Kathy. "The Forgotten Fifteen Million: Black Radio, 'The Negro Market,' and the Civil Rights Movement." *Radical History Review* 76 (2000): 115–35.

New York State School of Industrial and Labor Relations. "White Workers and Black Trainees," by Joseph Shedd. *Key Issues*, no. 13, 1973.

Noble, Charles. *Welfare as We Knew It: A Political History of the American Welfare State*. New York: Oxford University Press, 1997.

Norgren, Paul, and Samuel Hill. *Toward Fair Employment*. A project of the Industrial Relations Section, Princeton University. New York: Columbia University Press, 1964.

Norgren, Paul, et al. *Employing the Negro in American Industry: A Study of Management Practices*. New York: Industrial Relations Counselors, 1959.

Northrup, Herbert R. *Boulwarism: The Labor Relations Policies of the General Electric Company*. Ann Arbor: Bureau of Industrial Relations, Graduate School of Business Administration, University of Michigan, 1964.

_____. *Negro Employment in Basic Industry: A Study of Racial Policies in Six Industries*. Philadelphia: Wharton School of Finance and Commerce, Industrial Research Unit, 1970.

Northrup, Herbert, and Richard Rowan, eds. *The Negro and Employment Opportunity: Problems and Practices*. Ann Arbor: Bureau of Industrial Relations, Graduate School of Business Administration. University of Michigan, 1965.

"One Company's Answer to the Negro Job Problem." *Business Management* 25, no. 5 (February 1964): 42–45.

Orfield, Gary, and Edward Miller, eds. *Chilling Admissions: The Affirmative Action Crisis and the Search for Alternatives*. Cambridge, MA: Harvard University Civil Rights Project, 2000.

Ozanne, Robert. *A Century of Labor-Management Relations at McCormick and International Harvester*. Madison: University of Wisconsin Press, 1967.

_____. *The Negro in the Farm Equipment and Construction Machinery Industries: The Racial Policies of American Industry*. Report No. 26. Philadelphia: Industrial Research Unit, Department of Industry, Wharton School of Finance and Commerce, University of Pennsylvania, 1972.

Park, Robert. "Human Migration and the Marginal Man." *American Journal of Sociology* 33, no. 6 (May 1928): 881–93.

_____, ed. *Race and Culture*. Glencoe, IL: Free Press, 1950.

Park, Robert, and Ernest Burgess. *Introduction to the Science of Sociology*. Chicago: University of Chicago Press, 1921.

Perry, John. "Business – Next Target for Integration." *Harvard Business Review* 41, no. 2 (March–April 1963): 104–15.

Piven, Frances Fox, and Richard Cloward. *Poor People's Movements*. New York: Pantheon, 1997.

Plotke, David. *Building a Democratic Political Order*. New York: Cambridge University Press, 1996.

Quadagno, Jill. "Social Movements and State Transformation: Labor Unions and Racial Conflict in the War on Poverty." *American Sociological Review* 57 (October 1992): 616–34.

Reed, Bernice Anita. "Accommodation between Negro and White Employees in a West Coast Aircraft Industry 1942–44." *Social Forces* 26 (October 1947): 76–84.

Reed, Merl. *Seedtime for the Modern Civil Rights Movement*. Baton Rouge: Louisiana State University Press, 1991.

"Renovation in the NAM." *Fortune*, July 1948.

"Re-thinking Weber: The Business Response to Affirmative Action." *Harvard Law Review*, 102 (1989): 658–71.

Roediger, David. *The Wages of Whiteness: Race and the Making of the American Working Class*, rev. ed. New York: Verso, 1999.

Rosen, D. B. "Employment Testing and Minority Groups." *Key Issues*, no. 6 (1970).

Rosen, Hjalmar. *A Group Orientation Approach for Facilitating the Work Adjustment of the Hard-Core Unemployed*. Final Report to the U.S. Department of Labor, Manpower Development and Training Administration. Detroit: Wayne State University, 1969.

Rosenberg, Bernard, and Penney Chapin. "Management and Minority Groups: A Study of Attitudes and Practices in Hiring and Upgrading." In *Discrimination and Low Incomes*, edited by Aaron Antonovsky and Lewis Lorwin. New York: New York Interdepartmental Committee on Low Incomes, 1959.

Ross, Malcolm. *All Manner of Men*. New York: Reynal and Hitchcock, 1948.

Rosswurm, Steve, ed., *The CIO's Left Led Unions*. New Brunswick, NJ: Rutgers University Press, 1992.

Rutledge, Aaron, and Gertrude Zemon Gass. *Nineteen Negro Men: Personality and Manpower Retraining*. San Francisco: Jossey-Bass, 1967.

Schermer, George. *Employer's Guide to Economic Opportunity*. Washington, DC: Potomac Institute, 1966.

Scranton, Philip. "Large Firms and Industrial Restructuring: The Philadelphia Region, 1900–1980." *Pennsylvania Magazine of History and Biography* 116, no. 4 (October 1992): 419–465.

Schulman, Bruce J. *From Cotton Belt to Sunbelt: Federal Policy, Economic Development, and the Transformation of the South, 1938–1980*, rev. ed. Durham, NC: Duke University Press, 1994.

Schuyler, George. *Black and Conservative: The Autobiography of George S. Schuyler*. New Rochelle, NY: Arlington House, 1966.

The Selection and Training of Negroes for Managerial Positions: Proceedings of the Executive Study Conference. Held November 10–11, 1964. Princeton, NJ: Educational Testing Service, 1965.

Self, Robert O. *American Babylon: Race and the Struggle for Postwar Oakland*. Princeton, NJ: Princeton University Press, 2003.

Seligman, Daniel. "The Norris Enigma." *Fortune*, January 23, 1984.

Sewell, Stacy Kinlock. "The Best Man for the Job: Corporate Responsibility and Racial Integration in the Workplace, 1945–1960." *The Historian* 65 (Fall 2003): 1125–46.

———. "The 'Not-Buying Power' of the Black Community: Urban Boycotts and Equal Employment Opportunity, 1960–1964." *Journal of African-American History* 89, no. 2 (Spring 2004): 135–51.

Silberman, Charles. "The Businessman and the Negro." *Fortune*, September 1963.

Sitkoff, Harvard. *New Deal for Blacks*. New York: Oxford University Press, 1978.

Skrentny, John David, ed., *Color Lines: Affirmative Action, Immigration, and Civil Rights Options for America*. Chicago, University of Chicago 2001.

_____. *The Ironies of Affirmative Action: Politics, Culture, and Justice in America*. Chicago: University of Chicago Press, 1996.

_____. *The Minority Rights Revolution*. New York: Cambridge University Press, 2002.

Sloan, Alfred P. *The Adventures of a White Collar Man*. New York: Doubleday, 1941.

_____. *My Years with General Motors*. A new introduction by Peter Drucker. New York: Currency Books, 1990. (Originally published in 1963.)

Social Research and the Desegregation of the U.S. Army. Two original field reports by Leo Bogart, John Morsell, Robert Bower, Ira Cisin, Liela Sussmann, and Elmo C. Wilson. Chicago: Markham Publishing, 1969.

Soffer, Jonathan. "The National Association of Manufacturers and the Militarization of American Conservatism." *Business History Review* 75 (Winter 2001): 775–805.

Southall, Sara. *Industry's Unfinished Business: Achieving Sound Industrial Relations and Fair Employment*. New York: Harpers, 1950.

Sovern, Michael. *Legal Restraints on Racial Discrimination in Employment*. New York: Twentieth Century Fund, 1966.

Stebenne, David. "IBM's New Deal: Employee Policies of the IBM Corporation, 1933–1956. *Journal of the Historical Society* 5, no. 1 (Winter 2005): 47–77.

Stein, Judith. *Running Steel, Running America: Race, Economic Policy, and the Decline of Liberalism*. Chapel Hill: University of North Carolina Press, 1998.

Sugrue, Thomas. "Affirmative Action from Below: Civil Rights, the Building Trades, and the Politics of Racial Equality in the Urban North, 1945–1969." *Journal of American History* 91 (June 2004): 145–73.

_____. *The Origins of the Urban Crisis: Race and Inequality in Postwar Detroit*. Princeton, NJ: Princeton University Press, 1997.

_____. *Sweet Land of Liberty: The Forgotten Struggle for Civil Rights in the North*. New York: Random House, 2008.

Sullivan, Patricia. *Days of Hope: Race and Democracy in the New Deal Era*. Chapel Hill: University of North Carolina Press, 1996.

Sundstrom, William. "The Color-Line: Racial Norms and Discrimination in Urban Labor Markets, 1910–1950." *Journal of Economic History* 54, no. 2 (June 1994): 382–96.

Svonkin, Stuart. *Jews against Prejudice: American Jews and the Fight for Civil Liberties*. New York: Columbia University Press, 1999.

"Taking Adversity out of Diversity." *BusinessWeek*, January 31, 1994.

Theoharis, Jeanne, and Komozi Woodard, eds. *Freedom North: Black Struggles Outside the South, 1940–1980*. New York: Palgrave Macmillan, 2003.

Thomas, William R. "Problems under the FEPC." *Personnel Journal* 30 (May 1951): 14–19.

Thompson, Edgar T., and Everett C. Hughes, eds., *Race Individual and Collective Behavior*. Glencoe, IL: Free Press, 1958.

Thurber, Timothy. *The Politics of Equality: Hubert H. Humphrey and the African American Freedom Struggle*. New York: Columbia University Press, 1999.

————. "Racial Liberalism, Affirmative Action, and the Troubled History of the President's Committee on Government Contracts." *Journal of Policy History* 18, no. 4 (2006): 446–75.

Truman, David. *The Governmental Process.* New York: Knopf, 1951.

Tye, Larry. *The Father of Spin: Edward L. Bernays and the Birth of Public Relations.* New York: Crown, 1998.

"The Unhappy Parent of New Hiring Rules." *BusinessWeek,* January 24, 1970.

U.S. Census Bureau. *Statistical Abstracts of the United States, 2006.* Washington, DC: U.S. Government Printing Office, 2006.

U.S. Congress, House Committee on Labor. *To Prohibit Discrimination in Employment.* Washington, DC: U.S. Government Printing Office, 1944.

U.S. Congress, Senate. Committee on Labor and Public Welfare. *Antidiscrimination in Employment.* Hearings before the Subcommittee on Civil Rights of the Committee on Labor and Public Welfare, United States Senate, February and March 1954.

U.S. Congress, Senate Committee on Labor and Public Welfare, Subcommittee on Employment, Manpower and Poverty. *The JOBS Program: Background Information,* April 1970.

U.S. Congress, Senate, Committee on Labor and Public Welfare, Subcommittee on Employment, Manpower, and Poverty. *Manpower Development and Training Legislation,* May 1970.

Valien, Preston. "The 'Mentalities' of Negro and White Workers: An 'Experimental School' Interpretation of Negro Trade Unionism." *Social Forces* 27 (May 1949): 433–38.

Wallace, Henry. *New Frontiers.* New York: Reynal and Hitchcock, 1934.

Ware, Gilbert, and William Hastie. *Grace under Pressure.* New York: Oxford University Press, 1984.

Warner, W. Lloyd. "American Caste and Class." *American Journal of Sociology* 42 (September 1936): 234–37.

Warner, W. Lloyd, and Buford H. Junker. *Color and Human Nature: Negro Personality Development in a Northern City.* Washington, DC: American Council on Education, 1941.

Warner, W. Lloyd, and J. O. Low. *The Social System of the Modern Factory.* New Haven, CT: Yale University Press, 1947.

Watson, Denton, ed. *The Papers of Clarence Mitchell, Vol. 1, 1942–1943.* Athens: Ohio University Press, 2005.

Watson, Thomas, Jr., with Peter Petre, *Father Son & Co.: My Life at IBM and Beyond.* New York: Bantam Books, 1990.

Watts, Jerry G. "On Reconsidering Park, Du Bois, Frazier and Ried: Reply to Benjamin Bowser's 'The Contributions of Blacks to Sociological Knowledge.'" *Phylon* 44 (1983): 273–91.

Weaver, Robert. "Negro Employment in the Aircraft Industry." *Quarterly Journal of Economics* 59 (1945): 597–625.

————. *Negro Labor: A National Problem.* New York: Harcourt Brace, 1946.

————. "Relation of Social Change to the Economic Bases of Society." *Journal of Educational Sociology* 23, no. 6 (February 1950): 351–62.

Weems, Robert, Jr. *Desegregating the Dollar: African American Consumerism in the Twentieth Century.* New York: New York University Press, 1998.

Weiss, Nancy. *The National Urban League.* New York: Oxford University Press, 1974.

"Where Civil Rights Law Is Going Wrong." *Nation's Business* 53, no. 11 (November 1965): 60-67.

White, Ralph, and Ronald K. Lippitt. "Leadership Behavior and Member Reaction in Three Social Climates." In *Group Dynamics: Research and Theory*, edited by Dorwin Cartwright and Alvin Zander, 2nd ed., 527–33. Evanston, IL: Row, Peterson, 1960.

White, Walter. *A Man Called White.* New York: Viking Press, 1948.

Whyte, William Foote. "Human Relations Theory – a Progress Report." *Harvard Business Review* 34, no. 5 (September–October 1956): 125–32.

_____, ed. *Industry and Society.* New York: McGraw Hill, 1946.

_____. *Participant Observer: An Autobiography.* Ithaca, NY: ILR Press, 1994.

_____. *Pattern for Industrial Peace.* New York: Harper, 1951.

Whyte, William H., Jr., *The Organization Man.* Garden City, NY: Doubleday-Anchor, 1957.

Whyte, William H., Jr., and the editors of *Fortune. Is Anybody Listening? How and Why U.S. Business Fumbles When It Talks to Human Beings.* New York: Simon & Schuster, 1952.

Wilson, Logan, and Harlan Gilmore. "White Employers and Negro Workers." *American Sociological Review* 8, no. 6 (December 1943): 698–705.

Workman, Andrew. "Manufacturing Power: The Organizational Revival of the National Association of Manufacturers, 1941–45." *Business History Review* 72, no. 2 (Summer 1998): 279–317.

Worthy, James C. *Big Business and Free Men.* New York: Harpers, 1959.

_____. *William C. Norris: Portrait of a Maverick.* Cambridge: Ballenger, 1987.

Wright, Gavin. "The Civil Rights Revolution as Economic History." *Journal of Economic History* 59, no. 2 (June 1999): 267–89.

_____. *Old South, New South: Revolutions in the Southern Economy since the Civil War.* New York: Basic Books, 1986.

Yu, Henry. "Ethnicity and Race." In *The Encyclopedia of American Cultural and Intellectual History Social Sciences*, edited by Mary Kupiec Cayton and Peter W. Williams, Vol. 3, 109–20. New York: Scribner's Sons, 2001.

Zieger, Robert. *The CIO, 1935–1955.* Chapel Hill: University of North Carolina Press, 1995.

_____. *For Jobs and Freedom: Race and Labor in America since 1865.* Lexington: University Press of Kentucky, 2007.

Acknowledgments

I would like to thank Skidmore College for its generous financial support in the form of faculty development grants, sabbatical opportunity, and conference funding.

I owe thanks as well to all of those who offered suggestions and helped me find items in their archives, including Roger Horowitz and Marge McNinch of the Hagley Museum and Archives in Wilmington, Delaware; Stephanie Horowitz of the Charles Babbage Institute, University of Minnesota, Minneapolis; Kris Bronsted and Sonia Yaco of the Wisconsin Historical Society, Madison, Wisconsin; and Patrizia Sione at the Kheel Center for Labor Management Documentation and Archives, Cornell University Library, Ithaca, New York. Barbara Norelli, Amy Syrell, and others at Scribner Library tracked down innumerable items for me and I am grateful for their patience and ingenuity.

Linda Hall, Mason Stokes, John Brueggemann, and Ben Alpers all read parts of the manuscript for me, kindly pointing out comma splices, unsupported claims, and overstatements. Despite – or perhaps because of – their disagreement with many of the arguments in this book, they were exceptionally useful critics.

Eric Arnesen read this manuscript with a sharp and critical eye. His comments and skepticism made this book stronger. While I am sure there remains much with which Eric will disagree, I have appreciated his open-mindedness and willingness to entertain points of view very different from his own.

My greatest debt is to the remarkable Pamela Laird. Pam took an early interest in the project, and with her encouragement and support, I was able to proceed with confidence and purpose. Her comments and suggestions were always judicious, and more than anyone, she helped me make the transition from political history to business history. I find it fitting that someone who has written so much about mentorship should be such a wonderful mentor herself. It doesn't always happen that way.

Index